Notational Knowledge
Historical and Developmental Perspectives

Edited by

Eva Teubal
David Yellin Teachers' College, Jerusalem, Israel

Julie Dockrell
Institute of Education, London, UK

and

Liliana Tolchinsky
University of Barcelona, Spain

SENSE PUBLISHERS
ROTTERDAM / TAIPEI

A C.I.P. record for this book is available from the Library of Congress.

ISBN 90-77874-77-1

Published by: Sense Publishers,
P.O. Box 21858, 3001 AW Rotterdam, The Netherlands
http://www.sensepublishers.com

Printed on acid-free paper

Notational Knowledge

TABLE OF CONTENTS

The Multiple Functions of External Representations: Introduction   1
Liliana Tolchinsky

Historical Perspective

Historical Evolution of Number Systems and Numeration Systems   13
Carlos E. Vasco

Natural Language, Artificial Language and the Representation of Time
in Medieval Music   45
Dorit Tanay

Writing: The Story of a Cognitive Revolution   65
Jesús Tuson

Developmental Perspective

Restructuring Conceptual Intuitions through Invented Notations   81
Jeanne Bamberger

Distinguishing Numeracy from Literacy: Evidence from Children's
Early Notations   113
Julie E. Dockrell and Eva Teubal

Writing and Written Numbers as Source of Knowledge   135
Liliana Tolchinsky

A New Framework for Understanding How Young Children Create
External Representations for Puzzles and Problems   159
Lara M. Triona and David Klahr

Graphing Hagan Creek   179
Wolff-Michael Roth

Learning from Video: Early Understanding and Use of a Symbolic
Medium   209
Georgene L. Troseth

The Impact of Notation on Cognition & Its Development:
Theoretical Perspectives & Empirical Evidence   233
Michelle Eskritt and Kang Lee

Index   257

LILIANA TOLCHINSKY

THE MULTIPLE FUNCTIONS OF EXTERNAL REPRESENTATIONS: INTRODUCTION

Logotypes, tattoos, drawings, maps, musical scores, figures, graphs, writing, numerals, hallmarks, and signatures all these forms of external representation are part of our daily landscape and permeate most social activities from the moment we are born. In western societies the first institutional act is a representational one, parents inscribe the name of their child in the civil registry office. The means "we use to present and re-present our thoughts to ourselves and to others, to create and communicate records across space and time, and to support reasoning and computation, constitute a central part of any civilization's infrastructure" (Kaput, Noss and Hoyles, 2002). This book is about humans' creation, appropriation, understanding and use of external representations.

External representations may look very different; consider, for example, how different the map of your country and its written title look in their graphics. They may also refer to a diversity of domains; drawings might depict the shape and color of objects, musical scores denote tunes, writing represent language and tattoos might denote tribal identity.

Some kinds of external representation have become highly conventionalized, they form systems with clear boundaries in which new elements are hardly if ever accepted and in which combinations are regulated by rules and norms, others are unique creations or ad hoc inventions to solve a particular problem or represent a particular content. Conventionalized external representations use a limited set of elements of distinctive form which are recognizable despite the alterations different users may introduce in their appearance (e.g, an alphabet). It is in conventionalized notation where the distinction between *actual realizations* and *conceptual categories* becomes crucial. This distinction termed *inscriptions* and *characters* by Goodman (1976) is crucial because it enables users of notations to recognize the same despite the different. Strictly speaking the term 'notation' should be reserved to conventionalized external representations.

In spite of the differences in graphic features, domain of reference and degree of conventionality, external representations share three crucial features. First, they all have a "double face" (Sebeok, 1996, p. 34); they are what they are; yet, at the same time, they evoke something beyond them. Numerals are ink or graphite on paper or chalk on a blackboard but they can be used to refer to discrete quantities. Having a "double face" is common to every symbolic object – this is the *sine qua non* condition of a symbol.[1]

E. *Teubal et al. (eds.), Notational Knowledge*, 1–10.

This duality was turned into a triad by Pierce (1935–1966) who included the interpreter in the notion of symbol and brings about the second feature shared by external representations: *intentionality*. Representations do not stem spontaneously, they are produced by human agents intentionally. Intentionality is always true for production; but, it is not always true for interpretation. External representations must be intentionally produced for symbolizing whatever they symbolize, but a graphic shape or a numeral may evoke a particular person or event to an occasional interpreter. Any object must be created as a representational object in order to be symbolic but any object can be turned into a symbol in the act of interpretation.

Another feature that external representation share is that they have physical/material permanence, they are not ephemeral. This feature clearly distinguishes external representation from spoken language and sign language because their expression is fluent and does not last for off-line examination, unless of course it is recorded. This feature also separates external representations from any form of internal representation or concepts, the subject matter of cognitive psychology. Although a dialectical interaction is supposed between internal and external representations (Tolchinsky, 2003).

These three features: *double face*, *deliberateness*, *endurance* enable a peculiar kind of interaction with this kind of objects. We can produce them and look at what we are producing in the very process of production (Willats, 1985). The results of movements can be monitored, contemplated, and adjusted while they are still being produced, immediately after production and much later on. This kind of interaction explains why lasting and deliberate representations can be turned into a problem-space, not only after being completed, but also while they are produced.

Lasting and deliberately created representations can be separated from the producer and from the situation of production; they become detached from the process, the context of production and the time during which they were produced (Lee & Karmiloff-Smith, 1996). However, the producer, the context, the process, and the moment of production, all these aspects, somehow become embedded in the product so that this product means in the absence of the producer and in a different context and time.

These three features make of external representation a multifunctional kind of object. They function as communicative referential tool encoding a diversity of contents and being used in many different activities. From buying and selling to the most holy rituals, most social acts involve the creation and interpretation of external representations. Besides communicative referential tools, external representations are also epistemic tools, *objects to think with*. We can perform the same mental actions or linguistic activities online or off-line. The perspectives from which these actions are performed are multiplied when the same person is both the producer and the interpreter or when the situation is repeated at different times and spaces, individually or in groups. That is, external representations multiply our cognitive exercising under changing perspectives.

2

On top of being functional-communicative and epistemic tools, external representations constitute a domain of inquiry. In the initial lines of this introductory chapter I have taken this perspective by pointing at the differences between external representations and then at the features that are shared by every kind of external representation. To accomplish that, I have taken a synchronic- descriptive perspective on external representations. That is, I have reflected on the features of notations in a particular point in time.

There are other perspectives from which this domain of inquiry can be approached. From an evolutionary perspective we may ask for the extent to which production and interpretation of external representation is strictly human or rather it is a capacity shared by other species. There is strong evidence about chimpanzee's ability to distinguish numerals and to use arbitrary symbols for communication and rats can learn how many times they need to press a lever in order to receive a reward (Boysen & Capaldi, 1993; Dehaene, 1997). That is, interpretation of notations even of a conventionalized type is possible for apes, monkeys and rats. However, to the best of my knowledge, deliberate production of double-faced durable marking is not part of repertoire of other species except *homo sapiens*.

External representations can also be approached from an historical perspective. Some forms of external representation were born with humanity whereas others are much more recent. There are indications of human symbolic thought from almost 80,000 years before the present as reflected in the rest of used ochre and the deliberately perforated red-stained shell beads found at the Blombos Cave, in South Africa. Ochre is known as a source of color for ceremonial, decorative purposes and the shell beads are interpreted as personal ornaments or jewellery for the occupants of Blombos (Hirst, 2005). Maps, on the other hand, even taken in their most embracing sense as "... graphic representations that facilitate a spatial understanding of things, concepts, conditions, processes, or events in the human world" (Brown, 1977; Harley & Woodward, 1987) are very recent.

The ten chapters included in the book are devoted to the study of representational objects that were purposefully created as such where the purpose might be very broad and involve the whole society or serve a single individual in the act of solving a puzzle. These representational objects are viewed from different perspectives. Three authors approached these objects from a diachronic perspective in an attempt to trace the emergency and development of different systems in the history of human societies whereas the others took a developmental perspective; they trace the path of different systems in the history of individuals. Among the chapters that took a developmental perspective, three concentrate in conventionalized notations whereas the other three focus on invented external representations. Finally, the last chapter is dedicated to analyzing the effect of external representations on human development.

All the referred systems of external representation function as "extracortical" records (Donald, 1991) but their processing obviously has cortical support. Nevertheless, except for some scarce references to neurological studies on the effect of handling alphabetic materials and numerals, the neurological basis of notational knowledge is rather absent from the book. Having put forward what we have and what we miss we shall move to outline the content of the chapters in the book.

OUTLINE OF THE BOOK

The first three chapters of the book look at writing, number and music notation from an historical perspective. The idea is to learn *the reasons* that led to the emergence and subsequent evolution of certain systems, how *the principles* underlying the different systems evolve and *the processes* that enabled different cultures to move from one system to another. Each author, however, approaches the historical view with differing purposes.

Carlos E. Vasco's chapter "Historical evolution of number systems and numeration systems" aims at providing a re-reading of the history of numbers and numeration systems to help future research and practice in mathematics education. With this purpose in mind Vasco approaches the origins and development of number systems and of systems of numerical notations and compares those origins with research on children's actual use of those notations. Of particular interest is his discussion of the role that the need to represent succession of events in time – besides that of counting or subitizing of discrete objects in space – has played in the configuration of number systems.

Drawing on a distinction between number systems as conceptual constructions and numeration systems as semiotic registers – close to the notion of external representation – he advances the assumption of a conceptual underpinning of notational development. "Once we start developing mental (noetic) constructions like sizes of groups, duration of time-intervals, shrinking or expanding operators, mental comparison ratios, oriented placers, sliding operators, etc., we can exercise our semiotic powers to get any available tool from surrounding or remote cultures and invent semiotic registers to represent them". That is why, in spite of focusing on the history of written numerals, Vasco highlights the importance of oral and gestural registers before and after the invention of writing, in particular the use of these registers in children developing understanding of number.

Jesús Tuson in his chapter "Writing: The story of a cognitive revolution" traces the path of writing from its origin in the Near East some five thousand years ago to the deployment of modern alphabets in the Mediterranean region. Dwelling on the analysis of the precursors of writing that function as accounting systems, the author suggest strategies and mental processes that could be at the basis of the emergence of writing. After "a short typological tour" through the possible forms of writing systems, the author puts forward a number of purported practical steps that may have been involved in the development of syllabaries and alphabets. Although, according to Tuson, writing did not add anything substantial to our condition of *sapiens*, it solves crucial social problems of register and storage of information and illustrates the range of human ingenuity to solve these problems. The invention of writing implies also a "semiotic revolution" for the fixation of ephemeral speech creates intermodal links – involving a transfer from the auditory to the visual sense – that might be considered theoretically impossible. Because of its centrality and its rather chimerical nature this semiotic transfer is analysed in some detail showing the different steps that were involved in linking the two sensory domains for attaining the regulating principles of writing.

Both Tuson and Vasco highlight the emergence of writing and numerals to solve social needs, and the process of semiotic abstraction and separation of physical references that both writing and numerals suffer throughout history. Both authors emphasize as well the diversity of "semiotic registers" in which similar content can be expressed and the cognitive work involved in treatment and translation from one semiotic register to the other.

In "Natural language, artificial language and the representation of time in medieval music", Dorit Tanay explores the nature of the difference between the old and the new system of rhythmic notation and the driving forces that bring about these differences.

In the old system – before the fourteenth century – "the atomic unit of meaning is the whole rhythmic phrase. Only in the context of the phrase as a whole do the various signs, composing the phrase, acquire a definite rhythmic meaning. In the new modern system of rhythmic notation, however, each rhythmic value is represented by its own note-shape, yielding a one to one, invariant relation between the signifier and the signified. This is to say that the atomic unit of the temporal/rhythmical meaning is the discrete rhythmical duration as independent from the broader musical context".

Thus, the differences between the two systems are not just technical. They evolved gradually as a response to the changing musical taste and the growing quest for individuality and creative musical thinking and, at the same time they were driven by "a major shift in the concept of the relation between signifier and signified". This major shift is also reflected in the conceptualization of mathematical notation and language. In mathematical notation there is an increasing separation from matter and objects, allowing its practice to be completely abstract. And, in linguistics there is liberation of meaning from extra-linguistic context and increasing reliance on the relation between elements in every possible linguistic context.

The next three chapters explore the same notational domains – writing, written numbers and music notation – but from a developmental perspective. There is an important difference between the two chapters devoted to writing and written numbers and the one devoted to music. While the two first look at development taking into account the features of conventional systems and analyse the extent to which the child notational proposals come closer to conventional uses, the later focus on the child's notational attempts without taking as a frame of reference conventionalized forms of music notation.

Moreover, and unlike most previous work on notations, that focus on the development of writing or number notation separately, the two chapters focus on the relations between systems. Assuming that long before the advent of formal schooling the socio-cultural environment provides children with many opportunities to be exposed and to learn about a diversity of notational functions and forms, both chapters agree on the theoretical importance of discovering how children make distinctions between notational domains, how do they discover the specificity of each domain and what kind of relations do they establish between domains.

Julie E. Dockrell and Eva Teubal's chapter "Distinguishing numeracy from literacy: Evidence from children's early notations" present research that focuses on pre-schoolers' early production of notations for content that would typically be represented by numerals and writing. The studies presented in the chapter provide evidence that even the youngest children are able to differentiate the forms and functions of the two systems. They can use different notational systems in a meaningful way to communicate different kinds of information. They are not necessarily accurate, however, in their use of the system as a referential-communicative tool. Both the difficulty of the task and the referent to be represented have a significant impact on the child's notations. Thus, children's construction of notational systems needs to be considered as a continuous process that begins with initial discriminations between domains but requires developmental time and notational experience to attain both communicative efficacy and choice of appropriate notation for the referent within a particular task context. According to the authors, this process "will be firmly based in the communicative contexts in which the children find themselves and by the extent to which they are culturally valued".

The main claim of Liliana Tolchinsky's chapter "Writing and written numbers as source of knowledge" is that writing systems and written number systems are not only powerful communicative tools once they have been learned, rather they also serve as a source of knowledge about their own functioning throughout the learning process. Children's acquisition of two features, one from the writing system, the other from the written number system – the convention of graphic separation between words in current use of alphabetic writing systems, and the principle of place value in written numeration – are used as "case analyses" to support this general claim.

Jeanne Bamberger's chapter "Restructuring conceptual intuitions through invented notations: From path-making to map-making" presents a deep single case analysis of the transformations that occurred during one brief session as one child worked with a set of tuned bells to construct, reconstruct, and play a nursery tune. The observed transformation are qualified by the author as a move from path-making to map-making. Path-makers build tunes by building a cumulating bell-path. They look for correspondence between a bell and a tune event. When they find a bell that matches the next tune event, they place it to the right of the previously found bell. "The result is a bell path where each bell has been added in *order of occurrence* in the tune". The notations invented by the path-makers for the tune are basically "iconic" trail-maps. The bells on the table are "copied" onto the paper as stick-pictures or sometimes simplified copies of the bells.

Musical map-makers differ from path-makers in that they create an outside fixed reference. The construction of this external structure based on the basis bell property, that of pitch, enables the identification of a pitch unit that facilitates the application of the same schema to different tunes. Unlike the path-makers that create a unique instrument for each tune, map-makers create a schema that can be applied for playing different tunes. The notation invented by map-makers is not an iconic representation for the bells but a more abstract representation of the pitch properties and its ordering. In contrast to many learning perspectives, Bamberger suggests that "the goal of learning is not to *overcome* the behaviours associated with path-making, but rather to have access to both action and symbol such that one is able to choose depending on when, where, and what for".

The three other chapters that take a developmental perspective focus on children's invention of external representations. As suggested by Lara M. Triona and David Klahr in their chapter "A new framework for understanding how young children create external representations for puzzles and problems", children are often faced with the need to create representations for new situations that require encoding information in the form of an external representation. However, the processes involved in children appropriation of notational systems and those involved in creating external representation differ. For conventionalized representations children growing in literate communities have at their disposal examples of the graphic marks on different surfaces – the notational elements – that are part of the systems. Children most probably listen to the ways these forms are named and share many of the communicative situations in which they are used. Acquiring conventional systems is a process of appropriation in which children come to negotiate their own ideas with the particular (conventional) features of the systems. For invented external representations children must select which aspects of the event or situation they are going to take care of in their representation and, in many cases, the kind of graphic forms – line drawings? written words? graphs? – they are going to use for representing the selected aspects. Thus the interest of examining the external representations that children create in new situations.

Lara M. Triona and David Klahr review previous work on this domain and suggest future research that will be useful for gaining a more accurate picture of development. Of particular interest is their reflection on how amount and type of information that children need to encode affect children's ability to generate adequate notations. Although the picture of children's notational abilities varies substantially depending on this these two variables, there seems to be a general pattern of notational development. Children are first successful with the object symbolization tasks, then with simple sequences tasks, and finally with the problem solution sequences and location mapping tasks.

Beyond the influence of task constraints, the notational strategy children use whether it is figural or linguistic affects their ability to create successful representations. This suggest that many other aspects of children's approach to notations should be addressed on top of the differences in task constraints in order to gain a full understanding of their developing ability to create representations. The chapter presents a useful framework to guide future research on the development of children's creation of representations.

The domain of external representations is a dynamic one. There is a constant introduction of new tools that provide increasing computational resources but create, at the same time, new problems and revisited conceptualization of known media. The inclusion of video-images as a form of external representation deserving to be explored developmentally is a clear proof of the dynamicity of the domain.

Georgene L. Troseth's chapter "Learning from video: Early understanding and use of a symbolic medium" focuses in a kind of external representation that so far has received little attention: Video. This media fulfils the conditions of *double face*, *deliberateness*, *endurance* and video images are some of the first symbolic artefacts that many young children encounter. Therefore, the evolving understanding of this media is part of the domain of knowledge of external representation. Indeed, there are many functions of video images and specific "challenges" that children must face for gaining a full understanding of video. These include the need to interpret conventional devices such as cuts, pans, montage, and camera angles that convey spatial and temporal relations as well as *aspect* or viewpoint. In spite of the specific features of video images the author reports that understanding video follows a development very similar to that found for static pictures. Moreover, Troseth entertains a domain general view of notational development advancing the hypothesis that experience with one type of symbol (e.g., video images) may prepare children to recognize and use another (e.g., written or number notation).

Wolff-Michael Roth's chapter "Graphing Henderson Creek: A case of relations in sociomaterial practice" explores the many variables that are put into play in interpreting a graph. Assuming that "knowledge is not an entity that can be acquired but rather that knowing is equivalent to acting in the world", the author provides an in-depth case analysis of the interaction between a water technician and a mathematician while interpreting a graph. Because graphs have sign functions, the chapter also provides a concise overview of a semiotic approach to graphing followed by a presentation of activity theory, the framework in which the study is embedded. The author shows the many relations that form part of the water technician's knowledge and interpretation of the graph. It is not just how the time period, the level of the flow, the rain that fell down on a particular day are read from the graph but also the extent to which other personal and situational variables are involved in the interpretation. Finally, the author discusses the implications of this work for developmental issues in mathematical knowing.

The study shows that no act of interpretation is literal decoding. Creators and interpreters can infer and recover aspects of the original process, the context, the time, or the referents; however, what is inferred from the external representation is never identical to the original referents or contexts.

A common feature of these chapters is that authors approach external representations in general and, notational systems in particular, as a domain of development. Children's interaction and conceptualization of language, number, tunes and space change as they grow older. There is a long tradition of developmental psychology exploring the development in every such domain and researchers may have used external representations in the form of drawings or graphs, as a window to access children's ideas in a particular domain of reference.

But, the authors in this book are also interested in children's evolving notions on writing, video-images, graphs, music notation, and numerals as such and not only as expression of cognitive changes in the domain of reference. They do not relate to external representations as a derivation or direct reflection of children's understanding of the notation's domain of reference but rather look at the particular interactions that are established between the features of notations and the constraints of the domains of reference.

In Jeanne Bamberger's and Carlos Vasco's chapters we will find vivid examples of external representation functioning as an epistemic tool. Both at an individual level, when a child is elaborating his understanding of the entities and relations of a tune and when a community is expanding its understanding of number and numeration systems, external representation mediates processes of conceptual restructuring.

However, Eskritt and Lee caution us about being too enthusiastic about the effect of the use of external representations on cognition. In the last chapter "The impact of notation on cognition and its development: Theoretical perspectives and empirical evidence", Eskritt and Le examine the existing theoretical discussions on the relationship between notation and cognition from a historical and evolutionary perspective and review evidence from educational and cognitive psychology. They put forward the many possible reasons and ways that external symbols may influence cognition and its development. For example, external symbols can aid in organizing the display of otherwise disorganized information, such as the list (Donald, 1991). External symbols can also reveal relationships and structures about the information they encode and, hence, make explicit knowledge that may have been implicit (Karmiloff-Smith, 1992). Novel information can be 'discovered' in the development of the external symbols themselves, such as metalinguistic awareness (Olson, 1994) or musical knowledge (Bamberger, 1982). Moreover, experience on one kind of external representation may prepare children to gain insight in another system as advanced by Troseth (this volume) with respect to video images. However, in spite of this potentiality there are neither conclusive results nor enough research to separate the pure effect of external representation, whatever their kind, from other cultural and social variables.

NOTE

[1] The word symbol is derived from the Greek word *symbolon*. In ancient Greece it was a custom to break a slate of burned clay into several pieces and distribute them within the group. When the group reunited the pieces were fitted together (Greek *symbollein*). The two parts of *symbolon* become differentiated and turned into the most famous duo of semiotics and related disciplines: *signifier* and the *signified* (Saussure, 1916). The signifier is the formal side of the sign and the signified is the content side of the sign *inextricably* linked like "the two sides of a paper page".

REFERENCES

Bamberger, J. (1982). Revisiting children's drawings of simple rhythms: A function for reflection-in-action. In S. Strauss (Ed.), *U-shaped behavioral growth*. Academic Press.

Boysen, S.T. & Capaldi, E.J. (Eds.) (1993). *The development of numerical competence: Animal and human models*. Mahwah, NJ: Lawrence Erlbaum.

Brown, L.A. (1977). *The story of maps*.

Dehaene, S. (1997). *Number sense*. London: Allen Lane.

Donald, M. (1991). *Origins of the modern mind: Three stages in the evolution of culture and cognition*. Harvard University Press.

Goodman, N. (1976). *Languages of art*. Indianapolis: Hacket Publishing Co.

Harley, B. & Woodwar, D. (1987). Volume 1: Cartography in prehistoric, ancient, and medieval Europe and the Mediterranean. In B. Harley & D. Woodward (Eds.), *The history of cartography*. University of Chicago Press.

Hirst, K.K. (2005). http://archaeology.about.com/.

Kaput, Noss & Hoyles (2002) Developing new notations for a learnable mathematics in the computational era. In L.D. English, M.B. Bussi, G.A. Jones, R.A. Lesh & D. Tirosh (Eds.), *Handbook of international research in mathematics education*. pp. 51–80.

Karmiloff-Smith, A. (1992). Beyond modularity: a developmental perspective on cognitive science. MIT Press

Lee, K. & Karmiloff-Smith, A. (1996). The development of cognitive constraints on notations. *Archives of Psychologie 64*, 3–26.

Olson, D.R. (1994). *The world on paper*. Cambridge University Press.

Pierce, C.S. (1966). Collected papers. In C. Hartshorne, P. Weiss and A.W. Burks (Eds.), (Original work published 1935).

Saussure, F. de (1987). *Curso de lingüística general*. Madrid: Alianza Editorial. [Original work published 1916.]

Sebeok, T. (1996). *Signos: Una introducción a la semiótica*. Barcelona: Paidos. [Original: *Signs: An introduction to semiotics*. 1994. University of Toronto.]

Tolchinsky, L. (2003). *The cradle of culture and what children know about writing and numbers before being taught*. Mahwah, NJ: Lawrence Erlbaum.

Liliana Tolchinsky
Department of Linguistics
University of Barcelona, Spain

HISTORICAL PERSPECTIVE

CARLOS E. VASCO

HISTORICAL EVOLUTION OF NUMBER SYSTEMS AND NUMERATION SYSTEMS

Psychogenetic, Didactical, and Educational Research Implications

INTRODUCTION

Do you think writing down the number eighty-nine is easy? So it seems: just write an '8' and a '9', and there it is: '89'; but one child might think that you just wrote seventeen; another one might take the '9' for a '6' after a quick mental rotation, and confuse it with eighty-six or with sixty-eight, and a third might firmly believe it is ninety-eight. What if a German child hears "Neun-und-achtzig" in that order? Why write '89' instead of '98'? What if a French child hears "Quatre-vingt-neuf"? Maya children in ancient Mexico would have also heard something like that: "Four-twenties-and-nine", but they would actually have written a line and four dots on top of it inside a small square, and in another square above it, the four twenties as four dots. What if the old Romans would say "undenonaginta" (one-from-ninety)? Would the Roman child write 'IXC', or 'LXXXVIIII' or 'LXXXIX'?

There are many detailed and readable histories of mathematics, all of which begin with the same stories of the beginnings of number.[1] Why then attempting a short chapter on the same material, now so easily available? One answer could be the apparent failure of at least fifty years of research in mathematics education and didactics of mathematics to provide teachers and researchers with some workable models, theories, methods and materials to help children overcome the difficulties in reaching what has been aptly called "numeracy". It still takes too long, hurts too much, and produces too many allergies – even phobias – towards mathematics in too many children. Can a re-reading of the history of numbers and numeration systems using the appropriate magnifying glasses help future research and practice in mathematics education? This chapter is an attempt to cast a decisive vote in favor of the "Yes" answer.

Lauren Resnick used to say we shouldn't spend much time teaching or researching what is easy in mathematics, but rather concentrate on what is hard. She might have been right, but there is a catch. What is easy? Addition would be easy, but only if the coding of numbers were easy, which is not the case. Thus, we must begin by going as far back as we can in the search for the origins and development of number systems and numerical notations and compare those origins with research on children's actual use of those notations.

In spite of a general agreement among researchers about rejecting the Haeckelian (sometimes called "Piagetian") parallelism between phylogeny and ontogeny (or between sociogenesis and psychogenesis, see Piaget & García,

E. Teubal et al. (eds.), Notational Knowledge, 13–43.

1983), at least in the case of mathematics one cannot deny that many parallels are striking. This attempt to retrieve and interpret the past as it might have happened: the synchronic reading of history, must also be reframed and rechecked by a back-and-forth movement from the present to the past in a diachronic reading that attempts to place each past period in the course of the whole history of mathematics from the obscure pre-historic past to the ever-changing present.[2]

A SEMIOTIC FRAMEWORK

A first difficulty in re-reading the history of numbers – and the now very extensive educational research on numbers, numeration and numeracy – is terminology, and deeper down, the directly unobservable conceptual constructions in the minds of those who use or invent terminology. We need a magnifying glass to separate thin lines that, at first sight, seem to be just one. The first obvious magnification step in the proposed semiotic framework is to distinguish concepts as mental artifacts from signs as amphibious artifacts, sometimes mental and directly unobservable, sometimes materialized and directly observable. A parallel second step is to distinguish numbers as concepts from numerals as signs. But what is a sign? And, what is a concept? Are not concepts themselves just a particular type of mental signs internalized from the language of adults?

Noesis and Semiosis

The word 'semiosis' as a human activity of expression, representation and communication is intended to be opposed to 'noesis', the mental, cerebral, internal activity of thinking. The ideas – sometimes wrongly attributed to Piaget – that thinking (noesis) was a purely mental activity, without images, internalized words or symbols, and that language was only an outward expression of thought (semiosis), have become obsolete. The ideas – sometimes wrongly attributed to Vygotsky – that language, social expressions and cultural tools were the main components of human reality, and that thinking (noesis) was only internalized language, are fortunately becoming just as obsolete. The dialectics of noesis and semiosis is complex, dynamic and creative; there can be no refined individual noetic and semiotic activity without language and other cultural tools, but there can be no refined culture and language without individual, often idiosyncratic, creative and unpredictable noetic and semiotic activity (see Martí & Pozo, 2000; see also Tolchinsky, 2003).

Raymond Duval's use of 'semiosis' (Duval, 1995/2004) can be taken to include both the production or externalization activity (projective semiosis or the coding way) and the interpretation or internalization or activity (injective semiosis or the decoding way).

Semiotic Registers

Duval showed the need for clearly separating external, materialized representations (tokens, not types; see below) from internal representations and semiotic registers. 'Register' is a polysemic word. It is not used here in the usual sense of an electronic register to store information nor in the legal sense of a record kept by the city or school registrar. It is a metaphoric term used in the sense an organ player would use it: he or she pulls a register, and the same melody sounds different; there is a flute register, others for trumpet, violin, tuba or "vox humana". This metaphoric term was used in linguistics by Douglas Biber (1995, 1998) to distinguish functional variations in language (functional registers) and in didactics of mathematics by Raymond Duval (1995/2004) to point to the variety of coding and decoding processes. Hence, to avoid ambiguities, in this chapter the word 'register' will not be used alone, but in the combination 'semiotic register' (except to avoid clumsy repetitions).

When you are trying to express something you are thinking about (an idea or concept, an internal mental product of your noesis, like a number as the size of a group of nine people), you unconsciously choose a semiotic register and you search for an appropriate type of representation belonging to that register that would best represent your idea. Then you raise nine fingers, write '9' or call "nine" out loud.

Instead of looking only at tokens of numerals produced by ancient cultures, however exotic, striking and ingenious, our attention will be also directed at the numeration system as a semiotic register behind that token, and at the semiotic activity or semiosis that allowed the child, speaker, gesturer, painter, sculptor or writer to think about that number, to select that specific semiotic register, to choose the pertinent numeral type from the available types in it, and to produce the perceptible tokens of that type. These tokens configure an external representation belonging to that semiotic register.

As hinted above when introducing the word 'semiosis', a semiotic register must manage at least two processes: the production, externalization or codification process (projective semiosis or 'the coding way', more easily seen as active), and the interpretation, internalization or decodification process (injective semiosis or 'the decoding way', which, again, is not passive at all, because both types of semiosis are active).

Looking more closely at the decoding way, we can schematically say that the activity of interpretation usually starts from the perceptual detection of external sign tokens, always immersed in micro-, meso- and macro-contexts. In our case of numerals and numbers, the external sign token could be a gesture, a row of incisions, a knot, an oral word numeral, a token of the numeral '9', etc. This token triggers an internal pattern-recognition process that selects a sign type that matches the percept and also selects a plausible semiotic register; the selected type as used in that semiotic register is matched with possible internal meanings. For instance, to a child, the numeral '1' might mean the number one, but it could also mean a hook, and the numeral '2' might mean a swan. Combinations and associations of memories might increase the number of associated meanings (neurologists speak of "spreading activation" in a model of memory attributed to Quillian and developed by Collins and Loftus, 1975. See also chapter 7 of Goerzel, 1993).

In the coding way, the model works in the reverse direction, starting from what one wishes to express, finding an internal way of representing what is meant to be expressed by choosing a semiotic register and a representation type; then, the activated semiotic register as a cognitive-motor coding procedure produces an external representation by means of gestures, sounds, oral or written tokens of that type. For the purposes of this chapter, the concept of semiotic register allows us to ground a precise distinction between number systems as conceptual or noetic constructions and numeration systems as semiotic registers.

Treatment and Conversion

The activity of transforming an external representation into another belonging to the same semiotic register is called *treatment*, and the activity of transforming an external representation belonging to one register into another one belonging to another register is called *conversion* or translation (Duval, 1995/2004). Thus, paper-and-pencil addition of nine plus nineteen involves transforming a representation of the numeral type '9' and another of the numeral type '19' into a representation of the result of the addition of the represented numbers using the Western decimal written register. This is a treatment of the representations, yielding the result '28'. Changing this result to the Roman written register (or to the written hexadecimal alphanumeric register used in computer science) would be a conversion, yielding 'XXIX' (resp. '1C').

A skilled counter, using a tabletop abacus, like the Roman, Medieval or Renaissance counting table with engraved lines as guides and pebbles as counters, could often beat the algebrist's way of calculating with a pen. The counter's action of setting up the counters on the lines as the customer recites a verbal oral numeral is a conversion. Then, the treatment can be purely automatized on the part of the counter; at the end, the counter reads off the settings of the counters and lines on the surface of the counter and converts those visual patterns into another representation in the oral word register.[3]

Similar semiotic registers are associated with the Chinese counting board, with the Chinese abacus ("*suan pan*") and with the Japanese abacus ("*soroban*"). The Incas had also developed a counting board called "yupana" (see Selin, 2000, pp. 199–202), which indirectly shows the invention of an associated semiotic register. In these semiotic registers, the numeral tokens themselves are not easily visible to the untrained eye. They are distributed among counters, lines or wires, regions of the tabletop or the wooden tray. Properly speaking, the numeral tokens are not even *written*: they are *set*.

In contrast, a knot-register like the Inca "quipu" and the Chinese "bookkeeping knots" mentioned in Chapter 27 of the Tao Te Ching (according to legend, invented by the fisherman Fu Xi Shi before the invention of Chinese characters), and also found in a few North American native cultures, is not designed to allow a treatment of the represented numbers, because the knots are intentionally tightened, sometimes even treated with grease or glue to prevent changes in the recorded numbers.

In this sense, when Hindu-Arabic numerals were invented and the results of additions and other operations could be calculated by juggling tiles with the numerals on each one, or by writing and erasing numerals on papyrus, parchments, sand or dust trays, slates, paper, black or whiteboards, our cultures could use a semiotic register with which one could actually do arithmetic with little or no cognitive load between the initial setting of the numerals and the final read-off of the result.

The first reckoning books, later called with long titles involving "algebra" or "abacus", did not deal with algebra in the sense we know it today but with arithmetic. There was no difference between algebra and arithmetic until the time of the mathematical challenges ("disfide") in the Italian Renaissance, when algorithms to solve harder riddles were differentiated as "algebra" from the algorithms for the easier riddles, branded "arithmetic procedures".[4]

NUMBERS AND NUMERALS

The second magnification step in the semiotic framework involves two more distinctions patterned after the general semiotic distinctions explained above. The first requires us to distinguish *numbers* as concepts from *numerals* as signs; the second leads us to distinguish – among numerals as signs – numeral *types* from numeral *tokens*.

There are numerous instances (such as Colombia and Israel, to name two) in which the attempt to introduce the distinction between numbers and numerals in new syllabi from first grade on was rejected by many teachers who piloted the new syllabi. They perceived the distinction as useless and confusing. So did many mathematicians who reviewed the syllabi drafts: they thought this distinction was too formalistic, a relic of the then waning "New Math" era. The distinction was erased from the syllabi, but the controversy has not been settled.

Be it as it may for elementary school curricular materials, for the purposes of this chapter it is necessary to distinguish *numbers* as mental concepts from *numerals* as signs, and among numerals as signs, it is also necessary to distinguish mental numerals as sign *types* from materialized numerals as sign *tokens*.[5] Thus, when I speak about the number nine, I will be talking about the concept of nine, whatever that may be. It is customary to say that I am using the word 'nine', not *mentioning* it. When I say, "The word 'nine' in English is written with four letters" I am mentioning the numeral word 'nine', not using it, and I am using the numeral word 'four', not mentioning it. Single quotation marks will be used to mention words, other symbols, word numerals and symbolic numerals as types.[6]

For the second distinction between types and tokens a new notation will be needed. When I write about the word numeral 'nine' or about the symbolic Hindu-Arabic numeral '9' for the number nine, I am referring to a *mental* numeral type, not to a token of it, not even to the token just written in this sentence between single quotes. Specific tokens of a type will be written in square brackets. For instance, when I say that the following [9] is a token of the Hindu-Arabic numeral '9', I intend to direct your attention to that specific trace left by the ink on the paper in which this page you are now reading was printed. When I write again [9], this is another token of the same numeral type '9' for the number nine. Those two tokens might look identical at first sight, but they are situated in different places of the page and perhaps might be distinguishable if we used a magnifying glass, and certainly would be if we used a microscope.

A mental numeral itself as a type *cannot* be spoken, written or pointed to. A numeral type is a mental cognitive-motor procedure to write and recognize tokens of that numeral. Numeral types are operational cognitive-motor components of semiotic registers. Tokens of the same numeral type *can* be spoken, written or pointed to. They might differ somewhat from one another, up to the point where a child might write a token of her type '9' not as we usually write them, like the following token: [9], but upside down, making it look like the following token: [∂], or after a mental half-turn in a way that looks like the following token: [6], or after a reflection on the vertical midline, etc., but she still may recognize it as a token of the same numeral '9'. In bank checks, the machine-readable tokens of '9' would have a closed oval (rather a rounded-off square) and a straight stem.[7]

Research on children's rendering of numbers using oral or written numeral words or symbolic numerals often suffers from obscurity and didactical inapplicability because of the lack of clear distinctions and unambiguous notations for number systems as complex noetic constructions and numeration systems as semiotic registers; for numbers as concepts and numerals as signs; among numerals, for numerals as sign types and as sign tokens, and among types and tokens, for verbal oral, verbal written, symbolic written, and other types and tokens to come.[8] These ambiguities raise serious obstacles to meta-analysis and evaluation of such research.

"DO NUMBERS START AT ZERO, OR AT ONE"

In a chapter written 20 years ago I reported a recurrent question asked by teachers all over the world: "Do numbers start at zero, or at one?" Readers will find there my favorite answer to that question: "Number starts at two!" (Vasco, 1985). Why would I say that?

Obviously, if I say that a number of people agree with me, I cannot mean that there is only one person agreeing with me: at least two! Fortunately, I am not alone in answering "At two!" Any old arithmetic text, from Greek papyrus rolls to medieval parchments and 19th-century textbooks on paper will tell you that number starts at two, because one is not a number (see Aristotle,[9] Euclid,[10] and Boethius' *Institutiones Arithmeticæ*). For an 18th-Century arithmetic, you still can find in Harvard's Widener Library an arithmetic textbook of 1777, where right at the third page we learn that one is called 'one' because, "being as it is one and indivisible, it has no composition, nor is a number, but principle and foundation of all number" (Taboada y Ulloa, 1777). For all of them, one is not a number, but only the origin of number. In mathematics, we still say that one is neither a prime number nor a composite number. We do now say that one is odd, not even. The Greek and Latin sages would say it was neither prime nor composite, and neither odd nor even, simply because it was not a number at all. We have changed that story for the pair odd/even. Why haven't we changed it for the pair prime/composite? That, certainly, is odd.

At any rate, practically everybody today agrees that one is a number. Two is certainly a number in all cultures and times we know of. Special words related to 'two', like 'the dyad' or 'the couple', are very old, and in some ancient languages (Sanskrit, Hebrew, Greek, Arabic, Old Slavonic, etc.), there used to be a separate grammatical category between the singular and the plural: the dual. Relics of this "dual number" are still alive in English in the adjective "dual", and in the use of "either" and "both" (in Spanish, "ambos"). Semitic languages still keep dual forms, at least for paired body parts. Some Australian, Polynesian and Melanesian languages are said to contain not only dual forms, but also trial and quadrual (see Gullberg, 1997, p. 4).

When did one become the first number? Or is it true that now zero is the first number? Those are difficult tasks for every historian of arithmetic, and puzzling tasks for many teachers – and for every child.

IS THERE A GOOD DEFINITION OF NUMBER?

One cannot answer the question "Do numbers start at zero or at one?" or accept or reject my favorite answer "They start at two!" – which I still consider the more historically attuned – if we don't know what number is. Do we know? What concept of number do we have? For most of us today, one is a number; for many, zero is a number, and at least for some, negative numbers are also numbers, and non-integer rationals between zero and one are numbers too. Algebra and calculus students think they know what real numbers are, and of course, they believe they are *real* numbers, as if the other numbers were not real, or as if the real numbers were not as imaginary as imaginary numbers or as complex as complex numbers. How do people understand number?

Much work has been done for decades on the starting point of our present understanding of number. From archaeology, anthropology and history; from ethology, neurology, psychology, cognitive science and artificial intelligence, from didactics of mathematics – and even from pure mathematics – much has been gleaned, inferred, studied and analyzed about the counting numbers, significantly called "natural numbers", and about the way animals and human children start using those first few numbers. This chapter cannot even remotely summarize so much work (see for instance Dehaene, 1993, 1997; and Tolchinsky, 2002). Its purpose is rather to select a few examples from deeper and larger works – some of them treated in other chapters of this book – and hint at possible psychogenetic, didactical, and educational research implications of them.

An example from ethology: it is well known that some animals, including birds, can subitize low numbers, at least two, three or even four, clearly distinguishing them in laboratory trials or when a researcher removes one egg from a nest (for a full treatment, see Boysen & Capaldi, 1993; see also Davis & Perusse, 1988).[11] Five-year-old children can easily subitze up to five or six (witness the faces of dice), and Glen Doman reportedly can teach babies to subitize up to 60 or more orange spots on a poster.[12]

Thus, initial number systems seem to have been based on a few subitized or counted integers, over which addition would be practically the only binary operation; one can infer that the unary operation of going from one number to the next was also present, and that the usual additive ordering would be the only binary relation recognized by the users of that system. The pioneering work of Stanislas Dehaene has connected the neural basis of cognitive functioning to the higher-order processes of subitizing, counting, speaking, reading and writing of the first few integers (see a summary of his own work in Dehaene, 1993, 1997).[13] This means that for an initial concept of number it is not necessary to know how to count with words or gestures, against some extreme socio-cultural constructionist claims. Small numbers can, in principle, be conceived without words or external symbols.

Here lurks another fundamental problem in re-reading the history of mathematics and interpreting research in mathematics education. Numbers and numerals are considered as isolated objects, not as inserted in a systemic network where relations and operations are just as important as any specific number or numeral. There is no good definition of number because any definition would depend on what number system we are talking about, and there seems to be no overarching definition of number that encompasses all currently accepted number systems.

Compare this system of low-valued counting integers with the ordered ring of integers as considered today by mathematicians: the differences are enormous, even though the word 'integer' is often used for both types of number systems. The same integer three as a counting number might later become plus three in the signed integers, or become a trebling rational amplifier in the rational numbers; it could also be a real number or a complex number. There seems to be no definition that would cover all those so-called "integers" belonging to a chain of more and more complex number systems, not to mention algebraic integers.[14]

Parallel statements can be made about systems of numerals. Numerals never go around alone, even when they look like isolated tokens in print: [9]. Numerals are always part of a system with its basic elements, its assembling and decomposing operations, and its spatiotemporal relations. The tokens produced by speakers, writers or gesturers are the products of a very complex cognitive-motor system that produces and interprets tokens from within a limited range of allowable representation types: that system is one of Duval's semiotic registers.

For the purposes of this chapter, we will restrict our study to the so-called "counting numbers" or "whole numbers" or "integers" (the ordinary integers, that is; not yet the signed integers). We will study only some numeration systems for those numbers, which we identify with the semiotic registers related to them. The history of rational number systems and their numeration systems as semiotic registers would take another chapter, and so would the history of systems of signed integers, or of real numbers or complex numbers, and other candidates for the title "number systems".

IS THERE A GOOD DEFINITION OF NUMBER, AT LEAST FOR WHOLE NUMBERS?

Set theorists and logicians proposed late in the 19th century that any given whole number was not a first-order property, that is, a property of elements, but a second-order property: a property of sets of elements. In fact, so they said, each number was a property of all those sets and only those sets that can be put in a one-to-one correspondence to each other. This property was called "the cardinality" of the given set, sometimes also called "the numerosity", "the size", "the power" or "the potency" of that set (Cantor's "Mächtigkeit").[15]

Once you accept that – as a product of a refined noetic activity – there is such a mental object as a set formed by one and only one element, but distinct from the given element, then you realize that this kind of number could start at one: the cardinality of singletons. If you further allow – after an even more convoluted noesis – that there is such a mental object as a set formed by no elements whatsoever, being still a set, then you are forced to accept that this kind of number could start at zero: the cardinality of the empty set.

Numbers so defined were called by Cantor "cardinal numbers" or simply "cardinals". They deserve to be called "Cantorian cardinal numbers". Cantor himself extended them from finite sets to infinite sets and created a dizzying world of transfinite cardinal numbers. For the humble case of finite sets, the finite cardinal numbers starting at zero were soon identified as "the natural numbers". This unnatural definition via equi-cardinality of sets won the day, and those monstrous entities became natural.

There is much to be said in favor of such definition of cardinality and of Cantorian cardinal numbers, if only that – after strong initial resistance – they gained practically universal acceptance among mathematicians in a short period of time. To normal people, of course, the set-theoretic definition seems much too convoluted and anti-natural for something as obvious and natural as a plain old counting number, which they take to be just a member of a culture-friendly standard list to measure the size of groupings of loose, discrete, directly perceivable objects that lend themselves to be counted. In fact, there has always been a resistance to the acceptance of zero as a number, because nobody counts 'zero, one, two, etc.' In this sense, zero is not a counting number.

Hans Freudenthal devoted a long section of Chapter XI, "The number concept – Objective accesses", of his book *Mathematics as an educational task* to criticize the numerosity or potency or cardinality concept of number. Among many sharp observations, he states:

> Maybe the five on the die still reminds one of a potency, but nobody connects a numerosity idea with a 5-dollar bill, with 5 o'clock, with 5 minutes, with

grade 5, with platform 5, with the age of five, or the point 5 on the number line. (Freudenthal, 1973, p. 194)

We may see here the rational number 5 as an expander of a measure, the ordinal number 5 (without the ordinal number words, but one could also say 'fifth grade' instead of 'grade 5'), the coordinate placer 5 written under a tick on a number line, which is not necessarily an ordinal, etc.

A good summary of the pertinent literature and present research on children's cardinal and ordinal understanding of small numbers is found in Tolchinsky (2003) and in Bruce and Threlfall (2004). They distinguish well between cardinality and ordinality, and between subitizing and counting as two different ways of producing a number within the cardinality genus, which may or may not give rise to different species of that genus. The ordinality genus is more elusive (see below under "Kinds of whole numbers").

THE CASE OF ZERO

Children are often reluctant to accept that a single element could be or form a set or, equivalently, that a set could have one and only one element. Children are even more adamant in refusing to accept that no elements whatsoever could be or form a set or, equivalently, that a set without elements could be a set at all. They seem to reject the empty set. Would you say that you have a collection of stamps if you have no stamps at all? For me, this means that zero is not a number of objects at all. One (mental) thing is the concept of zero as the number of objects in an empty set, and another (material) thing is a written record of numerals for zero. These written records are ambiguous: they could refer to the concept of zero or be just empty-place indicators in a compound numeral. There are a few isolated Babylonian tablets that seem to have a numeral for zero. It was not necessary, as the numerals were written in rows and columns, and an empty cell was enough to signal the missing power of sixty; but there it is, perhaps only as a redundant empty-place indicator.

Chinese legend affirms that zero was invented in China before the Current Era, and that, much later, Buddhist monks transmitted this invention to Vedic scholars in India. In favor of this Chinese origin, we can read J.C. Martzoff's chapter (Grattan-Guinness, 1995, vol. 1, chapter 1.9, pp. 93–103) on Chinese mathematics, who says that oracle-bone ("*jiaguwen*") inscriptions of about the 14th century BCE incorporate decimal notation (Grattan-Guinness, 1995, vol. 1, p. 94). A similar statement is found in Karine Chemla's chapter on fractions (Grattan-Guinness, 1995, vol. 1, chapter 1.17, pp. 160–166). First she talks about the Babylonian solution of multiplying reciprocals of numbers of the form $2^p 3^q 5^r$, then the Egyptian solution of unit fractions, and then she says that the "Nine Chapters" or "*Jiuzhang suanshu*" can be dated to the first century CE, and that there are already numerals in decimal notation in it.

Joseph Needham, on the other hand, affirms that zero was imported from India to China about the 6th Century CE (see Crossley's statement in Grattan-Guinness,

1995, vol. 1, chapter 1.16, p. 156). Most historians attribute the invention of zero, at least as a dot to signal the absence of a numeral in a place where one could expect it, to Indian astronomers of the 5th century CE. The figures from one two ten, somewhat similar to ours, appear already in the 3rd Century CE in the Nana Ghat inscriptions, but without a clear positional value. The invention of the full positional notation with a zero (or its adoption from Chinese exemplars) must have happened in India in the first half of the 5th Century CE, assuming that the date given for the treatise on the parts of the Universe "Lokavibhaga", written in Sanskrit about 458 CE, is accurate. There, one finds, written in Sanskrit script, the word numerals for a number we would write '14,236,713' (Guedj, 1998/1996, p. 51).

Maya astronomers invented their zero independently about the 6th century CE (see Closs' study in Grattan-Guinness, 1995, vol. 1, chapter 1.16, pp. 143–149). The first clear mention of zero in the West seems to be a letter of the Mesopotamian Bishop Severus Sebokht to a European colleague about the year 662.

The Arabs knew about the Indian numeration system as early as the reign of Al-Mamun, who started a rich library of manuscripts in Baghdad. Around the year 773 CE, an Indian scholar brought there a copy of the astronomical treatise "Siddhanta", which was promptly translated. The new numerals were not easily received, and the old Arabic numeration system with the aliphatic letters as numerals was used for at least one more century.

Muhammad-ibn-Musa al-Khowarismi wrote a treatise on addition and subtraction according to the Hindu method, early in the 9th century, and the Hindu-Arabic numeration system quickly spread with the Arab conquerors through the Middle East, North Africa, and Spain. Gerbert of Aurillac, soon to be Pope Sylvester II (999 CE), used this system for documents and inscriptions, without much success or followers. Its use started spreading to Western Europe through the translation of Arabic manuscripts in Toledo from the late 11th to the end of the 13th Century. Although al-Khowarismi clearly acknowledged the Indian origin of the system, his translators referred to these numerals as "Arabic numbers". From this denomination stems the common name of our ten digits in all European languages. The decimal notation with a specific numeral for zero had to wait until the 13th century to spread through Italy and then the rest of Europe, when Mediterranean commercial routes, money exchange, loans and small quantities of precious metals, jewels and spices forced the merchants to switch from Roman numerals to Hindu-Arabic.

ORAL NUMERALS FOR WHOLE NUMBERS

Every child after five or six knows a good initial segment of the standard list used in the surrounding culture to measure the size of groups. Let us call "a count" the successive formulation of an initial segment of that list, starting at the word for 'one' (or whatever word starts the count in a given language and culture), and stopping at some later word.[16] The first count would then be, in English, saying 'one, two'; in Spanish, 'uno, dos', etc. Saying 'one' or 'none' would not be a count, but a failure to count. This standard list is like the tailor's measure tape, but instead of carrying it in our apron pockets like tailors do, we carry it in our memories. If the size of a group of objects needs to be measured, we just pull out our standard list step by step from memory, and we count mechanically to produce a measurement of the size of the group. Oral word numerals are the words in that standard spoken list, and the counting numbers are the sizes of groups of objects we could count by using that list.

The relevant pattern emerges from invariance of the count: if carefully counted,[17] no matter from what object you start, and in what order you make the successive objects correspond to the successive members of the standard list, the last numeral of the count is always the same. That last numeral of the relevant initial segment of the standard counting list is a numeral for that conceptual counting number, but there might be many other numerals related to the same number.

If we would reflect on why the last numeral of the count is always the same, we would arrive at a conclusion similar to the now-common set-theoretic definition of cardinal numbers; but that has to be taken as the conclusion of a long process, not as its starting point. If that were not the case, how could we agree that the convoluted set-theoretic definition of cardinal number captures the common notion of 'the size of a group' and gives a new insight into the reasons for the invariance of the count?

IS ARITHMETIC TIME-BASED OR SPACE-BASED?

There is another plausible historical origin of number besides the synchronic spread of groups of loose, discrete objects in space before our eyes, which we can subitize or count. It is the rhythm of events in time. The count of days is much older and natural than the proverbial count of sheep, which would require hundreds of thousands of years of hominization until the first few animal species were domesticated and the count of heads would become socially valued. Long before agriculture, the diachronic count of days until the Moon waned again or until the Sun returned to its solstice must have been well known. Time-related numbers may be as old as culture.

The historical record starts with notches on bones and shells well before the beginnings of writing, which can be roughly set in the fourth millennium BCE. There is a famous 37,000 year-old bone found in Swaziland with 64 markings, 29 of which could represent various phases of the moon; there is a 32,000 year-old bone found in Moravia with 54 markings, where five groups of five are clearly set apart. Bone and antler pieces with knife slashes and notches date at least to 15,000 years ago. The famous Ishango bone, about 11,000 years old, has two rows of sixty marks and a row of forty-eight. Marked clay tokens go back to the eighth millennium BCE (see Grattan-Guinness, 1997, pp. 24–25).

These carvings, notches and markings are one-to-one semiotic registers: they are designed to represent each object in the group by one token or incision. We could speak of notch registers, where the basic numeral is the incision, and recorded compound numerals are the spatially separated groups of incisions.

In writing, painting or sculpting, there are one-to-one bar, stroke or dot registers; primitive knot registers would add one knot to a string for every counted object. In this sense, Pythagorean figural numbers, which are represented and classified according to the geometric shape of dot groupings, correspond to recognizable compound numerals of a one-to-one dot register.

KINDS OF WHOLE NUMBERS

For the purposes of research and practice in mathematics education, it is worth rescuing many pages of the old arithmetic textbooks. From the early printed arithmetics of the 15th century to the school textbooks of the beginning of the 20th century, their authors used to start by distinguishing concrete from abstract numbers, and cardinal from ordinal numbers.

Let us start by the first distinction: concrete and abstract numbers. Historians and anthropologists have maintained that ancient cultures had specific number words for specific categories of objects, animals, and people. Archaeological dissection of existing languages, like Inuit, Chinese or Thai, give support to the distinction between these concrete numbers tied to specific groups of specific perceptually similar objects, and the separation of verbal oral or written numerals from their ties to concrete elements of a group, until they referred only to the abstract size of it, whatever its elements.

Children might go through short or not so short periods of conceptualizing number-of-years, number-of-people and number-of-objects as different from each other, not yet subsumed under an abstract concept of number, although I have not found specific research on this topic. Sociogenesis of the abstract number concept is not necessarily reflected in psychogenesis, but it could well be.

The second distinction is between cardinal and ordinal numbers. Counts have a neat order structure: the word numerals in any count have the total or linear order every mathematician admires the most, as revealed by the label they use for systems ordered like counts: "well ordered systems". In the history of mathematics, the linear order of the word numerals in any count must have played a powerful role in ritual, feasts, trade and war. Marching or standing in rows, lining up in queues, religious processions, hierarchical rankings and other culturally regulated activities might suggest to members of all cultures the construction of two different sequences of numbers. One would be associated to the standard list of counting words, like "one, two, three … ", and the other to a parallel list of placement-indicating words like "first, second, third …", different from the sequence elicited by the counting words and meant to designate each place in that prototypical order. The members of theses lists are called in older arithmetic textbooks "cardinal numbers" and "ordinal numbers". They could occur without envisaging an umbrella concept of number suggested to us by the final word in those two expressions (see again Bruce & Threlfall, 2004).

The history of these two lists must be as long and irretrievable as the history of spoken languages. To my knowledge, there is no way to document which one is older or whether they were just one and then drifted into two, and when. Modern cultures concentrate on teaching children the list of cardinal numbers, neglecting the ordinals, but their role is powerful enough to merit explicit recovery in mathematics education. I call them "ordinal placement numbers", as a species in the genus of placement indicators. A difficult problem is that ordinal placement numbers are attributed to chunks of space or time, not to lines or points, as mathematicians are wont to require. This creates a specific problem in the learning of the number line and of Cartesian coordinates, as most children prefer to write the numerals between the ticks on the number line, not directly under it.

Ordinal placement numbers have to be learned by heart, and, in many languages, including English, their abbreviations are not easy: '1st, 2nd, 3rd, 4th, 5th, etc.' In English, the word 'one' is the first count word; the word 'two' is the second; the word 'three' is the third, and then the Anglo-Saxon culture would have to invent ordinal words to match the rest of the count words. The fourth was clearly related to 'four' by a dental ending '-th' similar but not equal to the '-t' in 'first' or the '-d' in 'second' and 'third'; the fifth was a phonetic variant of 'five' with the same ending '-th'. From there on, one can simply add '-th' or '-eth' to the last sound of the count word. One must learn only the first five ordinal words by heart, and then assemble the rest of them from 'sixth' on.

In French, one only needs to learn the first two ordinal words 'premier, second', and then one can just add '-ième' to the count words. In German, one needs three words 'erste, zweite, dritte', and then one can add '-te' to the count words (except 'sieben').

In Spanish, there is a special list of ordinal words coming from Latin, only somewhat related to the usual count words: 'primero, segundo, tercero, cuarto, quinto, sexto, séptimo, octavo, noveno, décimo', which one must learn by heart. After the tenth ordinal word, one has three choices: going on with an easy list of ordinal words using the count words and ending in '-avo': 'onceavo, doceavo, etc.' or with two kinds of old ordinal words: 'undécimo' or 'décimoprimero', 'duodécimo' or 'décimosegundo'. The memory load is quite heavy for Spanish-speaking youngsters, and even worse for non-native learners of Spanish.

Some old arithmetic textbooks also distinguish a third type of numbers beyond cardinal and ordinal numbers. They are seldom noticed but clearly distinct from cardinal and ordinal placement numbers; they are called "distributive numbers". The classic Latin list of distributive numerals is "singuli, bini, terni, quaterni, quini, seni, septeni". In English, we would say, "one-by-one", "two-by-two", etc., and in Spanish, "de a uno", "de a dos", etc. I have found no research on the use of distributive numbers by children.

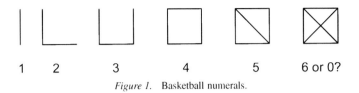

Figure 1. Basketball numerals.

MANY-TO-ONE CORRESPONDENCE REGISTERS

The lines or notches carved on wood or bones were one-to-one registers, in the sense that there was a mark for every object in the group. This is still clear in the first nine Egyptian numerals, the first four ancient Greek and Roman numerals, and the first three Chinese numerals (with horizontal strokes). Our numerals '2' and '3' could well come from streamlined continuous strokes for the old Chinese numerals. In other types of old and contemporary Arabic numerals for our two and three one can still see that they come from streamlined one-to-one vertical-stroke numerals.

The bar- or notch-numerals are not practical for large numbers, and require careful recounting. Very soon, all known writing cultures started to combine strokes and other icons to produce compound numerals for larger numbers. One still sees today in children's games or informal store inventories that the first four items are recorded by successive vertical strokes, but the fifth stroke crosses out the former four. The Roman numeral "V" could have come from this type of practices or just from a simplified icon of a hand. In children's games and youth's sports one also sees one-to-one registers that could easily become new numerals, like the recording of fouls in a basketball game from one (a vertical bar) to five (a slashed square; see Figure 1).

This practice could provide numerals for numeration systems base five, base six, or base seven, by crossing out the slashed square once more as a numeral for six, as above, and using a circle for zero.

Once the new abbreviating numerals are invented, the distinction between digits as basic elements of a numeration system, and one-digit, two-digit, or n-digit numerals became useful. One thing is to list the digits of a numeration system, and another one is to produce numerals for given numbers larger than the list of digits. With our ten different digits in the base-ten register, we can produce one-digit numerals for the numbers up to and including nine; from ten on we need two-digit numerals, etc. Thus, digits can be thought as simple or atomic types or as tokens thereof and their juxtaposition to form compound or molecular types and tokens requires a very refined semiotic register.

Oral-Word Semiotic Registers

The problem with concentrating attention on the history of written numerals is that we are forgetting the whole history of numbers and numerals before the invention of writing. Children begin to use finger numerals about the age of three, often before they speak them out, and much before they can write them out. A very

27

successful elementary arithmetic program in Colombia has as one of its tenets that children do not have to write anything during the first grade.[18]

With the diachronical reading of history, fortunately, mathematics education researchers' attention soon turned to oral-word semiotic registers, but not so much to gestural registers. We have no tape or videotape recordings of preliterate times. We must do careful archaeology and ethnology of present-day oral and gestural numeration systems. We must precisely delimit minimal basic-word or gesture lists; memory load; combination rules, and possible limits to the largest numeral that can be spoken or signaled in a given oral or gestural numeration system.

The power of combining a few known words to stretch the count is remarkable. When does the recurrent pattern start? It varies much from language to language. Take English: 'twelve, thir-teen, four-teen', etc. Because of the phonetic variant, one must learn the word 'thirteen' by heart, and the recurrent pattern starts only at 'fourteen'. In Latin: 'decem, undecim, duodecim', etc., the pattern starts right after the word numeral for ten. Compare with German: 'zwölf, dreizehn', etc.; with Spanish: 'quince, dieciseis', etc; with French: 'quinze, seize, dix-sept', etc. Latin has another trap up the line: 'septem-decim, duodeviginti, undeviginti', breaking off the recursive pattern after the numeral word for seventeen.

The order in which oral-word numerals are spoken out (try to think of the times before writing) also changes from language to language. There is the high-low reading, like ours vs. the low-high reading: Arabic, Hebrew, German up to 'neun und neunzig', and from there on there is a mixture of low-high and high-low readings, very confusing to foreigners. Think again in high-low terms when you read in Latin 'septem-decim': you follow a low-high reading, but from 'vigintiunum' on, you follow a high-low reading. It is not difficult to find other interesting archeological traces. In French, 'soixant-dix' reminds us of a sexagesimal past; 'quatre-vingt', of a lost base twenty.

Gestural Registers

There are also finger registers, finger-and-toe registers, and body-touch registers. The most impressive body-touch register was documented in the Sibiller tribespeople of New Guinea. After counting on the left-hand fingers up to five, they count from six to thirteen on the left wrist, forearm, elbow, biceps, collarbone, shoulder, ear and eye; the nose is touched for fourteen, and the sequence goes down the right side at the reversed gestural steps to keep counting from fifteen to twenty-seven (see Bergamini, 1963, pp. 18–19).[19]

Bede, the English monk of the 8th Century CE., invented a body register that allowed him to count up to a million. Chinese reckoners of the 15th Century CE. could count to a billion with an even more sophisticated body-count register. One can easily surmise that not many people could use such complicated semiotic registers, but they are the overdeveloped descendants from the finger-count registers any child quickly learns.

It is easy to observe different finger-numeral registers in pre-school children. I have found it very productive to ask for their age or the age of a little brother or

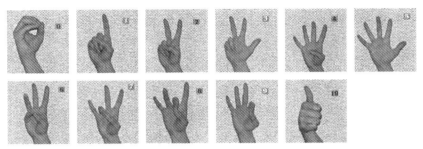

Figure 2. ASL finger numerals.

sister. Very young children usually do not answer in words and seldom know how to draw a numeral, but they seem to know exactly what I am asking, because they extend or bend the right number of fingers. One can then ask how old they were a year ago or how old will they be at their next birthday. Often they cannot clearly distinguish 'last' and 'next', but what they understand from my question is pretty clear by what they do with their fingers.

In theory, finger-numeral registers can be distributed in a three-by-three matrix, with the columns labeled 'extending registers', 'bending registers' and 'touching registers', and the rows labeled 'index-anchored registers', 'little-finger-anchored registers' and 'thumb-anchored register'.

By far the most frequent register I have observed is the index-anchored extending register. The child starts by extending its index finger up, then the middle finger, then the annular, then the little finger and then, but not always, the thumb to show a five. Folding registers are similar, but they start by extending all fingers and then bending in the index finger first, the little finger first, or the thumb first. Touching registers start by touching with the tip of the thumb of the same hand either the index finger first, and then touching the other fingers from the inside out, or the little finger first, and then touching the other fingers from the outside in.

It has been suggested that the dozen is a natural base if the finger count is carried by the thumb touching in order each phalanx of each of the four remaining fingers, either starting from the index or from the little finger. I have never observed the phalanx count. If you keep track of the dozens you have counted in the phalanxes of your right-hand fingers by doing the same with your left hand, you can see how a dozen dozens or a gross could be easily counted with just a finger-touching register. As far as I know, this type of count has not been factually observed; it remains purely hypothetical.

The usual finger figures used by hearing-impaired persons, and incorporated into the American Sign Language ASL are the main elements for another gestural register; any decimal numeral can be translated to or from it (see Figure 2). For numerals of four or more digits, the memory load is very heavy, because each additional digit signaled by a hand gesture changes the place value of the former digits. In this case, the low-to-high reading would decrease the decoding effort.

Iconic Registers

The beginnings of writing in 4th millennium BCE are now traced to Sumerian "bullæ", clay receptacles for carrying tokens inside, by means of which the receiver in a distant land could be sure that the goods delivered by the caravan leaders were really those intended by the sender. Soon, it was seen as useful to print the tokens also on the outside before closing the "bulla" and firing it.[20] After that, it must have been a short evolutionary change to realize that the tokens inside the cavity were redundant, and that only a flat piece of clay was needed for a complete record of the wares. Initially, the number of wheat sacks or sheep was recorded on the outside of the "bulla" by repeated impressions of the same token with an icon for a sack or a sheep. One could save space by impressing a line or dot for each item, preceded or followed by the respective icon. This variation seems slight, but it marks the transition from concrete to abstract numbers. These registers were still one-to-one, until specific icons for larger numerals were used.

Recently, Merce García-Milá, Ana Tebersoky and Eduardo Martí replicated and reframed a long line of research that came from earlier work of Bialystock and Codd (1996, 2000), who in turn continued the pioneering work of Martin Hughes (1986) on how children would mark on the outside of a box the number of cookies, buttons or pieces of candy inside it. This newer research led to the rediscovery of many "Sumerian children" among Catalonian Kindergartners, at distinct stages of symbolic compression of numerals (García-Milá, Teberosky & Martí, 2000; García-Milá, Martí & Teberosky, 2004).

Pythagorean figural numbers show an interesting iconic evolution, where the one-to-one register could easily evolve into a many-to-one register. The arrangements of triangular and square dots were at the same time aesthetically pleasant groupings of dots and icons of equilateral triangles and squares, as well as other geometric figures. Here, one sees how the semiotic register allows an internal distinction among numbers. Each sequence of figural numbers exerts a perennial fascination on mathematically inclined persons of all ages and nationalities.

One can easily see that a triangle, a square, a pentagon, etc. could have evolved into numerals of their own, but at that late age (7th century BCE), numeration systems based on groups of ten were firmly established. The ensuing need for nine distinct numerals would have made the use of these polygonal figures very cumbersome, as polygons of seven, eight or nine sides are very difficult to distinguish.

The die numerals in the six faces of dice are an articulated mix of a one-to-one register that can also be seen as possessing six different iconic numerals that can be read off without counting (or subitizing).

Phonic Registers

Oral word registers are not the only semiotic registers related to sounds. One can easily think of clap, finger-snap, whistle, lip- or cheek-click numerals for low numbers. Longer numerals can be obtained by rhythmic sequences of claps, as Jean Bamberger explores in this volume.

One could also count Morse code as a phonic semiotic register, where numerals and letters are expressed by long and short beeps. The printed or perforated dots and dashes configure a different semiotic register of the same Morse code. More recently, touch-tone telephones have introduced a new semiotic register based on beep pitch. Before touch-tone, there were people who could listen to the beeps of a pulse phone and decode the number dialed. After touch-tone, modem codes have introduced new semiotic registers that allow for a very fast communication of numerals and letters.

Visual-Tactile Registers

Abacus registers provide a mixture of visual and tactile experience: sliding-bead registers and movable-counter registers can be read by looking at the patterns, but may be produced and interpreted by blind persons. Notch registers, knot registers, and Braille-code registers can also be listed as visual-tactile registers.

Letter Registers

The invention of letters to correspond to syllables and then to isolable sounds was certainly one of the most crucial moments in the history of culture. We can say that letters were so valued, that they soon began to be used as numerals. There were at least three routes to this use.

First, independently invented numerals were identified with some of the later developed letters. This seems to have been the case in the Roman register; old numerals were only the icons 'I', 'V', 'X'. Second, the initials of numeral words were used as numerals. This seems to have been the case for the Roman 'C' for 'centum', and 'M' for 'millia'. How the letters 'L' and 'D' came to be used is not clear; 'L' could be an angular version of the lower half of a 'C', and 'D' seems to have evolved by just dropping the left semicircle of a circle-like icon split in half by a vertical segment, like '(|)', an older symbol for a thousand, later displaced by the convenient mnemonic of 'M' for 'millia'. Thus, for the letter 'M' we see an indirect path, starting with a special cipher for a thousand, and then the vague similarity of this cipher to the letter 'M', and the initial sound of 'millia', ended in the use of 'M' only.

In the older Greek numeration system, the initial of 'penta', not in the newer form 'Π' but in the old form with a shorter right vertical stroke (see Figure 3, adapted from Cajori, 1928, Sections 33–38, pp. 22–26, with the help of St. Andrew's website on the history of mathematics), seems to be the base for the numerals for 5, 50, 500, 5000. The initials of 'deka', 'hecto', 'xilia', and 'myria' were clearly chosen as numerals for 10, 100, 1000, and 10,000. These numerals are also called "acrophonic" ("initial-sound") numerals.

Third, the order of the letters of the alephat or alphabet, when it settled down, led to an easy extension of the use of the first ten letters as the first ten numerals, with or without a special marking to distinguish them as numerals. This was the case in Phoenician, early and late Hebrew, Aramaic, Palmyran, Syriach, and other ancient languages.

Γ	△	H	X	M
Pente	Deka	Hekaton	Khilioi	Murioi
Πεντε	Δεκα	Ηεκατον	Χιλιοι	Μυριοι
5	10	100	1000	10000

Figure 3. Old Greek numerals.

A	B	Γ	Δ	E	Ϛ	Z	H	Θ
α	β	γ	δ	ε	ϛ	ζ	η	θ
1	2	3	4	5	6	7	8	9

I	K	Λ	M	N	Ξ	O	Π	Ϟ
ι	κ	λ	μ	ν	ξ	ο	π	ϟ
10	20	30	40	50	60	70	80	90

P	Σ	T	Y	Φ	X	Ψ	Ω	⋔
ρ	σ	τ	υ	φ	χ	ψ	ω	ϡ
100	200	300	400	500	600	700	800	900

Figure 4. Greek letter numerals.

A second set of ten letter numerals served to represent multiples of ten from ten to one hundred. If available, a third set of ten letters would be needed to represent multiples of one hundred up to nine hundred or one thousand.

The fact that this use was started very early after the fixation of the respective alphabet is documented by the survival of three letters that later disappeared from the Greek alphabet (the "episemata": the digamma or vau, the koppa, and the sampi), that were still used for our '6', '90' and '900' long after those letters were dropped from the phonetic coding of Attic and Ionian Greek (see Figure 4, adapted from Cajori, 1928, Section 36, pp. 23–25, also with the help of St. Andrew's website on the history of mathematics).

This semiotic register had an upper limit at one thousand. One could start anew with a special marking to multiply by one thousand, but then, a million was the limit, unless one started to write letter numerals above an 'M' for 'myria' (10,000). Old Hebrew writers had to use the final variants ("sofit") of some of their letters to complete the character set from five hundred to nine hundred, and needed to start a new thousand-count (which could produce ambiguity when placed to the left or right of the first count) in order to go from one thousand to one less than a million. Using the myriad myriads (our '100,000,000') as a basis for a series of numerical combinations, Archimedes invented a complex set of word numerals to compensate for that limitation in his famous "Arenarius" or "The Sand Reckoner", a system that allowed him to estimate the count of grains of sand that would fill his spherical model of the Universe at our order of magnitude $10^{\wedge}64$.[21]

Cipher Registers

Ciphers are basic numerals that are distinguished by the culture as different from the letters of the shared alphabet. Our cipher '1' might look like a capital 'i', and our cipher '0' might look like a capital 'o', but numerals and letters belong to different symbolic sequences.

The history of ciphers in different cultures is well known, and hundreds of ciphers are recorded in plates and figures of various books of history of mathematics. Perhaps the attraction to these numerals has been an epistemological obstacle to studying the respective semiotic registers that produced them.

The evolution and the permanence of different types of Hindu-Arabic numerals are interesting on its own. It might be surprising to many readers that the Arabic numerals used today in the Middle East are quite different from ours, especially the numerals for '0', that looks like a dot; for '5', that looks like an 'O'; and for '7' and '8', which look like a 'V' and an inverted 'V' or lambda 'Λ'.

The apices or cones of Boethius had a variant of the numerals engraved at their tops or bottoms (see the apical numerals in Cajori, 1928, Section 80, Figures 22–23, pp. 49–50). We could today point at the numerals printed in the lower edge of bank checks as another variant of our numerals, redesigned to facilitate automated optical character reading.

Handwritten numerals have also different types, as any postal service employee will attest. OCR-software failed miserably when trying to distinguish the ways people, especially Hispanic people, would write very different tokens for '1' or '7'; worse yet, the tokens for the crossed-out variant of '7' – the usual one in Spain and Latin-America – could be read as tokens of '7', or of '2', or of '4'. Only cleverly designed and patiently trained neural networks managed to do the job with more reliability than human readers, even though nobody really knows how they do it.[22]

The sole introduction of special ciphers instead of letters still does not tell much about the numeral system and the semiotic registers that can use those basic ciphers to produce numerals for large numbers. For the study of the projective and injective semiosis using those registers one must look closer at the way basic numeral tokens are aligned on the surface of the medium. This is usually referred to as "place value".

Place Value

What is "place value"? Did Romans, late Romans, that is, use place value? My answer is "Yes". One could argue that from the beginning, when they started to write numerals for smaller numbers to the right of numerals for larger numbers, place value was already active as a syntactic rule: a reversal in order would be considered as (syntactically) wrong. In that incipient sense, place value was present, and it was active operationally from the earliest semiotic registers involving ciphers like 'I', 'V', 'X', etc., stipulating that numerals written to the right of others at a short distance from one another would indicate that the decoder must add the corresponding numbers to the accumulated total. Numerals written at longer distance from the tight groupings or starting another row or column would not have to be added to the previous ones. But one could also argue that place value was not yet active in the sense that writing to the left or to the right was not necessary to discriminate between two mental operations, addition and subtraction. We can set a threshold for the place value: the additive convention to form combined numerals would not yet be a case of place value, because the placement of the numeral must mean more than addition. The test is that if you scramble the numerals, the total number represented will still be the same.

When Romans began to write 'IV' instead of 'IIII', 'IX' instead of 'VIIII', 'XL' instead of 'XXXX', etc., they started to use place value in an operationally discriminating way: If a numeral token is written to the right of a numeral for a higher number, the place-value indicates you should add; if written to the left of a numeral for a higher number, the place value indicates you should subtract. Now you could no longer scramble the numerals and pretend they would represent the same number. If that is not place value, I do not understand that expression.

Still, one often reads that there is no place value until we have a base; but what is "a base"? There are, again, different levels of activation of the base for different numeration systems. The first level is the culturally preferred grouping for counts when numeral words or symbols for the successive count-from-one begin to tax the counter's memory. In that case, there could be multiple bases; one could say that a hand (a handful of fingers, noted 'V') was a natural base for Roman numerals, and so was a double hand (noted 'X'); for many American Indian groups, like for the Aztecs and Mayas, a "man" or "person" of twenty fingers-and-toes would be the next larger natural base.[23]

Babylonians clearly combined bases ten and sixty in their counts. One should not expect Babylonian children, even the cleverest of the priestly elite, to know by heart sixty distinct unrelated numerals for the sixty possible tablet rectangles. Now, if instead of using iconic numerals, we count out loud in word numerals, the hand or five disappears as a base, and the double hand or ten becomes the base of the count right from the beginning of the list after 'decem': 'un-decim', 'duo-decim', etc. But wait! For our 'nineteen', the Romans would say 'undeviginti', indicating a fossilized natural stop at twenty, just as in English we have 'four-score', and in French, 'quatre-vingt'.

For these phenomena at the first level, one should speak of additive bases. The next level would be to combine multiplication and addition to form large numerals. This would be the level of additive-multiplicative bases. One could say that the Mayan numeration system had an additive-multiplicative combination of bases five, twenty and three-hundred-sixty: five is an auxiliary base to write a strip instead of five dots; then, four strips would be erased by a numeral that might resemble a closed eye or a closed fist, and the following base would be twenty, written with one dot in the square above the cipher for zero; this sign need not be considered as a numeral for a number, but only as an indicator that there are no dots or strips to be marked in that square cell. Now, it is clear that the base of their numeration system is not yet at the third level, the level of the polynomial base, because the next Maya grouping is not twenty-squared, or four hundred, but a 'tun': a year or three-hundred-and-sixty, the number of days of the averaged year.[24]

The next Maya grouping would be at twenty years, a 'k'atun', and the next, in our notation, at 400 years (a 'baktun'; see Selin, 2000, pp. 210–229), corresponding to our '144,000', but it could have also meant a year of years, our '129,600'.

This cycle of five, twenty and eighteen twenties would classify this base as additive-multiplicative. It could be argued that the 360 for the units at the third level would be used only for calendrical calculations, but that there was a parallel count in strictly polynomial base twenty, so that the next unit would be our '400' and the 'k'atun' would correspond to our '8000'. This can be disputed in the Mayan case, but it is clear that the Aztecs also consistently used base twenty in a strictly polynomial way: they used a flag to represent our '20', a hair or feather ("tzontli") to represent our '400', and a bag of cacao beans ("xiquipilli") to represent our '8000' (Selin, 2000, p. 233).

This is the next level after the additive-multiplicative bases: the polynomial base, where the successive powers of the base yield the next higher groupings. Now we can see how refined a polynomial semiotic register for the natural numbers might be, and also see how cultural the word 'natural' is.

Alphanumeric Registers

They started when computers could no longer be programmed using only base two, with ones and zeros. The packaging of four bits to compose one byte allowed the use of the octal base. Then, a flag bit and a check bit were introduced in each byte, but still using numbers base eight. Wasting an extra bit to directly use decimal numbers was too memory-expensive in those days. Thus, when the next bit was introduced, it was more economic to use the hexadecimal numerals (base sixteen). Now, specific symbols for the numbers ten to fifteen were needed, and the letters 'A' to 'F' were selected as the required numerals for humans (computers just keep grinding the five-bit packages without paying any attention to the sixteen numerals from '0' to '9' and from 'A' to 'F'). Two octal bytes were sufficient for the first alphanumeric code, the old ASCII code of 128 symbols. Now, it is no

35

longer important to distinguish letters from numerals, as a double byte can contain the binary code of a letter or of a numeral. The computer does not care what it is, unless at some stage it must translate the content of the double byte into a printed decimal numeral or a printed letter of our alphabet.

The 10-Trap

One finds often in textbooks and papers on mathematics education a reference to our customary base ten by writing 'base 10'. That is a test case for the need to separate numbers, numerals as types and numerals as tokens. Assume we know the usual Hindu-Arabic numerals from '0', '1' on. What is the numeral for two if we use base two for binary coding? The answer is '10'. What if the base is eight in octal notation? The answer is '10'. What is the numeral for ten if the base is ten? We seem to know the answer too well, so well, indeed, that this knowledge makes us fall into the epistemological 10-trap. My bet is that you read "ten-trap", but I wrote "one-zero-trap". Let the usual Roman numeral 'X' be the next in the list of digits after '9'. What are the numerals for ten and eleven if the base is eleven? They are 'X' and '10'. If we let 'A' be the numeral for ten, 'B' for eleven, up to 'F' for fifteen, sixteen would correspond to the numeral '10' in the usual hexadecimal base preferred by computer hackers. If we go on with 'G' for sixteen, up to 'Z' for thirty-four, we could set the base at thirty-five, and after 'Z' we would also have to write '10' for our thirty-five. In general, we would find that the numeral for the base b, written in the base b, is always '10'. Failing to realize the polysemic nature of the numeral type '10' is the 10-trap. Compound numeral types correspond to very different numbers, depending on the semiotic register they are articulated to.

Small Bases

Culturally, bases two and three seem to be too small for practical use, except as early steps for an intermediate additive base, like the count: 'one, two, two-and-one, two-and-two, a hand'. South Pacific aborigines are reported to count from three to six by using the equivalents of two-one, two-two, two-two-one, two-two-two (see Gullberg, 1997, p. 3).

Successively touching one of the remaining fingers with the thumb would be an easy way to count using base four; the base would be additive-multiplicative if you keep track of the fours counted in your right hand by touching the remaining left-hand fingers with your left-hand thumb. The test for true polynomiality would be what you do after you have four fours indicated by your left thumb touching the last of the four fingers in your left hand. Your culture could be at the additive-base level, at the additive-multiplicative level, or at the true polynomial level.[25]

It is now frequent in schools to use colored numeral tokens with color codes for units, tens, hundreds, etc.; small numeral tokens for units and larger numeral tokens for larger groupings, and small square plates for units, bars or flats for tens and large square plates for hundred. This usage does not correspond strictly to place value for polynomial bases, because the differentiation of tokens allows the decoder to forget the position of the numeral to indicate the degree of the grouping

Table 1.

Alphanumeric numerals base thirty-six.

Ø	1	2	3	4	5	6	7	8	9
A	B	C	D	E	F	G	H	I	J
K	L	M	N	O	P	Q	R	S	T
U	V	W	X	Y	Z				

in the polynomial ranking. Only the absence of differentiation between numerals for those higher-order groupings introduces proper place value.

Against the sincere belief of teachers (and perhaps even researchers in mathematics education), the use of perceptually differentiated numeral tokens introduces an unnoticed didactical obstacle in many schoolbook exercises, purportedly designed to master the polynomial base for our decimal numeration system. Changing the color or the size of numeral tokens to indicate tens, hundreds or thousands, or using small squares, plastic strips or flats equivalent to ten small squares, and large square plates equivalent to ten flats does not help children master the value of placing figures in a definite order; it rather hinders that mastery, as those distinguishable numeral tokens could be anywhere on the table and still the total number represented by a specific set of them would be the same. Place value vanishes.

Cipher-Letter Registers: Hexadecimal and Beyond

As hinted above, first or family names written in our alphabet can also be interpreted as numerals in the base thirty-six (or thirty-seven if the Spanish '$\tilde{N}$' were included). Let us group the English alphanumeric symbols in a table of four rows of ten cells (see Table 1 below. One must be careful to cross out the numeral for zero: 'Ø', to distinguish it from the letter 'O'):

Then, our ten would be written 'A'; our twenty would be written 'K'; our twenty-four would be written 'O'; our thirty would be written 'U'; our thirty-five would be written 'Z', and our thirty-six would be written '1Ø': the 1Ø-trap again.

In this base, the name 'ANN' would be a compound numeral indicating the polynomial written in our usual base ten as

$$10 * (36\char`^2) + 23 * 36 + 23 = 12,960 + 828 + 23 = 13,811.$$

Four-letter words would make numerals for much higher numbers, and the number corresponding to 'CONSTANTINOPOLITANS' would be astronomical.

If upper- and lower-case letters were to be distinguished, one would need a base at least sixty; base sixty-four would be enough to include a few other non-English letters. Extended ASCII codes for word-processor fonts would then constitute the current step in the ongoing history of numeration systems as semiotic registers.

CONCLUSION: THE PARALLELISM OF ONTOGENESIS AND PHYLOGENESIS

Once we start developing mental (noetic) constructions like sizes of groups, duration of time-intervals, shrinking or expanding operators, mental comparison ratios, oriented placers, sliding operators, etc., we can exercise our semiotic powers to get any available tool from surrounding or remote cultures and invent semiotic registers to represent them, communicate about them, calculate results of operations with them, and think more accurately about them, always streamlining and perfecting them, even to the extent of transforming our initial mental constructions beyond recognition.

Creating mental extensions of already constructed concepts, like extending counters to placers, counters to expanding operators, expanding operators to shrinking operators, counters to forward pushers, forward pushers to backward pushers, etc., force their creators to invent extensions of taken-for-shared semiotic registers to produce external representations of their new creatures. Without the new conceptual inventions, new registers would not be created, and without the new registers, no careful definitions, axioms and theorems about the newly invented concepts could be developed.

The newly invented conceptual extensions of the natural numbers were called signed integers, rational numbers, real numbers and complex numbers (hyper-real numbers and hyper-complex numbers were added to the list in 1960), each one expressed through different semiotic registers, interactively invented in the process of extending the concept of natural numbers.

Those newly invented semiotic registers still keep archaeological traces of the former concepts and earlier registers, and afford greater power of representation, but at the same time, they place boundaries and obstacles to further knowledge. External representations are not just expressions of what we have constructed in our brains: they acquire forceful dynamics of their own. They transform our personal thinking and propagate in the culture, allowing others to challenge and correct our statements, hone new tools of representation and find out about affordances or obstacles we alone could not have possible found in our short lifetimes.

The illusion of the individual constructive mind that could in principle perform the miracle of reinventing the history of mathematics if only given sufficient time – sometimes wrongly attributed to Piaget – is as mistaken as the illusion that communities and societies can construct tools and languages that will perform miracles in the minds of the younger generations if only internalized by them – sometimes wrongly attributed to Vygotsky. In the course of history, the dialectical interplay of creative combinations and permutations of images, concepts, theories and models at the individual mind's level, with creative combinations and permutations of artifacts, tools and symbols at the collective mind's level, is irreducible to either pole.

The individualistic illusion cannot account for the speed, diffusion and persistence of many cultural changes, and the collectivistic illusion cannot account for personal innovation and creativity, misunderstood genius and stifled inventions.

Discrediting history and anthropology as sources of lessons for psychology and education, or discrediting psychology and education as mere internalizations of historically documented societal tools, languages, practices and pressures, are two ways of depriving history, anthropology, psychology and education of powerful sources of insights, conjectures and recommendations.

A careful reading of Piaget makes it clear that accusing him of a Haeckelian belief in the parallelism between embryology and phylogeny is a total misrepresentation. Moreover, that misrepresentation obscures the power of his ideas about using historical sociogenesis to extract psychogenetic conjectures for psychological and educational research.

As I extensively argued elsewhere (Vasco, 1995), in a book whose title, *Software goes to school* (Perkins et al., 1995), makes it implausible to look for an epistemological and methodological chapter in it, the rejection of the parallelism between sociogenesis and psychogenesis or between ontogeny and phylogeny is warranted if taken as a law in strictly biological terms, but totally unwarranted if taken heuristically as source of research conjectures.

Piaget's fine remarks in his posthumous book *Sociogenesis and the history of science*, co-authored with Rolando García (Piaget & García, 1983), have helped me and many other thinkers and researchers not only to re-read history in a way that has proved to be mathematically, psychologically and educationally useful, but to use results in mathematics, psychology and education to research and reformulate the history of mathematics in deeper and finer terms (see the ICMI Study on this topic: Fauvel & van Maanen, 2000). A cautious heuristic use of historical data to infer conjectures in psychology and mathematics education is not only promising and reasonable, but has already begun to be fruitful.

NOTES

[1] Many of the later historical accounts stem from the monumental four-volume work of Moritz Cantor 100 years ago, of which we have a good reprint of the revised 3rd edition (Cantor, M., 1907/1965). Drawings and prints of old notations were collected in another monumental work: Florian Cajori's *A History of Mathematical Notations* in two volumes (Cajori, 1928). For Babylonian, Egyptian and Greek mathematics and astronomy, Neugebauer (1951) is invaluable. Specific histories of number and arithmetic are to be found everywhere from the most erudite to the most superficial. My favorite general history of mathematics is the second edition of Carl Boyer's history, carefully edited by Uta Merzbach (Boyer & Merzbach, 1968/1989). There are more recent and very readable histories of mathematics, like Grattan-Guinness' history book (Grattan-Guinness, 1997), and the companion encyclopedia (Grattan-Guinness, 1994), as well as Gullberg (1997); but there are many other interesting books on the history of arithmetic, and the never-ending fascination with numbers keeps them coming out year after year. My favorites are two French books, Ifrah (1991), the most erudite, and Guedj (1996/1998) the best illustrated. For mathematics of other cultures, Joseph (1991/2000) was the most carefully interpreted history book; the collection of monographs edited by Helaine Selin is now the main source (Selin, 2000).

[2] See my heuristics interpretation of Piaget's psychogenesis/sociogenesis parallelism in Vasco (1995). More on this topic at the end of the chapter.

[3] The attentive reader must have noticed the three different meanings of the word 'counter' in this last sentence. For two of those meanings, see Room (1986, pp. 72f) and Radford (2003, p. 124; note 4, p. 144), who seem to overlook the basic meaning of 'counter': the person who counts.

[4] See the MIT translation of Cardano's *Great Art of Algebra*, Cardano (1545/1968), where the translator, T.R. Witmer, gave up on the readers' patience and used modern algebraic notation instead of the specific numbers and the one- or two-letter abbreviations used by Cardano. More details on these topics can also be found, in Spanish, in my book on Renaissance Algebra (Vasco, 1985).

[5] As a reason against those who might reject these distinctions, I must say that the controversy between those who advocate the distinction between numbers and numerals in elementary school materials, and those who reject it, could not possibly be settled by theory, research and practice without clearly marking off those two distinctions to start with.

[6] The word 'symbolic' is plagued with difficulties and ambiguities, and is used differently by different authors. Here it will be avoided as much as possible. In the last line of the paragraph above, and in similar contexts below, the expression 'symbolic numeral' corresponds to a cipher, like '9', as distinguished from a written numeral word, like 'nine', that captures the corresponding oral numeral word I cannot write here but the reader can easily pronounce.

[7] The reader can profitably consult Hofstadter (1995) and look up tokens of the type we call "lower-case *a*" in different fonts and texts, printed or handwritten, in children's stories and newspaper advertisements.

[8] To test your magnifying glass, think of the difference between a telephone number, a telephone numeral as a verbal oral type, as a verbal written type that only renders the oral sounds, and as a symbolic written type, and try to produce a token of each of the last three.

[9] See for instance Metaphysics XIII, 1, 1088a: "Therefore it is also with good reason that the one is not a number; for neither is a measure measures, but a measure is a principle [arché], and so is the one." See also Metaphysics X, 6, 1057a: "The one and number are opposed, not as contraries but as relatives."

[10] See Definitions 1 and 2 of Book VII of the Elements: A unit is that by virtue of which each of the things that exist is called one. A number is a multitude composed of units.

[11] A newer version of Boysen and Capaldi's 1993 survey, *The Development of Numerical Competence: Animal and Human Models*, is now in press, with a slightly different title: *The Emergence of Numerical Competence: Animal and Human Models*.

[12] Glen and Janet Doman have created a large organization to spread their controversial methods of teaching mathematics (and many other subjects) to babies. Their publisher prints a set of orange-spot posters (registered as "Dot Cards") and a book on how to use them and other teaching strategies: Doman & Doman (1993). *How to teach your baby math* (4th edn.). Wayne, NJ: Avery Publ. Group.

[13] Or visit Dehaene's webpage at the Cognitive Neuroimaging Research Unit to retrieve many of his original research papers, plus 30 or more recent scientific publications, most of them available there in pdf-format. The URL is: http://www.unicog.org/main/pages.php?page=SDpublications.

[14] Etymologically, the word 'integer' comes from 'integrum' ('whole'), as opposed to 'split', 'broken' or 'fractional'. The word makes little sense if it is not opposed to the fractions or rational numbers. Nowadays, mathematicians seem to contemplate only two choices: either they agree to identify the natural numbers with the positive integers, or with the non-negative integers. The second agreement seems to be the most extended. Practically all mathematicians today would agree that the integers (sometimes explicitly called "signed integers" or "relative integers") encompass the negative integers, zero, and the positive integers. Nevertheless, the ordinary use of 'integers' in everyday life, in Kindergarten and elementary schools is still synonymous with 'positive integers'. To avoid ambiguities, the word 'integers' will not be used in this chapter, reserving it for the more sophisticated number systems of signed integers, but it is useful to be reminded of these ambiguities when reading history books and old arithmetic textbooks, not to mention some research reports.

[15] "Jeder wohldefinierten Menge kommt danach eine bestimmte Mächtigkeit zu, wobei zwei Mengen dieselbe Mächtigkeit zugeschrieben werden soll, wenn sie sich gegenseitig eindeutig, Element für Element einander zuordnen lassen." See Section 1 of the *Grundlagen* in Cantor, G. (1883/1980).

[16] Within the same culture, like the Chinese, the Inuit or the traditional Thai culture, the first few numeral words might change when we count people, animals, fruit or other culturally selected groups of objects. See the distinction between concrete and abstract numbers below.

[17] If we counted correctly, if objects did not form or disappeared during the count, and if other subtle conditions for the applicability of the mental model of counting numbers hold; see the classic account

in Gelman and Gallistel (1978), in Fuson (1982), or in her chapter in Grouws' *Handbook* (Fuson, 1992).

[18] This program is called "Aléxima": "Al Éxito Matemático", and it was invented and developed by Margarita Barbosa in Bogotá, Colombia. Teachers find this proscription of writing the most objectionable part of her program, and no matter how number-proficient their children become, they still think students should write page after page of numerals and show their work in writing.

[19] The pictures found on p. 19 of the volume on Mathematics of the LIFE Science Library (Bergamini, 1963) are credited to the Spaarnestad Publishing Firm of Haarlem, Holland.

[20] See Schmandt-Besserat, D. (1996). *How Writing Came About*. Austin, TX: The University of Texas Press. Schmandt-Besserat, D. (1992). *Before Writing*. Austin, TX: The University of Texas Press. See also samples of bullæ in the Schøyen collection, items MS44631 MS4632 MS4638 MS 4523. Retrieved 2005-08-15 at the URL: http://www.nb.no/baser/schoyen/5/5.11/.

[21] The Greek text of The Sand Reckoner or Arenarius is in vol. 2 of the definitive edition of Archimedes, Opera Omnia, with commentary by Eutocius, edited by I.L. Heiberg and additional corrections by E.S. Stamatis. B.G. Teubner, Stuttgart, 1972. An annotated English version can be retrieved at the URL: http://www.calstatela.edu/faculty/hmendel/Ancient%20Mathematics/Archimedes/SandReckoner/SandReckoner.html.

[22] See the article "Handwritten digit string recognition" in Michael Arbib"s Handbook: Arbib, M.A. (Ed.) (1998). *The handbook of brain theory and neural networks* (pp. 447–450). Cambridge, MA: MIT Press.

[23] In Spanish, as in many other languages, there is no distinction for fingers and toes, the latter being referred to, if necessary, as "dedos de los pies" (literally "foot fingers").

[24] That is a nicely rounded average between the lunar year and the solar year, used in many ancient civilizations to divide the continuous horizon into 360 steps – in Latin, 'gradus' means 'step' – for the Sun and the Moon to walk back and forth during their year.

[25] For politically correct people who feel uncomfortable with words like 'level' or 'stage', these words imply no aspersions cast on the culture that creatively found the appropriate level of complexity for the environment they co-evolved with. On the other end of the spectrum, note that ascribing a very high level of Byzantine refinement to a culture would indeed cast very negative aspersions on ancient Constantinopolitans and recent Istanbulians.

REFERENCES

Bergamini, D. (1963). *Mathematics* (LIFE Science Library). New York: Time, Inc.

Bialystock, E. & Codd, J. (1996). Developing representations of quantity. *Canadian Journal of Behavioural Science, 28*(4), 281–291.

Bialystock, E. & Codd, J. (2000). Representing quantity beyond whole numbers: Some, none, and part. *Canadian Journal of Experimental Psychology, 54*(2), 117–128.

Biber, D. (1988). *Variation across speech and writing*. Cambridge: Cambridge University Press.

Biber, D. (1995). *Dimensions of register variation: A cross-linguistic comparison*. Cambridge: Cambridge University Press.

Bourbaki, N. (1950). The architecture of mathematics. *American Mathematical Monthly, 57*, 221–232.

Bourbaki, N. (1968). *Elements of mathematics: Theory of sets*. Reading, MA: Addison-Wesley.

Boyer, C.B. & Merzbach, U.C. (1989). *A history of mathematics* (2nd edn. Original edition published 1968). New York: John Wiley & Sons.

Boysen, S.T. & Capaldi, E.J. (Eds.) (1993). *The development of numerical competence: Animal and human models*. Mahwah, NJ: Lawrence Erlbaum.

Bruce, B. & Threlfall, J. (2004). One, two, three and counting: Young children's methods and approaches in the cardinal and ordinal aspects of number. *Educational Studies in Mathematics, 55*, 3–26.

Cajori, F. (1928). *A history of mathematical notations* (2 vols.). La Salle, IL: Open Court.

Cantor, G. (1980). Grundlagen einer allgemeinen Mannigfaltigkeitslehre. In E. Zermelo (Ed.), *Gesammelte Abhandlungen mathematischen Inhalts* (pp. 165–204). Berlin: Springer-Verlag. (Original work published 1883.)

Cantor, M. (1965). Vorlesungen über Geschichte der Mathematik (4 Bd., 3. Aufl.). New York/Stuttgart: Johnson Reprint Corp./B.G. Teubner Verlaggesellschaft. (Original work published 1907.)

Cardano, G. (1968). *The great art or the rules of algebra* (Translated and edited by T.R. Witmer). Cambridge, MA: MIT Press. (Original work published 1545.)

Collins, A.M. & Loftus, E.F. (1975). A spreading activation theory of semantic processing. *Psychological Review, 82*, 407–428.

Davis, H. & Perusse, R. (1988). Numerical competence in animals: Definitional issues, current evidence, and a new research agenda. *Behavioral and Brain Sciences, 11*, 561–615.

Dehaene, S. (1993). *Numerical cognition*. Oxford: Blackwell.

Dehaene, S. (1997). *The number sense*. Oxford: Oxford University Press.

Duval, R. (2004). Semiosis y pensamiento humano: Registros semióticos y aprendizajes intelectuales. (2a. ed. Trad. Myriam Vega Restrepo. Primera edición en español: Peter Lang/Universidad del Valle, 1999). Cali: Peter Lang/Universidad del Valle. (Original work published 1995: *Sémiosis et pensée humaine*. Bern: Peter Lang.)

Fauvel, J. & van Maanen, J. (Eds.) (2000). *History in mathematics education: The ICMI study*. Dordrecht/Boston/London: Kluwer.

Fuson, K.C. (1982). An analysis of the counting-on solution procedure in addition. In T.P. Carpenter, J.M. Moser & T.A. Romberg (Eds.), *Addition and subtraction: A cognitive perspective* (pp. 67–82). Hillsdale, NJ: Lawrence Erlbaum.

Fuson, K.C. (1992). Research on whole number addition and subtraction. In D.A. Grouws (Ed.), *Handbook of research on mathematics teaching and learning* (pp. 243–275). New York: Macmillan.

García-Milá, M., Teberosky, A. & Martí, E. (2000). Anotar para resolver un problema de localización y memoria. *Infancia y Aprendizaje, 23*(2), 51–70.

García-Milá, M., Martí, E. & Teberosky, A. (2004). Emergent notational understanding: Educational challenges from a developmental perspective. *Theory into Practice, 43*(4), 287–294.

Gelman, R. & Gallistel, C.R. (1978). *The child's understanding of number*. Cambridge, MA: Harvard University Press.

Goerzel, B. (1993). *The structure of intelligence: A new mathematical model of mind*. New York: Springer-Verlag.

Grattan-Guinness, I. (Ed.) (1994). *Companion encyclopedia of the history and philosophy of the mathematical sciences* (2 vols.). Baltimore/London: The Johns Hopkins University Press.

Grattan-Guinness, I. (1997). *The Norton history of the mathematical sciences: The rainbow of mathematics*. New York/London: W.W. Norton.

Guedj, D. (1998). *El imperio de las cifras y de los números*. Barcelona: Ediciones B. (Original work in French published 1996: *L'empire des nombres*. Paris: Gallimard.)

Gullberg, J. (1997). *Mathematics from the birth of numbers*. New York/London: W. W. Norton.

Hofstadter, D. (1995). *Fluid concepts and creative analogies: Computer models of the fundamental mechanisms of thought*. New York: Basic Books.

Hughes, M. (1986). *Children and number: Difficulties in learning mathematics*. Oxford: Blackwell.

Ifrah, G. (1981). *Histoire universelle des chiffres*. Paris: Laffont.

Joseph, G.G. (2000). *The crest of the peacock: Non-european roots of mathematics* (2nd edn.). Princeton/Oxford: Princeton University Press. (Original work published 1991.)

Martí, E. & Pozo, J. I. (2000). Más allá de las representaciones mentales: La adquisición de los sistemas externos de representación. *Infancia y Aprendizaje, 23*(2), 11–30.

Neugebauer, O. (1952). *The exact sciences in antiquity*. Princeton, NJ: Princeton University Press.

Perkins, D.N., Schwartz, J.L., West, M.M. & Wiske, M.S. (Eds.) (1995). *Software goes to school: Teaching for understanding with new technologies*. New York/Oxford: Oxford University Press.

Piaget, J. & García, R. (1983). *Psychogenesis and the history of science*. New York: Columbia University Press.

Quine, W. van O. (1951). *Mathematical logic* (2nd revised edn.; 1st edn.: 1940). Cambridge, MA: Harvard University Press.

Radford, L. (2000). Signs and meanings in the student's emergent algebraic thinking: A semiotic analysis. *Educational Studies in Mathematics, 42*, 237–268.

Radford, L. (2003). On the epistemological limits of language: Mathematical knowledge and social practice during the Ranaissance. *Educational Studies in Mathematics, 52*, 123–150.

Room, A. (1986). *Dictionary of changes in meaning*. London/New York: Routledge & Kegan Paul.

Selin, H. (Ed.) (2000). *Mathematics across cultures: The history of non-western mathematics.* Dordrecht/Boston/London: Kluwer.

Taboada y Ulloa, J.A. (1777). *Antorcha aritmética práctica.* Madrid: Antonio de Sancha.

Tolchinsky, L. (2003). *The cradle of culture and what children know about writing and numbers before being taught.* Mahwah, NJ: Lawerence Erlbaum Associates.

Vasco, C.E. (1985). *El álgebra renacentista* (2a. ed.). Bogotä: Empresa Editorial Universidad Nacional de Colombia.

Vasco, C.E. (1986). Learning elementary school mathematics as a culturally conditioned process. In M.I. White & S. Pollak (Eds.), *The cultural transition: Human experience and social transformation in the Third World and Japan* (pp. 141–175). Boston/London: Routledge & Kegan Paul. (Spanish translation: Vasco, C.E. (1990). El aprendizaje de las matemáticas elementales como proceso condicionado por la cultura. *Comunicación, Lenguaje y Educación (Madrid)*, 6, 5–25.)

Vasco, C.E. (1995). History of mathematics as a tool for teaching mathematics for understanding. In D.N. Perkins, J.L. Schwartz, M.M. West & M.S. Wiske (Eds.), *Software goes to school: Teaching for understanding with new technologies* (pp. 54–69). New York/Oxford: Oxford University Press.

White, M.I. & Pollak, S. (Eds.) (1986). *The cultural transition: Human experience and social transformation in the Third World and Japan.* Boston/London: Routledge & Kegan Paul.

Carlos E. Vasco

Instituto de Educación y Pedagogía. Programa de Doctorado en Educación
Universidad del Valle, Cali, Colombia
Centro de Investigaciones y Estudios Avanzados en Niñez y Juventud. Programa
de Doctorado en Ciencias Sociales, Niñez y Juventud
Universidad de Manizales-CINDE, Manizales, Colombia

DORIT TANAY

NATURAL LANGUAGE, ARTIFICIAL LANGUAGE AND THE REPRESENTATION OF TIME IN MEDIEVAL MUSIC

Temporal experience in general and rhythm in music in particular are very perplexing topics for discussion. Temporal events are by definition ephemeral, intangible, and elusive. Considering the fact that, even today, musical theorists find it difficult to describe the organization of time within musical compositions, it should come as no surprise that the evolution of a clear and unambiguous rhythmic notation persisted throughout centuries of trials and experimentation. Prior to the seventeenth century, the rhythm of Western music was organized by a system that did not, indeed could not, do two things that, today, are at the heart of modern rhythmic notation. It did not use bar lines to demarcate metric cycles, that is, to separate equidistant points in time, and it did not use distinct symbols to represent each time interval, in order to make clear whether a given note should be prolonged throughout, say, two time units or four time units. Bar lines mark off the grouping of the basic pulse into regularly recurring units and distinct symbols represent the specific time allotted to each musical note. Bar lines, in other words, make it possible to visualize and represent the conceptual and practical division between rhythm – the given sequence of different durations or note values – and the rather abstract organization of musical time at the deeper level, according to metrical accentuation. Musical meters refer to the grouping of regularly recurring beats to form repetitive cycles of a constant number of beats. Most common are the division of time into uniform cycles of duple meters (for example 2/4, 4/4) and triple meters (3/4, 9/8). In modern notation the meters (also called time signatures) are indicated right after the clef at the beginning of the musical piece of a printed score 4/4, 3/4, 3/2, etc. and, together with the bar lines, make the temporal structure (that is the metric structure) of the musical composition clear to the eye. However, in the old system of rhythmic notation, rhythmic units were encoded via a semiotic code, which used the same figure or sign for representing two different rhythmic values.

The difference between the old and the new system of rhythmic notation is not merely a small technical change. It demarcates a major shift in the concept of the relation between signifier and signified. In the old system the atomic unit of meaning is the whole rhythmic phrase. Only in the context of the phrase as a whole do the various signs, composing the phrase, acquire a definite rhythmic meaning. Detached from a musical phrase the single sign cannot be understood, in the sense that its specific rhythmic meaning has not been determined. Here we are

E. Teubal et al. (eds.), Notational Knowledge, 45–64.

reminded of Gottlob Frege's important principle, according to which the meaning of the single word in a natural language, as distinct from an artificial language, is only determined within the context of the whole sentence (Frege, 1949, p. 86). In the new modern conventional system of rhythmic notation, as used in the modern edition of, say, Mozart's piano sonatas, each rhythmic value is represented by a distinct sign, yielding a one to one, invariant relation between the signifier and the signified. This is to say that the atomic unit of the temporal/rhythmical meaning is the discrete rhythmical duration, considered as independent from the broader musical phrase. Here, in the modern system, the framework (consisting of time signature presented at the beginning of the musical piece, and marked down bar-lines) in which the individual signs are embedded determines the desired metrical accentuation, and the relative temporal meaning of each rhythmic sign or note-shape.

To illuminate further the conceptual difference between the old and the new system we may recall Ludwig Wittgenstein's famous elaboration, in his *Tractatus logico-philosophicus*, on the relation between sign and symbol as a key to the distinction between natural and artificial language (Wittgenstein, 2001). Like other philosophers of language, Wittgenstein believed that natural language consists of signs, such as letters and words, and that language ultimately refers to physical objects. However, Wittgenstein claimed that the referential relations between signs and objects in natural language are often problematic. It is quite common, for instance, that the same sign refers to different objects, and that several signs refer to one and the same object. For example, the sign "star" may refer to a celestial object or to a well-known and successful singer or actor, depending on the context in which the sign appears. Similarly, to recall Frege's paradigmatic example, the two different signs: "the evening star" and "the morning star" refer to one and the same celestial object – in this particular case, not a star at all, but the planet "Venus".

In order to solve this problem, Wittgenstein hypothesized the existence of an intermediate layer between signs and objects, consisting of what he called symbols. The symbols constitute the logical infrastructure of language. The symbols are perfect and unproblematic representations of the logical structure of the world. Each symbol refers only to one object, and each object is represented by one symbol. Thus, in the symbolic level, language represents reality perfectly.

Signs, according to this theory, are merely the sensual representation of symbols. However, for all practical purposes, language is communicated by signs, such as letters, spoken words and musical notes. According to Wittgenstein the ambiguity of natural language is not the product of the referential relations of symbols to objects, but rather of the unclear and opaque relations between signs and the symbols they represent. In order to avoid the philosophical errors caused by this ambiguity, he suggested using artificial languages wherein each sign represents only one symbol and thus has only one reference, and vice versa. Springing from Wittgenstein's observation I suggest that the modern system of rhythmic notation in which every rhythmical sign has its fixed, invariant meaning, imitates the idea of artificial language, unavailable before the birth of the modern symbolic algebra in the seventeenth century. The old rhythmic notation on the other hand, imitated natural language in which every sign can potentially signify several different objects, depending on the context of the whole phrase or sentence.

In fact, the old system of rhythmic notation can be taken as a very special and fascinating case-study of the earliest attempts to quantify time, and find an adequate semiotic field to represent the various time units, used in the musical compositions of early modern Europe. As the following survey will show, rhythmic ideas and their written representations evolved gradually as a response to the changing musical taste and the growing quest for individuality and creative musical thinking. With the growing emphasis on new rhythmic inventions came the construction of a new man-centered rather that God-centered mentality. Before the fourteenth century, music was of value only insofar as it revealed some aspect of the eternal word and the nature of God. Music was worthy of rhythmic notation only to the extent that it reflected and revealed some aspect of the Divinity. Medieval music, then, derived its importance from what it represented and not from how it represented. Hence, during this early phase of rhythmic notation music was notated by conventional patterns standing for a very limited arsenal of rhythmic values. Repetitive rhythmic patterns, maintaining triple meters were conceived as symbols of the Trinity and music measured by time reflected God's perfection by evoking the Trinity unity through its temporal articulations. A Trinitarian unit, that is, a unit composed of three equal smaller units, became the uniform measuring "tool" of music. This fundamental Trinitarian unit divided the indefinite flow of time into equidistant points in time, each demarcating a rhythmic cycle that was a trinity and a unity; it was one cycle that contained within itself three units.

Around 1300 the analogical manifestation of transcendent Trinitarian perfection ceased to be the only and ultimate goal of music. Composers enriched their music using increasingly more complex and variegated rhythmic ideas, notated by new note-shapes. Yet this process of transition from conventional to original rhythmic ideas, from patterned to distinct note-shapes, and above all, from notation taken as a testimony to God's signature in musical composition to notation taken as vehicle for the articulation of man's creative power does not represent a break from enchantment with the image of the Trinity. Rather, it represents the transformation of such enchantment into a new notational practice that remains "Christian" but no longer wedded to the idea that rhythmic signs are symbols, reifying in musical compositions the idea of the Trinity.

There are many questions that may arise about the evolution of rhythmic notation. When did composers and theorists think about rhythmic theory for the first time? Where and why did the idea of quantifying musical time emerge? Why did it take such a long time for bar lines, which illustrate the metric structure of the music in question, and which are so helpful for reading music, to be adopted? And, more to the point, how was music notated before the invention of bar lines and metric signatures? The driving forces behind the quantification, regulation and standardization of the different duration of musical sounds time for musical must be connected to the revolutionary transition from monophony to polyphony – from the performance of music by a soloist, who can "take his time", improvise and play with the notes as he wishes, to music performed simultaneously by several independent voices singing at once or music performed by a whole chorus. More specifically, the evolution of rhythmic notions and notation took place in thirteenth-century Paris, in close association with the polyphonic music that enhanced the Christian service at the Gothic cathedral of Notre Dame. While polyphonic music was hardly a common contemporary means of evoking the glory of God, the development of polyphonic music that called for several voices singing together and simultaneously in the Parisian cathedral necessitated the durational relations being written down, in order to guarantee harmonic co-ordination between the vocalists. It might come as a surprise that the earliest rhythmic structure imposed on musical composition took the form of recurring patterns borrowed from the Augustinian theory of quantitative poetical meters (Treitler, 1979, pp. 524-0545). The rudimentary and experimental notation of these repetitive patterns is termed "the rhythmic modes", or "modal notation".

The system of modal notation is based on six patterns composed of two fundamental elements, the basic rhythmic value coined the breve (brevis) and its duplication the long (longa). Arithmetically the relation between the breve and the long is 1:2. The six modes describe six ways in which longs (L) and breves (B) can alternate with each other. Both the breve and the long can appear in two values: the breve can indicate one or two time units, and the long can indicate either two or three time units. Hence the first pattern involved the repetition of the patters LBLBLB, when L=2 and B=1. But what was taken to be a rhythmic unit? Was there an intuitive or conventional sense of pulse, equal to or slower, or faster than one's heartbeats? In fact, we are still far from a complete understanding of the rhythmic concept of medieval composers and music theorists. Theorists, which codified the rhythm system, did not make relations between any of the rhythmic values and the notion of a biological or physiological pulse. We do know, however, that rhythmic notions and notation evolved within a predominantly oral musical culture, in a way that writing did not replace oral communication but rather coexisted alongside with it. Early notators were performers who tried to remind themselves how to perform musical compositions, which they already internalized through their aural experience. Early writers of musical treatises were not performers but scholars trained to communicate everything related to magnitudes and quantities through the language used generally in all the mathematical discourses of the Middle Ages, namely, the language of proportions. Rhythmic notation was confined to the expression of the relative durational value of each single note and this information sufficed for the experienced performer who probably counted more on his memory and aural training than on writing music.

The following table (Figure 1) shows the six rhythmic patterns of the six rhythmic modes, the way they were notated, and a transcription of the medieval method of rhythmic notation to modern notation. The numbers stand for proportional relation between the breve and the long:

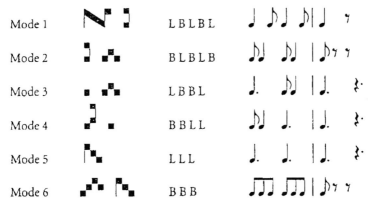

Figure 1.

As can be seen, the rhythmic modes show a certain level of complexity. Some of the longs signify two time units, while others signify three time units. Some breves represent one time unit but others represent two time units. It can be seen that the representation of the modes through this type of notation was grounded on an arbitrary grouping of notes in ligatures: the first mode, for example, was identified through its peculiar combination of a ligature that binds together three notes, followed by chains of two-note ligatures, that is, chains of groups of two notes bound to one another (Berger, 2002, pp. 629–631). Not only was the notation contextual, but it was also ambiguous. A ligature comprised of three notes could indicate LBL, BBL, LLL, BLB, or BBB. It is interesting to see that the notation of the first mode, denoting the trochaic pattern of a long followed by a breve, actually turns into the iambic pattern of a breve followed by a long. After the first isolated ligature of three notes, LBL, the eye sees the repeated ligature of two notes, BL. According to Jeanne Bamberger, there is a basic perceptual phenomenon according to which short values go to long values which then form a grouping boundary (Bamberger, 2000, pp. 121–122) Bamberger shows that with notation and without notation listeners tend to transform mentally the pattern; LB, LB, L to LBL, BL, BL. In the same vein, she argues that if one plays LBB, LBB, one almost invariably hears L BBL, BBL, BB ending so to speak "up in the air", to use Bamberger's own words (Bamberger, 2000, p. 122). One could speculate that, for the French, the second mode starting with a short value is more natural because of the iambic rhythm of the French language. But in the light of Bamberger's research on musical perception and cognition, the patterned "modal notation" of thirteenth-century Paris becomes a fascinating example of Bamberger's profound and universal perceptual principle.

Turning to the efficacy and semiotic behaviour of the modal notation, one sees immediately that longs and breves were not differentiated graphically; therefore, per se, they were meaningless. Why? – Because the unit of reference was the pattern as a whole and not any of its parts independently. It is then, difficult not to see the lack of any correlation between the symbol and its denotation at this early stage of rhythmic notation. Performers were supposed to differentiate between six different "pictures", each representing a specific rhythmic pattern. Modal notation was invented for the very restricted purpose of writing down music based on repeated patterns. Furthermore, modal notation was used for pure melodies sung without text. It served its purpose as long as musicians were satisfied with music that was rhythmically restricted and formulaic, and also free of any association with a French or Latin text, which had its own rhythm. When musicians became interested in adding texts to their polyphonic compositions, they faced two problems. They had to find a way to accommodate the melodies to the changing rhythms of the text, and they also had to indicate how the syllables of the text would fit the melody. Music with text called for the need to align between the syllables of the text and the notes of the melody. It forced composers and theorists to invent a new system of notation that would be flexible enough to accomodate the changing rhythm of the text, while allowing for a clear representation of the relationship between the notes and the syllables of the text.

For this purpose, thirteenth-century musicians invented a system of notation based on separate symbols. The codification of the new system is ascribed to the musical theorist, Franco of Cologne. In his treatise *Ars cantus mensurabilis* ("The Art of Measurable Melody"), written in about 1270, he expounded a revolutionary standard of musical notation, namely, that distinct graphic symbols should be used to notate the different rhythmic durations of individual musical events. In this differentiation of symbols, Franco laid the foundation of Western musical notation. His theory was widely distributed and was perceived as being highly authoritative. Despite its many deficiencies, Franconian notation survived until the late seventeenth century (Caplin, 2002, pp. 658–660).

Franco's new system consisted of three distinct signs, each indicating more than one rhythmic value:

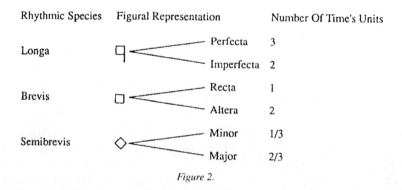

Figure 2.

Franco transformed the schematic and repetitive modal system into a flexible system governed and unified by the rhythmic value of the long, which prolonged throughout three time units. He called this long "perfect" (*longa perfecta*) because of its correspondence with the Holy Trinity. The perfect, ternary long became the first and principal unit for measuring time in music, and musical time turned into a symbolic image of divine perfection (Franco, 1952, p. 142). Like his predecessors Franco gave only the relative durational value to every single musical note-shape. The breve, like the long, could be divided into either three equal parts or two unequal parts, dividing the breve into 1/3 + 2/3. In practice, musical time was divided into equidistant points in time that articulated the recurring cycles of the perfect long. Each such cycle was conceived as a rhythmic whole, diversified through substituting the whole with its part. During the thirteenth century the division of the rhythmic whole – the perfect long – was restricted to three equal parts or two unequal parts, to maintain the reflection of the Trinity in the music.

As shown in Figure 2 Franconian notation operated with three types of note-shapes: longa, brevis, and semibrevis. Oddly enough, the system is both economical and cumbersome. Two different graphic symbols account for the distinction between a long and a short value, while short values are further differentiated into breve and semibreve. But each of these three signs actually denotes more than just one rhythmic value: the figure of the long could signify a prolongation throughout three units of time (i.e., three breves constituting a perfect long), or throughout two units (a long that includes two breves).

Likewise, the figure of the breve could indicate two different short values, one containing a single part, the other containing two such parts or units. This is to say that binary values had no separate representation. Franconian notation is beset by the shortcomings of its immanent ambiguities. One could attribute such inadequacies to the immaturity of rhythmic notation and lack of experience, or to the anticipated anomalies typical of the formative stages of any theoretical enterprise. One might also say that the theory merely reflects composers' practice and, therefore, the problem lies in the musical imagination of thirteenth-century composers, and has no bearing on the broader cultural presuppositions of those theorists who codified and expounded the system. But even if practical considerations were behind the state of the art, theorists explicated the practice using the terminology and system of reasoning they saw fit. In the thirteenth century it was generally the Aristotelian system that dominated intellectual endeavours.

How did rhythmic notation relate to thirteenth-century Aristotelianism? What did rhythmic notation, a system of symbols, share with other systems, such as that of discursive language, as understood by late medieval thinkers? And what were the deepest and broadest tenets that dictated the way symbolic representations were made and conceptualized? Before attempting to answer these questions, it is crucial to recall that throughout the thirteenth-century musical notation was developed under the influence of the Aristotelian qualitative rather than quantitative physics. Aristotelian physics denied the possibility of expressing mathematically intense changes, acceleration, retardation, diminution, augmentation, and the like. Aristotelian physics focused on qualities and their description, definition, and classification. Unlike modern physics, it did not involve any calculation but, rather, took the form of a dictionary or inventory of beings and their various predicates. How, one may wonder, could musical theorists have created a system of symbols that could represent time values or temporal quantities under the constraints of a scientific school of thought that was unable to provide a theoretical foundation for the quantification of durational values in music?

To understand their approach we need to differentiate between the note-shapes, that is, the rhythmic symbols denoting various durations or time units, and the theoretical frame, wherein musical theorists located their discourse and teaching of rhythmic notation. While the note-shapes referred to quantities, theorists abstracted the notion of duration into a general distinction between the long versus the short, taken as qualities rather than quantities. "Duration" became the essential "predicate" of the "subject", which is sound itself. Once reasoned into the status of predicates and abstracted into the only two options of duration, the long and the breve became categorically differentiated as distinct qualities, or even better, as distinct species of duration. As species, so argued Franco, the long and the breve can be manifested in more than one form: "Of simple figures there are three species: long, breve and semibreve, the first of which has three varieties, perfect, imperfect and duplex ... the breve may be divided into *brevis recta* and *brevis altera*. Regarding the semibreve, one is said to be major, the other minor" (Franco, 1952, p. 142). The evaluation of the Franconian symbols is determined by the surrounding context. As indicated in Figure 3a, a long preceding a long is a perfect long, consisting of three units or parts. But a long preceding a breve (Figure 3b) is an imperfect long, consisting of only two parts or units. In this case, the breve that follows the long causes its imperfection. In other words, the Aristotelian dichotomy between "being" and "privation", infiltrates the discourse of thirteenth-century musical theorists in their distinction between the two types of longs. The binary and, therefore, imperfect long is denied perfection, falling short of the perfect triple long. Imperfection is a kind of a default: it comes about only when a long is followed by a breve, as if one part of a ternary long is extracted and figured independently, whereby the long becomes binary rather than ternary, and thus loses it perfection. Let me repeat that according to the Franconian notation it is impossible to notate an imperfect long *per se*. A binary imperfect long can never appear alone, and, as a rule, is always followed by a breve, to round off the perfection. Notation, then, reflected the medieval theological point of view and discloses modes of understanding that transcended the boundaries of the given discipline: in the Christian culture of the thirteenth-century music was perceived as a mirror of divine perfection – and imperfection, that is, independent binary rhythmic values, had no place within musical works and its semiotic field.

Turning from the long to the breve, we see in Figure 3b that a breve before or after a long consists of one unit of time, but, if followed by another breve (Figure 3c) the second breve is altered and becomes a breve containing two time units. Thus, Franconian notation has two different signs denoting the same value. An altered breve is quantitatively equal to an imperfect long. From our point of view, it is illogical; from the point of view of thirteenth-century man who viewed the world through the prism of Aristotelian philosophy it made perfect sense. This is to say that apparent inconsistencies and illogical notational practice can be explained once reasoned in the context of the Aristotelian school of thought (Tanay, 1999, pp. 35–47). The mathematical aspect was simply irrelevant, a mere

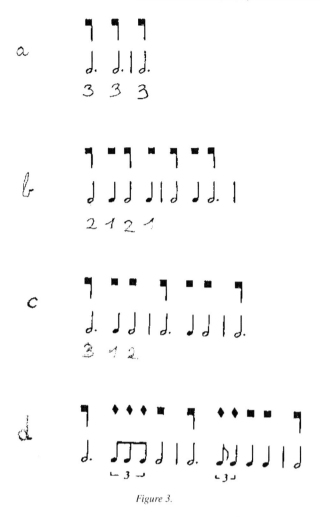

Figure 3.

accident, because an imperfect long and an altered breve were conceived of as being qualitatively different; one is a kind of long, the other a type of breve.

Another kind of anomaly regards the relation between the breve and its constitutive parts. As shown in Figure 3d the breve can be replaced by three equal parts or by two unequal parts, called *semibrevis*. But, unlike the long (Figure 3b), it cannot be rendered imperfect by its third part; this is to say, it cannot be replaced by a breve followed by a semibreve (2/3 + 1/3). At this point in music history, rhythmic notation represents durational hierarchy organized on three levels: the long, the breve, and the semibreve. But these levels operate independently. They do not relate mathematically as parts of a larger whole; each level is governed by its own set of rhythmic procedures. Such semiotic behaviour fits in well with the Aristotelian qualitative discourse that informed the musicians who developed rhythmic notation in the thirteenth century.

A closer scrutiny of Franconian notation reveals its formulaic nature: each symbol, in itself, is ambiguous. Its meaning can be determined only by considering the broader rhythmic phrase. More often than not, the rhythmic phrase consists of the same patterns of the previous pre-Franconian modal system. In other words, the vocabulary remained more or less limited to the six rhythmic modes that still functioned as the basic unit of rhythmic meaning. Writing music with differential system of note-shapes, rather than utterly arbitrary chains of ligatures, composers were free to navigate between the modes, and shift from one mode to another. It is true that Franconian notation does not use bar lines to clearly demarcate where or when a rhythmic cycle begins and terminates, yet it implies that the perfect long, the ultimate principle of rhythmic order, is both immanent in relation to the rhythmic variety found in music, and also transcendent, articulating time on the deeper level of the rhythmic organization (Treitler, 1979, pp. 524–558; Tanay, 1999, pp. 35–47). The regulative function of the perfect long is clear from its divine connotation. Theorists as well as composers considered it to be the root and the origin of all the other rhythmic values. Franco therefore rearranged the rhythmic modes to reflect this priority. In the old system the perfect long was the fifth mode (the first mode was the trochaic pattern of a long followed by a breve). In the Franconian system the perfect long became the first mode, the point of departure for all the other rhythmic options, and that to which all the other modes are reducible (Treitler, 1979, pp. 524–558; Tanay, 1999, pp. 35–47). It is not difficult to see now that the Franconian theory of notation formed the basis for the modern distinction between rhythm – the actual successive deployment of note values on the surface – and the underlying division of time into equidistant points in time known as meter, and further organized by binary or ternary metric accentuations.

It is important to understand the difference between the old ligatures and the Franconian system of rhythmic notation. The chains of ligatures that represented the six rhythmic modes reflect the fact that the principle of rhythmic order was an immanent, that is, intrinsic principle: this was the unvarying succession of rhythmic values of each of the different six rhythmic modes. With the perfect long, however, a new principle of rhythmic organization emerged, reflecting a new level of conceptual abstraction replacing the mere account of note-values as deployed on the surface with a new principle, which is both abstract and concrete: all rhythmic combinations derive from it, all being reducible to it. In comparison with the pre-Franconian system of the six rhythmic modes, the innovative aspect of the Franconian notation was not so much a matter of a richer rhythmic vocabulary but, rather, a new rhythmic motion: the monotony of the repeated patterns gave way to a new, more interesting and diversified rhythmic texture.

Let us now return to the question posited earlier: what do musical notation theories share with medieval linguistic theories? Both systems of representation, the musical and the linguistic, shared the profound belief that language is a mirror of reality (De Rijk, 1982, pp. 189–193). Let us reconsider the concept that the perfect long is made imperfect, turning from a triple/perfect long into a binary imperfect long, when it is followed by a breve. This regulative principle of Franconian notation presupposes that notes undergo change and may thereby suffer imperfection. The discourse as to whether notes are or may become perfect or imperfect reveals the natural foundation of medieval notation. In fact, both modal rhythms and the Franconian system of rhythmic notation refer to something concrete and absolutely determinate: namely, the rhythmic modes. Providing mere prescriptions for writing down a restricted set of rhythmic patterns, Franconian notation lacks the generality that is so essential to the mathematical and musical notations of the last four centuries. Franconian notation also lacks the absolute simplicity of modern mathematical or musical notation. It is economical but not elegant: with its economy come ambiguities. A profound connection between the development of musical and mathematical notation sheds light on the evolution of rhythmic notation.

In his classical analysis of the difference between the old and new mathematical methods of notation as developed during the seventeenth century, Jacob Klein observed that in the old schools of mathematics (from the Greeks until the turn of the seventeenth century) the notation of numbers always represented concrete physical/natural objects from which numbers were abstracted (Klein, 1968, pp. 117–123). The new mathematics used letters of the alphabet to represent magnitude as a general concept, free of any ontological commitment. The new mathematics, in other words, liberated mathematics from matter and objects, allowing its practice to be completely abstract. Hence, the new mathematical notation of the seventeenth century no longer related to a commodity, a tangible, tenable, and familiar substance. Present-day theories of language stress even more sharply the difference between traditional and current understanding of how a language confers meaning, using the distinction between the old referential language and the new relational language. According to the old wisdom, words were understood as referring to pre-existing objects: corresponding to things, words stand for these things in common discourse. In the new linguistic theories, meaning is not determined by reference, but is, rather, constituted through language. Accordingly, meaning depends on usage and on the functions of the manifold relations that every word may have with other words in every possible linguistic context. Given the natural foundation of Franconian notation it is easy to see that medieval rhythmic notation reflects the intuitive character of the old school of mathematics. To explore further the impact of linguistics on rhythmic notation, let us now compare the semiotic behaviour of the Franconian symbols with contemporary theories of semantics and grammar.

Medieval philosophers believed that linguistic elements and structures had counterparts in thought and reality. Thus, language was understood as an image of reality – a representation of pre-existing things, and not merely a tool of communication. Already in the twelfth century, logicians understood that meaning is not simply a matter of understanding isolated words, detached from their context, but, rather, depends on the linguistic context within which a given word is situated (De Rijk, 1982, pp. 161–164). This concentration on the meaning of a given word in a given context gave rise to a theory that focused on the effect of different categories of words on meaning. Even unequivocal words, words with a single and very clear meaning, could stand for different things in different contexts. For example, the word "man" is understood as referring to a being, made of flesh and blood, in the phrase "A man is running", but in the phrase "man is a noun", the word "man" stands for a linguistic category or grammatical part of speech. Hence, medieval logicians concluded that a word's actual meaning depends ultimately on the combination of its basic meaning (derived from its grammatical root) and its relationship to other words in the phrase or sentence. Since logicians assumed that language reflects reality, they argued that words – like things or beings – have properties, both essential and accidental (De Rijk, 1982, pp. 164–173). They recognized the essential property of every word to reflect its meaning in a sentence (the quality of *suppositio*). Among other qualities, they stressed the capacity of some words to amplify or restrict the meaning of adjoining words. Thus, for example, quantifiers such as "all", "some", "no", "every", may restrict or expand the number of the individual referents implied by a term, as in "every man" as against "some man" or "no man". In other words, logicians considered linguistic notation in terms of their extension: the number of individuals about which a given proposition is true. It is important to note that this theory was intended to clarify linguistic ambiguities or equivocations through the exhaustive mapping of the various meanings that a given word might have in different linguistic contexts. It concentrated on the notion that the actual referent of a given word is determined by the presence or absence of other words that have the potential to change the referent of the word in question. What is already noteworthy is the affinity between medieval linguistics and the Aristotelian worldview. In line with Aristotle's basic classification of every being according to its individual essential quality and possible accidental attributes, logicians claimed that words, like natural beings, have essential as well as accidental qualities. While the basic meaning – based on the word's grammatical root – is its essential quality or property, the various meanings that it may acquire in different contexts reflect its accidental properties. Moreover, quantifiers such as "all" or "some" are endowed with the power to amplify or restrict the number of referents in question (Spade, 1982, pp. 188–200). Here we are reminded of the parallel projection of Aristotelian ontology onto rhythmic figures. Musical notation, then, manifests the fundamental medieval belief that language (as a mirror of reality) reflects the structures of reality. The rhythmic symbol that indicates the long bears the property of perfection as its essential quality, and becomes imperfect only accidentally if followed by a breve. Furthermore, like contemporary logicians, musical theorists also argued that meaning is determined by the basic significance of each note and the consideration of the context within which a given rhythmic symbol is situated. As already noted, medieval logicians argued that the word "man" stands essentially for a human being, and accidentally for a grammatical category in the phrase "man is a noun". Similarly they divided words into those which have meaning in their own right, as for examples verbs and nouns, and words which are meaningful only when joined to words of the first kind, namely, words such as all the various propositions. These two opposing classes of words were conceived as analogous to natural things which are active without the assistance of anything else, vis-à-vis natural things which cannot move or change or act unless they have been moved or made changeable.

Stripped of its philosophical setting and examined from a practical viewpoint, Franconian notation was first and foremost a rudimentary solution for a new notational challenge. Based on distinct graphic signs, it enabled composers and theorists to correlate between the rhythmic signs indicating pitches and durations and an underlying syllabic text that prevented the use of ligatures. This is the place to recall that melodies with texts call for a clear visualization of the correlation between the syllables of the text and the notes that compose the melody. This is why ligated notation was replaced with separate note-shapes, yet ligatures binding one note to another did not disappear. The polyphonic music of the thirteenth century combined melodies with text and textless melodies, for which ligatures were still considered the proper notational representation – but now ligature turned into a highly sophisticated type of notation (Apel, 1961, pp. 312–315). If the old type of ligature was completely arbitrary – in the sense that the various different external shapes of the notes comprising the ligatures had no bearing on the meaning of the notes – the new type of ligature was differentiated according to the external form of both its prefix and suffix. Figure 4 shows some examples:

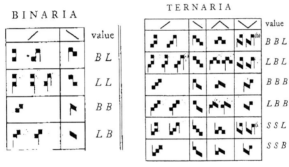

Figure 4.

It will come as no surprise that fourteenth-century composers and theorists broadened the scope of rhythmic possibilities, and developed a new arsenal of rhythmic signs to represent their new rhythmic concepts. The fourteenth century was the age of the sign. Fourteenth-century philosophers developed a particular interest in logic and linguistic analyses (Murdoch, 1978, pp. 51–71). Focusing on the relationships between language, reality and pre-existing ideas, they debated about the existence of universals, about the relation between universals and particulars focusing on individuating principles that serve to distinguish one particular being from another. Philosophers associated with the movement known as Nominalism challenged traditional Christian belief, which dictated that all signs refer ultimately to God, the subject and interpreter of all discourses, and argued that words refer to concrete and transient singular objects of the here and now. Fourteenth-century Nominalism is especially famous for its sweeping use of the theory of Ockham's "razor". Armed with Ockham's "razor", philosophers cut

away the metaphysical construction that, for generations, had created a wall between rational objects and man's cognition of particulars. Rejecting the existence
of universal concepts and reducing the world to concrete transient and singular
objects, Nominalism argued that knowledge is no longer guaranteed by universals,
but depends on the logical validity of written protocols about particulars and their
unique qualitative or quantitative properties (Murdoch, 1978, pp. 51–58). The
switch from abstractions to reality marginalized the typical thirteenth-century
Scholastic method of mapping things in their exact place within an ontological
hierarchy. In the fourteenth century, notably, descriptions became defined in terms
of the thing itself, or as compared with other similar particulars. Significantly,
the new fourteenth-century epistemology induced measurements, for if one looks
at a particular thing and sees that it is whiter, or bigger, than other particulars
of the same kind, one is driven to express through some kind of measurement
how one thing is whiter or bigger than another. The issue of representing reality
in all its varied manifestations and by means of an efficient and clear language
shifted to the forefront of philosophical interest. Focusing on linguistic representation, Nominalist philosophers aspired to a transparent and as far as possible
unambiguous language (Funkenstein, 1986, pp. 57–63).

The obsessive concern of the fourteenth century with variability and suitable
representation is echoed in the musical practice and theory of the period. The new
art of rhythmic notation was coined *ars nova*, reflecting the musicians' awareness
that new musical facts were being established that broadened the vocabulary of
rhythmic variables. To notate the new vocabulary, composers and theorists invented new note-shapes to represent rhythmic units that were shorter than the
semibreve of the thirteenth century, and reinterpreted the old signs for the long,
the breve, and the semibreve, so as to allow for new rhythmic values as well
as combinations of values not available in the older Franconian system (Apel,
1961, pp. 338–343). As shown in Figure 5, the new note-shapes included (from
the longest to the shortest duration) the *longissima*, the *longa*, the *brevis*, the
semibrevis, and the *minima* (Muris, 1972, p. 79).

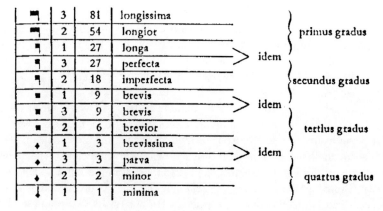

Figure 5.

The new system was constructed from the bottom to the top, starting with the new minima, defined as the smallest and indivisible rhythmic unit, and culminating with the maxima, which denoted a rhythmic value lasting throughout 81 minims.

Let us take a closer look at the table shown in Figure 5. The table is extracted from the *Notitia artis musicae*, dated 1321, a treatise written by the French mathematician, astronomer, and musical theorist, Johannes de Muris. The treatise describes the new rhythmic terminology of the early fourteenth century. The table represents the latitude and the limits of rhythmic durations. The latitude of prolonged sound is divided into four levels: *primus gradus*, *secundus gradus*, *tertius gradus*, and *quartus gradus*. Each level is further subdivided into three sections in the relationship of 3:2:1. Each level or gradus represents a continuum within a broader continuum, and indicates the possible variables of the given rhythmic level. Granting this continuity of time, Muris saw the various note-values as different parts of a single continuum. Deviating from his predecessors, he conceived the relations between the whole and its parts in mathematical terms. For him longer or shorter prolongations of different musical sounds were all measured according to one continuous dimension. While his predecessors argued that the long and the short differ in their rhythmic behaviour, Johannes de Muris emphasized the continuity and homogeneity of all rhythmic durations. He argued that the long as well as the breve and semibreve can all be turned imperfect, that is binary, and indicate two rather than three time units. Consider, for example, the first level, wherein the *longa* is taken as the unit of measurement, and is therefore numbered "1". In relation to the whole continuum of rhythmic values, however, it contains 27 minims, and can be extended further to last throughout 54 minims, becoming "*longior*", that is, longer. It can also be prolonged to contain 81 minims, becoming the *longissima*, that is, the longest possible *longa*. As far as the notational signs are concerned, we see that Muris' new system of notation presupposes the basic preconceptions of Franconian notation. He broadens the vocabulary of musical rhythm, but perpetuates the ambiguity and economy of his predecessors. Hence, the long, the breve, and the semibreve can each be either binary or ternary; in other words, each note value, with the exception of the minim, can be divided into either two or three parts, and each rhythmic symbol stands for two possible rhythmic meanings. This is to say that Muris failed to carry out his new mathematical understanding of rhythmic durations. He could not put into effect his new conception. His new art of notation (*ars notandi*) used the same operative principles that had guided his predecessors: his new rhythmic values still had to be "understood" via the meta-category of rhythmic perfection. Notwithstanding this deficiency, Muris' table as shown in Figure 5, implies not only the idea of the mathematical commensurability of various durations, but also previews a multitude of possible rhythmic combinations. For example, in the Franconian system only the ternary perfect long can suffer imperfection, that is, be replaced and varied by an imperfect binary long followed by a breve, which together maintain rhythmic perfection [2 (imperfect long) + 1 (a breve)] = 3. In the new *ars notandi* of Johannes de Muris, each perfect value can be rendered imperfect (divided into

2/3+1/3). Furthermore, imperfection can be achieved not only by the removal of an immediate third part, but also by the third part of the part, for example when the long is made imperfect by a semibreve, hence diminished by 1/9 of its durational value. In other words, Muris' system of notation broadened the vocabulary of rhythmic notation, and made the texture of parts and whole richer and more subtle. But binary values were still not visibly differentiated from triple values, as shown in Figure 5. For example, the same note-shape represented both a breve of 9 units and a breve of 6 units. But why so? As already mentioned, in Muris' system of rhythmic notation ternary values were still conceptualized as a reflection of the perfection of the Trinity. Binary values were associated with imperfection and disorder and, therefore, could not be introduced overtly and officially, that is, through independent note-shapes in musical works. The notion of musical correctness in the period in question was defined in relation to cultural/theological constraints that dictated what ought to be reflected in musical compositions. Conversely, one may argue that since many new binary values were added, then, in fact, binary values were legitimized *qua* new rhythmic facts, while the rhetorical representation of these facts in theoretical treatises preserved the sacral resonance of music as an image of God's perfection.

How did performers know whether a given symbol was perfect or imperfect, triple or duple? And, since every note value could now be divided into either two or three equal parts, how did they know, for example, whether a given semibreve was equal to two or rather three minims? Johannes de Muris, like Franco, provided rules that explained how every note value should be read in various contexts. In addition, in his later treatise, *Libellus cantus mensurabilis* (ca. 1340), he introduced new notational symbols that encoded all the information needed in order to differentiate between triple and duple value. A complete circle: O, indicates that the breve contains three semibreves, and is therefore ternary and perfect, while a moon-like incomplete circle: C, indicates that the breve is imperfect, divisible into two equal semibreves. By adding three points in the center of the circle Muris indicated that the semibreve is perfect, containing three equal minims, and by adding only two points in the center of the circle Muris indicated that the semibreve contains only two equal minims, and is therefore, imperfect. These new signs were placed at the beginning of the musical composition or musical section wherein a new rhythmic division was in question. In fact, these signs can be regarded as anticipating the four fundamental modern musical meters: a ternary breve and ternary semibreve yield the modern meter 9/8, a ternary breve and a binary semibreve produce the modern 3/4 meter, a binary breve and a ternary semibreve are equivalent to today's 6/8, and finally the binary breve and the binary semibreve gave birth to the binary 2/4 meter.

During the second half of the fourteenth century, French and Italian composers and theorists shared a new quest for legibility and clarity. Curiously enough, it came with a desire to invent new rhythmic signs, to represent in an adequate semiotic sphere every duration and rhythmic variant that man could create, imagine, and perform (Tanay, 1999, pp. 185–206). Composers and theorists were especially interested in the possibility of exploring how far the vocabulary of rhythmic values could be developed if time is understood as a continuum, hence, in principle, divisible into as many parts as one desires. The system of Johannes de Muris, we may recall, was based on the absolute and indivisible minim, while all other values in the system were multiples of two or three of the basic minim. The new approach to musical time as a continuum could theoretically unleash any system of constraints, allowing free play with the theoretically indefinite subdivisions of any rhythmic units. This included the standard minimal rhythmic unit, now no longer conceived as an atom of time but rather as a continuum. Composers and theorists were particularly fascinated by the possibility of breaking the minim down. They invented new note-shapes to indicate fast and capricious rhythmic progressions. Most indicative of the new concept of time was the use of proportion to measure the rate of change in the rhythmic motions or divisions. A given proportion defined the numerical relationship between the various fractions of the standard minim, replacing, say, three minims by another group of four minims, which were denser, yet still equivalent to the standard group of three minims. Such *ad hoc* substitution of minims diminished the standard minims. Hence, a proportion of 4:3 replaced the standard three minims with four minims that were condensed within the segment of time allotted to the three standard minims. While the standard semibreve of Johannes de Muris' system was comprised of either three minims or two minims (Figure 5), the new semibreve, now understood as a continuum, could be composed of 4, 5, 7, or even 10 new, much shorter minims.

How were these new, mainly short durational values notated? Was there a unified method of creating and notating new rhythmic values? Before answering these questions, it is important to mention that these notational innovations reflected an eccentric rhythmic style, characterized by unparalleled rhythmic intricacies that undermined Johannes de Muris' unified system. Historians of music have interpreted these complexities as a special case of a musical system in disarray, to be explained by patterns that may satisfactorily account for phases of aberration from the stylistic norm, such as the notion of mannerism, or the fin de siècle phenomenon, understood literally as well as figuratively. These approaches to the rhythmic style in question gain further support from the proximity in time and space between the evolution of chaotic rhythm, significantly in Avignon, and the Great Schism (1378–1417) that followed the "Babylonian Captivity". This famous crisis in papal supremacy has been associated with strong tendencies to secularization in the papal court, when life styles became luxurious and even licentious (Günther, 1963, pp. 105–121). The music associated with Avignon reflects a sense of crisis. Composers abandoned the traditional system of signs, dismissed the idea of a rhythmic constant in relation to which all the other values were measured. In addition, they allowed each note to change its duration throughout the musical piece. In fact, all the notes simultaneously could change their duration in real time (Stone, 1996, p. 232). This new, extremely free and unstable rhythmic style included many new notational devices. Here I will focus on just one method of creating new rhythmic values: changing the color of traditional notes.

To diminish or augment the value indicated by a given note-shape, late fourteenth-century composers and theorists changed the color of given notes from black to red. Note-shapes, as a rule, were all colored black in the thirteenth and early fourteenth centuries. By changing the color of a given note from black to red, composers and theorists indicated that the value of the note-shape was diminished by one-third of its original duration or value. More often than not, red notes were used in groups that indicated proportional diminution: the time allotted to just two standard black semibreves, was now replaced by three red semibreves. A comprehensive discussion of these notational complexities is beyond the scope of present paper. Here it will suffice to say that red notation takes advantage of the new approach to time as a continuum and, in fact, composers used this method of coloring to diminish the value of a minim or a semibreve not only in the 3:2 ratio, so that 3 proportional minims are equal to two standard minims, but also in the following proportions: 2:1, 3:1, 4:1, 4:3, 9:4 and 9:8. In other words, red notation enabled the composer to switch from triple meter to duple meter, and to create a momentary feeling of a ternary meter within a composition written in duple meter or vice versa (Stone, 1996, pp. 139–144).

It is important to note that the various types of coloration testify to a new approach toward diminution and augmentation of note values. In the older systems, of both Franco of Cologne and Johannes de Muris, changes in duration – as in cases where perfect triple note values were made imperfect and reduced to two units – had to be understood through mental consideration of potential imperfection because of the adjoining values or other contextual considerations. In the new system, however, diminution and augmentation were expressed differently, that is, directly, by changing the note-shape through coloration (Tanay, 1999, pp. 234–237). In addition, composers and theorists invented new note-shapes, shown in Figure 6. Theorists and composers agreed neither on the name of these new rhythmic values nor on the meaning of each of the new invented note-shapes. Different theorists gave different names to the same figure, or, conversely, the same term might have been applied to several different values. But these inconsistencies should be seen in light of other, equally significant consistencies. Firstly, each theorist tried to work out his own theory of rhythmic notation using clear, unambiguous, and – as far as possible – context-free notational symbols. Secondly, the new figures were used consistently within certain musical pieces, and even within the whole repertory of a single composer. Recent transcriptions and editions of the repertory in question have confirmed that the principle of consistency prevailed, so that in a good number of compositions each of the new figures has an *ad hoc*, yet distinct and unequivocal meaning.

With all this in mind, it is possible to argue that the instability and high degree of experimentation in the theory and practice of the late fourteenth century bear witness to a process and struggle. The goal of this struggle was a system of presentation whose recognition did not depend – as did that of the old system – on the mediation of the concept of rhythmic perfection. The new system of notation was one for which nothing existed between each notated figure and its temporal significance. One cannot avoid thinking about this development as manifesting the culmination in the realm of music of the Nominalist rejection of mental constructs (the realm of abstract universals) that formerly mediated between man's perception and the world as given to the senses. As we already observed, the new emphasis on sensible particulars led to measurement and quantification: when scrutinizing particulars one can do nothing but compare between such particulars or singulars: which is bigger, stronger, whiter, denser, etc. It is clear then, that the Nominalists agenda – its quest for transparent language, on the one hand, and preoccupation with measuring the qualitative and quantitative differences between real, singular, and concrete objects, on the other – stimulated parallel developments in the field of music.

Rhythmic notation, therefore, was not developed within an intellectual void. To the contrary, fourteenth-century philosophers, mathematicians, and logicians were all preoccupied with analyzing the inner composition of *continua*, their limits (*minima* and *maxima*), and the relationship of the parts to the whole within continuous processes. Nourished by theological investigations of God's infinity, His infinite distance from our world, His ability to create infinities of all kinds as well as His power to divide a given continuum into all its infinite parts due to his infinite free will and supremacy, all fourteenth-century intellectuals were immersed in problems involving the measurement of the units and parts constituting the continuum of time and space. It is difficult to overstate the centrality of quantification and measurement in the various scientific, philosophical and theological discourses of the fourteenth century. It is this fresh empiricist attitude that made possible the inquiry into the inherent physical or natural properties of sounds of different duration. Investigating the nature and limits of their own musical language, and inventing an adequate notational representation for each of the new rhythmic variants, composers and theorists of the late fourteenth century fulfilled a visionary quest already set out in Johannes de Muris' *Notitia artis musicae* of 1321: "Everything which is uttered singing, with a normal, whole and regular voice, the knowledgeable musician must write by appropriate notes".

REFERENCES

Apel, W. (1961). *The notation of polyphonic music, 900–1600.* Cambridge, MA: Medieval Academy of America Press.

Bamberger, J. (2000). *Developing musical intuitions, A project-based introduction to making and understanding music.* New York: Oxford University Press.

Busse-Berger, A.M. (1993). *Mensuration and proportion signs: Origins and evolution.* Oxford: Clarendon Press.

Busse-Berger, A.M. (2001). The evolution of rhythmic notation. In T. Christensen (Ed.), *The Cambridge history of western music theory.* New York: Cambridge University Press.

Caplin, W.E. (2001). Theories of musical rhythm in the eighteenth and nineteenth centuries. In T. Christensen (Ed.), *The Cambridge history of western music theory.* New York: Cambridge University Press.

De Rijk, L.M. (1982). The origins of the theory of the properties of terms. In N. Kretzmann, A. Kenny & J. Pimborg (Eds.), *The Cambridge history of later medieval philosophy.* Cambridge: Cambridge University Press.

Franco, of Cologne (1952). Ars cantus mensurabilis. In O. Strunk (Ed.), *Source reading in music history.* London: Faber & Faber.

Frege, G. (1949). On sense and Reference. In H. Feigl & W. Sellars (Eds.), *Readings in philosophical analysis*. New York: Appleton-Century-Crofts.

Funkenstein, A. (1986). *Theology and the scientific imagination from the middle ages to the seventeenth century*. Princeton: Princeton University Press.

Herlinger, J. (2001). Music theory of the fourteenth and early fifteenth centuries. In R. Strohm & B.J. Blackburn (Eds.), *Music as concept and practice in the late middle ages*. Oxford: Oxford Univeristy Press.

Klein, J. (1968). *Greek mathematical thought and the origin of algebra*. Cambridge, MA: MIT Press.

Murdoch, J. (1978). The development of critical temper: New approaches and modes of analysis in fourteenth century philosophy, science and theology. *Medieval and Renaissance Studies 7*, 51–79.

Muris, Johannes de (1972). *Notitia artis musicae et Compendium musicae practicae*. Corpus scriptorum de musica, 17. Holzgerlingen: Hanssler Verlag.

Parkes, M.B. (1992). *Pause and effect: An introductiion to the history of punctuation in the west*. Aldershot: Scholar Press.

Spade, P.V. (1982). The semantics of terms. In N. Kretzmann, A. Kenny & J. Pimborg (Eds.), *The Cambridge history of later medieval philosophy*. Cambridge: Cambridge University Press.

Stone, A. (1994). *Writing rhythm in late medieval Italy: Notation and musical style in the Manuscript Modena, Biblioteca Estense, Alpha.M.5.24*. Ph.D. Dissertation, Harvard University, Cambridge, MA.

Tanay, D. (1999). *Noting music marking culture*. Musicological Studies and Document, 46. American Institute of Musicology. Holzgerlingen: Hanssler Verlag.

Treitler, L. (1979). Regarding meter and rhythm in the ars antiqua. *Musical Quarterly 65*, 524–558.

Wittgenstein, L. (2001). *Tractatus logico-philosophicus*. London: Routledge.

Dorit Tanay
Department of Musicology
Tel Aviv University, Israel

JESÚS TUSON

WRITING: THE STORY OF A COGNITIVE REVOLUTION

This chapter provides a brief overview of writing from its origins in the Near East, more than five thousand years ago, to the development of alphabets in the Mediterranean region. At the same time, and rejecting historicism, it outlines the mental strategies and processes involved in the birth of writing (arising from the old accounting systems developed in the Fertile Crescent), as well as the practical steps which enabled syllabaries and alphabets to be created. Two basic arguments are put forward. Firstly, that writing, where it appears, does not add anything substantial to our condition as *sapiens*, but it does solve effectively the problems of societies that need to preserve information beyond the limits of personal and collective memory. Secondly, it is argued – and this issue appears not to have received the necessary attention – that the written record of verbal acts implies a genuine semiotic revolution based on a large scale synaesthetic game derived from the human ability for representation.

BEFORE WRITING

In terms of biological evolution, *Homo sapiens* is a recent arrival to the animal kingdom, the species arising slightly over one hundred thousand years ago in the central-eastern lands of the African continent. It soon became a travelling species which extended all over the continent and fifty thousand years later reached the coasts of China; ten thousand years later it was to be found in Australia and soon afterwards appeared in Europe. The map of the earth was finally completed when in subsequent migratory processes *sapiens* crossed the Bering Strait and occupied the land of America. It is therefore a surprisingly mobile species that adapted, with its 1350 cm^3 brain, its Aurignacian tools and its language, to any habitat, the difficulties of hostile environments failing to restrain its survival instincts as a species. Astonishingly, however, writing only appeared in Mesopotamia some five thousand three hundred years ago (with the first clay tablets): this is a very late period in the history of *sapiens*, because, if we reduce our existence as a species to the manageable time span of a 24-hour day, writing only arrived at around 22.30. Consequently, we should ask ourselves why it arrived so late, and what needs led some human groups in the Near East to the written record; we should also consider what mental processes our predecessors had to employ to achieve this unheard of intersensory transfer from the oral and auditory domain of speech to the manual and visual dimension of writing.

E. Teubal et al. (eds.), Notational Knowledge, 65–78.

Although the very early stages of Upper Palaeolithic art have left some eminent examples of figurative representations (for instance, Lascaux, Altamira and the paintings in caves and shelters throughout the Mediterranean) these can in no way be considered precedents of writing. Whether they had a magical function, as reminders, or decorative purposes these works must be carefully set apart from the processes through which the recording of verbal activity properly speaking occurred. However, things are very different when we consider the proliferation of accounting objects or counters throughout the Fertile Crescent during the Neolithic and, more specifically, some nine to four thousand years ago. During these five millennia, the use of small clay tokens with different forms and marks became common, and their function appears to have been none other than to take down the amounts of the products that travelled the ancient trade routes between east and west.

These archaeological finds occurred in sites such as Ur and Uruk, following the course of the rivers Tigris and Euphrates up towards Nippur, Nineveh, Jemdet Nasr, Jebel Aruda and many other towns, and stretched as far as the easternmost Mediterranean lands: Ras Shamra, Megiddo, Jericho, etc. It should be pointed out that from the third millennium BCE these pieces became scarcer, as they were substituted for clay tablets which, without doubt, were much more practical since they included several information items on the same surface in independent boxes. It is clear, however, that the Sumerians had already developed the technique of taking down quantities (with rounded cuts, a precedent of Mesopotamian numeration) to refer to the products they traded with: animals, cereals, oil, etc. Here, for the first time, human groups applied their symbolic ability to establish agreements or deals through figures which replaced the real objects: to refer to one hundred sheep, for example, they did not need to have them within sight; it was enough to handle the symbol representing them. From this stage, writing is but a short step away.

POSSIBLE TYPES OF WRITING SYSTEM

Before proceeding to the historical review, it may be useful to expound briefly on possible forms of writing in order to evaluate adequately ancient finds and also to observe the changes which occurred from one type of writing to the other. Let us, therefore, attempt a typological classification (which does not always run alongside the development of events). Considering writing as recorded speech, and according to the characteristics of (existing) languages, writing can apparently only occur in three different ways: writing is either a representation of 'the word', a representation of 'the syllable', or the representation of 'the minimum sound units of language'. With this approach in mind, it does not seem possible to write morphological units (with global, specific and arbitrary signs for forms of 'gender', 'number', 'diminutive', 'comparison', 'relationship', etc.), nor is it possible to have signs for a syntactic structure (for instance, with written forms to mark 'passive', 'agent', 'object', 'mode', etc.). For writing to have assumed morphological and syntactic levels, an advanced analysis of the grammar of the language would have been required, and in its early stages the technique of writing did not include such tasks. Therefore, the logically and culturally possible types of writing are lexical, syllabic and phonological writing. The latter two in particular, by representing non-significant segments of languages, can account for the whole range of realities in the linguistic system, including the morphological and syntactic: for instance, using alphabetic writing we can write *farm* (a lexical element), *farmers* (a lexical element plus a 'relational' and a 'number' morpheme), and we can also account for syntactic values such as *from/of* (header of 'complement'), *thus* (indicating 'consequence'), *skilfully* (an element of 'mode' incorporated to the lexical morpheme), etc.

Lexical writing appeared independently in three different geographical areas: Mesopotamia, China and Mesoamerica. In these territories, the writing of words appeared quite naturally on the basis of pictograms: initially realistic figures with a dual value as both iconic representations of things and with a link to words, provided they were part of a writing system and not just isolated signs. Generally speaking, pictograms most commonly became logograms (previously called 'ideograms') through a process of defiguration produced by the need to write more quickly in less time, this introducing a degree of 'italicization' and reducing the number of strokes. This defiguration was, without doubt, of paramount importance since it broke the link between signs and the need to serve reality (they could no longer be representations of things). From that moment on, signs lost the dual value referred to above: they became exclusively arbitrary signals that could only be associated to words, to linguistic facts, and no longer to designated objects. As a consequence of this defiguration, realities which could not be drawn also received a graphic sign: after this process, words referring to abstract concepts such as 'good' or 'evil', 'intelligence' or 'harmony' could be represented arbitrarily with complete ease, should the scribes so decide. Nevertheless, a logographic system suffers from a serious drawback, since the number of figures needed soars rapidly (precisely because of its relationship to the lexicon) and hundreds and even thousands of signs are required: those contained in a dictionary.

Syllabic writings constitute the first great revolution in the history of writing, and although there is no proof thereof, we can imagine a scribe, overwhelmed by the need to use so many signs, discovering the possibility of representing some recurrent units (syllables) which, in languages, imply a lower number of syllables than words and their logograms. This discovery is naturally attributed to the use of the *de rebus* or hieroglyphic principle which allows for the division of a word into shorter segments, each corresponding to another word. For instance, before syllabaries *sea* would be represented by a figure, *son* by a different one and *season* by a third one; however, with the syllabary, *season* can be written with the signs for *sea* and *son*, and so on for all the other cases. Thus, the *de rebus* principle could be formulated as follows: the sign so far representing a word (*sea, son,* etc.) will from now on represent that sound sequence, a syllable, independently of where it is found. The implementation of the syllabic principle implied a decisive step from the point of view of economy, since only a few dozen signs were now necessary (for instance, Crete's Linear B syllabary, of 15 BCE, contains eighty nine; old Persian, of 6 BCE, sixty nine; Japanese katakana, from 9 BCE, seventy five); in addition, however, the great economy of syllabaries predetermined the last stage of many writings: the alphabet.

Phonological or alphabetic writings are (at least ideally and ignoring some cultural factors that may make the use of logographic or syllabic systems advisable) highly minimalist systems, which seem to have advantages from the point of view of their transmission and acquisition. This explains the success of alphabets in many peoples, and especially in the ancient Mediterranean, as we will see below. Just as the syllabary was organized according to the *de rebus* principle, alphabets could only possibly arise from the acrophony principle. The latter can be formulated as follows: the sign used until now to represent a word (or syllable) will from this moment on be reserved for representing the initial sound of the word (or syllable) wherever it occurs. This is exactly the resource we use when spelling out our names, for example: T for Tokyo, U for Uruguay, S for Scandinavia, O for Oslo and N for Norway; this is made possible with an instruction such as the following: "write A where you find the initial for *about*, B for *bell*, C for *close*, etc.". This artifice was put into practice by the ancient Phoenicians in their alphabetic order: A for *aleph*, B for *beth*, C for *gimel*, D for *daleth*, etc. (obviously the written signs correspond to the first stages); thus a list was created which, with minor changes, has been passed on to present-day alphabets. The discovery of the alphabetic principle reduced even more the number of signs needed for writing: between twenty and thirty in most cases.

This short typological tour must come to a close with two observations. The first is that the change from one writing system to another reveals the extent to which human ingenuity comes to the fore when it is necessary to provide graphic solidity to fleeting speech, inventing increasingly economical systems that are easier to acquire and quicker to write. The second observation has to do with cultural relativism, and requires us to avoid regarding our alphabets as sacred, not even because they are easier to acquire; in other cultures and for other languages (Chinese, for instance, with its high degree of homophony) a logographic system may be preferable. We should also bear in mind that in Japan, which has probably the most complex of existing writing systems, or in the case of *kanji*, of Chinese origin, and the *hiragana* and *katakana* syllabaries, there is zero illiteracy.

THE FIRST WRITING SYSTEMS: MESOPOTAMIA AND EGYPT

The birth of writing can be located, with almost complete certainty, in lower Mesopotamia, in the towns bordering the rivers Tigris and Euphrates, some five thousand three hundred years ago. Its appearance can only be explained by the absolute need for writing in terms of administering towns, which had reached a size that made it impossible to continue trusting the limited possibilities of human memory. Places like Uruk, with an estimated population of ten thousand inhabitants, needed registers for the distribution of cultivated land, to assign food rations, and to note down incoming and outgoing products in the temple warehouses. In addition, it was necessary to leave proof of business transactions and all kinds of deals, as examination of the first clay tablets reveals. Writing, therefore, came about in order to ensure the organization of a complex administration, and also as a form of accountancy and registry. Only later would writing be employed to record laws, scientific observations (astronomy and medicine, for instance), and the recounting of noteworthy facts: the precedent of literature.

The first Mesopotamian writing was pictographic (or iconic): the tablets featured figures of animals, cereals, containers, etc., with numbers marked by pressure in the shape of circles and semicircles. Tablets are divided up into boxes, each for the quantity and the kind of product. However, this elementary and realistic writing was followed by cuneiform writing (performed by a slight pressure of the stylus which left wedge-like marks) halfway through the third millennium, thus consolidating the defiguration that enabled, as pointed out above, writing practice to be linked exclusively to language facts. Thus, the schematic picture of an arrow could mean both 'arrow' and the notion and word for 'life', because both were pronounced *ti* in Sumerian. Alternatively, the name of the priest Dudú was written by repeating the schematic picture for 'foot', the graphic symbol meaning 'walk' which was pronounced *du*. It should be pointed out that one of the driving forces behind the development of writing seems to have been the need to note the names of people and towns, because although it is quite simple to draw the head of a cow or an ear of wheat the same cannot be done with the name of a person or place.

Cuneiform writing was omnipresent throughout the Near East, and for two millennia it was the basis for recording a number of languages: initially Sumerian and Akkadian, and then Elamite, Babylonian, Ugaritic and Persian. These languages also produced inscriptions by pressing the triangular stylus upon a soft surface, or by engraving wedges on stone and other hard surfaces. Examples of cuneiform writing can be found on hardened clay tablets, on walls such as the Behistun Rock, on the bases of statues, and on stellae like the one of the Code of Hammurabi from 1760 BCE and now in the Louvre Museum. The tablet collections in museums around the world number half a million items: a good indicator of how widespread this writing was.

Three centuries after these Mesopotamian origins, Egypt offered the first examples of another fascinating form of writing: hieroglyphs. As many experts have pointed out, they appeared in their prime from the outset, without any developmental stages, as if they were the work of an expert planner and outstanding artist, a master of schematic realism. The source for the inspiration of Egyptian writing was very likely Sumeria, which was well connected with Egypt by trade routes; it can therefore be assumed that the Egyptians knew the system for recording speech production. However, the facts also strongly suggest that what was involved was a transmission of ideas rather than mere copying: Egypt was acquainted with Mesopotamian writing and developed its own stable system which lasted three-and-a-half millennia, the first example being the Narmer palette (3000 BCE), where pictographic and syllabic writing interact.

Throughout its history Egyptian writing developed three stylistic and functional models: hieroglyphic, hieratic, and demotic. The first is the most well known and has been greatly admired; it was used mainly for sacred texts on both papyrus and temple walls. The other two forms of writing were used for administrative documents and everyday matters (especially demotic, or 'popular' Egyptian). In addition, Egyptian scribes (a privileged caste that most probably maintained a complex system, beyond the grasp of most people, as a way of protecting its own class) introduced the signs known as 'determinatives' to resolve ambiguities. Thus, there are hieroglyphic signs with a lexical value, others with a purely phonetic value (monoconsonant, biconsonant, and triconsonant), and, finally, determinatives to indicate whether a word is the name of a place, a person, etc.; together this makes up the most complex system ever to have existed in the history of writing.

It was in Egypt that, for the first time, a writing material and a technology were produced which differed greatly from simple clay tablets: papyrus. Papyrus was produced from the plant *Cyperus papyrus*, very abundant along the Nile delta and banks, by cutting thin sections of its stem and arranging them vertically and horizontally before pressing them together in sheets which could then be put together to obtain scrolls several metres long. Although common, however, this was not the only writing material used: as in the case of cuneiform, Egyptian writing appears on all kinds of objects and surfaces, and especially on statues, the inner and outer walls of temples, on obelisks, plaques, and many other objects of everyday use. It was often produced with a paintbrush in typical black and red.

For many centuries the ability to interpret hieroglyphs was lost because Egypt, unlike Greece and Rome, produced no grammatical works aimed at preserving the ability to learn the old language. Thus, it became a mystery, and this led to strange, magical explanations being put forward until, in 1822, Jean F. Champollion deciphered it using the Rosetta stone (on which the same text appeared in three different writings: hieroglyphs, demotic and Greek). Champollion's hypothesis was that Coptic was a late stage of Egyptian (just as Romance languages are a late stage of Latin) and also that most Egyptian writing was alphabetic rather than logographic. Once he located and translated several person names he was able to produce a table with a consonant alphabet, with which it was possible to read and interpret the texts that have enabled the reconstruction of the history of ancient Egypt, spanning three-and-a-half millennia.

THE ALPHABET AND THE FOREST OF ALPHABETS

The sphinxes from 1700 BCE found in some mines in the Sinai Peninsula, at Serabit El-Khadim, and which display on one of their sides brief votive inscriptions, mark the start of the productive extension of alphabets from their origin in Phoenicia to their widespread use in both east and west. These are figures with a woman's head and a lion's body, with the following votive text at their feet: LBALT (or *lb'lt*) meaning 'for the lady' or 'for Baalat', Phoenician goddess of the town of Byblos. Although the style of these letters is markedly Egyptian, they were revolutionary in that the Canaanites (the makers) only retained the monoconsonantal signs of the Egyptian writing system and eliminated everything else (hieroglyphs, and the monumentality associated therewith). This Sinaitic adaptation (subsequently Phoenician, Greek, Etruscan, Latin, etc.) set the bases for functional writing, which could be performed with any instrument, leaving imprints on any surface, and thus began the process towards the democratization of writing, freeing it from the elitist caste of scribes.

The nerve centre of the new alphabetic writing was located on the easternmost Mediterranean coast, in Phoenicia, towards the year 1000 BCE. Almost certainly it was through land and sea trade routes that the new system became widespread, involving in time not only the Greek, Latin, Arabic and Hebrew alphabets, but also some writing systems in India. A classic example of its diffusion can be found in the Greek trade colonies (Ugarit among them), which very likely were the origin for the spreading of the system in its various versions in Athens, Thera, Ionia and Boeotia some time in the ninth and eighth centuries BCE, until in the fifth century the Ionian variety (that spoken by Homer, Heraclitus, Herodotus, and Hippocrates) became official. The Greeks passed on the new writing system to the Etruscans (a flourishing people to the north of Rome) in the seventh century, as well as through the – by this time Greek – trade ports located along the coast of the Tyrrhenian Sea. Soon afterwards, writing travelled from Etruria to Rome, where a twenty-one-sign alphabet became consolidated and spread as a result of Romanization.

The expansion of the alphabet has given rise to many – at times radical – adaptations. As we know, writing can never be transferred mimetically into a different language, since languages have different phonological systems. This means that the model language may have writing signs matching the exact number of its phonological units, in accordance with a theory seldom proved for alphabetic writings, but the receptor language may have more or fewer vowels and consonants with a word differentiating function than the model (for instance, in French, an *e* can be either open or closed, producing different meanings). Initially, this produces a mismatch: some written signs in the model language may not have a sound correspondence in the receptor language (useless letters, therefore), and some differentiating sounds in the receptor language may require the creation of new written signs. It is also true, however, that it is not always necessary for all differentiating sounds to be identified by a specific graphic sign. For instance, some alphabetic systems do not represent vowels, and as for consonants we know there some letters represent no sound (e.g., letter H in Spanish) and that a sound has different written representations; there may always be a mismatch, due to what is handed down from – sometimes very old – orthographic traditions that seldom keep up with constant language change.

The differences between the phonological systems of the model language and those of the adopted language are the driving force behind alphabet adaptations, and also some radical restructurings. For instance, the Greeks received from the Phoenicians a twenty-two-sign alphabet and, as they lacked the aspirated sound symbolizing *aleph*, they used this sign, now called *alpha*, to represent the low central vowel /a/; the same happened with the other vowels: they recycled some signs and even invented the sign ω for *omega*. As for consonants, they created signs for *fi, khi* and *psi*: φ, χ, φ; thus, in the classical period, the Greek alphabet consisted of twenty-seven signs covering most of the phonetic distinctions in this language. The Romans later dispensed with Greek letters due to lack of correspondence in Latin, and soon established a twenty-one-sign alphabet, to which were added (around the turn of the millennium) the letters Y and Z to write Greek names. The Slavic peoples also used the Greek alphabet, although this required greater adaptations.

All these adaptations, from the Greek (truer to the original model) to those which moved further away from the model, such as the runes of Germanic peoples or the Celtic Ogham alphabet, show us the extent to which this writing system became widespread, a system which, without doubt, must have been considered the easiest, quickest and most practical way to capture speech. A similar conclusion can also be drawn about other writing systems not dealt with here, and which justify expressions like "the triumph of the alphabet": for example, the Iberian system, in the Mediterranean area of the Iberian peninsula during pre-Roman times; the Tifinagh, developed between 2 BCE and 5 CE in north Africa and recovered today; or the Hangul alphabet from Korea, promulgated in 1446 by King Sejong and considered by many as the most perfect writing designed to date.

TECHNOLOGICAL AND SEMIOTIC REVOLUTION

Writing, as described above, has a history spanning more than five thousand years, and is today adopted in one form or another (logographic, syllabic and alphabetic, and mixed systems) by most of the human population. Some peoples, however, live their lives away from writing simply because they do not need it, because it is not consistent with their way of life, or because it would be an artificial and useless addition to their societies. These human groups proudly live as *sapiens* without being troubled by the complications derived from the Neolithic revolution: they are agraphic, illiterate peoples (like the Yanomami of the Amazon or Zaire's pygmies), who have always lived in groups of a few individuals, taking from their environment what they need to survive on a daily basis, that is, hunting and fishing on a small scale, gathering fruits, without the need to store products, without pack-animals, and using wood or bone tools. These groups keep alive the memory of their past, and tell tales and sing songs that preserve their identity as a people without recourse to writing, which would bring no benefits to their way of life.

In contrast, where writing was able to solve serious problems it proved to be a spectacular innovation, and it has repeatedly been said that it was an enormous technological revolution. It should be added that this revolution took place on minimalist terms: inventing any instrument which could leave permanent marks on a likewise invented and sufficiently stable support. Styli, brushes, carved bird feathers, or chisels for stone inscriptions, on the one hand and, on the other, inscribed and hardened clay tablets, papyri and parchment as historical supports, or, nowadays, paper, have in turn accompanied the signs of writing over the millennia. Indeed, never has so much come from so little. Moreover, writing, a revolution of almost universal proportions, also fostered many other revolutions: printing, without which our present world would be hardly imaginable, the typewriter, the linotype, the rotary press, and electronic edition systems are all technological developments based on print, and have brought about the almost unlimited expansion of writing and reading. There is, however, a much deeper revolution about which much less has been said: the semiotic transfer involved in the change from orality to writing.

Writing must be considered as a very special case of a theoretically impossible intersensory representation (or semiotic transfer). No one would think of 'smelling a violin concerto' or 'listening to a famous picture' or 'feeling how rough a perfume is'. These three examples share a very special characteristic: with language we can produce diverse expressions, using a rhetorical figure called synaesthesia, through which we can relate two different sensory inputs (smell-hearing in the first, hearing-sight in the second, and touch-smell in the third). But although these expressions are possible, as proven by the fact we have been able to produce them, there is no possibility of carrying out the three actions mentioned, or even of actually conceiving of them. In contrast, the verbal flow, which is oral and auditory, is indeed fixed in writing by written signs which are captured through sight. This is the key issue that must be addressed: synaesthesia, impossible in practice, and yet involving a transfer from the auditory to the visual sense. Because 'seeing words' must surely be as chimerical as 'smelling a violin concerto'. Let us consider the matter step by step with the help of some diagrams where the sensory domain appears for each case.

A semiotic transfer is possible when we do not move from one sense to another and, therefore, we are faced with a case of intrasensory representation. In this situation a real apple can be represented by a picture of an apple, and a real bird's song can be imitated by a musical instrument:

Diagram 1. Intrasensory transfer

A **real** apple	$\longrightarrow$	the **picture** of an apple
(visual)	....	(visual)
the **real** bird's song	$\longrightarrow$	the **imitation** of the song
(sound)	....	(sound)

From visual to visual there is a continuous dotted line, which represents the viability of the transfer. Indeed, we recognize the corresponding referent in the picture, so that the picture is accepted as a representation of the real object. In contrast, let us consider the following diagram:

Diagram 2. Intersensory transfer

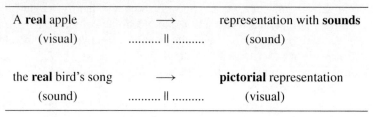

Here we are trying to represent a visual product (the apple) by means of sound, and also an auditory event, the bird's song of the second case, by means of a picture. As we can see, the dotted line is cut because this transfer is impossible: there is no possible way of achieving such representat ion. This would also appear to be the case of writing:

Diagram 3. The transfer of writing

The **real** flow of speech	⟶	the **graphical** representation
(sound)	.... ?	(visual)

This situation is completely analogous to the former one: we are attempting the transfer from the auditory domain to the visual domain, or to the graphical representation of the sound units of speech. If possible, let us position ourselves in a stage previous to writing, and delete from our world and our memory any notion or examples of writing. Let us add that our world has become very complex, that our ability to remember is limited, and that it has become essential that we find a way of stabilizing and lending durability to the products of speech. We can see in this diagram that the dotted line is not cut by insurmountable bars, but by a question mark: this represents a problem we must of necessity solve, since the semiotic transfer involved in writing is (and let us return to reality) an indisputable fact. Let us try to solve this problem step by step.

Diagram 4. Objects and icons

SYSTEM 'A': real vehicles (as referents)	$\longrightarrow$	SYSTEM 'B': the icons of the vehicles (as signs)
real tram	....	picture of a tram
real car	....	picture of a car
real bicycle	....	picture of a bicycle
etc.		etc.

Here, we have returned to the situation in Diagram 1: we stay within a domain, the visual domain, and we agree that the picture of a vehicle has a referent, the real car (as in ancient times when language was absent, the picture of a bull referred us, in a situation prior to writing, to the real bull and not to the word bull). But let us take a further step towards non-iconic representation and enter the symbolic domain through the use of an arbitrary system which can only work by establishing an explicit convention:

Diagram 5. Real objects and graphical conventions

SYSTEM 'A': real vehicles (referents)	$\longrightarrow$	SYSTEM 'B': conventions (signs)
tram	....	X
car	....	Y
bicycle	....	Z

Here we have substituted a series of symbols, the result of an explicit convention, for the icons (pictures of the vehicles). So now, when we wish to refer to a bicycle we can use Z, and so on for the other cases. But the problem remains to be solved, since by using icons (Diagram 4) or symbols (Diagram 5) we are still referring to visual referents with other visual elements, while our concern remains intersensory transfer.

The solution, however, is close at hand and is provided by language, each and every one of the languages spoken throughout the world, because language is an arbitrary or conventional referent system through which we name reality – regardless of its sensorial aspects – by means of sound symbols produced by the speech organs. The final solution to our problem is thus given as:

75

Diagram 6. Real objects and linguistic conventions

SYSTEM 'A':	$\longrightarrow$	SYSTEM 'B':
real vehicles		linguistic conventions
(referents)		(linguistic signs)
tram	....	*tram* (word)
(visual)		(sound)

This changes the whole picture, for *sapiens* have incorporated, naturally as a species, a mechanism of intersensory transfer to refer to reality (to real objects, their qualities, events, and all kind of relations such as causes, consequences and aims) by means of sound symbols which are obtained not from reality but from the linguistic human mind and the complex vocal system. These symbols are the result of mere natural conventions, so that the word *water* neither makes wet nor quenches thirst; the word *fire* neither burns nor heats; and neither does the word *because*, a marker of causal relationship, depend upon natural intent; it only depends upon the connection our mind establishes between two events: 'The road was closed because of a rock fall'. Nothing in *because* derives from factual reality: it is a mere convention that enables us to mark a mental relationship between two events by means of a sound label.

All that remains is one more step, guided by the sensory independence of language, and as depicted through the three stages of the following diagram:

Diagram 7. A ternary relationship

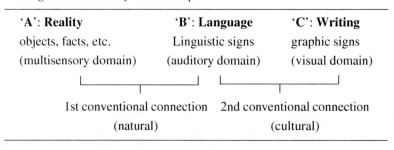

'A': Reality	**'B': Language**	**'C': Writing**
objects, facts, etc.	Linguistic signs	graphic signs
(multisensory domain)	(auditory domain)	(visual domain)

1st conventional connection   2nd conventional connection
(natural)   (cultural)

The consequences of this approach are as follows: language itself is a conventional system of intersensory transfer (A→B) which becomes a model for other types of conventional and intersensory transfer. Thus, step B→C (in the writing domain) is made possible, and once produced enables as many steps as are established by convention; C→D, if we want to move from the visual to the tactile domain, as in the Braille system; and D→B, if tactile writing is converted into a sound register. It is, therefore, the *sapiens* condition which includes the potentiality of writing, and certain compelling circumstances – such as the organization of societies from the Neolithic to the present – that determine whether writing occurs at all, freeing up the human ability to derive symbols from symbols. And symbols from symbols of symbols, and so on.

CONCLUSIONS

This chapter has considered, firstly, the three possible models of writing that are adopted in practice. Thus, this is not an indefinitely open field, nor even a domain with a large number of possibilities, but a very restricted area, since the structure of languages greatly determines the possible ways in which speech can be recorded. Writing, therefore, consists either in the graphical symbolization of words (pictograms and logograms), syllables (syllabograms), or minimal sound units (alphabets). In the latter, history and current practice seem to suggest that alphabets can represent only consonant relationships or articulations or both consonant and vowel relationships or articulations

Secondly, the chapter has offered a brief historical overview from Mesopotamic and Egyptian writings to the birth and expansion of the alphabet, especially in the Mediterranean area. The alphabet, notwithstanding other cultural considerations that may require the preservation of logographic and syllabic systems, appears to be the most economical system imaginable, which explains both its expansion and the praise that such writing has received: in various cultural domains it has been the source of inspiration for adaptations and even radically different formal creations. This historical overview has illustrated the range of human ingenuity, including the application of the *de rebus* principle in obtaining syllabaries and use of the acrophony principle to reduce drastically the number of signs and produce alphabets of about two dozen written signs.

Finally, attention was turned to an issue of concern that underlies all processes leading to the establishment of a writing system: the possibility of transfers between different sensory domains. These transfers cannot occur unless a system of conventions is produced (which has to be learnt explicitly): a system which functions as an agreement to organize informal correspondences, for example, 'the resulting sound of the articulatory movements corresponding to the voiced bilabial stop will be represented as B, and so forth'. This system of conventions, exclusively human, seems to originate in the conventional nature of speech, by which we attribute sound sequences to objects, to the qualities of objects, to events, to the states of things, and to the relationships formed in our environment; the human mind conceptualizes them and names them conventionally in each of the world's languages. This initial and natural linguistic transfer paves the way for other transfers, especially that of writing: the graphical representation (visual domain) of speech units (auditory domain).

REFERENCES

André-Leicknam, G. & Ziegler, Ch. (1982). *Naissance de l'écriture*. Paris: Éditions de la Réunion des musées nationaux de la France.

Bright, W. (Ed.) (1992). *International encyclopedia of linguistics*. New York/Oxford: Oxford University Press.

Daniels, P.T. & Bright, W. (1996). *The world's writing systems*. New York: Oxford University Press.

Gaur, A. (1987). *A history of writing*. London: The British Library.

Gelb, I.J. (1952). *A study of writing*. Chicago: The University of Chicago Press.

Harris, R. (1986). *The origin of writing*. London: Duckworth. Hooker, T.S. (Ed.) (1990). *Reading the past*. London: British Museum Publications.

Mangel, A. (1996). *A history of reading*. Toronto: Knopf Canada.

Ong, W.J. (1982). *Orality and literacy. The technologizing of the word*. London: Methuen and Co.

Sampson, G. (1985). *Writing systems*. London: Hutchinson.

Schmandt-Besserat, D. (1996). *How writing came about*. Austin: University of Texas Press.

Senner, W.M. (Ed.) (1989). *The origins of writing*. Lincoln, NB: The University of Nebraska Press.

Tuson, J. (1996). *L'escriptura. Una introducció a la cultura alfabètica*. Barcelona: Empúries.

Tuson, J. (2002). Imatges i paraules. *Anàlisi, 29*, 119–127.

Zali, A. & Berthier, A. (1997). *L'aventure des écritures. Naissances*. Paris: Biblioth'eque nationale de France.

Jesús Tuson
Departament de Lingüística General
Universitat de Barcelona, Spain

DEVELOPMENTAL PERSPECTIVE

JEANNE BAMBERGER

RESTRUCTURING CONCEPTUAL INTUITIONS
THROUGH INVENTED NOTATIONS

From Path-Making to Map-Making

INTRODUCTION

In this chapter I focus on a single, closely worked out example in which one child (whom I shall call Brad) invents a series of notations, each one a significant transformation of the one before. An Introduction, Part I, is followed in Part II by theoretical background, where I place the study in relation to relevant theoretical material and also describe the fundamental distinction between path-maker and map-maker. Part III includes a description of the tune building task and includes comparisons between typical path-makers and map-makers in both the music domain and in large-scale space. Part IV is the Story of Brad: Beginning with descriptions of the environment in which the study took place. I divide Part IV into 5 phases tracing Brad's evolution from path-making toward map-making. Part V, Conclusions, summarizes and draws some implications for teaching and learning.

The transformations traced in Part IV occurred during one brief session (about 45 minutes) as Brad worked with a set of tuned bells to construct, reconstruct, and play the nursery tune, "Hot Cross Buns". Each notation mediates a process of conceptual restructuring for Brad, while at the same time revealing to the observer his changing understanding of the entities and relations of the tune. Except for a few moments of interruption, all of Brad's work was recorded on videotape.

The transformations that occur in Brad's work in this one session closely resemble the kinds of restructurings that more commonly occur among children working on similar tasks over periods of several months and then only with adult interventions (Bamberger, 1995). Moreover, the developmental distinctions found among children's spontaneously invented notations at different ages are surprisingly mirrored in the specific developmental distinctions Piaget finds among children's descriptions of familiar walks through the city.

In tracing Brad's work in this single session, I argue that we follow him through a series of conceptual transformations that encapsulate and compress this process of moving from path-maker to map-maker. Moreover, I will claim that in following Brad we are able to watch one of those rare instances in which spontaneous and significant learning is actually occurring in real time.

E. Teubal et al. (eds.), Notational Knowledge, 81–112.
© 2007. *Sense Publishers. All rights reserved.*

PART I

THEORETICAL BACKGROUND: A PROPOSAL

My proposal for how this process may evolve is borrowed, in part, from Bartlett in his seminal book, *Remembering*:

> An organism which possesses so many avenues of sensory response as man's, and which lives in intimate social relationship with numberless other organisms of the same kind, must *find some way in which it can break up this chronological order and rove more or less at will in any order over the events* which have built up its present momentary 'schemata'. It must find a way of being dominantly determined, not by the *immediately preceding reaction*, or experience, but by some reaction or experience more remote. (Bartlett, 1932, p. 203)

Since we necessarily experience the world moving through time, our body actions as well as the flow of objects and events around us are necessarily experienced as successive and contiguous. Consider, for example, that the only way I can go from my desk to the door of my study is to walk from here to there. Each complex, integrated motion that we call walking is contiguous with, flows uninterruptedly into the next in both time and space. And as I walk, the objects I pass by – books on the bookshelf, pictures on the wall – necessarily pass by always in the same contiguous succession, as well. But if I choose to look selectively at some part of this complex of actions (does my left arm swing synchronously with my left leg?) I falter as I break up the meshed, chronological order to focus on a particular part in that sequence of events. And in doing so, I may also "liberate" from the meld, a new idea, a new concept.

My claim is that learning, in some very fundamental way, is learning to step off these temporal action paths, to selectively and purposefully *interrupt* the natural passage of contiguous actions/events by focusing on some chosen aspect, which then becomes the core of a new *succession*. For instance, if I choose to focus attention on just the books in my bookcase having to do with "paths", I will interrupt the contiguous succession of books to make a new, non-contiguous succession whose members represent a particular classification of all the books in my bookcase.

Drawing on Bartlett, I will argue that to construct a "concept", for instance, we must selectively interrupt the flow, the continuous succession of incoming sensory stimuli, to select, to pick out, and to recognize (by comparing backwards and forwards in time-space) a new succession made up of just those objects/events that are *congruent with our current field of attention*: all the "middle C's" in a tune, all the numbers (selected out of the "natural" sequential order) that are multiples of 4, all of the stones on the beach that have shiny sparkles.

Heinz Werner puts it this way:

> One who can shift his point of view in a purposeful grouping activity is no longer subject to the forces of sensory stimulation. He is able consciously to perceive that objects have different qualities, any one of which may be taken as the point of departure for an ordering process. (Werner, 1948/1973, p. 239)

This is also a way of talking about *classification*: we may choose objects for attention because they share a common selected aspect; these objects then become members of a particular class of objects. So, *selective attention* within the immediately (present) flow results in the construction of a *new succession*, a new ordering which includes just those objects selected, even though they are disjunct, non-contiguous in time and space. This is one way we have of learning something really new – of coming to see in a new way.

I further argue that this process of interrupting the unique, contiguous sequences of everyday experience is a necessary step (perhaps *the* necessary step) towards learning to understand, to give meaning to, and to use *the symbols, which populate notation systems*. This is because all descriptions, all sets of symbolic expressions, those invented by children as well as those associated with a community of professional users, are necessarily partial and they are so in two senses: they are partial in being *incomplete*, and they are partial in that they favour, or are *partial to* certain aspects of the phenomena while ignoring others. Philip Morrison has said of maps, the cartographers' working notation:

> Each map is in a way a theory that favours certain approximations. Procedures like selection, simplification, smoothing, displacements to make room, out-of-scale notation for bridges, streams, and roads so narrow that they would become invisible at true scale, enter inescapably. (Morrison, 1991).

To understand the "theories" implicit in these selective notation systems and to use their referents appropriately we must focus on the particular "favoured approximations" underlying these conventional notations. For instance, in order to give meaning to the symbol for "middle C", I have to jump around within the given succession of events in the tune so as to extract instances of that pitch from their unique position – the context in which they are embedded and their unique function within that context. As we shall see, to carry out this process becomes a major step for Brad as he travels the course from path-maker to map-maker.

Finally, and perhaps most important, I will argue that the goal of learning is not to *overcome* the behaviours associated with path-making, but rather to have access to both action and symbol such that one is able to choose depending on when, where, and what for.

PART II

PATH-MAKERS AND MAP-MAKERS: THE TASK AND THE MATERIALS

The task, as it has been presented to some 50 children between the ages of 8 and 12, and as it was presented to Brad, is as follows:

> "Build Hot Cross Buns with your bells, and then make some instructions so someone else can play the tune on your bells as you have them set up".

In preparation for the task, each child is given a mixed array of seven Montessori bells and a small mallet with which to play them (Figure 1).

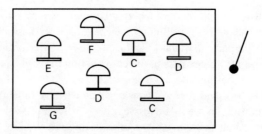

Figure 1. Seven bells and a small mallet.

The Montessori bells are a rather extraordinary technological invention. Unlike any other musical materials that play different pitches, *these bells all look alike*. This is in contrast to, for instance, a xylophone bar that is relatively longer and is also lower in pitch or a piano key to the right of another, which is also relatively higher in pitch. Thus, a child working with these bells must find differences in pitch *only by listening*.[1]

Each individual mushroomed-shaped metal bell is attached to a wooden stem, with bell and stem, in turn, standing on a small wooden base making it easy to move them about. Some stand on brown bases and others on white bases but this single difference has no significance to the pitch properties of the metal bells, themselves.

Path-Makers

Path-makers build tunes by building a cumulating bell-path. Searching through the mixed array of bells for a bell that matches the first event, they place the found bell in front of the mixed array on the table. Finding a bell that matches the next tune event, they place it to the right of the previously found bell. They continue on in this way, adding each found bell to their cumulating bell-path, next-next-next. The result is a bell path where each bell has been added *in order of occurrence* in the tune (see Figure 2).

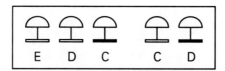

Figure 2. Hot Cross Buns – bell path.

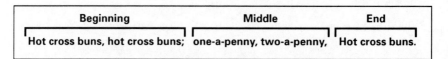

Figure 3. The three-part, figural structure of the tune.

As a result of the sequential building procedure, the sequence of bells in a path-maker's bell path makes a unique, "one purpose" instrument – it is made to play just this tune. Further, the spatial structure of the bell-path – three bells, a gap, then two bells – is a physical embodiment of the motivic grouping or *"figural"* structure of the tune – a "figure" being the smallest meaningful *structural* element or "chunk" of a tune (see Figure 3). The beginning figure, which goes with the words, "Hot Cross Buns", is embodied and played by the group of three bells. The middle figure, which goes with the words, "One-a-penny; Two-a-penny", is embodied and played by the second group of two bells. The ending figure returns back to the beginning figure again.

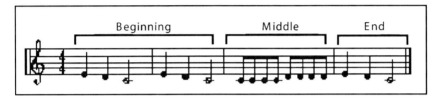

Figure 4. Hot Cross Buns.

With regard to *classifying* pitches, as shown in Figure 4, the middle part includes two of the pitches (C and D) that are already in the first figure. However, the *context* in which each of the matched pitches occurs is quite different when constructing the tune in order of occurrence and also in playing the tune. Most importantly, the *functions* of these matched pitches are entirely different within these contexts. For example, the C in the first figure has a longer duration and is last in a descending progression. As a result, this first C-pitch functions as an *ending*, the boundary-marker of the first figure. The C in the middle figure has a shorter duration, is repeated, comes after a figural boundary and as a result functions as a *beginning*, a start-up after the "gap" of the previous boundary. For all of these reasons, typical path-makers (children and musically untrained adults) consistently and understandably fail to recognize that these bells sound the same pitch. However, *when asked specifically to listen for pitch matches*, they are surprised to discover that "same pitch" was embedded in the tune. This is strong evidence to support the view that path-makers do not listen *across* boundaries of figures and that their focus remains on the *function of events within the figures of which they are members* (Bamberger, 1995).[2]

To play the whole tune, path-makers make an action-path through their bell-path: As a consequence of adding bells left→right in the order of occurrence in the tune, the predominant direction of the action-path is also left→right. However, there are three notable exceptions mediated by the structure of this tune, itself (see Figure 5).

First, the repetition of the beginning figure, the first three bells, requires a "turn around" in the action-path, a move "back" or right→left. Second, since the tune ends as it began, another turn-around is required to "go back" to play the

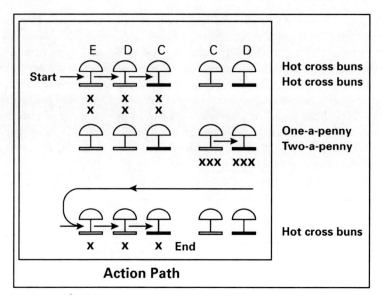

Figure 5. An **x** marks a tap on a bell, while the lines and arrows mark the direction of the path-maker's actions through the bells.

beginning figure, again. A third exception occurs in the middle part of the tune when single bells must be repeated even while the tune goes on.

These moments of interruption in the prevailing direction of motion form a sequential series of *landmarks* marking the boundaries of figures. The landmarks shape the structure of the action-path and it, in turn, coincides with the larger structure of the tune, itself.

Invented notations for "Hot Cross Buns" are basically "iconic" trail-maps, as shown in Figure 6.

Figure 6. Iconic trail path.

The bells on the table are "copied" onto the paper as stick-pictures or some-times simplified copies of the bells. But notice that the three bells on the table become nine marks on the paper. The group of 3 bells is first drawn again to show "coming after" – that is, to show the immediate repetition of the first figure, the three marks are drawn again after the middle part to show that the three bells are played again at the end. This is, of course, a notational convention – how else could we show that while objects may remain stationary, events played on them are coming after one another, are occurring through time? The notation for the middle section also shows the tension between static objects, the two bells on the table, and representations of events occurring on them. Here, the static objects are given precedence – each bell is drawn only once, even though each must be repeated several times. The difference here may be evidence, on one hand, for the strong sense of the three bells forming a group, and on the other to the difference between the player moving along on the bells, as in the three-bell figure, or the player staying put in one place as in the middle figure.

Musical and Spatial Path-Makers

As suggested earlier, there are interesting similarities between a musical path-maker's action path through the bells, and a path-maker who is a walker in the city. For instance, Kevin Lynch in his book, *The Image of the City* notices that a path-maker follows:

> ... a *sequential series of landmarks*, in which one detail calls up anticipation of the next and key details trigger specific moves ... In such sequences, there were trigger cues *whenever turning decisions* must be made and reassuring cues that confirmed the observer in decisions gone by ... (Lynch, 1960, p. 83)

Thus, changes of direction help to segment a journey and as such to mark the boundaries of spatial "figures". Just as these landmarks are clues for the walker in the city, so changes of direction in actions on the bells form a series of land-marks on the path through the tune. And like musical path-makers, walkers in the city simply go next-next-next within figures but do not construct relations across boundaries of figures or among landmarks.

The experience of musical path-makers, like path-makers in the real world, is of a journey that is paradoxically always in the immediate present while always going on. And the sense (both as feeling and as meaning) of this passing present is formed by the context of where the path-maker just came from, while the passing present forms the context, in turn, for where he/she is going. Thus, for path-makers, there is no comparing where they are to where they have been because there is no stopping, no stepping off the continuing path, and no means for comparing events that are distanced from one another in time/space. Christopher Hasty puts the situation this way in relation to musical experience:

> But because of [an event's] particularity of unrepeatability, we shall not be able to retrieve such a past event for a postmortem. It would seem, too, that its duration has also vanished. True, the event has not vanished without a trace, but that trace is the mark the past can make on the present – on a new event or events, each with its own individuality and freedom. (Hasty, 1997, p. 4)

Musical map-makers differ from path-makers right from the beginning of their work on the task. As if needing to put themselves in order, these players first search in the mixed array for a subset of the given bells which they *arrange from lowest to highest* proceeding from left (low) to right (high). Leaving alone any "doubles" in the given mixed array that match in pitch, the map-maker's arrangement forms an outside "fixed reference structure".

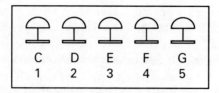

Figure 7. Fixed reference structure.

Much like seriating a mixed array of sticks that are graduated in height, each bell added to the right is "higher" than the one to its left, and each bell added to the left is "lower" than the one to its right. Thus, map-makers initially focus their attention on the *pitch properties* alone, rather than the path-maker's focus on order of occurrence and resulting situational function *within a particular tune.*

The property-ordered structure is an outside fixed reference in that it is *outside of any one tune and yet, its constituents are common to many.* And because its structure is based on the low-high ordering inherent in pitch properties, themselves, the structure also implies a "unit of pitch distance". This unit can be used to measure, along the reference structure, the distance between any two pitches – the "pitch interval". The intervalic relations among pitches within a tune help to compare the structure of one tune with another.[3]

Perhaps these map-making tune builders are like travellers who are dependent on their printed map for finding their destination – looking at it instead of the objects and events that, for the path-maker, shape the landmarks, the figures, and the feel of a particular moment along the way. Indeed, compared with a path-maker's bell-path, the pre-ordering of the bells can hardly be called a "path" at all; rather, like a map, it is an *ordered terrain on which to trace a particular action path* (Figure 8).

As might be expected, the map-maker's notation path is no longer iconic but rather symbolic. There are no pictures of bells, only numbers (Figure 9).

To construct their notation, map-makers first number their bells from 1–5 going low to high. Then, as they play the tune, they trace their action path along the pre-arranged bells "looking up" the number of the serial position *in the reference structure* for each tune-event in turn. They, so-to-speak, peel off each found number, "transporting" *it* to the paper. Iterations of this process result in a row of numbers that *designate*, or point to, a sequence of bell positions and these, in turn, target the player's moves to the sequence of bells that plays the tune.

Notice that map-makers need to use *only three bells* (C, D, E) instead of five to play the whole tune. In turn, mappers use only numbers 1-2-3 in their notation and these refer to just the three bells that they have used in building the tune. This is in contrast to path-maker's who use five bells including the two doubles – i.e. two C's and two D's. As pointed out earlier, the doubles are necessary for path-makers because each one – each C and each D, has its distinct function within the boundaries of the figure in which it occurs. These differences are critical to the transformations in Brad's work as he moves from path-maker towards map-maker.

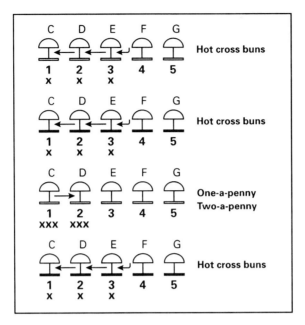

Figure 8. Map-maker action-path.

3 2 1 3 2 1 1 1 1 1 2 2 2 2 3 2 1

Figure 9. Mappers' notation.

The Builders Compared

The differences between musical path-makers and musical map-makers become more focused by comparing them with the differences that Piaget notices between younger and older children's descriptions of journeys through the city. Piaget says of younger children:

> ... each journey shows a particular vantage point and [the children] are unable to bridge the gap between the privileged vantage point of one journey and the next ... [E]*ach is unique* and therefore they cannot coordinate all the features in an area taken as a whole. (Piaget, 1960, p. 16)

While with older children:

> ... each vantage point *is no longer unique*. The link between any two land-marks can be conceived of as dependent on the *system as a whole*. [Children] can now relate any one part to all of the remaining parts. (Piaget, op. cit., p. 18)

Coupling Piaget's remarks with those of Lynch quoted above, we can say that musical path-makers like younger children, construct meanings in relation to the sequence and unique function of contextually situated *reference objects* or events (landmarks), where the occurrence of each object/event is a necessary condition for triggering the next move. Map-makers depend for meanings on the mental construction of *situation-independent reference structures* in which objects/events are linked to one another and placed in a single coordinate space, and where distances among them can be invariantly measured independently of their occurrence or function in any particular situation or sequence of actions (Bamberger & Schön, 1991).

However, unlike Piaget who associates these differences with age and stage of development, I will argue that experienced musicians make use of both paths and maps and, in fact, move effectively between and within them in order fully to participate (as listeners and performers) in the complexity of a complex piece of music.

PART III

THE STORY OF BRAD

The Setting

While the beginning and ending points of Brad's 45 minute session resemble the differences Piaget finds in children's earlier and later descriptions of their walks, the findings must be differentiated from Piaget's work not only in content, but also in experimental context.

— *Time*: Piaget gives us brief "snapshots" of different children at different times and at different ages and stages of development. Brad's work involves just a single child and the conceptual changes that take place over a single period of about 45 minutes.

— *Setting*: The setting is not a neutral one. Brad's work is carried out in the context of an alternative public school classroom called The Laboratory for Making Things. His notational inventions are influenced by the work of the 5 other eight and nine-year-old children who were also working in the Lab on the same task.

— *The Lab Culture*: Brad is also influenced by the characteristics of a culture that has developed in the Lab over the seven years of its existence.

As an integral part of this culture, children were accustomed to informal conversations in which they explained to one another or to an adult how they were making sense of their working materials – blocks, foam core, drums, Legos^{TM}, bells. They were also used to inventing some kind of graphic instructions/notations that could help someone else build what they had built. As in Brad's work, this collaborative reflection led to learning from one another– rethinking understandings and descriptions, subsequently even influencing work on later projects that involved quite different materials.

As another part of this culture, children moved freely between building working structures with hands-on materials, and building working structures (graphic designs and also melodies) using the computer as a medium. As a result of this movement back and forth, certain kinds of ideas became part of the culture, influencing and illuminating the children's understanding across all the media. For instance, there was the idea of "chunking" or grouping which initially emerged as they needed to "chunk" or parse a melody into workable "blocks"; these then became the "units of work" in composing melodies. The practice of "chunking" was also related to marking off elements that were to be named. This became most evident when we frequently heard one child asking of another as they looked together at a musical, Lego™, or other work-in-progress, "So what is a THING, here?" Indeed, the question became a very concrete way of posing a fundamental ontological question: What have you got here? What are the objects, the "things" that your house or machine or melody is made up of and what do you call them? The question quite spontaneously focused a child's attention on, for instance, functions, repeating objects, patterns, boundaries and groupings as they emerged.

I have grouped Brad's work into six phases. Each phase marks a stage in the transformation of Brad's tune-building strategies and his notation, and these, in turn, are evidence for changes in his way of understanding the tune, itself – its constituents and their relationships to one another.

Phase 1: Brad as Path-Maker

A. Labelling the Bells

While Brad, at the beginning of his work, is in many ways a path-maker, his first move already distinguished him from more typical path-makers. Apparently in anticipation of "making instructions", Brad begins the task of building "Hot Cross Buns", by giving himself another task – namely, labelling the bells. To do so, Brad cut out five paper squares, wrote numbers on them from 1 to 5, and *without playing the bells at all*, placed a numbered square in front of each bell (Figure 10).

Ordering the numbers right-to-left from 1 to 5, he ingeniously invented a way to name the undifferentiated, anonymous objects on the table (Figure 10).

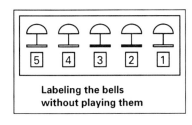

Labeling the bells without playing them

Figure 10. Lining up and labelling the bells.

While the sequence of Brad's number-names (1 2 3 4 5) may look similar to the sequence of map-makers' numbers, the meaning of the numbers is entirely different. Recall that map-makers' ordering and the numbers assigned to bells refer specifically to the perceived pitch properties of the bells: 1 2 3 4 5 refers to the low (1)-high (5) ordering of pitches. Brad's number-labels cannot, of course, refer to the hidden pitch properties of the objects (bells) they name since, remaining silent, these properties have not yet been revealed. Only the arbitrary positions they happened to take as he put them out on the table determine the number-names he gives to them. His numbers, like colour coded instructions for playing a tune, will instruct the player which bell-numbers, to play when. And like "paste-on" labels, the number-names are useful only as long as the labels stay attached to the bells.

B. Building the Tune

Playing the bells now, listening and searching for each bell *as it was needed in the tune*, Brad built up a cumulating bell-path (Figure 11). Being careful to keep the labels attached to the bells as he moved them into place, Brad transformed his initial silent line-up into a bell-path where the position of each added bell matches its order of occurrence *in the unfolding of the tune*.

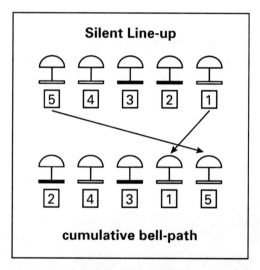

Figure 11. Building the tune.

As he worked, Brad *moved each number-label along with its bell*, working consistently from right to left (unlike more typical path-makers), Brad found that his bell-5 was the first one in the tune, while bell-1 played the second event in the tune. This process resulted in a cumulating row of bells accompanied by a cumulating row of numbers. While the row of numbers may appear to be a meaningless list, 2 4 3 1 5, going from right-to-left, the labels will serve Brad's purpose well as the basis for making his "instructions".

Brad's sequence of bells on the table "holds" the sequence of tune events in the order in which they appear in the tune, but his resulting bell-path differs from that of the typical path-maker in two ways: he consistently works right→left, and his bell-path has a corresponding "number-path" – the labels Brad arbitrarily attached to the bells.

C. Making an Action Path

Following his built bell-path, picking out the sequence of bells, Brad made an *action path* through his unique, one-purpose instrument that played the whole tune. Brad's *action path* was exactly the same as the typical path-maker except for its prevailing right→left direction (Figure 12).

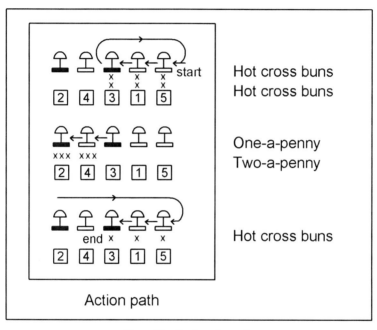

Figure 12. Brad's action path.

As with other path-makers, Brad's action-path included three notable exceptions to the prevailing direction (here, right-to-left), each of them mediated by the structure of the tune, itself: first, the repetition of the initial figure which requires a move back or left→right; second, repetition on single bells in the middle figure, and third, another move back (left→right) to play the first figure again.

D. The First Notation

Brad made his first instructions by so-to-speak "peeling off" each number-name from a bell and placing it on paper *in the order in which he played them*. In this way his sequence of actions through the bell terrain in table-space, becomes a sequence of numbers in paper space (Figure 13).

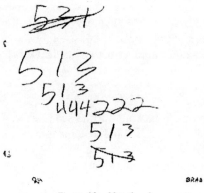

Figure 13. Notation 1.

Brad's notation strategy bears some similarity to map-makers' notation strategy in that he also "transports" *the number-labels, rather than a stick-figure pictures of the bells* to the paper. But a closer comparison shows critical differences (Figure 14).

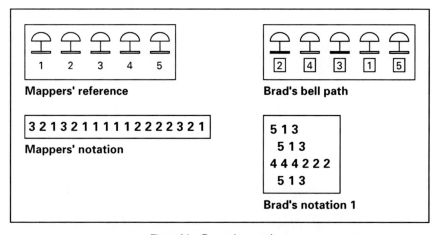

Figure 14. Comparing notations.

The numbers in map-makers' notation derive from and refer specifically to properties of the bells arranged in the fixed reference structure. Thus, seeing 3 2 1, the reader, following learned rules for playing on the all-purpose "instrument" will go "down stepwise" from high (3) to low (1) moving right→left along the fixed bell series. While Brad's numbers also tell the player to follow a series of numbers, his arbitrary number-names tell the player only where to go on this single-purpose "instrument" and nothing about the pitch properties of the bells they are playing.

And there is another significant difference: Brad *spatially groups* his numbers (Figure 13). The boundaries of Brad's spatial grouping also mark the boundaries of figures. These boundaries most noticeably coincide with *changes in direction* in his action path – i.e., the switchbacks in the prevailing right-left direction: the immediate repetition of the opening figure (**5 1 3**) and its return at the end. The changes in direction "bundle" these events helping to generate, along with the repetitions, themselves, the *figural or motivic grouping boundaries* of the tune. The middle figure which Brad notates as **4 4 4 2 2**, is bounded by the move to new bells, the repeated events played on single bells, and by the subsequent return to the beginning figure. The spatial boundaries in Brad's notation thus mark *landmarks* that shape the boundaries of melodic figures. In short, Brad's notation is a kind of structural analysis of the tune reflecting aspects that are not shown at all in map-makers' notations nor, indeed, in conventional staff notation.

Finally, it is interesting that in putting pencil to paper, Brad simply abandons the prevailing right-to-left direction of his *actions* and spontaneously invokes the left-to-right directional convention associated with writing. Apparently the left→right convention associated with "notation space" does not carry over to "action space" (Figure 15).

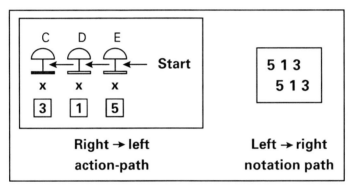

Figure 15. Action space vs. notation space.

Phase 2: A Discovery

In this phase Brad's surprising discovery gives us insight into the kinds of unexpected situations that lead to conceptual transformations and to the emergence of new kinds of entities and their relations.

The transformations were triggered by an accidental discovery made by another child, Celia. Working on the same tune building task, using bells with the same set of pitches, Celia set up her bells in a different configuration from Brad – 3 bells on the left side for the first part, two bells on the right side for the middle part.

After Celia had built and played the tune, she experimented a bit and discovered to her surprise that she could play the beginning of Hot Cross Buns "in two different ways so it sounds just the same" (Figure 16, seen from above).

95

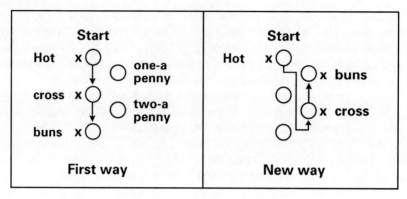

Figure 16. "... it sounds just the same".

A. Adapting Celia's Route

The discovery remained simply a mystery for Celia. But in the spirit of collaborative learning in the Lab, I showed Celia's new way to Brad and asked, "How do you explain this? See if it will work on your bells?"

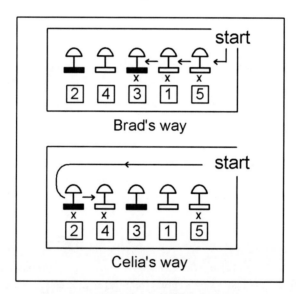

Figure 17. Celia's way on Brad's bells.

Brad played the first figure of the tune in his usual way and adapted Celia's new action-path to the shape of his bells for the repeat. Then pausing for just a moment he went on to play the middle part of the tune in a new way, as well (Figure 18).

Using the two bells labelled **3 and 1**, Brad played the middle part of the tune *with the same bells that he had previously used only to play the first part of the tune.* To complete the tune, he played the return to the first part in his usual way.

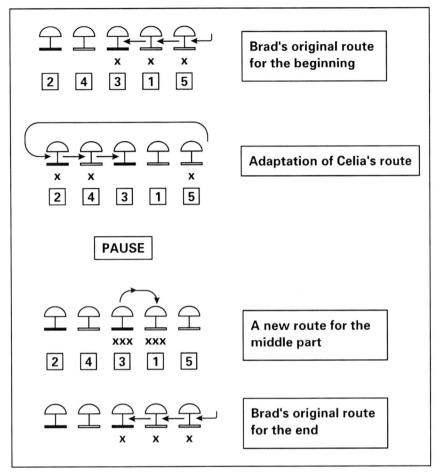

Figure 18. Brad's new action path.

At this point, Brad stopped, looked up with an expression of puzzlement and surprise, and said: "Oh, this is weird! I can play it with just three bells!" And he pushed aside the bell-pair labelled **4-2** (Figure 19).

Instantiating my earlier proposal, Brad has come to see in a new way: Mediated initially by adapting Celia's alternate route, he stepped off his familiar temporal action path, selectively and purposefully *interrupted* the natural passage of contiguous actions/events and focusing on a chosen aspect, formed the core of a new succession. Specifically, adapting Celia's alternative path, Brad crossed over (violated) the boundary of the first figure in the tune, leaping (rather than stepping) from the beginning bell-5 over the remaining members of his initial bell group [1-3] to the pair of bells at the other end of the bell-path [2-4] (Figure 20).

He thus displaced bells [2–4] from their previous function as members of the middle figure giving these bells new meaning as constituent members of the first

Figure 19. A discovery.

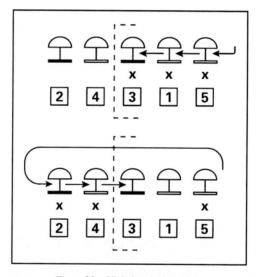

Figure 20. Violating the boundary.

figure. I argue that the events leading to this cognitive leap are an embodiment of what Bartlett described as "a crucial step in organic development". Brad found a way to "break up the chronological order [of his bell and action paths] and rove more or less at will in any order over the events" (Bartlett, op. cit., p. 206).

Piaget also comments on the important effect of taking "detours" on children's evolving conceptions of large scale space. Piaget says of children's alternate paths in getting from home to school:

Operations ... are found formed by a kind of thawing out of intuitive structures, by the sudden mobility which animates and co-ordinates the configurations that were hitherto more or less rigid despite their progressive articulation. Each detour leads to interactions which supplement the various points of view. (Piaget, 1960, p. 38)

Piaget's insights including the conceptual leaps that detours portend, and the logic implicit in them, bear an eerie similarity to Brad's "detours" in travelling in the very small space of his bell terrain.

B. Brad Explains

While it might seem to those who read and perform music from standard notation, that Brad simply recognized the bell-pairs 4-2 and 3-1 as matched pitch-pairs – both pairs of bells play pitches C and D. But jumping ahead a bit to Brad's own explanation, he makes it clear that this is not the case. When asked by Mary Briggs, his teacher, "How'd you discover it? All of a sudden you said, 'Wait a minute, I can do it with three'", Brad explained (Figure 21):

... I was realizing that if I could play it one way – like 5 1 3 (pause).

Then I realized that two of these (pointing to the pair [1 3]) could be used in a different way instead of these two (points to the pair [4 2]).

Figure 21. "... two of these could be used in a different way ...".

That is, the two bell pairs, **1-3** and **2-4** could be effectively swapped: they work as members of the first figural group or as members of the middle figural group. And since they are exchangeable in this way, they are *functionally equivalent* *pairs*. Brad articulates that principle in his expression "... could be used in a different way instead of ..." (Figure 22).

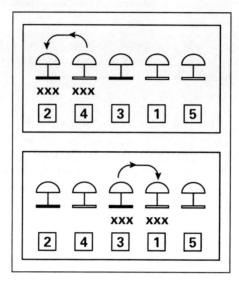

Figure 22. Functionally equivalent pairs.

And the final logical leap: since the two bell pairs are functionally equivalent, it is unnecessary to have them both; leaving aside one pair (**4-2**) just the other pair (**1-3**) plus the single 5-bell is enough, and that makes just 3 bells in all.

I argue that the events leading to this cognitive leap are an embodiment of what Bartlett described as "a crucial step in organic development". Specifically, Brad has found a way to "break up the chronological order [of his bell and action paths] and rove more or less at will in any order over the events" (Bartlett, op. cit., p. 206). Moreover, Brad's sudden leap instantiates my earlier proposal: initially mediated by adapting Celia's alternate route, Brad stepped off his familiar action path, interrupted the passage of contiguous actions/events and formed the core of a new succession. Brad had come to see in a new way.

Looking back, at the sequence of events in this phase of Brad's work, I will argue that Brad's insights provide evidence that constructing a class of functionally equivalent objects/events is perhaps a necessary intermediary step towards, but is not the same as, recognizing matched pairs of de-contextualized pitch properties-here, the class of all C's and of all D's.

But I want to emphasize that, as in most on-the-spot learning, Brad's reasoning was emergent in real time and as such was almost entirely embedded in his actions. Indeed, judging from the way he expressed his discovery, "Oh, that's weird; I can play it with just three bells", his insight apparently felt to him, at the moment, more like magic than a series of logical steps such as I have proposed.

Phase 3: Making the 3-Bell Theory Work

Phase 3 marks the working out of transformations that were imminent in Phase 2.

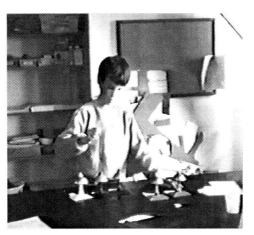

Figure 23. Pushing aside the two extra bells.

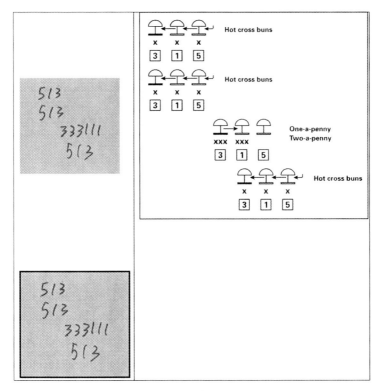

Figure 24. Notation 2: Just three bells.

Pushing aside the two "extra" bells (**2 & 4**), Brad successfully plays the whole tune using just the three remaining bells labelled **5 1 3** (Figure 24). His second notation gives instructions for how to go on just those three bells.

Brad's 3-bell notation might seem in some ways to resemble a map-maker's notation, but again there are important differences. The number-labels Brad uses, [**5 1 3**], are still the arbitrary labels he attached to the bells at the outset; as such, they do not refer at all to pitch property or fixed reference numbers. And perhaps more important, Brad's spatial grouping of his numbers continues to reflect the figural/motivic structure of the tune – something not represented in the typical map-maker's notation (Figure 25).

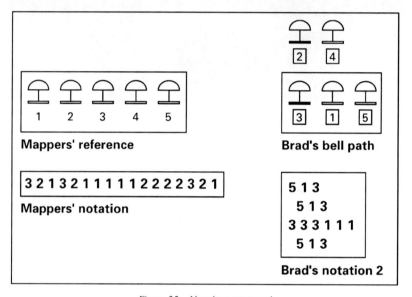

Figure 25. Notations compared

Looking with Brad at the finished notation, Mary's probing question leaves no doubt about these groupings. Circling the middle row of numbers, Mary asks:

M: *"Now, Brad, how come you put all those together?"*

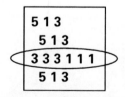

Figure 26. "kinda together".

B: *[rather haltingly] Because they're kinda together ... 'cause it's kinda the same ... it's the same as these three (Brad points to the previous three numbers, [5 1 3]).*

Brad's use of "the same" is noticeably different from conventional usage in relation to pitch. The events numbered [**3 3 3 1 1 1**] are "the same as" those numbered [**5 1 3**] in just one critical respect: the events "go together" to form gestures or structural entities. To use the children's expression, events that form a group, constitute the functional "things" of this small universe – what we would call the structural entities of the tune.

Phase 4: Brad's Reflections Produce a Third Notation

A notation for music lends itself to insight in part because it is a kind of spatial version of a temporal sequence, but it has the advantage of "holding still" so that it can be scanned in any order and even out-of-order. Holding still *to be looked at as a whole*, the notation becomes a conduit towards the emergence of what Brad describes as "... seeing a pattern". As pointed out earlier, invented notations, like conventional notations associated with a community of professional users, are partial in being incomplete, and also in being partial to certain features while ignoring others. In turn, the maker's choice of aspects and the related names given to them is revealing of how the maker is mentally representing the phenomena – what he/she is choosing to notice and the assumptions inherent in the larger framework in which these aspects are embedded. Turning that idea back on itself, Brad's third notation not only reveals how he is re-thinking the constituents and relations of the materials. The new notation also reveals the surprising potential that an *invented* notation has to uncover assumptions hiding in our *conventional* notations, as well.

Brad's next moves seem clear evidence for the significance Bartlett has given to "turning back" on one's own "schemata" and constructing new ones:

> [An organism] has somehow to acquire the capacity to turn round upon its own 'schemata' and to construct them afresh. This is a crucial step in organic development. (Bartlett, op. cit., p. 206)

A. Seeing a Pattern

Mary helps Brad to "turn round" by referring to a conversation that had occurred just a moment before: Mary says, "Now, Brad, you told me you saw a pattern. What was the pattern you saw?" Pointing to each of the three bells on the table as he gestures, still going right→left, Brad says in quick response to Mary's question: "Well you could really number them one-two-three; one-two-three" (Figure 27).

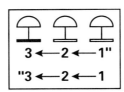

Figure 27.

And re-assigning his numbered paper squares, Brad re-labels the bells accordingly.

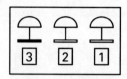

Figure 28. Re-labelling.

In doing so, Brad has replaced his *ad hoc* number-names (5-1-3) with conventional ordinal numbers that refer to and correspond with the sequence in which the bells enter the song as tune-events. In giving up the arbitrary number-names, Brad creates a whole new reference system. These are numbers that refer unambiguously to an apprehended world – a row of objects on the table that, when played, create events as they occur in the tune in real time. Using this new reference entity, Brad's verbal instructions for playing the tune along with his gestures, become an embodied, action notation. And with this, the numbers and the bells suddenly take on directional meaning. He says, gesturing to show the directionality, "Let's say this was 1".

This episode and its evolution raise new puzzles and new issues. For instance, Brad speaks as if asking "you", the receiver of his instructions, to walk along his numbers and bells, "going up" and "going down". But numbers do not literally go up or down, and we are not literally "going up" or "going down" either as we follow Brad's directions.

Notice that Brad's description, "So you go up ..." corresponds exactly to our conventional usage when we say of the number line, the numbers "go up".[4] Animating numbers, putting them into motion we are, of course, invoking a metaphor: a static list, a chronology stuck in space, comes alive as if acting in time and motion. But these metaphors are so deeply embedded in our language that we have forgotten that the terms, "up/down", "high/low" literally only refer to *visible, tangible objects that can move or can be moved up and down through time in space.*

Further, in adopting this new notation, Brad wipes out a central feature of his previous "instructions" – the notation as a physical embodiment of the tune's figural structure. Recall that Brad's initial bell-path was constructed in synchrony with the chronology of events in the tune. In turn, his initial notation-path was spatially grouped to reflect the tune's motivic structure. Over the last set of moves, Brad has gradually broken this synchrony apart. And now, with his ordinal numbering of the bells and his focus on directionality, he almost entirely abandons any reflection of this figural grouping structure.

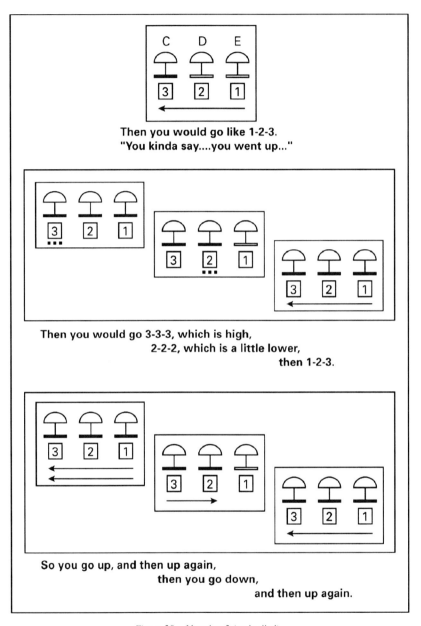

Figure 29. Notation 3 (embodied).

105

B. Metaphors, Meanings, and Notations

Brad's newly invented number scheme and his use of metaphoric spatial/temporal language reveals a paradox and the paradox, in turn, helps to reveal aspects of notational conventions that ordinarily can remain comfortably hidden in their common use and practice. Dead metaphors can come alive under conditions of uncertainty and confusion.

The paradox arises because similar spatial, directional, and motion metaphors are embedded in the terms we use to refer to *pitch relations*, as well as numeric relations. Just as we speak of numbers "going up" or "going down", so we speak of pitch "going up" or "going down".

Carrying this sense of apprehended movement into our language, we come to believe it – we attribute movement to melody, itself, as if pitch and melody were self-animated. And in similar ways, we attribute self-animation to numbers when we encourage children to say as they move along a number line, "The numbers are going up".[5]

But the sense we have of a melody "moving" is a mental construction like the frames in a moving picture that give the impression of movement. However, taken literally, it is performers who move, not pitches: Once built, neither the bells, their pitches, nor the notation on paper literally move anywhere. It is Brad who moves.

In making his new instructions, Brad is focusing on the self-animation we attribute to numbers, not the direction of pitch motion as you sing or play the tune. And here the potential for confusion in metaphoric meanings becomes intense. Looking back at the map-maker's notation based on the "motion" of the pitches *within the fixed reference structure*, the beginning of Hot Cross Buns in fact goes *down*, not up. The first two figures are numbered **3 2 1 3 2 1**. To make Brad's notation which he consistently writes right-to-left match conventional notation, which is, of course, written left-right, the sequence of numbers under the bells, as well as the direction of motion in his notation would have to be exactly reversed (Figure 30).[6]

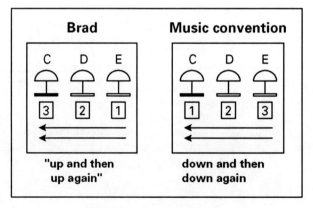

Figure 30. Crossed metaphors.

So the paradox that seems inherent in Brad's comment that the tune "goes up" when in fact it "goes down", is really not a paradox at all. Rather we see a beautiful example of a difference in *focus of attention*. Brad has numbered the bells according to their order of occurrence in the tune – the numbers are ordinals – (**1 2 3**) are the first, second, third events. But once applying the numbers to the bells, the numbers change who they are – they become elements in a number-line and Brad is moving "up" along that line. With a focus on conventionally represented *pitch direction* and assigning numbers according to music notation conventions, the sequence of pitches at the beginning of Hot Cross Buns, is "going down" [**3 2 1**]. Both designations are right; it just depends on what aspects you are "partial to".

Phase 5: Pitch, An Emergent Phenomenon

Thus far I have focused on Brad's actions, his notations, and his words as evidence for his changing understanding of the tune structure. Through these actions I have proposed analogies with movement through space, specifically with making and following paths–"bell-path", "action-paths", "notation paths", and alternate "routes" traversed. Moreover, I have attributed Brad's insights to inferences he has drawn from observing and mentally coordinating his actions as he both made paths and followed them. Most of all, I have given causal importance to the moments in which these paths have been interrupted and their chronologies, their contiguous actions/events broken up. Returning to Bartlett and my primary proposal, Brad, with the help of Mary and others, has indeed been able to "find some way in which [he] can break up this chronological order and rove more or less at will in any order over the events which have built up [his] present momentary schemata". It seems clear that Brad's invention of notations that hold still and that he can look at "out there", contributed to the possibilities for this "roving at will".

I have also emphasized the importance Brad gives to figures – these are the "things", the units of perception reflected in his written notations. But with his mostly verbal, gestural third notation, these figures as units of description have essentially disappeared.

While all of these transformations in action give evidence of emerging new entities and relations, none of Brad's notations referred to pitch or pitch relations, as such. Recall that with the bells all looking alike, pitch remains a hidden property of these unidentified objects. To build the tune Brad had to play the bells and listen for a match between the bells he heard and the tune in his head which he had sung and at times continued to sing as he went along. In building the tune and playing it, Brad necessarily did this pitch-recognizing entirely "by ear", in action, and in the local context of the tune in its becoming.

It is not surprising, then, that none of Brad's three notations referred to pitch or pitch relations, as such. The notations refer, in one way or another, to the ordering of bells as he has set them up in a row, to the sequence of tune events as coordinated with his actions, and, except for the last, to the grouping of these tune events into the figures of which they are members.

Watching Brad's work, I asked myself what on-the-spot intervention might help him account for his insights and for the inferences that led to them? It was my hunch that Brad would need to shift his focus of attention to pitch as an inherent and invariant property of a bell, independent of the functional role of that pitch within figures. Such an intervention might also help him account for the "weirdness" of his three-bell theory. This, in turn, could move him towards conceptual map-making, hopefully without losing the relevant functional attributes of his present representations. In Phase 5, through a series of interventions, I began the process of trying to carry out this program with Brad.

A. Matching Pitches – Another Surprise

Pointing to the two "discarded" bells, I asked Brad: "How come you don't need to use these bells? Do you know why it works?" Shaking his head, Brad said rather soberly, "No. I don't". This response tentatively confirmed my hunch that Brad was unaware of the duplicate pitches in his initial 5-bell collection. And the quality of his answer – pensive, reflecting some puzzlement – suggested that this was, indeed, something new for him to think about.

To help Brad isolate the pitch properties of the bells, taking them out from their structural functions when embedded in the tune, I made an intervention of a more directly instructive kind. Pointing to one of the "extra" bells standing apart from the three-bell tune-path, I said, "Can you find one (another bell) that sounds the same as this one?" This was a version of stepping off a well-trodden path of actions; instead of tune events, the bells could just play matching sounds (Figure 31).

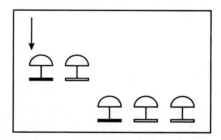

Figure 31. ... find one that sounds the same?

Playing the "extra" bell and testing each of the others, Brad immediately found a match for the designated bell. This was important proof that Brad had no problem actually recognizing matched pitches. However, he was visibly surprised to discover that matches were to be had – good evidence that this was a whole new view of the situation.

Quite spontaneously, Brad moved the matching "extra" bell over to position it together with its mate (Figure 32).

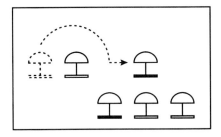

Figure 32. A match.

Having found one pair of bells that matched, Brad pushed the remaining "extra" bell over towards the bell he had labelled "3". And *without even playing it,* he said aloud, "And these probably do too".[7]

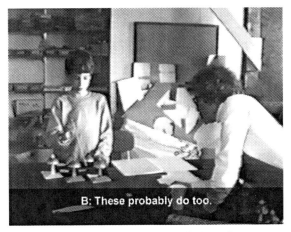

Figure 33. "And these probably do, too".

Testing the remaining bell with its hypothesized match, Brad positioned the new matches together to form pairs.

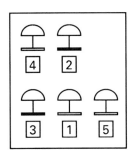

Figure 34. Bells that sound the same.

With the matches completed he had also completed a new kind of embodied notation: the bells no longer were (represented) objects that played tune-events but rather objects that "sound the same" as one another. The bells had once more changed who they are: once functionally equivalent, they were now simply pitch-matched pairs. And leaving no doubt as to his new understanding, Brad pushed the two extra bells away again, and said:

"So you really only need ... that's cool!"

Brad had made an important move from situation-dependent, functional meanings toward classification according to de-contextualized properties– a critical step (perhaps the critical step) in his evolving conceptual change from path-making toward map-making. And having plucked out from their functional context just those bell/pitches that share the same hidden pitch property, he had found reason to be convinced that his three-bell discovery was not so "weird", after all: you only do need three bells – "... that's cool!"

PART IV

CONCLUSIONS

Paths, Maps, and Educational Implications

I began the story of Brad with a proposal concerning learning: learning, I argued, is learning to selectively and purposefully *interrupt* the necessarily temporal passage of contiguous actions/events by focusing on some chosen aspect which then becomes the core of a new *succession* made up of just those objects/events that are *congruent with a current field of attention*. Looking back, what evidence do we find in Brad's work to instantiate this proposal? And what does Brad's work tell us more specifically about the process of transformation in moving between path-making and map-making? The initiating moment in Brad's evolution occurred when, mediated by Celia's alternative path, he was able to break up the chronological order of tune events and "rove more or less at will in any order over the events ...". Learning from this effect of this "break up" of his "felt path", Brad mentally coordinated in one representational space, objects/events that had belonged to separate spaces: bells could substitute for one another as "functionally equivalent". Constructing a class of functionally equivalent objects/events was a necessary intermediary step towards, recognizing matched, de-contextualized pitch properties. Through my intervention in the matching task, pitch property, as such, was seen as a differentiated "thing", an object of attention in itself.

Brad, with help, had made forays toward becoming a musical map-maker, but he was not yet there: He had yet to construct a whole new sequence based only on pitch properties – i.e. a functioning fixed reference grid in relation to which he could position any pitch, and measure its distance from others – an all-purpose instrument upon which he could play any tune, compare one with another, and unambiguously notate them.

Assuming as I have suggested, that Brad's work gives a glimpse into the conceptual change involved in moving from path-making toward map-making, we are left with a fundamental unanswered question: How can we help children acquire the security and the communicability of fixed reference, property invariance structures while continuing to develop the musically critical sense of figures and pitch functions in the unique context of an unfolding melody or even larger musical composition?

> Ideas of style, genre, and form; laws of harmony and counterpoint; analyses of the ideological determinations of music's production and reception – these and countless other imaginative constructions have enabled theorists to speculate on the determinacies of musical experience. But in our zeal to explain music, it has been tempting to forget the hypothetical and constructed nature of such categories and to imagine that it is these ideas themselves that have the power to produce our experience ... What can it mean in a truly temporal sense to say that the same is repeated? (Hasty, 1997, p. 8)

Finally, what are the more general educational implications of the distinctions between map-making and path-making? Consider that it is traditionally the case in schools, for instance, that *symbolic conventions* serve as the "spectacles" through which we see and judge a student's work. We look for either a match or a mismatch with convention and a match with conventional practice is judged correct.

But on this basis for evaluating student work, Brad's notational inventions would run a serious risk of being seen as simply wrong. Most important, such evaluation would miss seeing Brad's notations as a vehicle for revealing to himself and his teachers the cognitive work involved in his reasoning, his logical inferences, and the transformations they entail – in short, his learning.

What we are witnessing in Brad's multiple descriptions/notations is a stunning example of the multiplicity of criss-crossed intersections between notational conventions and inventions. Through these intersections and confrontations, we witness the possibility that *invention can illuminate convention*. However, questioning our notational conventions is a risky business because notational conventions shape our perceptions like eyeglasses that we look *through*. Reversing this habit, looking at our notational conventions through the glass of a child's inventions, we can begin to see aspects inherent in our conventional symbol systems that otherwise remain hidden from view. Perhaps this requires stepping off our well-trodden, well-learned symbolic paths to participate in and value the "felt paths" that we know best from moving about and being alive and well in the world of sensory experience. "Out of that tense multiplicity of vision {comes} the possibility of insight" (Bateson, 1994).

NOTES

[1] I have indicated the letter names of pitches in the mixed array of bells. However, this is obviously information that tunebuilders are not privy to and thus gives away information to the reader that is quite different in kind from that of the typical path-maker. As a result of becoming privy to such information, readers are also at risk of missing the cognitive work that is achieved and the transformations in understanding in the moves from path-maker to map-maker.

[2] See Tanay (Chapter 2, p. 45, this volume) for a comparison with early music notation: "In the old system the atomic unit of meaning is the whole rhythmic phrase. Only in the context of the phrase as a whole do the various signs, composing the phrase, acquire a definite rhythmic meaning."

[3] Since this collection of pitches includes only a subset of the possible (12) pitches used in Western music, and they are related by a non-constant interval, strictly speaking, this ordered collection does not provide an invariant unit with which to measure "pitch distance".

[4] This convention seems to imply some kind of quantitative meaning and with this meaning, the numbers would be considered cardinals instead of ordinals. That is, instead of next-next-next as with ordinal numbers, the expressions "going up" and "higher" could be understood as literally implying more-more-more. Wittgenstein describes a similar situation in the Brown Book in his discussion of "language games" (Wittgenstein, 1960. pp. 79–84). Indeed, we could see Brad as participating in language games of his own invention.

[5] K.S. Lashley in his classic paper of 1951, "The Problem of Serial Order in Behavior", speaks of the relation between syntax and action: "... the syntax of the act which can be described as the habitual order or mode of relating the expressive [symbolic] elements ... to the generalized schema of action, ... determine the sequence of specific acts, acts which in themselves or in their associations seem to have no temporal valence" (in Pribram, 1969, p. 525).

[6] Evidence that Brad was quite capable of distinguishing "up and down" in pitch was clear when, on hearing the beginning of the same tune played by the computer synthesizer, he said quite spontaneously, "Oh, it goes down".

[7] I use Brad's original labels for the bells, here, so as to make it easier to describe the inferences he now makes.

REFERENCES

Bamberger, J. (1991; 1995). *The mind behind the musical ear*. Cambridge, MA: Harvard University Press.

Bamberger, J. (1996). Turning music theory on its ear. *International Journal of Computers for Mathematical Learning*, *1*(1), 33–55.

Bamberger, J. (2000). *Developing musical intuitions; A project-based approach to music fundamentals*. New York: Oxford University Press.

Bamberger, J. & Schön, D. (1991). Learning as reflective conversation with materials. In F. Steier (Ed.), *Research and reflexivity*. London: Sage Publications.

Bartlett, F.C. (1932) *Remembering: A study in experimental and social psychology*. Cambridge: Cambridge University Press.

Bateson, M.K. (1994). *Peripheral visions: Learning along the way*. New York: Harper Collins.

Hasty, C. (1997). *Meter as rhythm*. New York: Oxford University Press.

Hasty, C. (2000). Music's evanescence and the question of time after structuralism. In M.P. Soulsby & J.T. Fraser (Eds.), *Time: Perspectives at the millennium*. Westport, CT: Bergin & Garvey.

Lynch, K. (1960). *The image of the city*. Cambridge, MA: MIT Press.

Morrison, P. (1991) Review of Mark Monmonier, How to lie with maps. *Scientific American*, July, 139–140.

Piaget, J. (1960). *The psychology of intelligence*. Patterson, NJ: Littlefield, Adams, & Co.

Piaget, J., Inhelder, B. & Szeminska, A. (1960). *The child's conception of geometry*. New York: Basic Books.

Wittgenstein, L. (1960). *The blue and brown books*. New York: Harper and Row.

Jeanne Bamberger
Professor of Music and Urban Education, emerita
Massachusetts Institute of Technology
Visiting Professor
Graduate School of Education
University of California, Berkeley, USA

JULIE E. DOCKRELL AND EVA TEUBAL

DISTINGUISHING NUMERACY FROM LITERACY: EVIDENCE FROM CHILDREN'S EARLY NOTATIONS[1]

INTRODUCTION

Children usually begin to put marks on paper at about the age of 18 months. In general these early marks are viewed as "presentations" rather than "representations" (Arnheim, 1956) and have typically been studied as precursors to drawings. Drawings are believed to be based on internal mental models, although the actual drawing may be constrained by other skills (Luquet, 1913; 1927). Investigations of children's developing skills to deal with iconic (drawing[2]) symbols have provided a rich data set for understanding the developing cognitive system. Until relatively recently, and in contrast to the wide ranging literature on children's drawings (Thomas & Silk, 1990), only intermittent attention has been paid to children's early inscriptions that were writing-like or number-like (non-iconic) (see Ferreiro & Teberosky, 1979, as an early example of such studies). By corollary early writing skills have often been conceived in narrow practical terms, with the focus being on the accurate production of letter and numerical shapes – handwriting. As a result of a series of insightful observations and a synthesis of a range of innovative studies, children's notations have proved to be a window into the development of representational capacities. Such studies have served to inform our debates about developmental processes more generally (Tolchinsky, 2003). This chapter, along with other chapters in this book, adds to this movement by examining the processes that underpin early notational productions.

Children realise that many different graphic marks convey some kind of meaning long before they are formally exposed to instruction in an educational context. However, while a child may know that a symbol conveys "meaning" they may not know the meaning at all or may have erroneous assumptions about the meaning. Studies of the development of children's notational abilities are currently viewed as both a way of examining the development of competence[3] with symbolic systems and as a means of identifying the mechanisms that influence developmental trajectories. It is argued that these young children understand symbolic notation as a formal problem space and can assign specific individual properties to the notation systems for writing letters and numerals (Tolchinsky Landsmann & Karmiloff-Smith, 1992). Yet mapping and understanding the semantics, that is the specific meaning, of particular forms is a more long-term affair.

Notational competence can be examined in two ways; we can consider what notations children typically produce and we can examine whether children differentiate between notations they are exposed to. The latter task might be seen as

E. Teubal et al. (eds.), Notational Knowledge, 113–134.

a comprehension or recognition task and the former task as a production task. The majority of studies have examined children's understanding of notations: only a few have focused on children's notational productions (see for example Hughes, 1986; Sinclair, Siegriest & Sinclair, 1983; Sinclair, Mello & Siegrist, 1988; Tolchinsky Landsmann, 1990). Comprehension tasks provide important data about the distinctions children use to discriminate between notational types but such results will be influenced by the contrasts provided by the experimenter. Such studies will not, on their own, provide information on whether children use these principles in creating their own notations.[4] Spontaneous productions allow us to examine notations that might not be encountered otherwise. In this chapter our research focuses on pre-schoolers' early production of notations for content that would typically be represented by numerals and writing. These early notations provide the basic infrastructure to support notations for the purpose of communication and notations for the organization of information while making notes (Mammana & Villani, 1998).

An understanding of the production of and the representational status of notational knowledge among 3, 4, and 5-year-olds becomes a crucial source of knowledge of the children's first ideas about the functions and rules of notational systems. In this chapter we describe two tasks which examine notational development. The first task – an identity card – examines the production of notations in the absence of any external notational stimuli to guide the children's responses. Thus, the task examines the children's production of notations to communicate information. The products derive from both the child's understanding of the task parameters and their experiences and interpretations of the notations they have encountered in particular socio-cultural contexts.

Our second task extends this line of investigation by considering children notations within a particular domain – numeracy. By designing a task that invites notations of numerals our second study – the dice game – provides the children with the opportunity to demonstrate their knowledge about numerical notations. Here we are primarily concerned with the ways in which tasks provide the children with opportunities to produce notations. By focusing on the domain of numerals we are able to consider task parameters specific to the domain (see chapter by Tolchinsky this volume) and how these parameters influence the child's subsequent notations. In both studies we consider development from the initial phases of the child's attempts to construct notations for numerals and writing to a point when they are entering a period dominated by the educational constraints imposed by the conventional primary school pedagogy.

BACKGROUND TO THE STUDIES

Notations systems can be conceived of as a subdomain of the more general domain of external representations (see Tolchinsky, 2003). The development of notational systems is considered to be one of the great advancements of human civilization. Their use extends memory and communication by leaving permanent traces that become independent of their creator, the place of creation and the time of creation (Lee & Karmiloff-Smith, 1996). The ability to select, organize and represent pertinent information as a notation and in note-taking is valued in our culture. Notations include written numerals, music, written language, maps and pictures. A unique set of constraints sets notations apart from other symbolic systems such as oral language (Goodman, 1976; Karmiloff-Smith, 1996). Drawing and modelling are symbolic since they are representational, written language and written numerals are considered as more arbitrary (less transparent) representational systems. These arbitrary representations can be considered as second order representations since writing does not represent meaning directly but through words and thus was, originally, conceived as inaccessible to the young child (Vygotsky, 1962; 1978).

Yet children's use of numeric and writing systems begins early. Enter virtually any pre-school provision and you will find young children using a range of different tools to make marks – marks on paper, marks in the sand, marks on the walls and in notebooks. "Children learn to follow text during story time, and recognize numbers in familiar places long before they are aware of these notations as symbols and long before any adult is explicitly attempting to teach the system to the child" (Bialystok, 1992a, p. 315). Thus the socio-cultural environment provides children with many opportunities to learn about notational functions and forms. Their use and interpretation are supported by interactions with parents, peers and siblings. Moreover unlike many of the other activities that children engage in, such as language and play, notations and constructions leave permanent traces. Children must learn about these different notational systems – what each system enables one to represent, what each system cannot represent and how each represents what it is supposed to represent (Ferreiro, 1986).

Children's production and use of notational systems have been regarded as an important aspect of cognitive development (e.g. Luria, 1928/1978; Vygotsky, 1962; 1978) but it was not until the 1980s that written language notations became a domain for psychological investigation in their own right. More recently explicit attempts have been made to investigate the nature and the role of these representations in cognitive development (see Lee & Karmiloff-Smith, 1996, for a review; Tolchinsky Landsmann & Karmiloff-Smith, 1992). The development of early notations is of importance in informing our understanding. There is accumulating evidence that young children understand written forms as entities but pass through a phase where they cannot yet assign them with symbolic value (Bialystok, 1992a).

In the first stage, children can recite the sequence with the correct name for each element in the sequence, that is the letters and numbers that make up the alphabet and counting sequence respectively. In the second stage they can recognize and produce the written form or notation that corresponds to each of those entities. They also know the names for those notations, such as "2" is "two" and "b' is "bee" and so on. It is not until the third stage, however, that they understand the meaning or significance of each of those written forms. (1992a, pp. 302–303).

Bialystok (1992b) defines these three phases[5] as the conceptual, the formal and the symbolic. The work reported here is designed to tap the link between the formal and symbolic.

In the formal phase the child is credited with understanding written forms as entities but cannot yet assign them with a symbolic value. What children seem to know is that something belongs to the domain of writing and something belongs to the domain of numbers. However while necessary this is not sufficient to induce or support a symbolic representation of the notations meaning. The link between oral and written representations for domains becomes important in the symbolic phase. Children can often solve problems in an oral domain before they can solve them in a notational domain (Lee, Karmiloff-Smith, Cameron & Dodsworth, 1998) but the symbolic representation of the notation presupposes knowledge of both the oral and the written systems and builds on that knowledge by linking the two (Bialystok, 1992a, p. 304).

Children know about some of the differences between iconic (drawings) and non-iconic (writing and numerals) symbolic systems without needing to be explicitly taught that they code meaningful differences. Children as young as three will differentiate conventional writing from drawing (Lavine, 1977). Further evidence from Tolchinsky Landsmann and Karmiloff-Smith, (1992) demonstrates that children understand symbolic notation as a formal problem space by 4 years of age and can assign specific individual properties to the notation systems for writing letters and numerals. Once this initial distinction is drawn children impose a number of formal constraints on what qualifies as writing. The subsequent differentiation of the non-iconic system is prolonged and the ages at which particular constraints are imposed on the system and the various categorisation systems used are less clear. For example, children's decisions about what qualifies as writing develops in phases (Teberosky, Marti & Garcia-Mila, 1998); both linearity and consistent direction are treated as important features of writing. However, it is not until children are five that children respect all the constraints in their recognition of notations, a finding that is consistent across different orthographic systems (Tolchinsky Landsmann, 1990).

Children's early knowledge of notations is also evident from their productions. Luria (1928/1978) is credited with carrying out the first systematic investigation of the emergence of writing by asking 6-year-old preliterate children to put something on paper that would help them remember dictated sentences. These skills

> ... can be studied in the child only experimentally and to do this the skill must be brought into being. The subject must be a child who has not yet learned to write; he must be put into a situation that will require him to use certain external manual operations similar to writing to depict or remember an object ... in the ideal case the psychologist might hope to force a child to 'invent' signs by placing him in some difficult situation. (in Martlew, 1983, p. 240)

This approach has been developed by a number of different researchers where children have been asked to "write", "put on paper" or note various elements of different tasks (De Goes & Martlew, 1983; Gombert & Fayol, 1992; Tolchinsky Landsmann & Levin, 1985; Sulzby & Teale, 1985). The results from production tasks do not always support a clear divide between iconic and non-iconic systems that is alluded to in the results of tasks that are based on recognition. There are a number of reports of young children producing mixtures of writing and drawings or drawings alone when asked to "write a letter to a friend" (McLane & McNamee, 1990) or to "write down information to help you remember it later" (Luria, 1928/1978). The nature of the instructions provided is clearly important. Asking children to "draw the object" or to "write the name of the object" resulted in marked differences in the proportion of drawing and writing behaviour (Brenneman, Massey, Machado & Gelman, 1996). The fact that such differences exist is indisputable; their interpretation is, however, a subject of some debate. Three possible explanations have been suggested. The most basic explanation is that such differences are simply a methodological artefact of the tasks used and tell us little about the children's notational competence. An alternative view is that those tasks that lead to the apparent confounding of notational systems, place demands on the children's referential-communicative use of notations. At this point in development, it is argued, notations can be considered either as a domain of knowledge or as referential-communicative tool but not both (Tolchinsky Landsmann & Karmiloff-Smith, 1992). Until children can use notations to signify specific meanings symbolically, performance will be particularly susceptible to the task demands. There is also the possibility that younger children use different notational forms to communicate different kinds of meaning perhaps size, for example, is more efficiently transmitted analogically.

An important fist step in disentangling these alternative explanations is to provide children with a set of instructions which do not afford particular notational forms. Thus, the children's productions will not be constrained by the instructions provided and they are free to produce a notation that they feel communicates the information required. Secondly if children are provided with tasks that elicit different notational forms in older children and adults, developmental differences can be evaluated. Finally if tasks are embedded in contexts where there is a purpose for the child in communicating information, that is the notation has communicative value, this will enhance the authenticity of the tasks and permit an examination of the link between the symbolic and the referential-communicative tool.

This analysis highlights the key methodological issues to be considered when designing notational tasks. Vygotsky was surely correct in highlighting the difficulties that exist in studying the developmental history of written language. Methodology has always been considered a critical factor in investigations of children's cognitive skills. Many theoretical explanations have been challenged because of failures to address the specific methodological consideration which impact on children's performance (see Donaldson, 1978, for a particular example of the importance of the "sense of the task"). Karmiloff-Smith has argued in a similar vein that

> depending on whether knowledge is required directly as a goal, or as the means to a goal also effects the level of explicitness at which knowledge needs to be defined ... in a block building task, children unable to balance blocks when this was the goal were able to balance the very same blocks where this was the means to a goal. (1996, p. 145)

It is surprising that so little has been written about the possible methodological confounds of studying children's non-iconic notations. There are two major concerns. From the child's point of view certain notational tasks and their inherent constraints may be ambiguous. Indeed tasks that provide little ambiguity (e.g. Brenneman et al., 1996), provide more transparent developmental performance. By corollary given that the referents of the notations produced by children can be ambiguous to the reader, experimenters' interpretations require corroboration and ideally reliability checks. In contrast to this relative lack of concern about methodology around children's notations, children's drawings have been considered from a number of critical methodological perspectives (see Thomas & Silk, 1990, for a general review, and Thomas & Jolley, 1998, for more detailed commentary). For example, both context and communicative purpose influence the types of drawings children produce (Davis, 1983). Moreover, as in other tasks investigating cognitive development the instructions the child receives are important (Neilson & Dockrell, 1981). Providing a goal is made explicit in the instructions, young children can represent in their drawings specific information about a particular object (Davis, 1983). Clarifying the impact of materials and instructions on children's notational performance is central to a valid understanding of the "problem space".

There are thus three specific parameters that need to be considered when we investigate children's notations: the nature of the task demands; the linguistic labels used to guide the children's notations; and the purpose of the task from the child's perspective. Linguistic labels guide and facilitate children's knowledge construction about notations (see also Teberosky, Marti & Garcia-Mila, 1998). Of particular importance is the lack of systematic attempt to characterize the nature of the task from the child's perspective. There is an extensive literature that emphasizes the importance of the pragmatic demands of the task in influencing children's performance (Donaldson, 1978; Clark, 1997). Given the role of notations as representational systems it follows that the purpose of the task may be crucial to the child's performance – "writing should be meaningful for children so that an intrinsic need should be aroused in them, and writing should be incorporated in to the task that is necessary and relevant" (Luria, 1978, p. 291).

From the child's point of view sorting writing-like and numeric notations may be fundamentally different to creating a notation for communicative purposes. If we are to understand the child's unfolding notational competence both the theoretical and methodological considerations point to the need to develop tasks that require the child to produce notations within an experimental format that are pragmatically appropriate and which legitimately demand the production of notations.

There is, therefore, a general consensus that children's early notations are an important area for developmental investigation. Results of such studies should specify the conceptual and contextual factors that underpin the development of symbolic functioning and the parameters that are barriers to the production of effective notations. Discovering when and how children make distinctions between symbolic domains is of considerable theoretical importance. But these discoveries need to occur within a broader framework of children's participating in contexts in which the notations involved are relevant to the interaction taking place in that context. Thus an important additional consideration to the current studies is the ways in which children produce notations in pragmatically transparent contexts where there are no additional cognitive demands. Our first study addresses some of these issues; we ask children to complete an identity card. The task stretches their notational competence but, we would argue, is meaningful for the child. In Donaldson's (1978) term the task makes "human sense". In the studies described the children's notations are subject to a rigorous coding that is checked for reliability. If the criticisms raised above are valid a task that possesses a referential communicative function and neutral instructions should *not* produce the confusions between iconic and non iconic notations that have previously been reported in the literature.

STUDY 1: CHILDREN'S NOTATIONS FOR THEIR PERSONAL CHARACTERISTICS

Numerals and letters are different in the type of meaning they represent and in the syntactic rules that establish how they must be read and written. However, there is an intricate relationship between them "two different but also related systems" (Ferreiro, 2000, p. 17). To what extent are children aware of the different types of meanings that can be represented? Central to our concern is the possibility that certain kinds of stimuli and tasks may support the production of different notational forms. Thus, even though the notation produced by the child may be "inaccurate" with respect to the adult form, children may provide evidence of intending to communicate and this intention can inform us about their understandings and representations of notations. Thus, the problem of mapping between notation and representation becomes one of both (a) identifying referential communicative function, and (b) learning to use the consensually agreed forms. Our identity card task aimed to allow for the production of different types of notations, writing, numerals and iconic. The children were asked to enter their personal information into an "identity card". The identity card required the child to produce information that is either conventionally presented in writing or in numerals. This task allowed us to evaluate whether children used notations in a referential communicative fashion while respecting domain constraints.

The identity card task provided an opportunity for a group of pre-school children to communicate relevant and meaningful information by creating a mapping between a referent and a form. Each child came to play a game with a puppet. Prior to commencing the game the child was asked to help the experimenter by completing an identity card. To emphasize the communicative value of the identity card children where told that the card would allow people who didn't know the child "*to learn a lot about them even when they were not there*". To allow for the production of different types of notations, the task was designed to contain some items implicating numeric notations and other implicating verbal/written notations. To allow the child to generate their own representations the instructions were open ended and no images or examples were provided (Teubal & Dockrell, 1998). For analysis purposes we divided the items into two equal sets: set A were deemed to require writing responses (henceforth called verbal) and set B were deemed to require responses involving numerals (henceforth called numerical). Set A included the child's name, street on which the child lived, the city in which they lived, the colour of their eyes, the colour of their hair, the name of their brother/s (if applicable) and the name of their sister/s (if applicable). Set B included the child's age, the age of their brother/s if applicable, the age of their sister/s if applicable, their telephone number, the year in which they were born, their weight, their height and the number of brothers they had and the number of sisters they had. Children were presented with a sheet of paper that had space at the top to draw a picture of themselves and beneath a series of boxes (as one finds in an application form) to complete their answers. The children were read the questions and asked to "put down on paper" the response. The appropriate space was indicated with a gesture.

We tested 80 English[6] children ranging in age from 3;0 to 5;5. To tap the development of their notations the children were banded in four groups: group 1, $N = 19$, $M = 44$ months; Group 2, $N = 21$, $M = 51$ months; Group 3, $N = 22$, $M = 56$ months; Group 4, $N = 18$, $M = 62$ months. We expected older children to perform in a similar fashion to adults – providing a "conventional" notation for items that afford the use of writing and items that afford the use of numerals. In contrast we predicted that the youngest children would maintain this distinction only for items which they encountered regularly in the environment that is where there was a significant socio-cultural support. For items where children were less familiar with numeral or written representations we predicted that iconic representations would be used to convey elements. Thus we expected differential responding across types of items and individual items.

There were statistically significant differences between the children's responses to the verbal and numeric tasks ($p = 0.001$). Children provided more writing-like notations for the verbal tasks and numeral-like notations for the numeric tasks. Figure 1 illustrates the percentage of canonical responses for the two stimuli sets for the four age groups. For both writing and numerals there was a significant developmental trend with the older children providing a greater proportion of "*conventional notations*" where numeric responses were provided for items implying numeric responses and writing-like responses for items implying writing-like responses ($F_{3,79} = 4.0$, $p < 0.01$, partial Eta squared $= 0.14$) and numeric tasks ($F_{3,79} = 4.85$, $p < 0.01$, partial Eta squared $= 0.30$). Nonetheless,

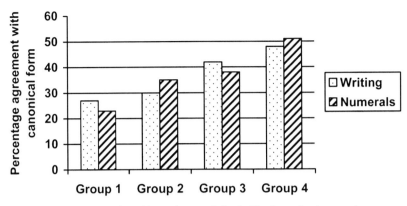

Figure 1. Percentage match for writing and numerals for the identity card task across the age groups.

over 20% of the two youngest age groups were providing appropriate notations for the numeric and verbal tasks while over 45% of the oldest children were providing appropriate notations for the two types of stimuli. There is thus preliminary evidence that even in the youngest children there are the initial signs of differentiating the functions of the two systems.

The 16 items covered a wide range of different data sources. It was clear from a visual analysis of the data that the numbers of appropriate responses varied across items. For example "the year in which they were born" resulted in a significant number of omissions or ambiguous responses. Therefore, a more detailed analysis of the children's notations of 10 items where sufficient responses occurred was carried out to provide further evidence of the ways in which the children's conceptualizations and understandings impacted on the notations they provided. The final coding frame consisted of the following four categories:

1. AMBIGUOUS – Marks on paper that did not resemble any known sign or marks that combined writing-like and number-like elements or iconic elements.

2. WRITING LIKE REPRESENTATION – Letters or letter-like forms isolated or linked or writing like notations, termed Verbal.

3. NUMBER-LIKE REPRESENTATIONS – A single mark which resembled conventional digits termed Numerical.

4. ICONIC – A drawing to represent the required element in the identity card-pictorial Response for names and ages of brothers and sisters were excluded from the analysis because of significant numbers of missing data for these categories. Tables 1 and 2 present the percentage distribution of the children's responses for these verbal and numeric tasks.

As Tables 1 and 2 illustrate the total number of iconic (drawing) responses for both questions requiring writing notations and those requiring numerals was low. As a whole these results indicated that children do not rely on iconic responses in this task but the distinction between writing and numbers is less clear. However, a closer examination of the items illustrated that there were specific items where

Table 1.

Percentage of children's notation types for the tasks implying writing responses.

	Writing-like	Numeric	Iconic	Ambiguous	Missing
Own name	90	1.3	0	7.5	1.3
Colour of eyes	43.8	3.8	20	26.3	6.3
Colour of hair	45	3.8	23.8	20	7.5
City name	50	6.3	1.3	20	22.5
Street name	57.5	2.5	5	10	25
% response	47.7	3	8.4	14	10.4

Table 2.

Percentage of children's notation types for the tasks implying numeral responses.

	Writing-like	Numeric	Iconic	Ambiguous	Missing
Own age	11.3	73.8	0	12.5	2.5
Phone number	15	60	0	10	15
How tall?	17.5	25	12.5	27.5	17.5
How heavy?	18.8	22.5	6.3	22.5	30
Year of birth	31.3	17.5	0	16.3	35
% response	15.7	33.1	3.1	14.8	16.7

iconic responses occur – "colour of eyes and hair" and "height" and to a lesser extent "weight". When the children's responses for hair were considered 15% of the oldest children produced iconic responses. For these young children certain characteristics "invite" an iconic notation which provides information to the reader. Note that as we have seen this does not mean children cannot produce verbal and numeric notations appropriately in other contexts. As the tables illustrate, only 3% of the children produced numeric responses for the items that we deemed to require writing-like responses. A greater number produced writing-like responses for the tasks requiring numeric responses (15.7%). However, a large proportion of these were accounted for by the responses to the child's year of birth and also the height and weight items where children produced utterances like "I am too heavy for mummy to carry me now". These results highlight that some uses of text involving numerical information can be inherently fuzzy. In these cases written words could be used appropriately to provide quantitative information. The reverse rarely occurs; incidences of numerals occurring for writing stimuli were virtually non existent. Children's responses reflect the variability in both the ways in which numbers can be represented and the types of quantities that numbers denote. This ambiguity was evident through their increased use of iconic representations and the high proportion of ambiguous and writing-like responses.

Importantly, the children's notations matched their verbal responses with numeric tasks on the whole generating responses that were numerals and writing tasks generating words. The significant exceptions to this pattern were the children's responses in the "height" and "weight" questions where gestures were sometimes provided. These gestures further suggested that for young children referring to height and weight was strongly governed by the appropriateness and acceptability of the iconic mode of representation. When people talk they gesture and those gestures often reflect thoughts not expressed in their words (Goldin-Meadow & Wagner, 2005). Initially the high rate of iconic responses to colour of hair and eyes (over 80% in both cases) might seem to contradict this analysis yet drawings are useful for representing colour as well as the size, and shape of objects. Children's responses to the items dealing with weight and height elicited a small proportion of verbal responses *both* in an oral form and a notation. It is, therefore, possible that the children were marking these as qualities and not quantities. Only over time does the child perceive these as quantities and at a later stage they become quantities to be dealt with numerically. In addition both height and weight are frequently described in the children's environment with relative terms such as heavier or lighter and taller or shorter rather than absolutes such as 100 grams or 10 metres. The literature on the development of number concepts identifies a similar distinction where children's grasp of discrete quantities is earlier than the grasp of continuous quantities (see Piaget, 1952).

The results of the identity card task demonstrated that children as young as three differentially use notations to symbolise different domains when the task makes sense to them. The children provided evidence, not only of the ability to discriminate between notational domains, but also of an intention to use the notation in a communicatively effective fashion. Perhaps most importantly, these results suggest that where confounding appears to occur across domains it can reflect the sensitivity of the child to represent the referent in different ways. Thus it appears that young children's notations reflect their representations of different referents as well as formal notational knowledge about the domain. It is also important to consider the developmental trends in the children's responses. The data demonstrate that the domain of notations is an unfolding area for these children; performance differed between children and across items.

Our data suggest that children do not move simply from drawing to other notational forms. In contrast these notational forms existed in parallel. They were used to differentially represent items. What bearing do our data have on current understandings of children's notational development? In the first instance they challenge the view that there is a general notational domain, fostered initially by drawing as a first order representation (Martlew & Sorsby, 1995). From this perspective children's early writing is conceived of as "drawings of writing". Vygotsky explicitly talks about the move from the drawing of things to the drawing of words. There was little evidence from our analysis to support the view that these pre-school children were "drawing writing" or "drawing numbers". Even our youngest children differed in the representations of themselves and in their attempts to fill in the boxes to provide descriptive information about themselves.

However, a significant proportion of the older children used iconic forms to represent particular kinds of information. The data were consistent with the conclusions of Brenneman et al. (1996), who identified reliable and systematic differences between drawing and writing through an analysis of videotaped action sequences.

Is it the case then that drawings and writing reflect domain specific knowledge from the outset (Gombert & Fayol, 1992; Karmiloff-Smith, 1992)? Our data suggest not; notational forms reflect both knowledge and pragmatic expediency that is influenced by the nature of the task and the context it which it occurs. On the whole, the children understood the communicative value of particular kinds of symbols but many had not mastered the specific mapping between the notation and the specific symbolic value of that symbol. In effect it should come as no great surprise that mapping the relationships between symbols and values and being able to put them consistently into use may be an extended process. Children know from an early age the referential powers of words yet they spend many years mapping out the denotations of lexical items (Dockrell & Campbell, 1986; Dockrell & Messer, 2004). This mapping process is influenced both by the domain to which the lexical item refers (Braisby & Dockrell, 1999) and the contexts in which the term is initially encountered (Clark, 1997). One might wish to argue from our data that the children's notational responses indicated that they had learnt from experience to pair particular notation forms with particular familiar information (age, name) but as yet they had not developed a representational status that stood for specific meanings. Such an interpretation would suggest that the process was child governed. However the children's productions for other items indicated that there is a case to argue that both environmental support and the cognitive complexity of the "to be represented item" are influencing the children's productions.

STUDY 2: CHILDREN'S NUMERAL NOTATIONS – THE IMPACT OF CONTEXT AND STIMULI

The data from the identity card study extend the claims that pre-school children distinguish between different notational domains. Moreover the children's inscriptions indicated that certain notations were preferentially used to represent particular kinds of information. While our knowledge of children's use and structure of the written language system is increasing significantly (Tolchinsky Landsmann & Levin, 1987) we know very little about how children begin to grasp the function and structure of the numeral system. The data from the identity card task supported the view that the development of numerical notations may provide different challenges to that of notations for writing. In the identity card task there were nearly twice as many ambiguous and missing data points than there were for the writing items suggesting that numerals are more complex for the children. Secondly in the identity card task only 3% of the responses to the writing elements were numeric while 22% of the responses to the numeric items were writing-like suggesting that the children were uncertain about the conventional use of numerals in these situations. Both results suggest that children have not mapped out the extended uses and meanings for numerals. Such results might be seen as giving further credence to the claims that children can recognise and write numerals without understanding that those notations also serve a referential function (Hughes, 1986; Sinclair, Mello & Siegrist, 1988). This hypothesed developmental trajectory for numerical notations would parallel trends in oral number use where children can count without understanding the cardinal number of the last number word uttered (Fuson, 1988; Sophian, Wood & Vong, 1995; Sophian, 1997). To what extent are the children's numeric responses a function of the complexity of the numerical domain or the demands of the task?

Study 1 does not allow us to differentiate between these two alternatives. Firstly, unlike other kinds of words, number words can be represented correctly by both numeric and verbal notations: the response "3" or "three" would be equally correct for the age question of a 3-year-old. So it may be that the nature of the task leaves open alternative appropriate modes of responding. If this were the case then a task that only invited the use of numerical notations would be less likely to generate writing-like responses.

Children in literate cultures are exposed to numerals in many different contexts which confer upon them different functions, such as labelling (Aubrey, 1994). Ewers-Rogers and Cowan (1996) have shown that children were more familiar with some purposes of numeral-use than with others. Knowing what the numerals were used for typically preceded spotting that they were missing in a representation or including them in a task that required completion. Thus, numerals are present in the environment, children are differentially familiar with their purpose and by corollary they constitute a domain of potential knowledge for the developing child. Our next task assessed the performance of the same children studied in the identity card task to explore the ways in which different input stimuli affect children's numeric notations. This was done as a game that required the children to produce notations to denote number (Teubal & Dockrell, 1997; Teubal & Dockrell, 2005). We asked all of the 80 children who had completed the identity card to play a dice game with a puppet. The child's task was to record the results of the dice throw on a record sheet. The children were told that the participant with the largest number was the winner so it was important to mark down the scores to decide the winner. The data for the recording of six different throws were analysed: two throws were with a die that had a numeric representation (either a low number < 5 or a high number 5 or 6); two throws were with a die that had dots representing the number (either a low number < 5 or a high number 5 or 6); and two throws represented a null quantity (either a 0 or the blank face of the die). The children were also required to sum the total of two throws – their throw and that of the puppet. Thus, a task was designed in which numerical notations were required and tapped at different levels of complexity (recording single quantities, the null quantity and addition).

What kinds of notations did the children produce? A researcher, who was blind to the particular exposures the child had received, coded all the children's notational productions. From the researcher's codings it was possible to ascertain whether the coded response produced matched the die. The same coding frame that was used in the identity task was used for this task. Codes were combined for consistency with the present task and the final coding frame consisted of the following six categories:

1. AMBIGUOUS – Marks on paper that did not resemble any known sign or marks that combined writing like and number-like elements.
2. WRITING-LIKE REPRESENTATION – Letters or letter-like forms isolated or linked or writing like notations.
3. NUMBER-LIKE REPRESENTATIONS – A single mark which resembled conventional digits but was not an accurate reflection of the stimuli (or sum) presented.
4. CORRECT DIGIT – Digit notation corresponding to the quantity or digit displayed in the die or the sum of the die in the sum tasks.
5. INCORRECT ITERATIVE – Iterative representation in which the number of marks did not correspond with the quantity displayed.
6. CORRECT ITERATIVE – Iterative representation in which the number of marks did correspond with the quantity displayed.

The distributions of the notations produced by the children are presented in Table 3. The first point to note about the results is that the majority of children completed the task and they did so by producing a notation that was appropriate to the domain of number. A total of 4% of the children's responses were writing-like. This is strong evidence that children have marked the task as one where representations of numerosity are required and this governs the types of notations they produce. There was also strong support for developmental trends in children's notation types for the small numbers of dots and the small numbers in digits. As might be expected, overall children's iterative responses declined with age with a parallel increase in digit notations (see Figure 2, and Bialystok & Codd, 1996). The digit zero and the blank face of the die did not produce similar developmental trends. The blank face of the die produced the highest number of writing-like responses 11% overall and 23% of the oldest group's responses. Given the difficulty that children purportedly experience with the concept "zero" this is perhaps not surprising. There were two cases where the children described their responses in ways that would support this interpretation – "a circle", "a round". Yet for the majority of children their spoken responses demonstrate that they are well aware of what the display represents. The performance of Maddy (3;0) is a case in point. When presented with the 0 she produces 0 and says "*naught*"; presented with the blank face of the die she produces 0 and says "*nothing*". In fact the majority of children in the youngest group (68%) referred to the blank face of the die with the words "none" or "nothing", not a single child called it zero. In contrast 22% of the children in the oldest group used the term "zero" to refer to the blank face of the die. The blank face of the die caused specific notational problems (see Table 3) and it may be that it is extremely difficult for the child to produce "something" to stand for "nothing". Ferreiro (1986) has described similar difficulties in emergent verbal writing when the child has to represent "in writing" verbally formulated negatives. In contrast the digit zero appeared to encourage

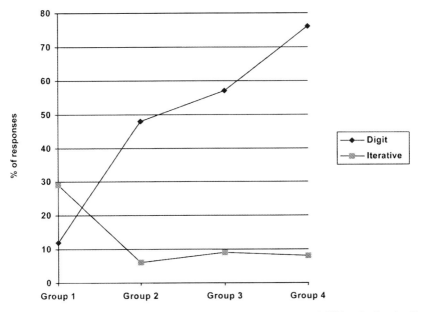

Figure 2. Provision of iterative and digit notations by the four age groups of children for the stimuli.

copying. The primary nature of the circular shape and the occurrence of this in the children's environment may have increased the copying response.

Overall, there was a highly significant positive correlation between response forms produced for small dots and digits and those produced for large dots and digits. Thus, irrespective of their accuracy, when children produce number-like representations for dots they tend to do so for digits as well; equally, if children produce iterative forms for digits they tend to do so for dots as well. These results further indicate that children are working within a single notational mode for numerosity, irrespective of the nature of the display. However, although the display does not determine the type of notational output, it contributes to it. The significant association between notation and display type for the small numerosities supported this. Similar trends were found for large numerosities but they were not significant (see Teubal & Dockrell, 2005).

By considering the children's notations in general, we have provided further evidence that children are sensitive to the specific notational constraints for numerals and have provided evidence that these notations are reflecting the children's knowledge of what the symbol stands for. Results from the identity card were indicative of a gross link between domain and notation but the accuracy of their symbol use was not established. In contrast the dice tasks allowed the assessment of the extent to which children's notations accurately reflected the display. Data from the dice task indicated that even some of the youngest children were aware of the value for which the symbol stands. The results support a developmental progression in notations, with children producing a greater number of accurate notations as they get older. Children were significantly less accurate at

127

Table 3.

Distribution of notational responses across the different displays.[7]

Notations	Digits Small	Dots Small	Digits Large	Dots Large	Digit Zero	Blank Face of the Die	Total
Ambiguous	4%	5%	8%	5%	6%	5%	5%
	(3)	(4)	(6)	(4)	(5)	(4)	(26)
Writing-like	1%	3%	1%	5%	0	11%	4%
	(1)	(2)	(1)	(4)		(9)	(17)
Number-like	21%	24%	20%	15%	15%	13%	18%
	(17)	(19)	(16)	(12)	(12)	(10)	(86)
Correct digit	56%	44%	50%	43%	69%	26%	48%
	(45)	(35)	(40)	(34)	(55)	(21)	(230)
Incorrect iterative	8%	0	1%	9%	5%	10%	5%
	(6)		(1)	(7)	(4)	(8)	(26)
Correct iterative	4%	17%	3%	11%	0	26%	10%
	(3)	(13)	(2)	(9)		(21)	(48)
No response	6%	8%	18%	13%	5%	9%	10%
	(5)	(6)	(14)	(10)	(4)	(7)	(46)
Total	80	79	80	80	80	80	479

producing correct notations for the sum task than producing correct notations for the single quantities. As was the case with single numerals there were no significant differences in performance across the two displays. There was, however, a statistically significant age group effect with only the oldest children performing significantly better (see Teubal & Dockrell, 2005). So while children in both the older groups performed more accurately in the single numeral condition, it was only the oldest children who were more accurate in the sum condition. As with the null quantity display these data support the view that it is important to draw a distinction between the difficulty of a task at the notational level and the difficulty of a task at the problem solving level (see also Lee & Karmiloff-Smith, 1996; Lee et al., 1998). Task difficulty at the problem solving level appears to be a key factor that impedes children's notational adaptations (see also Deloache, Uttal & Pierroutsakos, 1998).

The children's spoken responses confirmed the results of a number of previous studies that support the view that oral responses occur before notational forms (Bialystok & Codd, 1996; Lee et al., 1998). In every age group and in all but one experimental condition the percentage of correct spoken numerals was higher than the percentage of correct notations. In addition there were only a few cases in which the child's notation was correct and their spoken response was wrong. In contrast the data from our zero stimuli did not conform to this pattern.

Data were also collected about the children's oral responses in solving the sum task. For all ages the use of counting as a strategy varied with type of stimulus presentation: significantly more counting was associated with the dots than with the digits presentation. For the digits 10 overt counts (14%) were recorded for the small numerals and 12 overt counts (15%) for the larger numerals. In contrast, for the dots 46 overt counts (58%) were recorded for the small numerosities and 38 overt counts (49%) were recorded for the larger numerosities. But the older children when dealing with large quantities use the counting strategy more than the younger children regardless of kind of stimulus presentation. When one of the addends is zero there was no difference in the strategy used between age group, rather the difference appeared with the kind of input. There was more counting when the blank face of the die depicted the null quantity and was added to a die with dots.

The ways in which children create notations for numerosities is of importance both theoretically and practically. From a theoretical position, data about developing notation systems provides information about the ways in which cognition is influenced by internal and external representations. From a pedagogical position notations might provide a complementary path for developing children's numerical competence. The present results provide confirmatory evidence about the role of notations as representations in the domain of numerosity. The data demonstrate a clear developmental pattern in children's accuracy of notation performance and in the types of notations produced. Children become both more accurate with age and produce more digit-like notations. Analysis of the percentage of correct responses indicated that there was a discrete jump for accuracy of single notations from the age of 4;6 and for accuracy of sums from the age of 5;0. Yet in all cases some children of younger ages were providing accurate notations.

Developmental trends in children's notations are to be expected. A range of factors could explain such developments. If these were solely explained by increasing motor competence accuracy should be positively associated with our measure of motor skill. This was not the case in our study since the children's responses were unrelated to a standardised measure of motor skill. In addition the finding that there were no significant differences between correct responses for dots and digits provides indicative evidence that children's notational performance originates in their internal (intervening representations), although subtle influences of input stimulus were evident. The increased difficulty with the larger numeral and dots displays reflect the trends evident in the oral data (that is children found these harder to identify correctly) and other studies on children's counting skills confirm this (Fuson, 1998). The differential impact of the stimulus type supports the view that the two stimuli for numerical operations afford the children different notational opportunities within the domain. In contrast when children were presented with a notation for zero copying did appear to occur possibly indicating that some children took the sign to stand for a shape and not a numeral. The present results thus suggest that a combination of internally-generated representations and the nature of the stimulus to be represented influence children's developing notations.

The zero task and the transformation task further explore the relationship between children's developing notations and task complexity. The notational requirement in the transformation task, that is the adding of two numerals and recording the result, involved the recording of the result of a transformation, not the recording of the transformation itself. Solving the problem required that children to perform a transformation that involved a computation from the original displays, presented either iconically or non-iconically and re-presented by means of the children's own notations.

CONCLUDING REMARKS

The children in these studies are using notations as representations and as representations that have communicative value. Moreover, the differentiation across tasks and task elements implies that the notations carry symbolic value for the children. If children can use different notational systems to communicate different kinds of information then the child's performance with the notations themselves can serve as a further support to cognitive changes. The children's implicit knowledge of notations is evident from the ways in which they respond to the different types of information they are required to produce. The children are using the system in a meaningful way although they are not necessarily accurate in their use of the system as a referential-communicative tool. Their failure in the referential mapping component occurs because they do not know what the exact meaning of each one of the notations is. On the whole their productions are different for representations of numerals and representations of written language. There is, therefore, clear evidence that, at least at the level of notational domains, children respect constraints in their productions. These productions are influenced both by the cognitive demands of the tasks and the meaning of the activity for the child.

We can see in both the identity card and the dice task that the difficulty of the task (sum and null quantity) and the referent to be represented (e.g. weight/height/year of birth) has a significant impact on the child's notations. Unlike the data presented by Bolger and Karmiloff-Smith (1990), where well-formedness constraints were respected, our data indicate that task difficulty alters both the "correctness" and the types of notations the children create. The data support the distinction drawn by Lee and Karmiloff-Smith (1996) between the difficulty of the task at the notational level and the difficulty at the problem solving level. We propose that the sum task and the null quantity task cause the children's difficulties at the problem solving level whereas some of the elements in the identity task raise problems at the notational level. Such an analysis supports our caution of the stage interpretation of development mentioned in the earlier sections. While there are general *phases* in our data there are differences in performance that depend on the task, the notational domain and the communicative demands placed on the child.

Learning is an individual process that is socially guided. A critical factor in this development is what the task affords. Children are sensitive to the domain-specific constraints operating on each notational domain but they use the pragmatic demands of the task to guide their efforts. In many ways the tasks seem to provide a scaffold on which the children hang their early notations. The contexts in which these notations are produced and interpreted support particular kinds of inferences and notational representations. Children learn to use and adapt notations to serve many different functions. Our data suggest that even at the early stages a degree of flexibility exists in the system.

Impressive as these accomplishments are, the pre-school child has much to learn about notation in terms of both structure and function (Nelson, 1996). At a basic level children need to learn about the unique referential function of particular symbols. Further there is little evidence in these tasks that the children can manipulate the symbols or use them in problem solving. For example, very few of the children used their iterative notations to perform a "count on" solution in the sum task. Children experience problems both with the notational representations generally (Lee et al., 1998) and with encoding specific elements within a notation e.g. the notion of sequence (Lee & Karmiloff-Smith, 1993). Children's construction of notational systems needs to be considered as a continuous process that begins with initial discriminations between domains and develops to more complex analyses of the cognitive demands of tasks (Lee & Karmiloff-Smith, 1993). In parallel, the children are able to utilize their notations as communicative tools (Dockrell, Teubal & Ralli, 2000; Klein, Teubal & Ninio, 2005). This knowledge is also developing. There are developmental challenges related to both communicative efficacy and choice of appropriate notation for the referent within a particular task context. This is knowledge that will be firmly based in the communicative contexts in which the children find themselves and by the extent to which they are culturally valued.[8] This supports an approach which sees the children's notational development as partly consisting of the process of appropriation of the notational systems offered by the culture. Thus a theoretical account of children's early notations must address the representational demands of the tasks, the context in which these notations are produced and the factors that assist children in their efforts to construct more powerful, more specialized mental representations for notations around them.

NOTES

[1] We are grateful to The Academic Study Group – Israel and the Middle East who funded exchange visits between England and Israel and all the children who willingly participated in the studies. Both Richard Cowan and Mina Ralli have been stimulating colleagues discussing issues relevant to this chapter. Jane Correa provided considered advice on the final draft of this chapter.

[2] Iconic representations hint to or point towards the symbolised item however, they do not need to be pictorial. A series of scratches representing a particular numerosity is iconic. Drawings can be described as either iconic or pictorial representations. In Luria's terms first order representations are iconic and therefore encompass both pictures and other forms of iconic representations. In contrast non-iconic representations do not possess this link or hint of a link with the "to be" represented element.

[3] We take the position that our ultimate concern is elucidating competence. Competence is inferred through the child's performance on particular tasks. Tasks, may of course, provide inaccurate information and result in faulty inferences about competence.

[4] There is considerable debate about the status of comprehension tasks. By their very nature the child is guided by the experimenter's range of options and constructs. Forced choice tasks are particularly likely to lead to spurious results where children may be credited with levels of cognitive competence that they do not actually possess (Dockrell & Messer, 2004).

[5] We choose to use the term "phase" rather than "stage". The term stage suggests a clear cut differentiation form when a child passes from one stage of representation to the next. Our reading of the literature and the data we present here suggests a gradual shift of representational capacity. Moreover, it is a shift that is influenced by the nature of the task.

[6] In England at the time of the study there were no identity cards thus the children's experiences did not lead them to expect particular formats or forms.

[7] Data from one child for the dots small was missing.

[8] Note that Hatano and Inagaki draw a similar conclusion about conceptual change. "We agree that the increased amount of knowledge is the necessary condition ... we would also emphasize the role of other people and tools as socio-cultural or external constraints in conceptual change" (1997, p. 125).

REFERENCES

Arnheim, R. (1956). *Art and visual perception: A psychology of the creative eye*. London. Faber & Faber.

Aubrey, C. (1994). An investigation of children's knowledge of mathematics at school entry and the knowledge their teachers hold about teaching and learning mathematics, about young learners and mathematical subject knowledge. *British Educational Research Journal, 20*(1), 15–20.

Bialystok, E. (1992a). Symbolic representation of letters and numbers. *Cognitive Development, 7,* 301–316.

Bialystok, E. (1992b). The emergence of symbolic thought: Introduction. *Cognitive Development, 7,* 269–272.

Bialystok, E. & Codd, J. (1996). Developing representations of quantity. *Canadian Journal of Behavioural Science, 28,* 281–291.

Bolger, F. & Karmiloff-Smith, A. (1990). The development of communicative competence. *Archives de Psychologie, 58,* 257–273.

Braisby, N. & Dockrell, J.E. (1999). Why is colour naming difficult? *Journal of Child Language, 26,* 23–47.

Brenneman, K., Massey, C., Machado, S. & Gelman, R. (1996). Young children's plans differ for writing and drawing. *Cognitive Development, 11,* 397–419.

Clark, E.V. (1997). Conceptual perspective and lexical choice in acquisition. *Cognition, 64,* 1–37.

Davis, A.M. (1983). Contextual sensitivity in young children's drawings. *Journal of Experimental Child Psychology, 35,* 451–462.

De Goes, C. & Martlew, M. (1983). Young children's approach to literacy. In M. Martlew (Ed.), *The psychology of written language: Developmental and educational perspectives* (pp. 217–236). Chichester: Wiley.

Deloache, J.S., Uttal, D.H. & Pierroutsakos, S.L. (1998). The development of early symbolization: Educational implications. *Learning and Instruction, 8,* 325–339.

Dockrell, J.E. & Campbell, R.N. (1986). Lexical acquisition strategies. In S. Kuczaj & M. Barrett (Eds.), *Semantic development*. New York: Springer Verlag.

Dockrell, J.E. & Messer, D. (2004). Later vocabulary Acquisition. In R. Berman (Ed.), *Language development across childhood and adolescence: Psycholinguistic and crosslinguistic perspectives*. Trends in Language Acquisition Research 3. John Benjamins Publishers.

Dockrell, J.E., Teubal, E. & Ralli, M. (2000). *The influence of task parameters on children's early notations*. Paper presented at the International Society for Behavioural Development, Beijing China.

Donaldson, M. (1978). *Children's minds*. London: Fontana.

Ewers-Rogers, J. & Cowan, R. (1996). Children as apprentices of number. *Early Child Development and Care, 125,* 15–25.

Ferreiro, E. (1986). The interplay between information and assimilation in beginning literacy. In W.H. Teale & E. Sulzby (Eds.), *Emergent literacy: Writing and reading* (pp. 15–49). Norwood, NJ: Ablex.

Ferreiro, E. (2000). *L'écriture avant la lettre*. Hachette Education.

Ferreiro, E. & Teberosky, A. (1979). Los sistemas de escritura en el desarrollo del ni. Mexico: Siglo XXI. English translation (1982). *Literacy before schooling*. Exeter, NH: Heinemann Educational Books.

Fuson, K.C. (1988). *Children's counting and concepts of number*. New York: Springer Verlag.

Goldin-Meadow, S. & Wagner, S. M. (2005). How our hands help us learn. *Trends in Cognitive Science, 9*, 234–241.

Gombert, J.E. & Fayol, M. (1992). Writing in preliterate children. *Learning and Instruction, 2*, 23–42.

Goodman, N. (1976). *Language of arts*. Cambridge: Hackett.

Hatano, G. & Inagaki, K. (1997). Qualitative changes in intuitive biology. *European Journal of Psychology of Education, 12*, 111–129.

Hughes, M. (1986). *Children and number: Difficulties in learning mathematics*. Oxford: Basil Blackwell.

Karmiloff-Smith, A. (1992). *Beyond modularity: A developmental perspective on cognitive science*. Cambridge, MA: MIT Press.

Karmiloff-Smith, A. (1996). Internal representations and external notations: A developmental perspective. In D.M. Peterson (Ed.), *Forms of representation: An interdisciplinary theme for Cognitive Science* (pp. 141–151). Exeter, UK: Intellect Books.

Klein, E., Teubal, E. & Ninio, A. (2005). *Young children's development of the ability to discriminate between different notational domains – Drawing, writing and numerical notation*. Paper presented at the 11th European Conference for Research on Learning and Instruction (EARLI Cyprus).

Lavine, L.O. (1977). Differentiation of letterlike forms in prereading children. *Developmental Psychology, 13*, 89–94.

Lee, K. & Karmiloff-Smith, A. (1993). The development of cognitive constraints on notations. *Archives de Psychologie, 64*, 3–25.

Lee, K. & Karmiloff-Smith, A. (1996). The development of external symbol systems: The child as a notator. In R. Gelman & T. Au (Eds.) *Perceptual and cognitive development* (pp. 185–211). New York: Academic Press.

Lee, K., Karmiloff-Smith, A., Cameron, C.A. & Dodsworth, P. (1998). Notational adaptation in children. *Canadian Journal of Behavioural Science, 30*, 159–171.

Luquet, G.H. (1913). *Les dessins d'un enfant*. Paris: Alcan.

Luquet, G.H. (1927). *Le dessin enfantin*. Paris: Alcan.

Luria, A.R. (1928/1978). The development of writing in the child. In M. Cole (Ed.), *Selected writings of A.R. Luria*. New York: M.E. Sharp. Reprinted in M. Martlew (Ed.) (1983). *The psychology of written language: Developmental and educational perspectives* (pp. 237–278). Chichester: Wiley.

Mammana, C. & Villani, V. (1998). *Perspectives on the teaching of geometry for the 21st century: An ICMI study*. Dordrecht: Kluwer.

Martlew, M. (Ed.) (1983). *The psychology of written language: Developmental and educational perspectives*. Chichester: Wiley.

Martlew, M. & Sorsby, A. (1995). The precursors of writing: Graphic representation in preschool children. *Learning and Instruction, 5*, 1–19.

McLane, J.B. & McNamee, G.D. (1990). *Early literacy*. Cambridge MA: Harvard University Press.

Neilson, I. & Dockrell, J.E. (1981). Cognitive tasks as interactional settings. In G. Butterworth & P. Light (Eds.), *Social cognition* (pp. 213–238). Brighton: Harvester Press.

Nelson, K. (1996). *Language in cognitive development: The emergence of the mediated mind*. New York: Cambridge University Press.

Piaget, J. (1952). *The origins of intelligence in children*. New York: Norton Library.

Sinclair, A., Siegrist, F. & Sinclair, H. (1983). Young children's ideas about the written number system. In D. Rogers & J. Sloboda (Eds.), *The acquisition of symbolic systems*. New York: Plenum.

Sinclair, A., Mello, D. & Siegrist, F. (1988). La notation numérique chez l'enfant. In H. Sinclair (Ed.), *La production de notations chez le jeune enfant, langage nombre, rythmes et melodies*. Paris: PUF.

Sophian, C. (1997). Beyond competence: The significance of performance for cognitive development. *Cognitive Development, 12*, 281–303.

Sophian, C., Wood, A. & Vong, K. (1995). Making numbers count: The early development of numerical inferences. *Developmental Psychology, 31*, 263–273.

Sulzby, E. & Teale, W.H. (1985). Writing development in early childhood. *Educational Horizons, 64*, 8–12.

133

Teberosky, A., Marti, E. & Garcia-Mila, M. (1998). *Early stages in the development of notational knowledge*. Paper presented at ISSBD, Berne, Switzerland.

Teubal, E. & Dockrell, J.E. (1997). *Children's developing numerical notations; The impact of input and function*. Paper presented at EARLI, Athens, Greece.

Teubal, E. & Dockrell, J.E. (1998). *The relationship between emerging literacy and emerging numeracy – Evidence from children's early notations*. Paper presented at ISSBD, Berne, Switzerland.

Teubal, E. & Dockrell, J.E. (2005). Children's developing numerical notations; The impact of input and function. *Learning and Instruction, 15*, 257–280.

Thomas, G.V. & Silk, A.M. (1990). *An introduction to the psychology of children's drawings*. London: Harvester Wheatsheaf.

Thomas, G.V. & Jolley, R.P. (1998). Drawing conclusions: A re-examination of empirical and conceptual bases for psychological evaluation of children from their drawings. *British Journal of Clinical Psychology, 37*, 127–139.

Tolchinsky, L. (2003). *The cradle of culture and what children know about writing and numbers before being taught*. Mahwah, NJ: Lawrence Erlbaum.

Tolchinsky Landsmann, L. (1990). Early writing development: Evidence from different orthographic systems. In M. Spoelders (Ed.), *Literacy acquisition*. Norwood, NJ: Ablex.

Tolchinsky Landsmann, L. & Levin, I. (1985). Writing in preschoolers: An age related analysis. *Applied Psycholinguistics, 6*, 319–339.

Tolchinsky Landsmann, L. & Levin, I. (1987). Writing in four- to six-year-olds: Representation of semantic and phonetic similarities and differences. *Journal of Child Language, 14*, 127–144.

Tolchinsky Landsmann, L. & Karmiloff-Smith, A. (1992). Children's understanding of notations as domains of knowledge versus referential-communicative tools. *Cognitive Development, 7*, 287–300.

Vygotsky, L.S. (1962). *Thought and language*. Cambridge, MA: MIT Press.

Vygotsky, L.S. (1978). *Mind and society: The development of higher psychological processes*. Cambridge, MA: Harvard University Press.

Julie Dockrell
Institute of Education, University of London
United Kingdom

Eva Teubal
David Yellin Teachers' College
Jerusalem, Israel

LILIANA TOLCHINSKY

WRITING AND WRITTEN NUMBERS
AS SOURCE OF KNOWLEDGE

Writing and numbers have a strong impact on learning and development. As referential-communicative tools written language and numbers enable us to transmit information. As recording tools they have expanded our cognitive powers and have strongly influenced our representation of reality (Bruner, 1966) providing the basis for "theory building", a way of knowing qualitatively different from other pre-literate ways of knowing (Donald, 1991). As epistemic tools, they provide invaluable help in clarifying ideas and grasping the hierarchical organization of arguments and problems.

Written language has shaped our way of speaking and thinking about language and written numbers contributed to a systematic and generalised concept of number (Wiese, 2003). Ever since written language entered human history it has impregnated spoken language so thoroughly that it can no longer be accessed as purely spoken language (Ong, 1982). From our perception of sounds in a word to our distinction of sentences in a piece of discourse, the different levels at which we, literate adults, analyze speech are rarely natural units of segmentation; we impose them on speech as a consequence of our experience with alphabetic writing. Once written numbers were invented and their use generalized they enabled the formulatation of purely formal rules for comparing, adding or dividing two numbers. "The scaffolding of mathematics can then rise, ever higher, ever more abstract" (Dehaene, 1997 p. 6).

The features of writing systems and written number systems are influential not only after they have been learned but throughout the whole learning process. The central claim of this chapter is that notational systems are an important source of knowledge about their own functioning. Put simply, the best way to learn the features of notational systems is through full interaction with them. I shall dwell on two such features, one from the writing system, the other from the written number system, as "case analyses" that serve to support this general claim: (a) the convention of graphic separation between words in current use of alphabetic writing systems, and (b) the principle of place value in written numeration.

Both conventions are specific to the written modality. People do not speak making pauses between words. In normal speech words are grouped in sort of intonational phrases and these rarely coincide with words (Nespor & Vogel, 1986). Thus, separating between words is a characteristic of the written modality and not of the spoken modality.

E. Teubal et al. (eds.), Notational Knowledge, 135–158.

It is much the same for the positional principle. If spoken numbers were positional we would say for 772 *seven-seven-two* and just from the order of pronunciation we would understand the differing class of each figure (that the first to be pronounced corresponds to hundreds, the second to be pronounced corresponds to tens and the third to be pronounced corresponds to units). In contrast, in speech 772 is said *seven **hundred** seventy two*, where the differing classes are expressed by morphemes suffixed or juxtaposed to the number words. To *seven* we add ***hundred***, to *three* the suffix *ty* that means tens, and the lack of any suffix in *two* indicates that it refers to units.[1] When writing *seven hundred seventy two* we put the numerals in a prescribed order 772 to indicate that, if there are three numerals on a row, the first on the rightmost side means (2) units, the following to the left means (7) tens and the leftmost side means (7) hundreds. The positional principle consists in using position to indicate the class of the figures (the class of hundreds, decades, and units respectively). Thus, in spoken numeration there are more explicit cues – special words – to express different classes whereas in the written numeration the only graphic cue is the different position; the different classes must be inferred from the differing position. In this sense the written system is more hermetic than the spoken one.

My goal is to show that these two conventions – the graphic separation between words in writing and the positional principle in the written system of numbers – are learned by immersion in the functioning of the system. As obvious as this claim may sound – that conventions of the systems must be learned through using them – it is by no means generally acknowledged. Until not so long some psychologists (Monoud, 1986) and many teachers still today insist on the need to fulfil a number of pre-requisites before letting children write. It was assumed that children must define their laterality, refine their visual and auditory discrimination and be aware of the phonemes of their language before learning to write. As for numbers, we can still find explicit suggestions to refrain from using written numeration and to look for alternative ways as the best solution to cope with children's difficulties for understanding the positional principle. In this chapter I will focus rather on how children find their way to these conventions by negotiating between their own ideas and the information provided by the notational systems.

THE CHILD'S PATH TO WRITTEN WORDS

Graphic Separation of Words in Writing

Alphabetic orthographies "conjure" (Aronoff, 1994) spoken language along three dimensions: (1) The *graphic* dimension includes the superordinate and ordinate features of writing, such as linearity, directionality, discreteness, relative size and letter shapes. This dimension guides our recognition of legible strings and informs about order of interpretation. (2) The *graphophonic* dimension relates to the links between graphic signs and the phonological segments the writing system represents such as consonants or vowels. This dimension constrains our interpretation of individual letters and letter combinations. (3) The *ideographic* dimension refers to the means by which the writing system reflects in direct ways derivational or inflectional morphology (Blanche Benveniste & Chervel, 1970; Catach, 1989). This dimension enables us to recognize that *medicine* and *medical* are related, despite the different pronunciation of the intermediate /c/ or that the difference between *niño* 'boy' and *niños* 'boys' is of number and not just of sounds. This difference is perceived even in those cases in which the final *s* in *niños* 'boys' is not pronounced.

In addition to these conventions, there are a number of graphic devices that are not part of the orthography but supplement crucial information when orthographies are used for writing texts. These graphic devices include different punctuation marks such as colon, coma, semi-colon and blank spaces. Although blanks between strings are not punctuation marks in the Latin sense of *punctum*, 'dot', they mark the boundaries between certain entities that people using the written language will call word (Catach, 1989; Parkes, 1993).

The history of writing shows that the creation of blank spaces between words is a relatively late acquisition in the development of writing systems. It was the practice at an early date for Ancient Greek and Latin (Desbordes 1990, p. 234). But, after that, the practice was abandoned. Although it may be considered a strange form of regression, writing with no spacing between words – *scriptio continua* – was widely practiced up to the 10th century and still evident in the Renaissance epoch (Blanche Benveniste, 1997 p. 38).

For us, silent readers, texts written without spaces are very difficult to follow. And although the task for reading *scriptio continua* was probably easier for readers who read aloud and who had to read few and well known texts, it still required specific preparation. Before the inception of silent reading, separating words was the task of the reader as he listened to his own reading. With the development of silent reading writers started to create blanks while writing texts. In the ninth century the first regulations requiring scribes to be silent in the monastic scriptorium began and that was the reason which led Irish scribes to start marking the separation between words in the text so as to simplify its reading. Initially, proper names and complex parts of speech were separated but, with time, "Irish scribes began isolating not only parts of speech but also the grammatical constituents within a sentence, and introduce many of the punctuation marks we use today" (Mangel, 1995).

The creation of blanks and the use of punctuation allowed for an easier identification of the different parts of the text and contributed to a "democratization" of reading. Even people who were not familiar in advance with the texts could attempt to read them (Sirat, 1994). It was only with the advent of printing, however, that separation between words became relatively established for every kind of text and similarly defined for any category of word or position of the word in a sentence.

The notion of what deserves to be separated by blank spaces is language dependent. In Chinese there is an almost perfect coincidence between spoken and written words, whereas in Eskimo no element, except proper names appears as an isolated word. In English, prepositions and articles are written with blanks on both sides, whereas in Hebrew, for instance, most of the prepositions and the only existing article are written as prefixes bound to the content word. Even in languages of the same family like Spanish and Italian, both Romance languages, the same elements "to" "the" would be written separately in Spanish *a la playa* but together *alla spiaggia* in Italian.

In short, words are quite easy to define in graphic terms – strings of one or more letters with a blank space on either side. The problem starts when we try to find *stable* correlates for this definition beyond a particular writing system or a particular language. Words, in common with many other linguistic constructs, elude clear cut definitional criteria outside writing. Linguists suggest that "in the case of terms (like 'words') which function as theoretical primitives, only lists of symptoms can be provided" (Zwicky, 1985, p. 285).

What are the symptoms that guide children for creating blank spaces in their written output? What ideas do children have about what must be written separately and what jointly?

Acquiring the Conventions of Writing

During the earliest stages of learning to write, the graphic space available is the limit. When writing, 3 to 4-year olds may start at any point on the page and stop at the edge of the paper; no matter how big or small the page is, there are no self-imposed limits to their writing. Since linearity is one of the first features to characterize preschoolers' writing their earliest productions are linear, discontinuous patterns of wavy lines. The first constraining factor is genre.[2]

To illustrate this point I will refer to a study in which Hebrew speaking preschoolers were asked to write a fairy tale *Ami ve'tami* 'Hansel and Gretel' and to describe what the chocolate house in the tale looked like. Their knowledge of phonographic conventions of written Hebrew was very poor; most of them knew how to draw Hebrew letters but they did not always know their phonic value. Nevertheless, their written outputs for narratives and for descriptions were segmented very differently. The narrative was written in long lines of one letter after the other with hardly any internal spacing between them, except for the name of the protagonists, which sometimes appeared with blanks on both sides. The description, on the other hand, looked very similar to a list of isolated words (Sandbank, 2001). Indeed, when asked to read what they had written they interpreted the long lines as full sentences, parts of the tale. When interpreting the description, however, they named the different elements in the house saying that there were "chocolates, candies and cookies". A similar graphic differentiation was found when comparing the way preschoolers wrote shopping lists with the way they wrote news or advertisements (Tolchinsky Landmann, 1993). Long before gaining a full command of the phonographic conventions of the written system, the graphic layout of their texts imitates the features of different genres.

The distribution of different syntactic categories of words is sensitive to genre. Descriptions contain more nouns and adjectives and can be reduced to labelling, whereas narratives require more complex predication and connectives. This seems to be reflected in the lay-out that children use. For genres in which isolated words, mainly nouns, are used, they put together strings of letters, usually each on a different line; for fuller utterances they were reluctant to create internal blanks among strings of letters.

Word-Category Counts

Genre appears as one of the initial constraining factors of the external boundaries of texts, the general lay-out of written productions of 4 to 5-year olds. The syntactic category of words seems to be a constraining factor of internal separations. Linguistic theories of all shades draw distinctions in at least two word classes – those denoting "material content" as opposed to those denoting a "relation" (Sapir, 1958). This distinction was differently termed, i.e. "lexical item" as opposed to "grammatical item" (Lyons, 1968); "content word" as opposed to "function word" (or, to include both free and bound morphemes, "functor" – Slobin, 1997, p. 266). Typically, the first class includes nouns and verbs, and usually adjectives; the second class includes free morphemes such as conjunctions, prepositions and bound morphemes such as affixes marking categories of number, case, tense, and so forth.

Quite a few psycholinguistic studies in Romance languages suggest that children's interpretations and production of blanks between strings of letters is in some way related to this distinction. Clemente (1984), asked children from 5 to 11 years old to write short stories and then to split them up into "the smallest possible parts". As a rule, 5 to 7-year olds showed difficulties in separating determiners from names, compound verbs, reflexive pronouns from their host verbs. It is only at a second grade, after the age of 7, that conventional spacing between words is achieved. Children from 5 to 7 years of age did not produce a blank within *aviaunavez*, 'once upon a time', or *superrito*, 'his little dog' which must be written in Spanish with internal blanks: two in the case of *había una vez* 'once upon a time' and one in the case of *su perrito*, 'his little dog'.

Using another procedure, Ferreiro and Teberosky (1979) obtained similar results. The experimenters wrote a simple sentence of the form N+V+det+N, like for example *Papa patea la pelota* 'Dad hit the ball', in front of the child, and asked him/her where each word was written. They concluded that children of different ages have different expectations as to the necessary correspondences between what is said and what is written. Children are not always expecting a correspondence between the number of written strings separated by blanks and the number of spoken words; the youngest do not even expect to find in the written sentence all the words included in the spoken message. The kind of words children expect to find follows a clear progression: first, at age 4 to 5, only nouns are expected to be written; later, nouns and verbs, and finally, every category of word, including articles. For these researchers, the reason for this is that children under 7 years old do not consider functional terms as proper words that deserve to appear isolated, with blanks on both sides. Forms such as determiners, verb particles, prepositions, auxiliaries, pronouns and conjunctions which have grammatical denotation but no referential content are considered inseparable from the content words they usually modify and therefore are written attached to them.

Ferreiro and Pontecorvo's study of the development of the separation of words in Italian, Spanish and Portuguese provides support for this claim. They asked second and third graders who already knew the phonographic conventions of their respective languages to write a well known fairy tale (Ferreiro, Pontecorvo, Ribeiro Moreira & García Hidalgo, 1996). As far as types of mistakes were concerned, comparative analyses across the languages included in the study showed that in spite of the difference in languages, and the different handwriting in which children are instructed (cursive linked, or printed), hyposegmentation – writing without a blank space where it should be one – was always more frequent than hypersegmentation – creating a blank space where it should not be one – and more frequent than hyper plus hyposegmentation. Moreover, problems of separation were related to the same kind of elements. Functional elements which are unstressed monosyllables such as *a* 'to' (preposition), *el, la,* 'the', *un la* (articles), *de* 'of' (preposition), *su* 'his/her/its' (possessive), *se* 'it', *le* 'him' (pronominal clitic[3]), *que* 'which' were found, as a rule, attached (hyposegmented) to the content words (nouns, verbs) they modify.

It is important to note, however, that the authors found a higher frequency of hyposegmentations of the preposition *a* 'to' in comparison to the conjunction *y* 'and'. Similarly, *la* 'the –fem./ her' (article and pronominal clitic) and *el* 'the –masc./ he' (article and personal pronoun) tended to hyposegment to the other graphic elements more often when they were functioning as articles than when functioning as pronominal clitics. This means that other factors besides the category of the element in terms of functional vs. content word may be influencing children's decision to attach or separate. In addition, the authors noted that, in hypersegmentations, the resulting strings of elements tended to correspond to possible written words in the respective languages. For example, they hypersegmented *bosque* 'forest' producing *bos-que* where the second part *que* 'which' is a very frequent written string. According to these authors hypersegmentations of this kind demonstrate a higher command of written language.

Summing up, during the first stages of acquisition of conventional writing, the likelihood of creating blanks on both sides of a string of letters is related to the syntactic category of words. Children hyposegment function words (e.g., determiners, auxiliary verbs) to content words (e.g., nouns, verbs). The decisions to join or separate elements will reflect, in order, what children conceive to be prototypical words: proper names, common names, certain adjectives and adverbs, and certain verbs. These appear to be considered "more words" than functional-class elements. (Reichler-Beguelin, 1990; Blanche Benveniste, 1992). The interpretation is very sound and is supported by what we know about the metalinguistic development of the notion of words (Berthoud-Papandropoulu, 1976). Note as well that a system based on this rationale could be linguistically very consistent. There are, however, some hints that the typical distinction lexical versus grammatical item does not provide a fully satisfying explanation of children's decisions to create blanks.

Syntactic Context Counts More

A series of recent studies we have performed with Spanish children showed this to be the case. Our aim was to trace the development of separation between words in written Spanish from preschool to third grade, so as to assess the effect of word category on children's creation of blank spaces in their writing. In particular, we wanted to explore the effect of the classical distinction between *content words* and *functional words*, and the consistency of this distinction in sentences of differing length and in short texts. As recall, *function words* were written with blanks on both sides less frequently than content words. Thus, the purpose was to determine whether these categories of words are consistently separated in every textual environment, or rather if these categories of word are more difficult to separate in one textual environment than in another one, or in one task but not in another.

With these aims in mind we asked 165 Spanish speaking children from preschool to third grade – 36 in preschool; 41 in first grade and 44 in second and third grade – to write two-word phrases and four-word simple sentences dictated orally and a short well known fable that was previously read to them. The dictation tasks were very controlled and the last one was a more open/natural situation of text-writing. In the dictation task half of the phrases and half of the sentences included constructions in which the target region (the first blank between words according to conventional writing) was located between a functional word and a content word. For example, in the sentence *el viento sopla fuerte* 'the wind blows strong', the target region is located between a determiner (*el* 'the') and a noun (*viento* 'wind'); in the sentence *Ella pinta cuadros rojos* 'she paint(s) pictures red'), the target region is located between a personal pronoun (*Ella* 'she') and a verb (*pinta* 'paints'). In the other half of sentences, the target region was located between two content words. For example, in the sentence *Luis lee libros tontos* 'Luis read(s) books silly', the target region is the blank between the proper name and the verb; in the sentence *hoy lava ropa sucia* 'today (s/he) washes cloth dirty', it is between an adverb and a verb. We compared determiners, reflexive pronouns (or other pronominal clitics) and personal pronouns as representatives of the category *function words* with adjectives, adverbs and proper names as representatives of *content words*. In the selection of words we controlled for number of syllables and grammatical gender. As for the text that the children were asked to write, it obviously included all the categories of word and the kind of constructions that were selected for the phrases and sentences.

The children's written productions were examined, looking for conventional separation and for different ways of unconventional separation (hyposegmentation, hypersegmentation in or outside the target region) and non-alphabetical or illegible writing. As in the previous study, by far the main form of unconventional separation was hyposegmentation. The mean number of hyposegmented words was 1.30 and 1.25 words for the four-word sentence and two-word phrase, respectively, compared to 0.71 and 0.76 for other forms of unconventional segmentation in the four-word sentence and 0.67 and 0.88 in the two-words phrase.

Table 1.

Means in conventional segmentation in the two dictation tasks.

Tasks	Preschool		First grade		Second grade		Third grade	
	Mean	SD	Mean	SD	Mean	SD	Mean	SD
Two-word phrases	10.08	16.28	36.91	15.57	46.55	4.41	47.40	0.85
Four-word sentences	5.97	11.32	26.73	19.37	44.75	7.77	46.40	4.35

(minimum score = 0, maximum score = 48)

Table 2.

Means in conventional segmentation in the re-writing task.

Tasks	Preschool		First grade		Second grade		Third grade	
	Mean	SD	Mean	SD	Mean	SD	Mean	SD
Short texts	0.83	1.37	3.19	2.29	4.77	1.50	5.80	1.09

(minimum score = 0, maximal score = 7.85 after transformation)

This study had three main findings. The first concerns the effect of the textual environment (a two-word phrase, a four-word sentence or a story) on children's separation of words. Table 1 presents the mean scores and standard deviations for conventional segmentation by grade in the two dictation tasks. We found that the amount of conventional separation of words decreases with sentence length. Children produce more conventional separation when writing two word phrases than when writing four word sentences.

The differences between tasks diminished with school-level. Second graders attained almost perfect separation according to the conventions of written Spanish.

As for the text production task, we will refer only to the results of analyzing the creation of blanks in the same kind of constructions as the ones that were dictated to the children. Due to the differences in the number of target elements that children used in their texts we had to transform the scores in each category in order to attain the homogeneity required for the analysis. Table 2 shows the mean scores and standard deviations in conventional segmentation by school grade in the text writing task.

As can be seen, children still have some difficulty separating words when writing a text until third grade. It is possible that the need to control for the content, for the wording and for the organization of the text releases children's control over the separation between words and this fact explains the difference in performance in the text-production task compared with the dictation task. In any case, the different results suggest that the conventions of writing, at least for graphic separation of words, are not acquired across the board, for every writing task, but rather by successive approximations.

Our second finding also concerns the effect of textual environment (two word phrases vs. four word sentences vs. short texts) but this time with respect to the distribution of conventional and unconventional separations as a function of the syntactic categories embraced in the target region. This finding was very important because it led us to the discovery of the role of syntactic context in guiding children's separation decisions.

In two-word phrases the highest score for conventional separation was obtained for those phrases in which the first element was a determiner (e.g., *el viento*, 'the wind'), these were followed by phrases that started with a proper noun and those that started with an adjective. That is, one functional word and two content-words scored highest for conventional segmentation. The lowest conventional segmentation score was obtained by sentences starting with a reflexive pronoun (*se pinta* '(3rd person sing) himself painted') followed by phrases starting with adverbs.

The results obtained in the four-words writing task showed a different pattern. In this task sentences containing proper names as their initial elements obtained the highest score on conventional separation followed by sentences containing personal pronouns. Sentences with reflexive pronouns had the lowest score on conventional separation and the highest on hyposegmentation; exactly the same pattern is repeated in each school year. (There was a main effect of word category $F(5.785) = 11.40$, $p < 0.000$ but no interaction). If we look at the two extremes – clitic pronouns and proper names – we should say that the distinction *content* vs. *function words* biases the children's use of separation. Indeed, when we compared conventional separation for *functional words* – determiners, reflexive pronouns and personal pronouns ($M = 14.75$, $Sd = 10.30$) – vs. *content* words – numeral adjectives, adverbs and proper names ($M = 15.20$, $Sd = 10.31$) – we found a significant difference in favour of content words. But a closer look at the mean hyposegmentation score suggests that there are internal differences both among *functors* and among *content* words; *content* words such as adverbs are closer to clitic pronouns than to proper names, and personal pronouns are closer to proper names than to reflexive pronouns. At the same time determiners had higher conventional separation scores and lower hyposegmentation scores than reflexive pronouns, despite the fact that both are *functional words*.

To interpret the findings in the two dictation tasks we must take into account the syntactic context – defined by the category of the preceding element – in which the target elements appear. In terms of syntactic environment, determiners and adjectives, fall in the nominal domain, reflexive pronouns and adverbs in the verbal domain, and proper names and personal nouns can appear in either. When the results in the two tasks are compared according to the syntactic context, elements in the verbal domain (reflexive pronouns and adverbs) differed significantly from elements in the nominal domain (determiners and numerals).

This finding is supported by results in text-writing. Obviously since this is a more open task we could not control for the exact wording and amount of occurrences as we had been able to do in the dictation tasks. Since proper nouns and personal pronouns were not in the original text there were none in the children's texts either. In this task, adverbs obtained the lowest scores both in conventional separation and hyposegmentation, and clitic pronouns had the next lowest conventional separation score but the highest hyposegmentation score. Therefore, the effect of the syntactic context is similar to that in the other tasks; elements in the verbal domain (reflexive pronouns, adverbs) were written attached to their verbal hosts more frequently than determiners and numerals to the nominals they are specifying. These findings show, therefore, that syntactic context is more relevant to explain children's initial decisions to create blanks than the syntactic category of the elements per se.

Writing Teaches about Written Words

There is no doubt that long before learning to write children have some internal representation of separability of elements; otherwise we would find a large number of segmentation mistakes in early language development, and this is not the case. This intuitive and pre-literate notion of word turns into a normative concept with the learning of writing.

When children start learning about written language they do not seem to believe that this separability must be necessarily reflected by blank spaces between strings of letters. However, the first attempts to separate strings of letters seem to be linguistically based; blanks are motivated by differences in the syntactic category of the elements they are supposed to separate. It is more reasonable to write proper names separately, as they have an existence outside discourse than to separate elements that are syntactically attached – like clitic to verbs. This rationale has to be abandoned in order to accept the particular conventions of the writing system they are exposed to. These conventions, however, are not always linguistically based. In many cases only historical reasons explain why some elements are written separately and others not. Children seem to move from a linguistically reasonable internal definition of what should be written separately and what should be written attached to a written language-based definition. Interestingly enough, this definition is what literate adults assume to be words. It is through learning to write that children have access to the notion of written words. And this notion seems to be the one reflected in most metalinguistic tasks. In the domain of separation between words as in other domains (e.g., phonological awareness) the features of writing guide the reflection on language. To be clear, I am referring here to the evidence in favour of phonological awareness being a consequence of learning how to read in an alphabetic system rather than an ability acquired outside the interaction with alphabetic systems (e.g., Bertelson, Cary & Alegria, 1986).

In the next section, I shall discuss another case in which the features of the written system of numeration are used by children on the way to discovering relations of order between numerals; in so doing, they grasp the importance of position in the numerical system.

CHILDREN'S PATH TO THE WRITTEN SYSTEM OF NUMBERS

The Principle of Place Value in the Written Number System

Our system of written numerals consists of a small set of primitive elements 0 to 9, that are visually well distinguished – 3 looks different from 4 which in turn looks different from 2 or 1. These elements can be concatenated to form any other numeral. Any numerals, say 3 and 4, can be concatenated to form a new numeral 34, this new numeral can be concatenated to any other numeral, say 5 forming another numeral 345 and so forth. The concatenation of numerals is governed by recursive rules making the set infinite. The set is ordered as a progression established by a function '<' that expresses the order of any numeral relative to other numerals (Wiese, 2003, p. 223). The basis for ordering is the set of primitives and, in our written system, the higher numeral in the progression is got by concatenating to the right. Thus, the number of numerals in a string is a good indicator of higher order. In our example, 345 is higher in the progression than 34. However, if two strings have the same number of elements, the first on the left side defines the order of a numeral relative to the other. In 445 and 346, 445 is higher in the progression because 4 is higher than 3 in the progression of primitive elements. If two strings have the same number of elements, and the first, on the left side in one string, is identical to the first on the left side in the other string – 346 and 347 – the second to the right decides and if these are equal (as in the example), the following to the right decides and so forth. There are some conflicting points concerning the use of zeros in this description, but I am going to leave them for the moment.

In short, if one knows the sequential order of primitives and takes into account directionality – from right to left – it is possible to infer the sequential order of any two complex numerals. This is not to say that one has necessarily to know the referential meaning of each numeral, either primitive or complex. For example, that the difference between a set of 346 pencils and another set of 345 pencils is only one pencil. Moreover, one does not need to be aware of the fact that the system is decimal and positional. One does not need to know that, the elements of the system are the nine digits smaller than the base ten and each position in complex numerals represents different powers of ten (the power of the base by which it must be multiplied). The rightmost position $= 10^0$, the following position to the left $= 10^1$; then – always to the left – the following position $= 10^2$, the next $= 10^3$, and so on. The position of each digit in the numeral indicates the power of the base by which it must be multiplied and the zero element is used to mark the absence of a given power of the base. Based on this *positional principle* numerals have two readings: a *face value* when they appear in isolation as elements of a sequence from 0 to 9 and a *positional value*, when they are integrated in a complex numeral indicating the class they belong to (units, decades, hundreds, etc.).

This *Principle* by which the value of a numeral changes according to its location in a string is not exclusive to our non-verbal systems of numerals. The Babylonian sexagesimal system (-1900 to -1800) marks the earliest appearance of this principle; the Roman system also makes use of position. For example, when I is placed before V as in IV it reads 'four' whereas after V as in VI it reads 'six'. The benefits of this principle are obvious, by using position to change the value of the same elements, we need less elements of different shapes – less primitive elements – for generating an infinite sequence.

This useful feature of written systems creates a number of problems for young children. It seems that children have difficulty understanding this principle until almost age nine. In the next section we shall discuss some of the explanations that were provided for this purported difficulty in the context of a more general picture of children evolving knowledge on written numerals.

Acquiring the Conventions of the Written System of Numbers

A few weeks after birth infants can perceive the difference between one array of three dots and another one of four. While it is true that they can do that only with small sets, they are able to do it with any shape: dots, rectangles or triangles, and even when the items are in motion (Antell & Keating, 1983; Starkey & Cooper, 1980; Strauss & Curtiss, 1981). At 6 and 8 months of age, infants are able to coordinate information presented visually with auditory information. Shown photographs of two and three dots while a drum is beating they looked longer at the photograph that matched the number of drumbeats (Starkey et al., 1983; although Moore, Benenson, Reznick, Peterson & Kagan, 1987, failed to replicate this finding). As they grow older so grows their experience with different numerical tools (Wiese, 2003) in many contexts. They raise their fingers to show how old they are, use counting words to count steps when going up on staircases, and push buttons on the elevator to get higher.

On top of infants' sensitivity to numerosities and children's experience with counting words, very early, children recognize the written numerals as being different from other visual displays such as drawings, or letters. Four-year olds say that figures are for counting whereas letters are for reading (Tolchinsky & Karmiloff-Smith, 1992). At this age written numerals and writing are viewed as two distinct territories. Children apply different rules to each territory. Nevertheless, on some occasions, boundaries between territories are crossed due to the need to convey a message.

In a study I carried out with Annette Karmiloff Smith (Tolchinsky Landsmann & Karmiloff Smith, 1992), we sought to determine whether children were sensitive to the different constraints inherent in the two systems of writing and numbers, or whether they considered both to be simply drawings. The participants were children between 3 years, 8 months and 6 and a half years from a lower middle class neighborhood of Barcelona. The task was very simple: we used two sets of cards, one set for the *writing-domain task* and the other for the *numbers-domain task*. For each set of cards we asked the children to say *which cards were not good for writing* or *not good for counting*.[4] The cards varied according to the following features: iconicity, linearity, identical elements, length of the string, conventionality of elements, and pronounceability of the string. The same features were used in the cards for the numbers-domain and for the writing-domain. Thus, there were cards with figurative drawings, others with abstract schematic drawings and still others with conventional letters or numerals. There were cards with strings of the same letter (or the same numeral) repeated many times and others including all different letters (or all different numerals), and still other cards with some letters repeated and some different. Some cards contained a single letter (or a single numeral) and others contained two, three, up to eight letters (or numerals). Finally, there were cards containing obviously pronounceable words, and others consisting solely of consonants, and thus unpronounceable.

We wished to determine whether the criteria children applied in admitting a card to one territory were similar to the ones they applied in admitting a card to the other territory. If they decided, for example, that a card containing the same repeated letter was *not* good for writing and that similarly a card containing the same repeated numeral was *not* good for counting, then we could conclude that the same criterion – "avoid repetition" – was imposed on both writing and numbers. If on the other hand repetition was accepted in one domain but rejected in the other, this would imply that children were applying a different criterion to each domain.

The results of the sorting task demonstrated that over 95% of the children at all ages clearly separated between exemplars belonging to writing or numbers and those belonging to drawing. They overwhelmingly concluded that cards containing drawings were good for neither writing nor number. Mixtures of elements from different domains [$M#&©] were also clearly rejected by 85% of the children as not being good exemplars of either domain.

However, the most revealing result was that the children drew a clear distinction between writing and number notation. Eighty percent of the subjects at all ages identified strings with repeated identical letters as not being good for writing, though they did not do so for number notation with respect to strings of identical numerals. They clearly imposed a constraint on writing that stipulates that strings must include a variety of different elements, while realizing that for number notation such a constraint does not hold. Moreover, they chose a card containing linked numerals imitating cursive writing as a bad exemplar of number notation, but accepted cursive writing for written notation.

Single elements, repetition of elements, and very many elements were accepted for numbers but rejected for writing, whereas linkage was accepted for writing but rejected for numbers. In the context of this task, 4-year olds were clear about formal distinctions between writing and number. We can see then, how successful young children are at distinguishing drawing from either writing or number notation and at using different formal constraints to distinguish the domain of writing from that of number notation.

This is not to say that they can use numerals to represent quantities, even small quantities; on the contrary, it takes some developmental time (and exposure to numbers) until children accept that, for example, five toy bricks can be represented with a single digit. Studies on the development of numerical notation have shown that until relatively late, sometimes after age 6 or 7, even children who know the name and shape of digits resort to analogical graphic representation (e.g., Teubal

& Dockrell, 2005; Hughes, 1986; Sinclair, Mello & Siegrist, 1988). In a playful context the experimenter put four toy bricks inside a box and six toy bricks inside another and ask children to stick a label on each box and put on it how many toy bricks are inside each one. They may use four tallies to show that there are four toy bricks and increase the number of tallies for showing that there are six.

This analogical way of representation already implies crucial quantitative ideas. They reflect a sort of iteration-in-act and an explicit term-to-term correspondence that are somehow directly manifested in the graphic outcome of analogical representation. Note, however, that both iteration and an explicit term-to-term correspondence will become cancelled in the use of single digits. It seems that young children need to perceive how many objects are represented and only later they are willing to accept the less expressive conventional numerals. Indeed, analogue notations persist when children attempt to communicate numerosity, at least as one of the possible graphic representations, sometimes after first or second grade. Analogical representation appears in referential-communicative situations, when children use numeral to show cardinalities but not when they are asked to write counting words on dictation. They may or may not hit at the correct figure but they will not attempt to produce an analogical representation. In the first case they are using the tallies as counting tools; in the case of dictation they are translating a verbal element from one sequence – the sequence of counting words – to a non-verbal element of another sequence.

Understanding the written system requires identifying not only the elements but also the relations between elements. A turning point in children's understanding of the written system of numbers concerns their grasping of the rules of concatenation, the ways in which complex numerals are formed from simple elements and the role of position in this concatenation.

Many researchers (Brun, Giossi & Henriques, 1984; Kamii, 1986; Richards & Carter, 1982, 1986; Sinclair & Scheuer, 1993) have explored the development of first and second graders' understanding of place value. They usually confront the child with a particular numeral, e.g. 18, and ask questions such as *How many does this number represent?* (pointing at 8) and *How many does this number represent?* (pointing at 1).

Four to six-year olds did not usually attribute the conventional numerical meaning to the whole numeral; if they did, they did not attribute any meaning to the individual digits. Slightly older children (5, 6, 7-year olds) interpreted meaning conventionally and attributed meaning to individual digits but the sum of the digits did not account for the whole collection. Each digit is read for its face value; the whole may be read correctly but the two readings are juxtaposed, and the children do not seem to be concerned by the "contradiction". For example, with the cue 27 they read *twenty seven*; when asked for reading each digit they may say that the first means *two*, the second *seven* and all together *it makes nine*.

It was only after 6, 7, 8 years that the relationship between the parts and the whole starts to be solved.[5] Individual digits are given values which, when added up, give the total amount of the numeral, but they are not based on groups of tens. Finally, the precise meaning of tens and units are interpreted. It is important to note that, here again, there is an effect of magnitude. Children's realization of the meaning of tens and units is very slowly generalized to hundred and thousands.

Until they reach almost 9 years of age children have difficulty understanding positional value. Fuson expresses the underlying representation of children's responses very clearly: "Initially children's conceptual structures for number words are unitary conceptual structures in which the meaning or the referents are single objects (as in counting objects) or a collection of single objects (as in the cardinal reference to a collection of objects)" (Fuson, 1990).

Nevertheless, to understand multi-digits and especially for the ability to operate with numbers above 20 "children need to construct multi-unit conceptual structures". That is, children must understand that each numeral in the string represents a different level of unit – units, decades, thousands, etc. – and that these different levels of units are represented at the same time in a multi-digit numeral. This is an important condition for understanding the meaning of multi-digits and for performing basic arithmetical operations. It is hard to understand what we are doing when we "carry one" in adding 38 + 3 if the additive composition of the system is not understood.

Why does it take so long to build this multi-unit structure? One explanation is that the difficulty lies in the need to deal simultaneously with figures whose value changes depending on placement in the string and this requires an operational understanding of the part-whole relationship. Kamii (Kamii & De Clark, 1985) explicitly suggests postponing explicit teaching of positional value and devoting time to concrete understanding of grouping and seriation. According to the Piagetian account, on which Kamii's ideas are based, when class inclusion and seriation are reciprocally assimilated the notion of number is constructed. Therefore, it is through these activities that children will grasp the concept of number and will apply this concept thereafter to any notational system. It might be better to postpone explicit teaching of positional value and devote time to concrete understanding of grouping and seriation (Kamii, 1986; Kamii & De Clark, 1985).

A second explanation posits that the comprehension of positional value is an outcome of children's understanding of addition. According to this interpretation, neither counting nor learning the written system will help them; only a change in children's addition procedures[6] – from *counting all* to *counting on* – can spur understanding of the base ten system (Nunes & Bryant, 1996). Nunes provides empirical support by exploring the relative effect of counting and addition to solve a version of the relative value task used to represent multi-digit number. Alternately, 5 to 6-year olds had to judge the relative value of two quantities of money either by units of the same order or by units of different order, and to solve simple addition problems. They had no difficulty solving the task that required only counting, but there was a significant correlation between the number of children who used the counting on strategy and those that showed an understanding of the additive structure of the system.

Finally, some researchers state that mathematics curricula prevent children from understanding the positional nature of the written system by ignoring their ideas and the sources of their mistakes. Therefore, different activities should be designed to materialize the hierarchical grouping of our system and to allow children to invent non-conventional notations for the different groupings (Bednarz & Janvier, 1986). Children are placed in situations which require creating different groupings for collections of objects. Once they have gained experience with different possible groupings, they are supposed to realize that it is not the same to talk about 'one' if we refer to a single object or to a package of ten grouped objects. Children are encouraged to represent each level of grouping using a different block; for example they may be encouraged to use cubes for representing grouping of tens, and strips for units. After they have decided on particular symbols for each level of grouping, they are asked to represent complex numerals using the symbols that they have chosen: for example, 77. They are expected to use 7 cubes and 7 strips or any other combination in order to represent this multi-digit number. As a rule this is a very difficult task until the age of 8 when children find a way with canonical partitions (7 cubes and 7 strips) yet found it more difficult to represent non-canonical partitions such as understanding that 77 stands for 6 cubes and 17 strips (Resnick, 1983; Bednarz & Janvier, 1984a, 1984b, 1988; Ross, 1986).

Faced with these difficulties, researchers' and many teachers' advice is to circumvent the written system. The reasoning seems to be that if the difficulty lies there (in the written system of numerals) it is advisable to look for alternative routes. Thus, at school children are deprived from a full interaction with the whole system (Fuson, 1990).

I would rather suggest looking at what toddlers and preschoolers know that may help them to further understand the functioning of the system and relating to written numeration as a source of knowledge. I will suggest that, if interaction is stimulated, children will find their way in the notational environment and will discover its underlying principles.

Discovering the Rules through Interaction with the Written System

A number of psychologists and teachers of mathematics (Lerner & Sadovsky, 1994; Martínez Ruiz & Tolchinsky Landsmann, 1993; Scheuer, 1996) assume that the possibility of understanding the system begins with using it. Based on this assumption, they looked at the criteria children use when comparing numerals in the context of regular class activities in preschool, with 5 year-olds, and first grade with 6 year-olds, or in the context of controlled or clinical interviews. For example, children may be asked to play card-games in which the winner is the one who got the higher number. They must decide which is the winning card and justify their decision; explaining, for example, why they think that 28 "beats" 19. Researchers used other similar tasks varying the number, variety and position of digits as well as the presence or absence of zeros to discover the strategies and criteria children apply for comparing between numerals. This task is unique in that, unlike those previously described, it does not require a referential use of the numerals for marking cardinality.

In other tasks children are required not only to compare numerals but also to produce numerals. For example, asking from them to jot down a "big number". As in the previous tasks, children are not required to communicate or to refer to any set of empirical objects, but to reflect on a certain element that, in their view, is a "big number". A close observation of children's responses, questioning and reactions in the contexts of these different tasks shows how children use the features of the written numerals: the number of elements in a string, the value of the elements, and their position, for deciding about the relations between numerals.

Number of Elements in a String Counts

In order to decide which of two cards displays the "larger" numeral, one criterion appears very clearly before six years of age: The more figures it has, the larger it is. In most cases the decision is based exclusively on the features of the notation – by looking at the numerals – since children do not know how to read these numerals. Certainly, when they are able to read the numerals they provide additional justification by reference to the oral sequence, like saying for example "this one is larger because *it comes after* this one". Note that this child is clearly referring to a sequence in which elements are located. Five-year olds have no problem in distinguishing higher from lower numerals among the lexical primitives and when it comes to compare complex numerals they apply this knowledge for deciding about the relation among them.

This idea, that it is the number of figures that makes a numeral higher than another, however, is not immediately generalized to every pair of written numerals. Children hesitate when facing pairs of numerals in which there is an extreme difference in the face value of the elements, for example when they had to decide between 112 and 89. Perhaps they are trying to coordinate two kinds of information, one provided by the absolute value of the figures, which they already dominate, and the other provided by their conviction that the number of elements in the string counts for deciding which number is "larger".

There may be another source of conflicting referential and syntactic information. Children may doubt between the purported value of the numeral as a whole and the amount of numerals in the string. They know that the string has a value as a whole but they do not have a clear idea of how the whole value is obtained. This was expressed clearly by one child who commented "two numbers form one number" (Lerner et al., 1994). Other children try to add the values of the figures and decide that 112 must be less than 89, "because the first is just four and the second is seventeen".

The number of elements in the string is a very useful criterion when it can be applied. But, what happens when the elements to be compared have the same number of elements? A close look at these cases in which children had to decide between pairs of numerals having the same number of figures shows that number of figures is not the only criterion children apply in order to decide between pairs.

Position of Elements in a String, Also Counts

This criterion appears especially when the number of figures in each pair differs and so children explain that, "the first starting from the left wins". This explanation reflects that children are taking into account the role of position in determining the value of a figure. Recall that in positional systems, the value of a figure is determined by its position with respect to other numerals in the strings. Therefore, if two numerals have the same number of digits the face value of the leftmost side will be decisive. This is what children are saying. They even go a step further and sustain that when the leftmost digits from the two numerals are the same, it is necessary to look at the following digit.

In general, independently of the magnitude of the numerals, children find it more difficult to determine the relation between pairs of numerals in which one of them had the highest digits in the rightmost position than to determine the relation with pairs of numerals in which the mere consideration of face value of the leftmost position was enough. For illustration, children found it harder to decide between 19–21 or 88–79 than between 50–40 or 301–501. In 19–21 the difference between 9 and 1 is so big that it provoked doubts, despite the fact that the leftmost side digit differ. In the second case 88–79 the conception of 9 as "a big number" is so strong that it also provokes doubt. Again, we are witnessing here an important effect of absolute value of the digits, and another example of the kind of conflicting information children have to coordinate in order to decide order relations between numerals.

Obviously, 5 and 6-year olds are not aware of the reasons underlying the "the first one wins" criterion. They do not know that since our system is positional and ruled by recursive grouping in base 10, in bi-digits the rightmost digit stands for two groups of ten whereas the leftmost stands for a power smaller than base 10. However, children do elaborate on the notational consequences of positionality and recursivity in base 10. Their interaction with numerals used in different situations allows them to perceive the regularities. In effect, the fact that sometimes numerals appear in isolation, sometimes in long strings suggests that the number of figures is of some significance. If only isolated digits were presented in the children's environment, they would never realize that this is a relevant criterion for differentiation. Then comes their search for justification of the observed regularities, a search that seems to be enhanced by the need to explain verbally to an interlocutor the reasons for winning or losing, in the context of the kind of games that were used in some of the mentioned studies (e.g., Lerner et al., 1994), or in general when children need to chose a particular numeral.

But if this is so, does a clear understanding of positional value and the additive composition of the system help to understand the functioning of written numbers, or does the use of written numbers facilitate understanding of positional value? To put it in more general terms, is it understanding the underlying basis of the system a condition for understanding how to use written numbers, or does the use of written numeration help to understand its underlying principles and, in a bootstrapping effect, improve its use? The next characteristic of children's path toward written numeration clearly reveals the role of written information.

Some Numbers Count More Than Others

In parallel to the construction of the numerical sequence it seems that children hit on some counting words and also on some written numbers that seem to function as organizers of the sequence but are not learned sequentially. That is, counting words such as 'million' or 'hundred' might be learned before 'sixteen' and numerals such as 100 or 1,000,000 before 16. There might be different factors that explain the ease by which they are learned. Hyperbolic uses of language include these number-words very frequently as in the expression "I've told you hundred times to take out your shoes ...". And these expressions are of very common use in English and in Spanish as well (Colston and O'Brien, 2000). Moreover, rounding numbers is very common in daily talk. We are more likely to say *He earns more than a hundred dollars* than *he earns more than one hundred thirty two dollars*. As for non-verbal numbers, exact tens, hundreds or millions have a clear notational pattern: a figure and zeros and they have an exact correspondence with counting words (in Spanish as well as in English). These characteristics may explain why "round numbers" serve to organize the sequence and sometimes function as prototype of "big numbers". Most 5-year olds' attempts to say "a big number" start with exact tens, or hundreds – round numbers, 10, 100, 500 or 1,000,000.

This task has also served to highlight the links children established between spoken and written numbers and shows in the so called "oral based notations". These notations are based on children's knowledge of "round numbers" and the idea that the order of written numeral follows the order of uttering. Children write for example (60020 for *seiscientos veinte* 'six hundred twenty') they know that six hundred is written 600, and twenty is written 20; following the verbal utterance, they put one after the other. This is the basic pattern, though, as we shall see, there are some important variations.

These "oral based notations" differ from what I have called "analogical notations"; they are obtained by means of different operations. Children use "analogical notations" to fulfil a referential – communicative function. They produce these notations when they are attempting to communicate certain content – – the cardinality of a concrete set of objects. The graphic outcome – the analogical notation shows explicitly, by term-to-term correspondence, how many objects are there in this concrete set. In contrast, oral based notations result from a mapping of one series of numerals (spoken) onto another series of numerals (written) but without implying a referential use. In this kind of notation a verbal numeral is transposed into a written numeral, non-referentially, just mapped onto each other, like in dictation – when a spoken numeral is rendered in a written form – or in a reading task – when a written numeral is rendered orally.

In the next section I will show how the process of understanding written numerals is qualitatively changed when the two kinds of information, the referential information – about cardinality, for example – and the information provided by transposing spoken into written numerals are confronted.

Coordinating Cues

Initially children have no problem with these inconsistencies between pieces of their own knowledge. A notation based on spoken numbers co-exists with a notation based on written numbers. Thus, preschoolers and first graders may use conventional numbers for bi-digits but strictly "oral based notation" for multi-digits. They may write 29 conventionally, but 209 when they attempt to write *twenty nine* (Martínez Ruiz & Tolchinsky Landsmann, 1995).

Is there any representation of magnitude underlying this notation? In other words, are children aware of the referential meaning of 209 in terms of magnitude, for example? Following Power and Del Martello (1990), is there a "semantic interpretation" of the notation that results from transposing a spoken word onto a graphic shape? According to the same authors, "From observational data it seems that children dissociate the transcoding activity from their knowledge about the numerical magnitude represented by the spoken numeral" (p. 100). To illustrate: children compare numerals they have just written: 1000 and 60020, they read the first *thousand* and the second *six hundred twenty* and say that *thousand* is more than *six hundred twenty*. However, when asked the same question for what they have just written they indicate that 60020 is "bigger" than 1000. That is, they accept that *thousand* is more than *six hundred twenty* and that, if a numeral has more figures than another one, it is "bigger", which is correct as far as the two assertions are considered for each sequence – the spoken – and the written, separately. It is correct that thousand is more than six hundred twenty, in the spoken sequence; it is also correct that 60020 is "bigger" than 1000, in the written system. If no referential uses in which consideration of numerical magnitude are involved and no systematic linking between the English counting words and the written representation of these particular words are established, the two assertions are perfectly acceptable.

The point is that, if interaction with the written number system is promoted and children are required to use numbers for different "number assignments" (Wiesse, 2003), a certain conflict starts to emerge. For example, a first grader producing an oral based notation of 10040 for *ciento cuarenta* 'hundred and forty' comments that "it has too many zeros". This may be the first indicator of his awareness of the conflict, certain uneasy feeling about his own production. Other children start to compare their own oral based notations and the notations they have produced for "round numbers". When children realize the conflict between what they know about magnitude and what they know about the role of number of digits in determining magnitude, they resort to a range of solutions. They may change their interpretation, or their written production. Concretely, they start reducing their written notation as a clear attempt to be consistent with the amount of digits that fits better with their idea of magnitude. They have found their way in the written system while using it in different situations.

ON THE ROLE OF WRITING AND WRITTEN NUMBERS

The particular conventions I have analyzed belong each to different notational systems: writing and written numbers. Although in a very abstract sense both conventions relate to the way notational elements are grouped in the graphic space in order to convey meaning, there is nothing about graphic separation between words that children can apply or generalize for understanding positional value or the other way around. The only reason for bringing them together in this chapter is because they illustrate the way in which children's ideas interact with the features of the notational systems and take advantage of their features so as to acquire each system's conventions.

The conventions I have dealt with must be acquired very early. The perusal of a text is rather difficult without separation between words and it is impossible to work out spelling rules without having defined word boundaries. Therefore, it is essential for the child to learn where to produce these boundaries. And, as we have seen, they manage to do this before third grade. However, the rationale under the convention "words must be written with blanks on both sides" is impossible to explain to a 6 or a 7-year old. The features of writing guide children's discovery of written words and also literate adult's conception of what is a word.

It is similar for the positional principle. Although it must be acquired very early in order to operate with numerals, it is very difficult to explain mathematically to a 7-year old. The only possible way of learning about them is by full interaction in use.

It is by being exposed to, and by using, written numbers that children will master numerical writing. Even before using numerals as communicative tools, before grasping the magnitude numerals represent, children are sensitive to the elements and the combinatorial regularities of numerals. Children's knowledge of round numbers, of the importance of number of figures and position in determining value demonstrates that they grasp the regularities of the system. They use both notational and verbal information and in trying to solve notational and arithmetical task they come to grips with the additive structure of written numeration.

If, on the other hand, children's interaction with written numbers and writing is controlled", the discovery of these conventions becomes very difficult. If their access to the full use of writing is regulated slice by slice in a piecemeal way, preventing them from experiencing text writing, because they have not been taught all the letters, they will deprived both of the opportunity to solve problems of separation between words and of the opportunity to learn how to solve them. If the access to the full number sequence is also regulated in such piecemeal way with the idea that understanding of the additive structure or positional value must first be acquired outside the system and only subsequently applied, they are turned into obstacles for understanding the written numeration. If, on the other hand, significant interactions with notational artefacts and with the use and reflection of writing and written numbers are not only allowed but encouraged, the discovery of the conventions of each system will be facilitated.

NOTES

[1] In daily speech it is seldom used *seven-three-two* for 732 but then, from the general intonation, the interlocutor understands that he has to treat this as a whole number and using his knowledge of the written system understand it as *seven hundred thirty two*.

[2] Genre refers to an organizational structure of information. It is a term borrowed from literary analysis and is used in the study of language development to distinguish, for example, between scripts, personal narratives, poetry, etc. in terms of their distinctive content, organization and linguistic features (Hudson & Shapiro, 1991).

[3] Pronominal clitics are unstressed object pronouns that can form a prosodic unit together with an adjacent accented word or they can be morphosyntactically bound, or both. Pronominal clitics must occur with a verb, as they are directly verb related as direct or indirect objects. They can be located preceding the verb as a proclitic, or positioned after the verb as an enclitic. The interest of the category derives from the fact that clitics appear to partake both of the properties of independent words and those of affixes. (Zwicky, 1977, 1985).

[4] Why did we ask for a card that "*is not good for writing (or counting)*"? By asking in that way, we were asking the children to choose a *negative* exemplar, that is, an exemplar that either lacked the features required to be part of the set or had some particular feature that prevented it from being part of the domain. We assumed that selection of negative exemplars would require more careful analyses of the cards than selection of positive exemplars. We reasoned that for selecting exemplars that were part of the domain the children would only have to identify prototypes. On the other hand, in order to decide which cards did not belong to the domain, they would be required to analyses the features, as the selection could not be based on mere identification of prototypical entities. The purpose was then to discover whether the features that lead children to select negative exemplars in the domain of writing are the same as those that lead them to select negative exemplars in the domain of number.

[5] The observed developmental changes do not strictly correspond to age differences that is the reason for the overlaps between the age groups.

[6] There are three basic procedures that children use when counting verbally: *counting all, counting on from the first*, and *counting on from the larger*. The *counting all*, or sum, procedure is analogous to counting manipulative except that the child does not rely on objects to keep track of the count. The procedure involves counting both the augend and the addend starting from 1. To solve the problem 4 + 3 for example the child will count "1, 2, 3, 4, 3, 6, 7, the answer is 7". The *counting on* from the first number involves stating the value of the first number and then counting a number of times equal to the value of the second number, for example, counting "4, 5, 6, 7", to solve 4 + 3. A child using this procedure will count, "3, 4, 5, 6, 7", to solve 3 + 4. The adoption of this more sophisticated procedure requires that the child understand that stating the cardinal value of the first number is in a sense a shortcut to counting that number and that counting does not have to start from 1. The most sophisticated, *counting on from the larger* requires not only an understanding of how the cardinal value that he adds on can be used to make verbal counting more efficient but also an understanding that the order with which numbers are added together.

REFERENCES

Antell, A. & Keating, D. P. (1983). Perception of numerical invariance in neonates. *Child Development, 54*, 695–701.

Aronoff, M. (1994). Spelling as culture. In W.C. Watt (Ed.), *Writing systems and cognition* (pp. 67–88). Dordrecht: Kluwer.

Auzias, M., Casati, I., Cellier, C., Delaye, R. & Verleure, F. (1977). *Écrire à cinq ans? [Writing at five?]*. Paris: Press Universitaire de France.

Bednarz, N. & Janvier, B (1984). La numération: Une stratégie didactique cherchant à favoriser une meilleure compréhension. *N, 34*, 5–17.

Bednarz, N. & Janvier, B. (1984). La numération: Les difficultés suscités par son apprentisage. *N, 33*, 5–31.

Bednarz, N. & Janvier, B (1986). Une étude des conceptions inappropriées dévelopées par les enfants dans l'apprentisage de la numération au primaire. *Journal Europeen de Psychologie de l'Education*, *1–2*, 17–33.

Bednarz, N. & Janvier, B. (1988). A constructivist approach to numeration in Primary school: Results of a three year intervention with the same group of children. *Educational Studies in Mathematics*, *19*, 299–331.

Berthoud-Papandropoulou, I. (1980). *La réflection métalinguistique chez l'enfant*. Geneva: Imprimerie National.

Bertelson, P., Cary, L. & Alegria, J. (1986). Literacy training and speech segmentation. *Cognition*, *24*, 45–64.

Blanche-Benveniste, C. (1997). The units of written and oral language. In C. Pontecorvo (Ed.), *Writing development. An interdisciplinary view* (pp. 21–46). Amsterdam/Philadelphia: John Benjamins Publishing Company.

Blanche-Benveniste, C. & Chervel, A. (1970). *L'orthographe* [*The orthography*]. Paris: Maspero.

Brun, J., Giossi, J. M. & Henriques, A. (1984). A propos de l'écriture décimale [On decimal writing]. *Math-École*, *23*, 2–11.

Bruner, J. (1966). On cognitive growth. In J. Bruner, R. Olver & P. Greenfield (Eds.), *Studies in cognitive growth*. New York: Willey

Catach, N. (1989). *Les délires de l'orthographe*. Paris: Plon.

Clemente, A.R. (1984). La segmentación de textos. El comportamiento evolutivo. *Infancia y Aprendizaje*, *26*, 77–86.

Colston, H.L. and O'Brien, J. (2000) Contrast of kind and contrast of magnitude. The pragmatic accomplishment of irony and hyperbole. *Discourse Processes*, *30*(2), 179–199.

Desborde, F. (1990) *Ideés romaines sur l'écriture*. Lille: Presses Universitaires de Lille.

Dehaene, S. (1997). *Number sense*. London: Allen Lane.

Donald, M. (1991). *Origins of the modern mind: Three stages in the evolution of culture and cognition*. Cambridge, MA: Harvard University Press.

Ferreiro, E. & Teberosky, A. (1979). Los sistemas de escritura en el desarrollo del niño. México: Siglo XXI. [Trans. 1982. *Literacy before schooling*. Exeter, NH: Heinemann Educational Books.]

Ferreiro, E., Pontecorvo, C., Ribeiro Moreira, N. & García Hidalgo, I. (1996). *Chapeuzinho vermelho aprende a escrever* [*Little Red-hood learns how to write*]. Sao Paulo: Atica.

Fuson, K. (1990). Issues in place value and multidigit addition and substraction learning and teaching. *Journal of Research in Mathematical Education*, *21*, 273–280.

Hughes, M. (1986). *Children and number difficulties in learning mathematics*. Oxford: Basil Blackwell.

Kamii, C. (1986). Place value: An explanation of its difficulty and educational implications for the primary grades. *Journal of Research in Childhood Education*, *1*, 75–85.

Kamii, C. & De Clark, G. (1985). *Young children reinvent arithmetics*. New York: Teachers College Press.

Lerner, D. & Sadovsky, P. (1994). El sistema de numeración: Un problema didáctico. In C. Parra & I. Saiz (Eds.), *Didáctica de las matemáticas* [*Didactics of mathematics*] (pp. 95–184). Buenos Aires: Paidos.

Lyon, J. (1968). *Theoretical linguistics*. London: Cambridge University Press.

Mangel, A. (1995) *The history of reading*.

Martínez Ruiz, S. & Tolchinsky Landsmann, L. (1993) La alfabetización numérica. *Cuadernos de pedagogía*.

Moore, D., Benenson, J., Reznick, J.S., Peterson, P. & Kagan J. (1987). Effect of auditory numerical information on infant's looking behavior: Contradictory evidence. *Developmental Psychology*, *23*, 665–670.

Nespor, M. & Vogel, I. (1986). *Prosodic phonology*. Dordrecht : Foris.

Nunes, T. & Bryant, P. (1996). *Children doing mathematics*. Cambridge, MA: Basil Blackwell.

Ong, W. (1982). *Orality and literacy*. London: Methuen.

Parkes, M.B. (1992) *Pause and effect: An introduction to the history of punctuation in the West*. Hats, UK, Scolar Press.

Power, R. & Del Martello, M. (1990). The dictation of Italian numerals. *Language and Cognitive Processes*, *5*, 237–254.

Resnick, L.B. (1983). A development theory of number understanding. In P. Ginsburg (Ed.), *The development of mathematical thinking*. New York: Academic Press.

Reichler Beguelin, M.J. (1990) La notion de "mot" en latin et dans d'autres langues indoeuropéenes anciennes. In M. Fruyt & M.J. Reichler Beguelin (Eds.), *Modeles linguistiques, 12*(1), 2246.

Richards, J. & Carter, R. (1982). *The numeration system*. Paper presented at the Annual Meeting of the American Education Research Association, New York, USA.

Ross, S.H. (1986). *The development of children place value. Numeration concepts in grades 2 through 5*. Paper presented at the Annual Meeting of the American Education Research Association, San Francisco, USA.

Sandbank, A. (2001) On the interplay of genre and writing conventions in early text writing. In L. Tolchinsky (Ed.), *Developmental aspects in learning to write*. Dordrecht: Kluwer.

Sapir, E. (1958). The grammarian and his language. In D.G. Mandelbaum (Ed.), *Selected writings of Edward Sapir in language, culture and personality* (pp. 150–159). Berkeley/Los Angeles: University of California Press. [First published 1924.]

Scheuer, N. (1996). *La construction du système de notation numérique chez l'enfant*. Unpublished dissertation, University of Geneve.

Sinclair, A. & Scheuer, N. (1993). Understanding the written number system: 6 year-olds in Argentina and Switzerland. *Educational Studies in Mathematics, 24*, 199–221.

Sinclair, A., Mello & Siegrist, (1988). La notation numérique chez l'enfant. In H. Sinclair (Ed.), *La production de notations chez le jeune enfant: Language, nombre, rythmes et melodies* (pp. 71–99). Paris: Press Universitaire de France.

Sirat, C. (1994). Handwriting and the writing hand. In W.C. Watt (Ed.), *Writing systems and cognition*. Dordrecht: Kluwer

Slobin, D. (1997). The origins of grammaticizable notions: Beyond the individual mind. In D. Slobin (Ed.), *The crosslinguistic study of language acquisition. Vol. 5* (pp. 265–323). Hillsdale, NJ: Lawrence Erlbaum Associates.

Starkey, P. & Cooper, R.G., Jr (1980). Perception of number by human infants. Science, 200, 1033-1035.

Starkey, P., Spelke, E. & Gelman, R. (1983). Detection of intermodal correspondences by human infants. *Science, 222*, 179-0181.

Strauss, M.S. & Curtiss, L.E. (1981). Infants' perception of numerosity. *Child Development, 52*, 1146–1152.

Teubal, E. & Dockrell, J. (2005). Children's developing numerical notations: The impact of input display, numerical size and operational complexity. *Learning and Instruction*, pp. 257–280.

Tolchinsky, L. & Karmiloff-Smith, A. (1992). Children's understanding of notations as domains of knowledge versus referential-communicative tools. *Cognitive Development, 7*, 287–300.

Tolchinsky Landsmann, L. (1993). *El aprendizaje del lenguaje escrito*. Barcelona: Anthropos.

Van Loosbroek, E. & Smitsman, A.W. (1990). Visual perception of numerosity in infancy. *Developmental Psychology, 26*, 916–922.

Wiese, H. (2003). *Numbers, language and the human mind*. Cambridge: Cambridge University Press.

Zwicky, A.M. (1977). *On clitics*. Bloomington, IN: Indiana University Linguistics Club.

Zwicky, A.M. (1985). Clitics and particles. *Language, 61*, 283–305.

Liliana Tolchinsky
Department of Linguistics
University of Barcelona, Spain

LARA M. TRIONA AND DAVID KLAHR[1]

A NEW FRAMEWORK FOR UNDERSTANDING HOW YOUNG CHILDREN CREATE EXTERNAL REPRESENTATIONS FOR PUZZLES AND PROBLEMS

INTRODUCTION

There are two main approaches to understanding the development of children's notational knowledge: (a) focus on children's learning of different notational systems whose features are based on cultural conventions; and (b) examine unique notations that children create in new situations that may use multiple notational systems. Several chapters in this book use the first approach. For example, Tolchinsky (this volume) focuses on children's use of writing and numerals as sources of knowledge, and Roth (this volume) examines how knowledge and contextual experience facilitate the successful use and interpretation of graphs of creek height. Each of these chapters investigates the ways in which children come to understand and use a notational system that has been invented and conventionalised by others. In this chapter, we use the second approach exploring how children create and evaluate notations in novel situations where multiple notational systems could be used.

This approach is important because children are often faced with the need to create representations for new situations: a science class experiment may require a new method of data representation, a history report may require novel arrangements or notations for different types of information, and both formal games and informal social discourse may require external notations for various kinds of record keeping. Such tasks require that some information is encoded into a representation – or notation[2] – and many different kinds of notations would successfully accomplish this result. The way the task is presented and a person's prior experience with similar tasks will influence how much freedom they will have in creating these representations; however, the tasks in and of themselves do not specify one particular kind of representation over another.

There has been some research that examined these types of tasks (e.g., Bolger & Karmiloff-Smith, 1990; Callaghan, 1999; Cohen, 1985; Eskritt & Lee, 2002; Karmiloff-Smith, 1979; Lee & Karmiloff-Smith, 1996; Triona & Klahr, 2002) but the specific tasks used vary extensively in the types and amount of information that children must represent, as does children's ability to create the representations. In this chapter we introduce a framework that allows systematic comparisons between the different notational tasks, and thereby provides a more coherent picture of the development of children's notational abilities. Our framework distinguishes between different types and amounts of information that

E. Teubal et al. (eds.), Notational Knowledge, 159–178.

must be included in representations and it begins to explore how these differences affect children's ability to generate adequate notations. The framework's most important contribution is to explain the previously incompatible findings, but it also identifies gaps in the existing literature that should be explored in future research.

In this chapter we first describe common features of the various notational tasks that have been studied. Second, we categorize the different kinds of notational tasks based on the types of information required in the representation. Third, we take each type of information and discuss children's experience with that type of information, relating it to the amount of information required for the representation to be adequate. We also examine how children's notational strategy influences their notational task performance. In the final section, we use our framework to suggest some new directions for research on children's notational abilities.

COMMONALITIES BETWEEN NOTATIONAL TASKS

Although there are many differences among the notational tasks, many of them use the same basic paradigm of presenting a task, for example a puzzle, that the children completes a few times and then the child is asked to mark something on paper so that another child could complete the task in the same way. The experimenter introduces the task to the child by describing the task characteristics (e.g., a musical sequence, a puzzle solution), the broad properties of the notation (i.e., the materials to be used, the medium of the notation, etc.), how the notation will be used and by whom. In most cases, memory demands are minimized by ensuring that the task is still present while the child creates the representation. The specifics of the task determine what must be included in a "successful" notation. The wide variability in these task constraints across the studies may partially account for differences between studies.

Both the knowledge about the user and purpose of the representation are needed to evaluate the adequacy of that representation. For example, if a child generates a notation that uses words, then the user of that notation must be able to read the words used in the representation. The user then applies the meaning of the words in the context of the task. If the user is successful in completing the task, then the representation has met its purpose. The purpose of the representation is also important when determining its adequacy because the purpose defines the types of information that need to be included. In many of the investigations involving children's representations, children are informed about some characteristics of the user (e.g., age) and how much the user will know about the task before being shown the representation. In others, the users' knowledge state is not specified explicitly, but is assumed by those judging the notation's adequacy (i.e., by the researchers who are scoring the child's responses).

Our framework organizes the differences in task constraints based on the content necessary in the representations (see Table 1). This method of organizing

Table 1.

Types and amount of information required in different kinds of notational tasks.

Task	Purpose of Representation	Age[a]	Information Type and Amount		
			Object	Location	Sequence
Object Representations					
Callaghan (1999)	Draw a picture that distinguishes among all the objects in a set.	4	5	n/a	n/a
Object and Location Representations					
Eskritt & Lee (2002)	Flip over pairs of cards until matches are found. Allowed to create representation to help child win game faster.	11	18	36	n/a
Sequence and Object or Location Representations					
Cohen (1985)	Observe a sequence of notes played on musical instruments and then create a representation adequate to reproduce the sequence of notes.	8	4	n/a	10
Karmiloff-Smith (1979)	Choose directions (right or left) along a route and record the selections that continue on.	8	n/a	2	20
Sequence, Object, and Location Representations					
Bolger & Karmiloff-Smith (1990)	Solve one of two puzzles and create a representation that another child could use to replicate the solution.	>10	3/6	3/3	7/5[b]
Lee & Karmiloff-Smith (1996)	Solve a puzzle and create a representation that another child could use to replicate the solution.	10	4	4	5-9
Triona & Klahr (2002)	Solve a puzzle and create a representation that another child could use to replicate the solution.	>10	3	4	7-11

[a]Approximate age at which at least 50% of the children created successful representations.
[b]Only minimum number of moves possible reported, average number of moves is unknown.

prior research clarifies the reasons for differing findings about children's ability to create representations. This framework also suggests the importance of analyzing individual representations for their informational content. As we will argue below, these differences account for the wide discrepancies in existing claims about children's notational abilities.

The notational tasks that have been used to study children's representational development can be divided up into four categories: (a) object representations, (b) object and location representations, (c) sequence and object *or* location representations, and (d) sequence, object, and location representations (Table 1, Column 1). Within these categories, which were developed based on the type of informational content required, there is surprising consistency in findings; this contrast the mixture of results seen when all of the studies are compared as one group. In this section we describe in detail the specific features of each of these task categories and how successful children of different ages are in creating adequate representations.

Object Representations

Children have shown the earliest success creating representations for novel tasks when asked to represent objects. Callaghan (1999) asked 2 to 4-year-old children to draw symbols that uniquely identified five objects. Each object differed from a standard object (a small ball) on one of four different dimensions: shape (line), size (large ball), number (three balls), or attachments (a "spider" ball). The purpose of the representation was to direct a second experimenter to choose the right ball when their ears were covered. On the children's first attempt to represent the objects, 20% of the 3 and 4-year-old children drew the objects with all distinguishing features. At the end of the session, 31% of the 3-year-olds and 50% of the 4-year-olds drew notations that uniquely identified each of the five objects. None of the 2-year-olds were successful in distinguished among all the objects, and only 18-25% incorporated any one of the four dimensions in their notations. The 2-year-olds' inability to produce distinctive symbols for the objects is not surprising because none of their free drawings resembled their description. These results suggest that between the ages of 3 and 4, children begin to learn the representational nature of notations. Moreover, about half of the 4-year-olds can provide sufficient information in their notations to distinguish multiple objects, once they are familiarized with the task.

Several other researchers have examined drawing (e.g., Cox, 1992; Golomb, 1981) but Callaghan's research is unique in that children are asked to draw specific objects that can be represented with their current repertoire of marks. Much of their prior research has had children draw complex objects (e.g., a man, tree, and flower) from memory. By having all children draw the same five objects when they are in front of the child, memory is not an issue. Overall, the research on symbolizing objects tasks suggests that children can represent objects in early childhood.

Object and Location Representations

This category of notational tasks requires children to map the locations of multiple objects. There has only been one study that has looked directly at children's ability to create object and location representations. Eskritt and Lee (2002) gave 6 to 13-year-old children the option to produce notations while playing a simple memory game, but notation production was not required. Sixteen pairs of cards were placed picture-side down and children turned over cards in pairs in order to find matching pictures. After playing a game once without the option of creating a notation, the experimenter reset the game and gave the child paper and markers telling him or her to "write or draw anything you want to help you win the game in fewer turns; if you can't think of anything that is okay" (Eskritt & Lee, 2002, p. 256). In order for children's notations to be useful in finding the matches, the notations needed to include accurate representations of the locations for multiple cards. Children under 10 years of age were less likely to produce a notation compared to older children (Eskritt & Lee, 2002) or adults (Eskritt, Lee & Donald, 2001). Even when the younger children did produce notations, most of the representations did not contain any useful information to aid the children's memory (e.g., pictures of people or the names of matches already found). These non-mnemonic representations did not improve performance on the memory game. Instead these children took slightly more turns to complete the game when creating the notation than when not allowed to take notes. These findings suggest that the 6 to 10-year-olds had difficulty knowing what to put into the representation that would help them in playing the game.

The older children (ages 10 to 13 years old) also found creating a useful representation difficult – only 20-25% of them produced notations that represented the locations of more than eight cards (out of a total of the sixteen pairs). In a prior study, even adults were more likely to choose to create a notation when producing it before rather than concurrently with the memory game (Eskritt et al., 2001). During a second experiment the children were allowed to first take notes of the card positions and then play the memory game. Eighty-five percent of the 12 to 13-year-olds, but slightly less than 50% of the 10 to 11-year-olds, produced notations that included a majority of the pairs of cards (Eskritt & Lee, 2002). These results suggest that separating the notation creation and game playing tasks increased the 12 to 13-year-olds' performance to a greater extent than the 10 to 11-year-olds. Overall children had difficulty creating representations for this task especially when compared to their success in other types of tasks. It is expected that if fewer cards and locations were used in this task younger children would be successful in creating representations. In the section describing the informational types, I provide more discussion about the effect of amount of information on children's ability to create representations.

Sequence and Object or Location Representations

Tasks requiring that children create representations of sequences have been used with children over a wide age range. Cohen's (1985) cross-sectional study of 6 to 11-year-olds explored the development of children's ability to notate a musical sequence. An experimenter played a sequence of 9 to 17 "notes" on four different percussion instruments, one at a time, as children marked the information on paper. Before marking, the experimenter told the children that they would need to use their representation to play the musical sequence with the experimenter. Cohen found that there was a significant change in children's ability to notate the musical sequence between age 6 and 8. Before 8 years, the majority of children's notations inadequately represented the musical sequence (i.e., the notation could not be used to replicate the sequence by the experimental raters). As many as 38% of the 6-year-old children produced "holistic" representations. These children would add marks on the paper as each of the instruments was played, but instead of representing the musical sequence, they created one complete picture (e.g., a tree) that did not appear to encode any information about the instruments that were played.[3] The other 6-year-olds had different difficulties when using the representation that they just created. About 24% ignored their own notations when asked to play the sequence, while another 24% used different rules when playing than when creating the notation. Of all the 6-year-olds, 14% created successful representations in which they used the sae rules when creating and using their representations. This lack of coordination between the production and interpretation of their notations suggests that, even though most children can create adequate representations of objects by age 4 (Callaghan, 1999), this ability is tenuous and cannot be extended to notations of sequences two years later.

Of the 7-year-olds, 50% used the same rules for production and interpretation of their representation; however, 83% of all their representations were inadequate – the representations could not be used to replicate the musical sequence. By 8 years and beyond, 5% of the children created adequate representations. Cohen provides little detail about the content of the inadequate notations, but her examples suggest that at least a few children omitted the sequential information about the order that instruments were played and instead included information about how often each instrument was played. In summary, although younger children found it difficult to create notations for the musical sequences, the majority of children created representations that could be used to replicate the sequences by 8 years of age.

Bamberger (this volume) has children create representations of musical sequences similar to Cohen's (1985) research. For this task children are given several bells that may have the same or different pitch, but they all look identical. Children can arrange the physical bells in the external world in whatever manner they choose. Then they create an external representation of a musical sequence based on the organization of the bells. The physical similarity of all the bells regardless of tone creates a dilemma for children in figuring out how to represent the differences and similarities in tone without other differences to use as a reference. An important insight described in Bamberger's chapter is the recognition that multiple bells play the same tone. The chapter does not report age-trends in children's success of this task so it is unclear how the findings of this research fit within the current framework.

Another study that examined children's sequence and object *or* location representations was Karmiloff-Smith (1979). In this study, 8 to 11-year-old children were shown a portion of a route and were asked to choose whether to go to the right or to the left. One choice always led to an immediate dead-end while the other continued on the route. Once a child chose which direction to follow, he or she was show the result of his or her choice, which had a new choice point if it was the direction that continued. Children were asked to mark down the directions as they moved through the series of choice points so that they could use the representation to drive an ambulance on the route and not hit any dead-ends. The route could be identified by referring to the direction (i.e., right or left) or landmarks that were present at most of the choice points. Most children were successful in creating a representation of the sequences of choices. Karmiloff-Smith focused her analyses on changes that occurred in already successful representations, providing little description of the unsuccessful representations.

Children were successful in creating sequence and object *or* location representations by 8 years of age. Younger children, although successful with object representations (Callaghan, 1999), had difficulties creating representations of sequences.

Sequence, Object, and Location Representations

The solution steps of puzzles are another type of sequence that children have been asked to include in notations. Research on sequence, object, and location representations has found that children have more difficulty creating these representations than the sequence and object *or* location representations. Bolger and Karmiloff-Smith (1990) had 8 to 10-year-old children solve modified versions of either the Tower of Hanoi (Klahr & Robinson, 1981) or the Missionaries and Cannibals task (Jeffries, Polson, Razran & Atwood, 1977). The two problem-solving tasks are similar in that both involve moving different objects to different locations in a specific sequence. Children often had difficulty solving the problem, but they did not create their representation until they solved the problem once unaided. The children were asked to create representations to communicate the solution to a peer (same age as participant) and a younger child (6 years old). Only 10% of children created notations that were adequate in encoding the solution. Most children failed "to include necessary spatial or temporal markers" (Bolger and Karmiloff-Smith, 1990, p. 266) in their representations. There is evidence that unsuccessful children were using an appropriate approach because they used one-to-one mapping between their symbols in the representation and the different objects in the problem-solving task. The authors provide no further information about what made the representations unsuccessful. The low rate of successful representations contrast starkly with children's ability to create sequence and object *or* location representations, for which most of the 8 to 10-year-old children created adequate notations.

One explanation for children's inability to create adequate sequence, object, and location representations in Bolger and Karmiloff-Smith (1990) was the complexity of the problems used. Lee and Karmiloff-Smith (1996) had 8 to 11-year-old children created notations of the solution to a simple block puzzle. To solve the problem four puzzle pieces were moved within a confined area to get

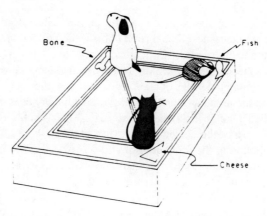

Figure 1. The apparatus for the Dog-Cat-Mouse problem. Each animal must be moved to its favorite food: the dog to the bone, the cat to the fish and the mouse to the cheese. Reprinted with permission from "Solving Problems with Ambiguous Subgoal Ordering: Preschoolers' Performance" by D. Klahr, 1985, *Child Development, 56*, p. 942.

one particular piece to a specific location. There were between five and nine total moves for children to include in their notation and the puzzle was easy for children to solve. As in Bolger and Karmiloff-Smith (1990), children were asked to create one representation for a peer (same age) and one for a younger child (6 years old). More than 90% of the 10 to 11-year-olds' notations contained enough information to communicate the sequence, but the majority of the 8 and 9-year-olds' representations were inadequate. The older children were able to show notational competency with this simpler problem-solving task, but the 8 to 9-year-old children still produced fewer adequate notations than the children in Cohen's (1985) study did for musical sequences.

For a notation of the move sequence to be successful, it needed to include sequential information. This information could be marked explicitly (e.g. numbers or words) or implicitly, relying on page conventions (i.e., left to right or top to bottom). Only 21% of the 10 to 11-year-olds' notations included explicit sequence information compared to 82% of the adults (Lee & Karmiloff-Smith, 1996).

Triona and Klahr (2002) also explored children's ability to generate notations for the purpose of communicating the solution to a puzzle. Children (ages 7 to 9) first solved the Dog-Cat-Mouse puzzle (see Figure 1). This simple problem, borrowed from Klahr (1985), has four corner locations that are connected to form a square with a single diagonal connection from the top-left corner to the bottom-right corner. Three different animals are each positioned in their own corner and can be moved, one at a time, by way of the connections to the empty corner. Children moved the animals around until they reached specific locations. Once children had determined the set of moves, the children were asked to "mark something down" so that another child their age could look at what they marked down and move the animals in the same way. Only 40% of the children successfully represented the sequence of solution steps. Children always created representations that included information about the task but unsuccessful representations were missing sequential information leaving the order to make the moves unknown.

Children as old as 9 and 10 had difficulty creating successful sequence, object, and location representations. But when only two types of information are required, as in the sequence and object or location representations, 8-year-olds are often successful in creating them. In the description of the informational content framework in the next section, we explain this contrast in more depth.

Summary

Children's ability to create successful representations varies substantially depending on which of the four types of tasks are used for the study. Even 4-year-olds are able to incorporate several distinctions between objects in their representations (Callaghan, 1999), but children under 8 years have difficulty creating successful sequence and object or location representations. Creating successful sequence, object and location representations is even more difficult for children; many 8 to 10-year-olds omit crucial information from their representations (Lee & Karmiloff-Smith, 1996). The amount of information needed in the one study of an object and location task made creating representations difficult for even 11 to 13-year-old children. The pattern that emerges from these different notational tasks is as follows: children are first successful with the object representations, then the sequence and object or location representations, and finally the sequence, object, and location representations and the object and location representations. By considering the notation task, a developmental progression in children's ability to create representations appears. This prior research provides evidence that the constraints of the task influences how difficult it is for children to create representations. In the next section, we describe each information type that these tasks required and consider how the amount of information related to children's success in creating representations. This new way of comparing the results of different notational tasks suggests it would be useful to analyze representations by focusing on the informational content.

COMPARING NOTATIONAL TASKS: INFORMATIONAL CONTENT

Children's ability to create representations for these four kinds of tasks relates to differences in the informational content required. In this section, we will elaborate on children's abilities to create and use representations that include each of the three different types of informational content: object information, location information, and sequential information. We also demonstrate that the amount of information necessary influences the difficulty of the notational task. This framework allows for systematic comparisons between the different notation tasks, and thereby provides a more coherent understanding of the development of children's ability to create representations. In the description of each information type, we provide an estimate of the age when children are able to include that type of information in their representations based on prior research.

Object Information

Almost all of the notational tasks required information about particular objects. For example, in Callaghan (1999) children needed to represent five different balls that had different features; and in Eskritt & Lee (2002) children needed to refer to the pictures on the cards in their representation. The one exception to this is Karmiloff-Smith (1979), in which the object (an ambulance) was constant for the tasks and only direction and sequence needed to be included.[4] The object representations only required object information, while all of the other tasks required multiple types of information to be included in the representation.

Although most of the tasks require object information, they differ in the amount of information needed to uniquely identify a particular object. Unfortunately, it is difficult to quantify how much information is needed to specify an object because the distinctiveness of objects varies across the multiple tasks. We address this problem by estimating the amount of information using the total number of objects that are included in the task. The more objects that are in the task, the more demand on the children's working memory to keep track of them. In many cases the more objects, the more information that is required to specify a particular object. In the fourth column of Table 1, the number of objects included in each task is specified. Notice that most of the tasks have between 3 and 5 objects. The one task that has many more objects to represent is Eskritt and Lee's (2002) memory game – this may partially account for the difficulty even older children had with this task.

Children's general ability to represent objects earlier than other kinds of information is not surprising when considering that most children are able to create representational drawings around their third birthday (Cox, 1992; Golomb, 1981). In addition, Callaghan (1999) presents data suggesting that representational drawing on a free drawing trial is related to their success in creating object representations for 2 and 4-year-olds. For 3-year-olds, this relation was not significant because children were more successful creating the object representations than they were in creating a free drawing that was symbolic (as opposed to just scribbling). Late, when children learn to write, they can use words or even design arbitrary symbols to refer to objects.

Young children's facility in including object information does not mean that this skill is fully developed by age 5. First only half of the 4-year-old children were completely successful in distinguishing all five objects in their final representation (Callaghan, 1999). Additionally, Reith and Dominin (1997) found that when asked to represent complex stimuli, children do not portray the figures accurately until age 7, possibly because of their limited fine-motor skills or their lack of knowledge about the stimuli's characteristic features. Children may learn which features are critical to specifying objects through everyday drawing experiences with parents (Bramswell & Callanan, 2003). Of course, children can use other methods besides drawing to refer to objects (e.g., words, arbitrary symbols). This research suggests that children's ability to include object information in their representations develops throughout early childhood.

In summary, object information is required in almost all the notation tasks and children's earliest success in creating representations occurs with tasks in which only object information is required. Over time children develop an ability to clearly identify particular objects by learning which features are crucial to include in the representation.

Location Information

A second kind of information that is required for several notation tasks is location information. The location to move the objects needs to be specified for three or the four types of tasks. Children were successful in creating representation that included locations when they were as young as 8 years old (Karmiloff-Smith, 1979), but had difficulty creating successful representation in more complicated tasks. Eskritt and Lee's (2002) memory game required mapping the locations of several cards that were in a matrix. Children found this task especially difficult – only one quarter of the 10 to 13-year-olds included enough card locations to make their representation beneficial. For each notation task, the number of locations possible is provided in the fifth column of Table 1. Most of the tasks only re-quired distinguishing between a few locations, but Eskritt and Lee's task required distinguishing a large number of locations. The quantity of locations might be another source of children's difficulty in creating successful representations for that task.

Most research on children's understanding of representations of location infor-mation has focused on their use of maps. Children sometimes show characteristic misunderstandings in the correspondence between maps and spaces (e.g., Liben & Downs, 1994, reported children sometimes asserted a road must be red because the line on the map is red). In addition, parents rarely provide deep explanation about the symbolic nature of maps – typically they talk as if young children already understand maps as representational objects (Callanan, Jipson & Soen-nichsen, 2002). However, children as young as 3 years are successful in using maps to determine target locations as long as landmarks can be used as a reference (e.g., Bluestein & Acredolo, 1979). Additional research has found that the use of maps improves children's understanding of large spaces (Uttal, 2000; Lehrer, Ja-cobson, Kemeny & Strom, 1999)). These researchers believe that children require instruction to learn to create mathematically accurate representations of space. Little research has been done asking children to create maps from scratch, so the influence of children's understanding of maps on their ability to represent locations is unknown.

Although children have difficulty in understanding representations of large-scale spatial locations, their capabilities with smaller spaces are most relevant for the notational tasks that have been studied. The research results on produc-ing representations suggest that 8-year-olds are capable of representing location information. For example, location information was often included even in un-successful representations (Triona & Klahr, 2002). Children's ease in representing locations may also be due to the limited number of locations included in the tasks, which allowed representations to refer to direction (e.g., right, left, up, bottom). In the task where children did have difficulty creating successful representations (i.e., Eskritt & Lee, 2002) there were thirty-six locations; thus referring to the direction was not enough information to specify a particular location.

The research on children's understanding of location information in representations finds that children have some difficulties when using maps, but, by 8 years of age, they can successfully create representations that incorporate location information for a variety of tasks. Success may be dependent on the small spaces used in the notation tasks and the limited number of locations that needed to be distinguished.

Sequential Information

The third type of information required for some of these tasks is sequential information. The primary difference between the two types of notation tasks that require sequence information is in the amount of other types of information that need to be included in the representation. Children have more difficulty with the tasks that require all three kinds of information (i.e., sequence, object, and location representations) than those that only require two types of information (i.e., sequence and object *or* location representations). Most 8-year-old children can create successful representations for the two information type tasks, but children of this age had difficulty creating successful representations for the tasks that required all three types of information.

In the set of studies reviewed here, complexity of problem appears to be more related to the difficulty of creating representations than the length of the sequence. Although the length of the sequences did not vary much across tasks (see last column of Table 1), children had less difficulty representing the longest sequence (Karmiloff-Smith, 1979) compared with the shorter sequences (Bolger & Karmiloff-Smith, 1990; Lee & Karmiloff-Smith, 1996). But children were less likely to create successful representations for more complicated problems, such as Tower of Hanoi (Bolger & Karmiloff-Smith, 1990), than for simpler problems, such as the blocks puzzle (Lee & Karmiloff-Smith, 1996). It is possible that children's difficulty in figuring out the solution to the problem left fewer cognitive resources available to design the representation.

The contrast between sequence and object *or* location representations and sequence, object, and location representations is interesting because the primary distinction between them is the total number of types of information to be included. Children are more successful in creating representations when the task only requires two types of information than when the task requires all three types of information. Another potential difference is that the sequence, object, and location representations use problem-solving tasks, which have children determine the sequence to be included in the representation, while the sequence and object *or* location tasks tend to use simple sequences that are provided to the children by the experimenter. However, Karmiloff-Smith's (1979) sequence and object *or* location task had children figure out the route that they were including in the representation. The distinguishing feature between the two types of tasks is the number of types of information needed.

The extra difficulty of three types of information relative to two types may be related to the availability of only two-dimensions on paper. For the sequence and object or location tasks, which only requires two types of information, children often will use one of the dimensions to implicitly include sequence in their representations. For example, in Karmiloff-Smith's (1979) children would often use the horizontal dimension to represent the direction and the vertical dimension to represent sequential information. Similar representations were created for Cohen (1985); a few children used one of the spatial dimensions for sequential information and different icons for each instrument. However, for sequence, object, and location representations, three types of information are required in the two dimensions. Children under 10 years often fail to include all three types of information in their representations for these tasks (e.g., Bolger & Karmiloff-Smith, 1990; Lee & Karmiloff-Smith, 1996). For many of these representations children would include both object and location information in the two dimensions, but failed to include sequential information (e.g., Bolger & Karmiloff-Smith, 1990; Lee & Karmiloff-Smith, 1996; Triona & Klahr, 2002). This depends on children relying on figural methods to represent the information, because if children use language, order conventions (e.g., left to right and top to bottom) provide implicit order and objects and locations can be described using words.

Another possible explanation for children's difficulty in including all three types of information in their representations is their focus on objects to the exclusion of sequential information. Lee and Karmiloff-Smith (1996) examined the hypothesis that children preferred redundant object information over explicit sequential information. They asked children to choose the best of two adequate representations: (1) a notation that redundantly referred to the objects (i.e., referring to the puzzle piece by both the colour and number) but only implicitly referred to the sequence (i.e., ordering moves from top to bottom), and (2) a notation that only used one attribute to refer to the object (i.e., color) and explicitly refers to the sequence (i.e., with numbers). It is important to recognize that both of these notations were adequate in the sense that the notation could be used to replicate the sequence. Participants' choice of the best notation reveals which kind of additional information they considered more useful: extra information about which puzzle piece to move or explicitly marking sequential information. An overwhelming majority of the children (8 to 11 years old) preferred redundant information about the object whereas the majority of adults preferred explicit information about the sequence.

For another pair of representations, the implicit sequential information was ambiguous (i.e., both left to right and top to bottom conventions were used for diagrams), making the redundant object information representation more difficult to use than the explicit sequence representation. For this choice, 8 to 9-year-old children still preferred redundant object information; however, the older children were at chance in choosing between explicit sequential information and redundant object information. The results from this forced choice task suggests that the reason children's notations are missing sequential information goes beyond a simple failure to remember its necessity when creating the notation. Explicit sequential information is less important to younger children than object references, but as they get older, children begin to appreciate the importance of including temporal information in their notations.

Overall, children have particular difficulty with the inclusion of sequential information, especially when all three types of information are required.

Summary

Table 1 presents the amount of each type of information that the different notation tasks required. It is clear from this table that the tasks in which the youngest children are successful require less information than the other notation tasks. The youngest children succeed in the task that only requires object information (i.e., Callaghan, 1999), while even older children found difficult the task that required many locations and objects (i.e., Eskritt & Lee, 2002), or that required all three types of information in the representation (i.e., Bolger & Karmiloff-Smith, 1990).

It is important to understand that the kinds of information required in a representation depend on the purpose of the representation. For example, Eskritt and Lee's (2002) object and location representations do not require any sequential information even though each pair of cards is turned over in sequence. A few of the unsuccessful representations included a list of the cards in the order that they were turned over. This representation would have been appropriate if the purpose was to use the representation to replicate the sequence instead of knowing the location. In a similar manner, some of the unsuccessful representations from Cohen (1985) showed how often each instrument was played in the musical sequence instead of the sequence to play the instruments.

In addition, other kinds of information could be required in different notation tasks. For example, none of these tasks required the quantity or duration to be specified but some research has examined children's invented representations of number (Bialystok & Codd, 1996), addition (Hughes, 1986) and rhythm (Bamberger, 1982). This framework does not provide an exhaustive list of kinds of information that can be included in representations. Instead it begins to clarify the differences in content that serve as possible causes for the variability in children's ability to create representations for these notational tasks.

BEYOND TASK CONSTRAINTS: CHILDREN'S NOTATIONAL STRATEGIES

The framework clearly correlates the demands of the notation tasks with age-related changes in children's ability to create successful representations. The easiest type of tasks – for which even young children are successful – requires only one type of information. The hardest tasks require three types of information or a large number of locations and objects in the representation. However, there are within-age differences in children's performance that are left unexplained by only taking task constraints into account. Examining the notational strategies that children use allows for the sources of these individual differences in success to be determines. Strategy use has been studied extensively in mathematics and other domains (Shrager & Siegler, 1998; Siegler & Svetina, 2002; Kuhn, Black, Keselman & Kaplan, 2000), but there has been limited consideration of strategy in notational research. This oversight is huge because the strategy constrains how information is included in the representation; these constraints could benefit or detract from children's notational success. In this section, we will go over the limited discussion of the influence of strategy on notational adequacy and briefly discuss some research from our laboratory that begins to address this issue.

Several researchers have created categories for the different kinds of representations that children create. For example, Karmiloff-Smith (1979) described five different kinds of representations that children created for the route task. This categorization focused on the overall organization of the representation particularly paying attention to whether the choice points were abstracted from the route. Bolger and Karmiloff-Smith (1990) took a different approach and instead counted the number of words and pictures in the representations. They focused on the particular elements used rather than on the overall organization of the representation because it was common for children's representations to include both pictures and words. Both of these studies used these categorizations as descriptive tools for understanding the kinds of representations rather than as correlated of the adequacy of the representations. However, the overall adequacy of participants' representations from both of these studies was at the extremes. Almost all of the children successfully represented the route task (Karmiloff-Smith, 1979) while almost none of the children successfully represented the problem solutions sequences used for Bolger and Karmiloff-Smith's (1990) study. The large variability in the children's notational strategies was not used to predict whether children were successful.

Another approach to categorizing different notational strategies distinguishes between figural representations, which use primarily pictures and figures, and linguistic representations, which primarily use words and sentences. This distinction is related to the notational system used, but is not exclusive; figural representations might include linguistic labels, and linguistic representations might include figural features (e.g., a color dot instead of the color name). Lee and Karmiloff-Smith (1996) separately evaluated the adequacy of linguistic and figural representations and found that children's linguistic representations were more adequate than their figural representations. They hypothesize that the difference is primarily due to the omission of sequential information from figural representations, but did not specifically test this by analyzing the informational content of the representations. Adults were just as likely to create figural representations as children; however, the adequacy of adults' representations did not vary by notational type.

In our research (Triona & Klahr, 2002), we examined the types of representations that children created for the solution to the Dog-Cat-Mouse problem (see Figure 1). In analyzing the representations children created, we coded adequacy as an overall indicator of how well the representation communicated the problem solution sequence. In addition, we coded the types of information that the child in-a)

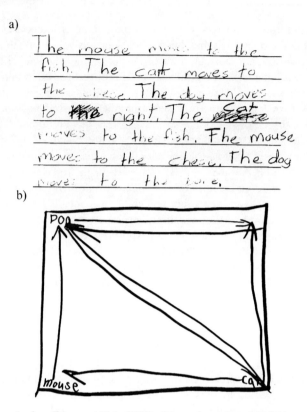

The mouse moves to the fish. The cat moves to the cheese. The dog moves to the right. The cat moves to the fish. The mouse moves to the cheese. The dog moves to the hole.

b)

Figure 2. Examples from Triona and Klahr (2002) of the representations that children created of the Dog-Cat-Mouse problem. (a) The linguistic representation includes object, location and sequential information, while (b) the figural representation includes only object and location information.

cluded in the representation (i.e., object, location, and sequential). Borrowing Lee and Karmiloff-Smith's distinction between figural and linguistic representations, we replicated their finding that linguistic representations were more successful than figural representations. Figure 2 shows typical examples of figural and linguistic representations. In analyzing the types of information that were included in their representations we found that both kinds of representations included object and location information. However, only 20% of the figural representations included sequential information. Of the three types of required information, only the sequential information was missing from the inadequate figural representations while 100% of the linguistic representations included sequential information.

In order to understand the difference in the inclusion of sequential information, we coded sequential information as implicit, based on English conventions of left to right and top to bottom, or explicit, using numbers to explicitly specify the order of the moves. The majority of linguistic representations included sequential information implicitly, while the few figural representations that included sequence did so explicitly. These results suggest the automatic implicit inclusion of sequential information in linguistic representations benefited the adequacy of children's representations.

In Triona and Klahr (2002), children created four different representations of Dog-Cat-Mouse solutions and used their prior representation before creating the next. Despite the poor adequacy of many of the representations, very few children switched the type of representation they created (e.g., from figural to linguistic) over the four trials. This intriguing finding means that the relation between strategy and informational content could not be separated from children's knowledge because children selected both. It is possible that children's knowledge about sequence guided their strategy choice, such that awareness of the need to include sequence lead children to choose a linguistic strategy whereas lack of this knowledge lead children to choose a figural strategy. However, it is also possible that it is the constraints of the strategy that influences the inclusion of sequential information – regardless of whether the children know about including sequence, it maybe that the implicit nature of sequential information in linguistic representations results in its inclusion, while the difficulty of figuratively including sequential information leads to its omission. To tease apart these alternative explanations, a follow-up study is needed in which children created both figural and linguistic representations.

Further research is needed to understand the role strategies play in children's ability to create adequate representations. Prior research suggests that strategies may influence the types of information that children include in their representation, but these studies have not teased apart children's knowledge and the strategy used. By using the framework to analyze individual children's inclusion of the various kinds of information, future research could better understand the interaction between children's notational strategy, adequacy, and informational content of representations.

FUTURE RESEARCH DIRECTIONS

The framework presented in this chapter reveals several gaps in the literature to date. Few studies have used multiple notational tasks and none have strategically examined the influence of different types and amounts of information required by the task. Research is also needed to examine how other informational types affect children's notational abilities. Further research is required to understand the role strategy plays in the types of informational content included.

The framework makes it clear studies that systematically vary the types and amount of information are needed. The review presented in this chapter provided a clearer explanation for disparate findings based on the framework, but the framework needs to be tested directly in a single study. Researchers can operationally define amount of information when the same task is used with more or less of the same information. Comparing children's ability to create representations with different amounts of information will help our understanding of why more objects are more difficult for children to represent. Because changing the types of information requires changing the task, systematically exploring the effects of having multiple types of information will be more difficult. One possibility is to have several versions of the same task in which the purpose of the representation is manipulated so as to make one, two, or three types of information necessary for representational adequacy. Another potential study could have three different tasks that all use the same objects. Although it will be challenging to design a study to explore the effect of different types of information, it is a crucial test of the current framework's assertion that different informational types influence children's ability to create representations.

As noted earlier, the three types of information that are described in the framework do not represent an exhaustive list of possible types of information that could be required in a representation. Research is needed that expands the number of required information types. One potential direction is to examine the need to include quantity information rather than sequence information. In addition, duration may also be a useful information type to examine. By exploring more types of information we will better understand the types of information that children are successful in representing and the types of information that they find difficult to represent.

Another important question the framework highlights is how notational strategy influences the informational content. Clearly children's ability to create notations varies by age depending on the type of information required, but within age variations in children's success maybe explained by the notational strategy that children use. Research is needed which has children use multiple strategies to create a representation of the same task. This would allow for the role of strategy to be separated from children's prior knowledge. This line of research would also link the research described in this chapter, which examines notations that children choose to create in new situation, to the notational research that focuses on children's learning of particular notational systems. Understanding how children's strategies affect the adequacy of their representations will begin to show how children connect their knowledge of multiple notational systems.

Throughout this chapter we have identified some key differences among different notational tasks that explain the divergent results of the various studies. By understanding the informational content required by the task, we can explain the developmental pattern of findings across a wide range of tasks. We also discuss the need to look beyond the task constraints to understand the variability in children's success within one particular task. Future research needs to explore the gaps in the literature highlighted by this framework. By systematically varying the types of notational tasks used in studies, we can better understand how children's ability to create representations develops with age and experience using different notational strategies.

NOTES

[1] This work was supported in part by grants from NICHHD (HD25211) and NSF (BCS 0132315) to the second author. The development of this framework was part of the first author's dissertation thesis and portions of this work were presented at the meeting of the Society for Research in Child Development, April 2003, Tampa, FL.

[2] We use the terms "notation" and "representation" interchangeably in this chapter, and our use of "representation" always means an observable external representation, rather than a hypothesized internal representation of the kind used in cognitive theories.

[3] In early art education, children are sometimes asked to create drawings while listening to music to help children develop their creativity. It is possible that children are overextending this behavior into the music task, which is supposed to be symbolic rather than just creative. It is unknown whether this practice was common in the schools that these children attended.

[4] Although there were landmarks that were along the route, which children could include as part of their representation, they needed to identify the direction to follow by indicating whether to go the direction with the landmark or without the landmark. This is why this task is considered to require sequence and location information only.

REFERENCES

Bamberger, J. (1982). Revisiting children's drawings of simple rhythms: A function for reflection-in-action. In S. Strauss & R. Stavy (Eds.), *U-shaped behavioral growth* (pp. 191–226). New York: Academic Press.

Bamberger, J. (2007). Restructuring conceptual intuitions through invented notations (this volume).

Bialystok, E. & Codd, J. (1996). Developing representations of quantity. *Canadian Journal of Behavioural Science, 28*(4), 281–291.

Bluestein, N. & Acredolo, L.P. (1979). Developmental changes in map-reading skills. *Child Development, 50*(3), 691–697.

Bolger, F. & Karmiloff-Smith, A. (1990). The development of communicative competence: Are notational systems like language? *Archives de Psychologie, 58*(226), 257–273.

Braswell, G.S. & Callanan, M.A. (2003). Learning to draw recognizable graphic representations during mother-child interactions. *Merrill-Palmer Quarterly, 49*(4), 471–494.

Callaghan, T.C. (1999). Early understanding and production of graphic symbols. *Child Development, 70*(6), 1314–1324.

Callanan, M.A., Jipson, J.L. & Soennichsen, M.S. (2002). Maps, globes, and videos: Parent-child conversations about representational objects. In S.G. Paris (Ed.), *Perspectives on object-centered learning in museums*. Mahwah, NJ: Lawrence Erlbaum Associates.

Cohen, S.R. (1985). The development of constraints on symbol-meaning structure in notation: Evidence from production, interpretation, and forced-choice judgments. *Child Development, 56*(1), 177–195.

Cox, M.V. (1992). *Children's drawings*. London: Penguin Group.

Eskritt, M. & Lee, K. (2002). "Remember where you last saw that card": Children's production of external symbols as a memory aid. *Developmental Psychology, 38*(2), 254–266.

Eskritt, M., Lee, K. & Donald, M. (2001). The influence of symbolic literacy on memory: Testing Plato's hypothesis. *Canadian Journal of Experimental Psychology, 55*(1), 39–50.

Golomb, C. (1981). Representation and reality: The origins and determinants of young children's drawings. *Review of Research in Visual Arts Education, 14*(1), 36–48.

Hughes, M. (1986). *Children and number: Difficulties in learning mathematics*. Oxford: Basil Blackwell.

Jeffries, R., Polson, P.G., Razran, L. & Atwood, M.E. (1977). A process model for Missionaries – Cannibals and other river-crossing problems. *Cognitive Psychology, 9*(4), 412–440.

Karmiloff-Smith, A. (1979). Micro- and macrodevelopmental changes in language acquisition and other representational systems. *Cognitive Science, 3*(2), 91–117.

Klahr, D. (1985). Solving problems with ambiguous subgoal ordering: Preschoolers' performance. *Child Development, 56*(4), 940–952.

Klahr, D. & Robinson, M. (1981). Formal assessment of problem-solving and planning processes in preschool children. *Cognitive Psychology*, *13*(1), 113–148.

Kuhn, D., Black, J., Keselman, A. & Kaplan, D. (2000). The development of cognitive skills to support inquiry learning. *Cognition and Instruction*, *18*(4), 495–523.

Lee, K. & Karmiloff-Smith, A. (1996). The development of cognitive constraints on notations. *Archives de Psychologie*, *64*(248), 3–26.

Lehrer, R., Jacobson, C., Kemeny, V. & Strom, D. (1999). Building on children's intuitions to develop mathematical understanding of space. In E. Fennema & T.A. Romberg (Eds.), *Mathematics classrooms that promote understanding* (pp. 63–87). Mahwah, NJ: Lawrence Erlbaum Associates.

Liben, L.S. & Downs, R.M. (1994). Fostering geographic literacy from early childhood: The contributions of interdisciplinary research. *Journal of Applied Developmental Psychology*, *15*(4), 549–569.

Reith, E. & Dominin, D. (1997). The development of children's ability to attend to the visual projection of objects. *British Journal of Developmental Psychology*, *15*(2), 177–196.

Roth, W.-M. (2007). Graphing Hagan Creek (this volume).

Shrager, J. & Siegler, R. (1998). SCADS: A model of children's strategy choices and strategy discoveries. *Psychological Science*, *9*(5), 405–410.

Siegler, R. & Svetina, M. (2002.) A microgenetic/cross-sectional study of matrix completion: Comparing short-term and long-term change. *Child Development*, *73*(3), 793–809.

Tolchinsky, L. (2007). Writing and written numbers as source of knowledge (this volume).

Triona, L.M. & Klahr, D. (2002). Children's developing ability to create external representations: Separating what information is included from how the information is represented. In *Proceedings of the Twenty-Fourth Annual Conference of the Cognitive Science Society*, p. 1044.

Uttal, D.H. (2000). Seeing the big picture: Map use and the development of spatial cognition. *Developmental Science*, *3*(3), 247–286.

Lara M. Triona
Department of Psychology
University of California
Santa Cruz, USA

David Klahr
Department of Psychology
Carnegie Mellon University, USA

WOLFF-MICHAEL ROTH

GRAPHING HAGAN CREEK

A Case of Relations in Sociomaterial Practice

INTRODUCTION

Over the past decade, it has almost become a truism to say that the mathematics in school and the mathematics in everyday settings are considerably different, and often incommensurable. However, it is much less evident what the competencies are that people bring to (implicitly or explicitly) mathematical tasks in everyday situations. In the following episode, Nadely, a beginning mathematics and science teacher visits a farm that is part of a movement in the valley to improve the health of a local creek and watershed. She meets with Karen, a water technician working on the farm and paid by – to a considerable extent – a grant from a governmental agency. Karen is also part of an environmentalist movement that has taken as its goal to improve the watershed and to design the creek, its riparian zones, and the practices of the people living in it.

One of the first things Karen shows Nadely is the water monitoring station, which essentially consists of a pen chart recorder that continuously inscribes water levels on a paper roll. In the following excerpt, Karen reads the graph and provides some explanations. In the process, she points and moves along the graph using deictic and iconic gestures (Figure 1).

```
01   K: So, this [b] is a twenty-four hour time period, so time's going this way on
02      the graph, so a day ago [a] the flow was about fifty liters a second higher
03      and each square going this way is about [b] thirteen liters a second. So,
04      we were kind of, I guess we had a bit of rain yesterday [a] or the day be-
05      fore, and we've got a bit of a peak from that rainfall event [a]. In the
06      summer, [c] the flow goes down to about ⌈here and        ⌉
07   N:                                         ⌊Oh, whoa!⌋
08   K: that's equivalent to about. . . . This summer was pretty good, about
09      twenty liters a second. But it can go down to about eleven, and that's, for
10      fish to survive in this creek, we need about twenty.
11   N: Oh, okay.
12   K: So, when we get low, the fish will find a pool somewhere to hide and if it
13      weren't for these deep areas, in little pockets, throughout watershed, they
14      are sort of hiding and laying low until volumes have come up.
```

E. Teubal et al. (eds.), Notational Knowledge, 179–207.

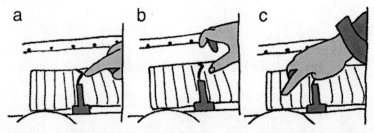

So, this [b] is a twenty-four hour time period, so time's going this way on the graph, so a day ago [a] the flow was about fifty liters a second higher and each square going this way is about [b] thirteen liters a second. So, we were kind of, I guess we had a bit of rain yesterday [a] or the day before, and we've got a bit of a peak from that rainfall event [a]. In the summer, [c] the flow goes down to about here.

Figure 1. Karen, the water technician, reads the graph to Nadely, the practicum teacher. The graph is "in-the-making", still on the pen chart plotter in the monitoring station at the farm where Karen works.

The first part of this reading (lines 01–10) is not unlike what one might expect a reading of a graph to look like. The reading appears to be able to exist by itself, no different from the decontextualized readings that are often required from students in research on graphing. But then it becomes quite clear that Karen's graph-reading practices exist with respect to much more.

Karen situates her talk about summer water levels (lines 08–10). Normally there are about twenty liters/second of water flowing past her monitoring site. In and of itself, this number does not tell us very much. Sense arises from the mediated relations that exist in activity settings. When summer levels can go as low as eleven liters/second, the value of twenty is already put into a new relation. Another time, she suggested that the volume, "last year was quite high, twenty-seven liters per second". For the innocent reader unfamiliar with the historical context of flow volumes, a graph that has volume values around twenty liters/second makes little sense. For Karen, on the other hand, the twenty liters/second do not exist independently of the other possible summer values, and the variations within and across seasons (see also Figure 6c). For her, the graph exists in relation to many other things she does and knows in this watershed and on her farm (Figure 2). In contrast to the eleven and twenty-seven liter/second volumes that are, in Karen's descriptive language, "low" and "quite high", we get a sense of the variability of summer flows. Furthermore, Karen's understanding does not stop with the numerical values of the volumes. She knows about fish and the conditions they need (lines 12–14). She is familiar with the temperatures that go with different water levels and, in turn, influence the conditions of the water as habitat. For Karen, all of this is part of what constitutes her competent reading of this graph at this time.

Karen also talks about fish, though these have little to do with her work on the farm. Yet the fish Karen talks about are not abstract objects somewhere out there. Rather, they are intimately related to her activities in her watershed-related world. She participates in capturing the trout in traps for measurement purposes,

Figure 2. Karen, the water technician, is intimately familiar with the valley (left), where her farm is located, and Hagan Creek (right), which she has studied closely as part of her involvement in the environmentalist group.

counts them making use of an electroshock device, and brings them to the surface by throwing small spitball-sized chewed paper into the pools. She knows that the trout prefer the areas below the riffles that she builds, where the water has a higher dissolved-oxygen (DO) content as indicated by her DO meter. She is familiar with the accounts given by elders from the nearby First Nations village. They still talk about the eighteen-inch cutthroat that they used to fish in the creek. Karen has read the notebook entries of the local priest who was able to capture a dozen trout in the course of one morning. That is, there is more to Karen's explanation than the graph as such. What she says here is only figure against a complex ground of embodied and distributed, practical understandings of this world. The object of her knowing is first and foremost the creek, knowledge *of* the creek, while the graph is *one* of the tools mediating her knowledge *about* the creek. Her talk is about the summer and about fish that need a certain amount of water. I suggest that Karen's reading of the graph – in fact, her competency – derives from a dense network of activities, practices, and facts. It is this dense network to other graphs, instruments, and practices that situates Karen's competency and allows these graph-related competencies to exist in the first place.

The excerpt shows two further aspects. First, without the gestures, it is virtually unknowable what the referent of Karen's talk is. So as a first step, we include these as part of our analysis. Furthermore, Karen's gestures and talk do not stand on their own but are over and about the graph. They are *about* the graph, that is, the graph is the topic of Karen's talk. But importantly, the talk is also *over* the graph in the sense that the latter serves as indexical ground. It therefore makes sense to use a cognitive unit of analysis that includes the entire performance, talk and gesture, and the graph. Second, graph reading exists in a social nexus: It matters whether a reading occurs as part of an interview for research purposes or whether it occurs as part of a person's ongoing work (Roth & Lee, 2004). In the present situation, the two participants contribute to establishing their mutual roles: Nadely constitutes herself, and is constituted, as a listener; Karen is the presenter, as she talks about her work and how the graph inscribes itself in the practices. But she does not just narrate irrespective of the listener. Nadely signals that she is still with the narrative at those points where breaks in the narration allow her to take a turn (lines 07, 11). This pattern is changed only once when Nadely expresses amazement about the extreme low levels of water during the summer months.

In the past, much research on mathematical knowing has focused on models of mind irrespective of the societal activity within which it occurs. This approach is being questioned, for it neglects the contexts that enable cognition to exist in the first place. Here, context is viewed as the historically constituted concrete relations within and between situations (e.g., Lave, 1988). I take the view that knowledge is not an entity that can be acquired but rather that knowing is equivalent to acting in the world; knowing is a process rather than a state. Knowing arises from historically constituted (concrete) relations within and between sociomaterial[1] situations and involves the individual body as much as the individual mind. The body-mind ensemble is an indissociable sociomaterial entity subject to be formed by the sociomaterial world to which it is connected and that embeds it. I am therefore interested in the position that "the relational dynamics [between sign and practice] are not created inter-subjectively in any simple sense, but are produced in relation to aspects of social practice which are culturally and historically specific" (Walkerdine, 1988, p. 12).

I begin by contextualizing my work in two ways. First, because graphs have sign functions, I provide a brief overview of a semiotic approach to graphing (see also Roth, 2003). Second, as the introductory analysis of Karen's work shows, graphs are embedded in numerous other relations requiring an expanded framework. I present one such framework derived from activity theory. After a brief exposition of the research context in which the data were collected, I provide detailed analyses of the relations that are constitutive elements in Karen's knowing. I end this chapter with a consideration of possible implications of this work for developmental issues in mathematical knowing.

SIGNS AND SIGNING PROCESSES

In the past, philosophy of language assumed two separate domains – world and signs (symbols, language) – separated by a deep gulf. This gulf had to be transgressed through correspondences (Figure 2a). Scientists presuppose a structural isomorphism between structure of the world and mathematical structure (signs). This isomorphism, expressed in the form of Wilson's couplet "Fundamental Structure ↔ Mathematical Structure" (Lynch, 1991), is embodied in the mapping of Figure 3a. However, there is evidence that this isomorphism is an illusion and that the isomorphism may be the outcome of scientists' work rather than a pre-existing condition. Thus, cognitive scientists faced a problematic gulf in the guise of the question, "How do the symbols [which are the basis of information processing] ever come to relate to the things in the world?" That is, cognitive scientists came to identify the "grounding problem" as its major challenge. In the psychology of mathematics education, the problem surfaced as referential isolation, the fact that for many individuals, the mathematics of the classroom existed

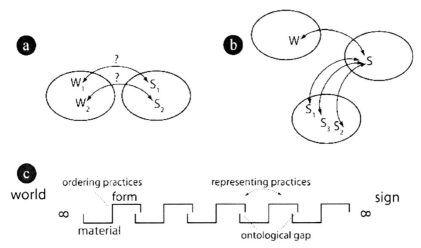

Figure 3. (a) Different views on the relationship between sign and the world. World and sign have long been considered to be separate domains, which were linked by correspondences, referential functions. (b) The relationship between a sign and its referent is elaborated by another relationship of the original sign with another sign, said to be its interpretant. Because there are potentially many interpretants, semioticians speak of an infinite process of interpretation, or infinite semiosis. (c) A potentially infinite chain of signification relates world to language (Latour, 1993). Each element is at the same time a sign for the previous element, and the referent for the subsequent element. Between elements, there is an ontological gap. Within each element, material can be given form. These gaps are navigated by means of shared social (representing) practices, which establish and control the relations.

separately from events in the world (e.g., Greeno, 1988). This separation was of particular importance in those situations where psychologists of mathematics education saw that mathematics could be applied (i.e., there was said to be a structural equivalency).

Researchers in the social studies of science have come to question the existence of such an isomorphism. They bracket Wilson's couplet and thereby make it to a phenomenon to be researched rather than to be accepted a priori. The resulting research focuses on the practices by means of which such things as soil samples, screaming rats, or defecating lizards come to be represented in mathematical (Roth & Bowen, 1999). At every step of the way, we encounter elementary forms of mathematical practices that always involve the physical body of the researcher. The gap seemingly disappears in the practices of the scientists who enact continuous series of transformations. This research aligns itself with semiotics, a line of research concerned with the relation between signs and things in the world relatively little consulted by mathematics educators.

For nearly one hundred years, semioticians (e.g., Peirce, Saussure, and Eco) have researched the relationship between world and language, signs and their referents (Nöth, 1990). They recognized that there existed an ontological gap between signs and their referents. Those following the path of Charles Sanders Peirce propose that while we cannot close the gap, we can always superpose another, sign-sign relation on top of the first relation. This second relation between a sign and another sign, its interpretant, elaborates the first relation, which remains inaccessible in principle (Figure 3b). For example, the sign /dog/ refers to some aspect of the world. The relation between the sign /dog/ and the class of entity, "dog", that it refers to can be elaborated by other signs such as a drawing, the equivalent in another language (e.g., chien [French], Hund [German]), a metaphoric use such as /fidelity/, and so forth. Here, each production of an interpretant sign constitutes a translation of the original sign. The process of translation (interpretation) is unlimited, because there are many, potentially an infinite number of interpretant signs (Figure 3b). Semioticians refer to this process as unlimited semiosis.

When we follow scientists (or any other individual involved in sign production), we begin to notice a series of (potentially infinite) translations. These translations turn, for example, living lizards caught somewhere in the mountains of the Pacific Northwest into a statement such as "there is a significant correlation between lizard sprint speed and leg length". This statement itself translates and is translated by a graph or statistical information (e.g., p, r, R^2). (For a detailed ethnographic study of such activities, see Roth, 2004.) For example, a two-column table of numbers and a Cartesian graph are equivalent because of established practices, not because there is an inherent logical connection between the two. Similarly, a mathematical function such as $f[x] = x^2 - 3$ and a parabolic curve on a Cartesian graph are equivalent because of established and shared mathematical practices, not because of some internal logical relation.

Following scientists around we come to see chains of elements – each of which plays the role of sign for the previous element and the role of thing/matter for the next, giving rise to a chain of signification (Figure 3c). That is, each element constitutes a map for the previous element, its territory; in turn, it becomes territory for the subsequent element. It is important to note, however, the consecutive elements are separated by an ontological gap. The links across each gap are established as a matter of sociomaterial practices common within and constitutive of particular communities. This view is commensurable with semiotic processes operating at multiple hierarchical scales in which elements to the right in Figure 2c are the objects of an element in the middle, which themselves are signs in a system of interpretants (Lemke, 2002). The semiotic processes relating to the lines of graphs themselves are inscribed in topological semiotics, whereas entities such as the variables (axes labels) inscribe themselves in typological semiotics (Lemke, 2000).

GRAPHING AND ACTIVITY SYSTEMS

Traditionally, sign-reference relationship was the primary object of research in mathematical cognition. More recently, it has been recognized that this relationship is not independent of the community of interpreters, which led me to a semiotic approach. But even considering the community of interpreters is insufficient to account for mathematical understanding; that is, a semiotic analysis is

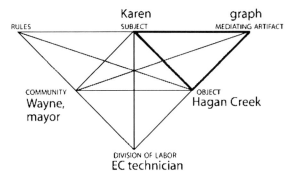

Figure 4. The activity constitutes the basic, irreducible unit of analysis in the present study: None of the parts can be understood on its own and each contributes to constituting all others. It shows the kind of mediations that exist between the elements isolated for heuristic purposes. Schools and research often only focus on the "primary" relation between subject, object (water level in Henderson Creek), and mediating artifact (graph).

therefore only part of the story. To capture the other parts, I draw on activity theory (e.g., Cole & Engeström, 1993). My introductory description and analysis of Karen in activity brought out a number of relations. Thus, Karen focuses on the creek that her farm needs as a water supply throughout the season, but this relation is mediated by the graph. Both the creek and the graph are historically and culturally situated. First Nations and other people have been drawing water from the creek for hundreds of years, and Western farmers have received licenses since the 1940s. The graph as the product of a pen chart recorder is embedded in scientific and technological culture as an important recording device. That is, the relations between graphs and some aspect of nature are not simply perceptual or functional. An important task therefore lies in carefully studying the way in which material, practical, and linguistic relations are produced in activity (systems).

In activity-theoretic terms, I focus on relations that arise from triplets of heuristically isolated entities including subject, object, mediating artifact, community, rules, and division of labor (Figure 4). These entities are not "elements", for this notion implies reducibility of the whole to smaller parts (Vygotsky, 1986); these entities function as "go-betweens" between two other entities, and therefore as mediators – in one sense of the term mediation.[2] For example, the graph (mediating artifact) mediates the relation between Karen (subject) and Hagan Creek (object), which means that Karen does not just know the creek through her embodied dealing with it as a material thing but that she *knows* it *in terms of* the graph. This relation is equivalent to the semiotic relations featured in Figure 3b. Here the subject, object, and mediating artifact find their correspondences in interpretant, referent, and sign, respectively. However, the point of an activity theoretic perspective is that this primary relation is stabilized and made possible by other mediating relations – in fact all of the relations that exist on the inside of the irreducible activity unit, which in Karen's case are constituted either in her work on the farm or through her participation in the environmentalist group. The division of labor with an Environment Canada technician mediates the relation between Karen and the creek. The different mediated relations displayed in Figure 4, as an ensemble, including material and social dimensions, constitute the basic unit of analysis of human behavior, an activity system.[3] The fusion of the material and the social (discursive) produces relations of signification and the individuals that are positioned, qua subjects, within practices.

Activities are oriented toward something and driven by something. This something, the object/motive, exists on two planes: as part of the sociomaterial world (*being-in-itself*) and in consciousness (Hegel, 1977). The object/motive is constantly in transition and under construction, and it manifests itself in different forms for different participants in the activity. We have also seen that objects appear in two fundamentally different roles, as objects and as mediating artifacts or tools. In both activity-theoretic and semiotic terms, there is nothing in the material constitution of an object that would determine which of the two roles it has in an abstract and decontextualized sense. It is the activity that determines the place and sense of the object (Marx, 1976).

In the present study, I show that Karen's reading of the graph in terms of the water levels of Hagan Creek is inscribed in many other relations, some of which are made thematic in Figure 4. For example, another configuration mediates the primary Karen – Hagan Creek – graph relation: the community, graph, and Karen. Yet another relation made thematic in this chapter is that between the Mayor Walter, the Hagan Creek watershed, and Karen. Still another mediated relation is that between Karen, the water levels, and the Environment Canada technician who comes to establish the calibration curve that allows Karen to read her graph in terms of liters/second although it really displays water levels. In another relation, the graph replaces Hagan Creek as the object and is, in turn, mediated by other graphs.

Graphs provide the basis whereby particular physical relations are inscribed as relations within the organization of practice. In such cases, we cannot simply speak of "representation", because signs represent more than physical relations (Walkerdine, 1988). As beings, we always come to a world where graphs, as signs in general, are always and already social (Heidegger, 1977). In Karen's work, the graph taps many other practices (signifying and material) within the valley, irrigation, damming the creek, fishing, habitat maintenance, building impervious surfaces, building riffles, planting trees in riparian zones, oxygenating the creek. It is in relation to these other practices that Karen's graphing exists. Looking at her graph reading in the absence of everything else, we could come to the conclusion that she competently reads it. But this is of little help for understanding the relations that make this graphing competence possible in the first place.

BACKGROUND OF THE STUDY

The data presented in this chapter derive from a large three-year study on the representation practices among scientists (almost exclusively ecologists) and environmental activists.[4] This study included both formal interview situations in which participants were asked to read and elaborate on graphs that we had culled from introductory university ecology courses and textbooks. My research team also conducted multiyear ethnographies in field research settings and in an environmental activist group that focused its activities on the Hagan Creek watershed and the community of Central Saanich. One of these activists was Karen, a water technician employed by a local farmer with funds from a government grant. The farmer had environmental concerns related to the water resources in the Hagan Creek watershed where his farm is located, and especially in regards to the creek from which he obtains much of the water for irrigating his fields. Among others, Karen operated a device that continuously monitors the water level in the creek by means of a pen chart recorder.

In addition to the research among the environmental activists, we also designed and enacted a science curriculum in which elementary children have opportunities to engage in (mostly mathematical) representation practices. The children constructed representations about the creek and its environs with the ultimate goal of feeding their understandings back into the community during an open house organized annually by the activists. As part of this work, Karen and the activists worked with teachers, such as the new teacher Nadely with whom I worked, to familiarize them with her work on the farm and among the activists.

The materials used in this chapter derive from four videotaped situations where Karen explained the water level graphs and talked about the graphs with teachers and visitors at the open house. In addition, I spent considerable time with Karen walking in and alongside the creek, studying the habitats from the mouth of the creek to its beginnings. We spent time talking about the watershed while standing far above the creek, or walking the fields of the farm. Furthermore, we spent considerable time together working with seventh-grade students in the creek, teaching them how to collect data, make observations, and how to understand the watershed as an ecosystem. Our conversations were recorded in the form of videotapes, audiotapes, and fieldnotes. Some materials on which I draw derive from grant proposals written by the activists to garner funds for their activities. I further draw on understandings deriving from my ethnographic work among the activists.

KNOWING GRAPHING: RELATIONS IN PRAXIS

In this section, I describe some of the relations within my unit of analysis. My primary focus is Karen, the subject at the base of the mediating triangle (Figure 3). My research on graphing suggests that relations such as those described here are fundamental to the constitution of competence. My detailed analysis shows that Karen was highly competent and each feature of the water level graphs provided her with a window into her world, the Hagan Creek watershed (Roth & Bowen, 2001). Here, I do not want to return to that analysis but rather provide evidence for the different kinds of relations that go with the knowledge that we had documented earlier.

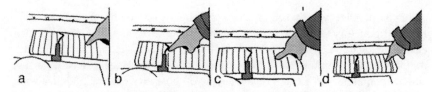

Figure 5. Karen explains where the graph would be given a major rainfall both today (d) and some-time in the past (a, c). As her finger moves back and forth on the page, it embodies the movement of the pen in response to the changing water levels.

Historical Context of Hagan Creek and Central Saanich

Karen and the graph she reads to the visitors on the farm and the yearly open-house event organized by the environmentalists do not exist in a vacuum. Rather, Hagan Creek and the community located within its watershed boundaries have their own political, social, and economic histories. Commuting into the community and working with the people that inhabit the watershed provides Karen with many opportunities to find out about past events and the historical evolution of water-related contexts. Thus, although she had been around for only four years, and although the water level monitoring station has existed for about the same time, she can make then-and-now comparisons of the amount of water coming through the creek after a specific rainfall event. (The positions of Karen's hands at four points are given in Figure 5.)

15	K: But in the winter, the rainfall times [a] what historically might have
16	been, a [b] say [c] a [b] two-inch [c] rainfall [c] event might have gone
17	up to about three thousand liters a second. What we're getting [d] is,
18	we're getting up here almost, almost off the graph paper, or up to five
19	thousand liters a second. That is, in a major rainfall, when all the water-
20	shed is saturated, nothing else is soaking in, either off the grass cover or
21	off the pavement.

For Karen, the graph does not exist in and of itself. Rather, it is mediated by the historical evolution of the watershed (lines 15–18). It is further situated with respect to other, larger watersheds and with respect to the season (winter) when such rainfall events occur contrasting (extremely) low water levels in summer when the farms need it most for irrigating their fields. Furthermore, elsewhere in the transcript Karen situates the increase from 3,000 to the projected flow rate of 5,000 liters/second, on the one hand, relative to small and large watersheds, on the other hand. Smaller watersheds suffer from flash floods, especially with the large number of impervious surfaces and straightening and channelizing of the stream (e.g., Figure 2, right) that Hagan Creek and the community as a whole have experienced in the past. Finally, the graph does not just show 3,000 or 5,000 liters/second, but these values exist in relation to the physical characteristics of the watershed, the grass cover and pavements (lines 20–21). Karen also knows that if more than twelve percent of a watershed is covered by impervious surfaces (e.g., pavement), its health will be seriously affected. In this watershed, the impervious surfaces have increased tremendously over the past two decades. The mediating relation of the community and its history is further highlighted in the following excerpt:

21   K: There are about twelve licenses on the whole creek. And that was all
22   made, all these decisions were done like in the late forties based on zero
23   knowledge of this creek, this watershed. So, we finally decided well,
24   they don't have the funds, so we're just gonna pay for one. The munici-
25   pality has gotten their own station just down stream at Stella's Road and
26   Wally's Drive. So, they're monitoring up there for changes in the fluc-
27   tuations of the flow, we're monitoring down here, so we've pretty much
28   covered the whole watershed.

Here, Karen's work with graph inscribes itself in a situation that has historical roots to the 1940s. At that time, her farm as well as eleven others received their water licenses, although, as she emphatically points out, little is known about the ecological complexity of watersheds, their watercourses, and the underground aquifers that feed them. Furthermore, what happens at her monitoring station is also linked to, and interacts with, what happens at other water monitoring stations. Thus, Karen's reading of the graph becomes meaningful in the ensemble of mediated relation to other currently existing practices and to the watering and communal water distribution practices from which they have evolved.[5] Karen's activity inscribes itself in a historical context – consistent with cultural-historical nature of activity theory, we cannot understand what she does and knows in her actions unless we consider these historical relations as well. The years she has spent as a water technician in the watershed have given her many opportunities to talk with farmers (other than her employer), First Nations people, and other local residents who have been living next to the creek for more than half a century. As a member of the environmental activist group, Karen also has access to the historical records that speak of plenty in terms of water resources (e.g., people used to canoe in the creek) and trout sizes and quantities no longer heard of.

There are farms with water licenses that take water from the creek between a monitoring station placed by the community and her own. The differences between Karen's readings and those coming from the station of the municipality are also important to her work. The water monitoring station and the graph it churns out also exist in the context of the entire water budget of the watershed. In fact, Karen and the other technicians and engineers she collaborates with have done calculations of the total rainfall on the watershed and compared it to the amount of water that flows out of it at the station, which is only 300 meters from the mouth of the creek.

Karen further is familiar with the relationship between the amount of rainfall and the response by the watershed in terms of the amount of water that will be shown on her graph. Here we have, embodied in her practices, another translation and semiotic connection which contribute to Karen's competent reading.

One of the questions asked by visitors related to the minimum water flow required by the fish, "Does the water level affect temperature or oxygenation levels?" Karen first did not address either temperature or oxygenation but responded that fish needed a minimum depth for navigating the creek. Then she picked up the question of temperature and oxygenation.

29   K: Yeah certainly, as the flow gets lower the temperature would get higher.
30   Because they only got this much water to heat up, it's gonna all get
31   warm throughout it. It but if it's this deep and there's a pocket that is
32   covered into the bank you can. . . . You gonna have a nice little hiding
33   spot. I think they need anywhere from eight to eleven parts per million
34   of oxygen. Most fish do. We have little sticklebacks that, actually they
35   eat them. They can survive at two parts per million oxygen completely
36   exposed sunlight areas. So where there is a food supply, there's still no
37   cutthroat trout because they are not gonna follow them into those areas.
38   In terms of temperature, anything around thirteen is a really nice tem-
39   perature, they will, the bigger granddaddy kind a cutthroat that hang out
40   here. In the summer, it's like twenty-seven. In this fully exposed area.
41   But down at the bottom, they've got a seven-foot depth to hang out
42   when the dam is in. And they got cool temperatures down at the bottom.

Karen is very familiar with the creek. We have walked along its bed numerous times, including other individuals interested in the restoration of Hagan Creek or consultants. Karen has constructed riffles from local rocks to improve the oxygenation rates, and she planted trees that eventually would provide habitat. She has used a dissolved-oxygen meter to determine the oxygenation of the creek water both above and below the riffles she single-handedly built on the farm property, or in collaboration with the other activists in other parts of the creek. When she reads the graph, it is against all of these experiences that have left indelible traces in her body and mind.

In this excerpt, we can recognize Karen's familiarity with the creek as an ecological and a physical system. First, the water flow will affect water temperature (lines 29–31), the temperature lowers the dissolved oxygen (lines 33, 35–36), and there are temperature gradients in deep water. All of these factors affect where cutthroat trout and sticklebacks (trout food) can live during different parts of the year and especially during the summer months (lines 37–41). Thus, Karen's reading of the graph is not independent of her familiarity and practical understanding of the creek, the physical characteristics of heat capacity, and ecological relationships between species that have different requirements on their physical environment. Karen's reading of the graph during the summer months exists in and as of the mediating relations in respect to the creek.

In the extensive network constituted by these relations, Karen navigates between the different representations of the creek (i.e., signifiers that characterize knowledge about the creek) and integrates the tools and history. Yet we must not forget that this integration is achieved in and through Karen's activity. We need to remind ourselves that the different representations (signs) Karen uses in her

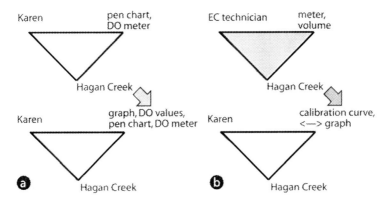

Figure 6. Changes in mediational relations. (a) Karen uses the tools at her hand to produce graphs, outcomes of her activity at some point in time. These graphs increase the number and range of mediational tools thereby constituting subject and object in and through new forms of relations. (b) As an aspect of the division of labor, the Environment Canada technician uses her tools to produce a calibration curve for water levels water volume conversions. This curve becomes one of the tools appropriated by and available to Karen, mediating her own relation to creek and the water level.

activity are nevertheless distinct and arbitrary. As she works in the creek, her familiarity with the setting increases. Furthermore, the outcomes of her activities provide additional mediating tools for understanding the creek. For example, Karen measures the water level in the creek using the pen chart recorder connected to the measurement device. As an outcome of this activity, she gets graphs that monitor the water level throughout the year. These graphs then become new tools that mediate her relationship with the object and in fact constitute Karen as a "more knowledgeable" subject and the creek as a "better-known" object. This development over time is represented in Figure 6a.

Mediating Artifacts, Tools, and Division of Labor

In all instances where Karen read the graph in public, she talked about water volumes. Yet the graph is directly proportional to water level but not to volume. Karen's reading therefore involves a translation, which is not linear in terms of the water quantity. The graph stands in a linear relationship with the height of the water in the central pipe, which is transferred from the floating device to the pen by mechanical means. However, because of the shape of the creek, the height-volume relation is not linear but some complex function.

Her work exists in the context of all activities of the watershed, the other farms, the efforts of the community to monitor the water usage in the community, etc. In part, of course, the work is divided up among people. On the farm, Karen is responsible for the work of monitoring water levels, replanting riparian zones, or building riffles while others are responsible for operating the pumps, drawing the water, and irrigating. Similarly, in the activities of the environmentalists, Karen may produce graphs but others write the proposal in which the graphs are used to get further funding for Karen's position. Furthermore, although Karen shows

191

how to get the volume data from the water level data, she did not establish the calibration curve that allows water level data to be translated into water volume curves. Here, there is a clear division of labor involving a different organization.

43   K: What the Environment Canada technician does is, he or she, comes
44   down three or four times a year, gets into the creek, and measures the
45   area across the creek, and based on the corresponding water levels . . .
46   And eventually get a calibration curve which means that someone like
47   me can come down and say that means X volume. And for example, at
48   one point to the line was here we got seventy-one liters a second.

The Environment Canada technician also gets into the creek, establishing cross section data, maps these against water levels, and constructs a calibration curve (lines 43–46). These curves are themselves an outcome of an activity and become mediating tools in Karen's work. Karen is familiar with major markers established by the calibration curve. In fact, when she reads the graph, she talks about water volumes rather than the water levels displayed. But she does not actually produce the water volume graphs (e.g., Figures 7a–c) herself. This, too, is done by the technician from Environment Canada, and as she repeatedly emphasizes, takes about a year to get done.

49   K: It kind of takes a year after the information collected to process it and for
50   six thousand dollar cost. So, an Environment Canada technician comes
51   down, scoops the whole roll up, takes it back to his office and calculates
52   what that line means.

Nevertheless, the resultant graphs come back to the community to be used by Karen, the farmer, and the environmentalists for a variety of purposes. For example, graphs may become part of a proposal that seeks further funding so that Karen can continue her work. Figures 7a and 7b show graphs taken at different places in the watershed. In respect to this figure, the main body of the proposal reads:

> Discharge measurements are generally 6 to 10 times greater at downstream site than at a flume site. The downstream site, a water survey station on Central Saanich Farm is roughly 2 km below the flume site on the Gooding's Farm. In between these sites, 7 small tributaries feed the main creek, yet there is negligible flow in them during the summer period. The inflow is believed to be due to the influence of the nearby bedrock aquifer just to the north of the valley. Bedrock is observed to form sections of the main streambed. (From proposal to fund Karen's position.)

Here, there is more discharge down river than at the upper site. As the activists' proposal states, the contributions by the seven tributaries are negligible: the differences are due to the aquifer. These differences constitute up new relations in that another graph relates to the amount of water in the aquifer (Figure 7c). Here, the graphs qua social objects embody the material properties of inscriptions. Inscriptions can be layered, transformed, juxtaposed to other graphs, and inserted into

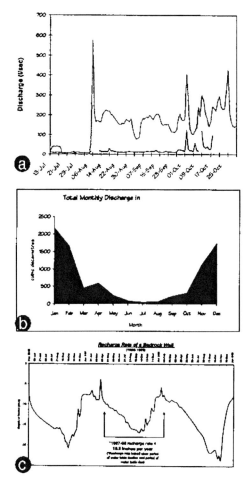

Figure 7. Artifacts mediate the understanding Karen has of the original graph. (a) The water volume graph constitutes a translation and was produced by another technician using a calibration curve. (b) Further translation produces a monthly discharge graph. (c) Changes in ground water levels parallel the seasonal changes in discharge levels [b]; ground water accounts for the differences in two other graphs [a].

documents. For example, there are relations to the third graph in that the discharge rate curve displayed in Figure 7b has maxima and minima that correspond to those in Figure 7c, both being related to the amount of rain fall onto the watershed. Figure 7c plots the depth of water in local wells, and therefore inscribes itself in the practices of drawing water for irrigation purposes. Figure 7b arises from integrating the transformed graphs over time, that is, $D = \int v(t)\,dt$ for one-month periods.

These graphs derive, in part, from operations that characterize inscriptions, including translations (non-linear), layering, scaling, and integrating. For example, graphs such as those in Figures 7a and 7b can be constructed from Karen's original graphs by transforming them using the calibration curve and translating the water levels into volume. (Mathematically, this volume v as a function of time is given as $v(t) = C_{v \to h}(h(t))$ where $h(t)$ is the water level and C the calibration function that maps height onto volume.)

In concluding this section, three points are to be noted. First, there exists a division of labor concerning the focal object of the activity (Hagan Creek). The actions of different individuals are interdependent all contributing to the overall project of coming to know the creek. Second, as part of this activity, Karen, the Environment Canada technician, and others produce representations that subsequently become part of the set of artifacts mediating the relation between subject and object. These activities have outcomes that change the relations in the mediational triangle with Karen as the subject (Figure 6b). Third, the graphs are themselves objects mediated by other graphs (mediating artifacts). That is, the graph Karen explains to Nadely (the teacher) or Walter (the mayor-visitor to Open House) exists in relation to other graphs that Karen, her activist colleagues, and others in the community work with. The three graphs displayed here exist in and through their relation with the graph at Karen's hand, but also with respect to each other. Evidence such as that provided in this section supports the contention that Karen's graphing competence is embedded in many other mediated relations (Figure 4). These mediated relations constitute the very context that establishes the sense of the graphs.[6] However, Karen's competence also involves a very physical, embodied component, which is described in the following section.

EMBODIMENT

Knowing the source of the data and the instruments by means of which data are collected was an important aspect of scientists' determining the level of competency (Roth & Bowen, 2001). When scientists were unfamiliar, their readings often involved mis-readings that shared similarities with those of high school students. This is also the case for Karen. In this subsection, I show that reading graphs is an embodied activity, against the graph as a ground. Gestures are used together with language so that the three constitute a communicative ensemble that is much more complex than talk would be by itself. It is not only the text, but Nadely can see embodied in Karen's gesture an iconic representation of the pen (shaded inverse "T" next to curve in Figures 1, 5) moving across the paper, inscribing the line that is the focus of the present interaction.

Karen knows the instrument that records the water level graphs and in particular the mechanism by means of which the curve is being taken. She knows the instrument so well that her body participates in communicating the functioning of the device. Consider her presentation featured in Figure 8a. Here, Karen's hand moves from right to left along the horizontal direction of the paper while uttering "hours go this way". Her hand follows the direction of the paper in the pen chart recorder, taking the same trajectory. The gesture therefore stands in an iconic relationship with the tracking paper. Time is not just a label on the axis, but is

Hours go this way

This is inside the equipment, the upright column. . . And it is
fluctuating between one point one meter and lately, at the end of
the graph, two point one meters.

Figure 8. The gestures of Karen embody the movement of pen and paper, and the dynamics of the
recording device. (a) The hand shows 'time" as elapsing in the direction in which the paper moves in
the recording device. (b) The hand embodies the pen tracking across the paper while the body moves
up and down in the way the floating body in the stilling well that ultimately drives the pen.

something that continuously unfolds and is indexed by the turning wheels and
moving paper. Karen has a very embodied understanding of time as it pertains
to her graphs. Interestingly enough, indicating the time through a bodily movement may depend on the circumstance, for in another situation, Karen's gesture
described a trajectory in the opposite direction. Here, her gesture described the
trajectory of the graph as it unfolds on the paper under the pen. Here, Karen's
hands track the apparent direction of the pen across the paper. In both situations,
time was something embodied in the (apparent) motion of the paper or pen, and
embodied in her gesture.

Karen does not just know the relationship between some sign (point on graph)
and the amount of water. Her gestures embody the working of the pen. As Karen
talks, her hand-finger movement (sequence Figures 5a–5d) moves along a trajectory similar to that of the pen. The trajectory of her finger, therefore, stands in an
iconic relation to that of the pen similarly to her movements portrayed in Figure 1.
Interrupted by the movement and gesture that indicated the distance on the paper
that amounts to one day, her finger moves, similar to the pen, across the paper.
In the same way, the to-and-fro movement of the pen is embodied in her hand
moving up and down along the now vertical side of the chart.

The involvement of her entire body in representing the recording in terms
of sensori-motor experience is even more pronounced in the following episode.
Here, Karen explains the source of the graphs to a visitor to the Open House
(Walter, the mayor of Central Saanich).

53   K: So, the way this works is there's pipes going across the creek and the
54   water comes into the still(ing?) well area and this is, the fluctuations in
55   that water level drive this wheel here and then this pen works.

As Karen talks about the well in which the water fluctuations drive a floater, her arms form a circle; she bends her knees, so that, as a whole, she describes a drumlike object. Immediately thereafter, Karen enacts the graph recording with her entire body, hand and body standing for (i.e., representing) the pen and floating device, respectively (Figure 8b). She begins to bend her knees so that her body moves downward like a piston "inside the equipment" in "the upright column", while her right hand follows in and amplifies the downward and upward movement of her body. But in this, Karen's sensori-motor actions are not just indexical to the floater, but to the fluctuations of the water level (the OBJECT in Figure 4) throughout the year (see utterances in Figure 8b). Karen performs the recording, her right hand embodying the pen movement; her entire body then enacts the up and down of the floater in the stilling well, her right hand constituting an iconic relation to the recording device.

In these examples, we see Karen not just talk about but move (parts of) her body through trajectories that stand in iconic relations to the graph, paper, or recording device. The movements of these entities, which she observed frequently over the four years preceding the episode, exist as sensori-motor representations in Karen's experience, and are available in public to her listeners. The movements of pen and paper, which exist in the material trace of the graph, are literally embodied. The meaning of "time goes this way" and Karen's up and down movement with her body, followed by her hand is simultaneously built on two types of meanings. First, it built on the sensori-motor action involving Karen's finger (hand) over (in front of) the plotting paper and the graphical space it defines. Second, Karen draws on the symbolic meanings associated with the marks and lines on the paper of the conventional graphical signs. The sensori-motor processes therefore constitute an important aspect of collective processes of meaning making, and the witnessing of the Other's subjective understandings. The graphs thereby constitute subjects and objects in referential ways as simultaneous, co-existing participants in the described events.

Sociologists and philosophers, and more recently artificial intelligence and cognitive scientists, view learning as the structuring of mind, which is fashioned during bodily interactions with the social and material world (e.g., Merleau-Ponty, 1945). Linguistic studies suggest that our language is deeply grounded in and arises from the mid-level (not too tall, not too small) entities that we encounter in the world (e.g., Roth, 2000). Here, my recordings of Karen constitute an exemplary case. Here understanding of the graphs is deeply linked to her understanding of the water level recording device.

To summarize, Karen's graphing competencies have a strong physical component, which I exemplified here in terms of the relation between her gestures, the recording device, and the graph. However, other physical relations also exist, for Karen's understanding of the creek is tied to her in-creek activities, building riffles, catching trout, planting trees, etc.

Before discussing the relevance of this work to mathematical cognition and development, I articulate an important aspect of graphing as it has arisen from my work. Until now, my description focused largely on different relations involving Karen and other aspects of the sociomaterial setting of Hagan Creek and its watershed. However, I have not yet addressed the role and importance of graphs in face-to-face interactions. Here, graphs can become sites where social interactions occur over issues that are relevant to the lives of the people living in the area. Both with the teachers on the farm and with the visitors to the Open House, Karen explained the graphs and her work. She was in what we might term a *knowledge display mode* (e.g., Roth & Middleton, 2006), and her audience provided but continuers, that is, turns at talk that allow the current speaker to continue speaking, such as "Yes", "Okay", or "Is that right". However, there are many instances in my transcripts with interactions beyond continuers. She has prepared her exhibit at the Open House of the environmental activist group. She intended to show and explain to people of what her work consists, how it inscribes itself in the life of the community, and what plans the activists have for improving water quality and quantity in Hagan Creek.

When a graph is a public object, there is always the potential that other persons will contribute their readings. In the following episode, a visitor to the open house (Walter, the Mayor of Central Saanich and principal of local middle school) does not just let her continue, but contributes in an active way. He begins to talk while Karen is still going, thereby making a bit to take a turn at talk. Walter injects his hypothesis based on his own reading of the graph. As a consequence, the episode does not just constitute mere knowledge display, and is not only about the graph. Rather, the episode is an exchange that takes the graph as its starting point and elaborates many related issues.

56	K: ((Gesture as in Fig. 9)) And then there is superimposed rainfall up there
57	and ⌈one of these ⌉
58	W: ⌊Does it say? ⌋
59	K: Pardon?
60	W: Does it say, "Now I know when that will peak?"
61	K: Aha, good. So, one of these little squares is two millimeters.

Karen did not expect Walter's interjection and she may not have heard what he said: her "Pardon?" requests a restatement. Walter thereby obtains a turn in which he elaborates his passing theory about the topic at hand. Karen then acknowledges his theory, but continues with an explanation of the conventions (scale) rather than addressing the relation of the rainfall with the peak of the water level.

Presenting her work in public, Karen navigates the tension between interacting with the audience and presenting the other with what she might consider to be the foundational knowledge required for being able to read the graph. Yet, there is always a tension involved in such relations. Here it is one of who owns the interpretation of the graph, and therefore the speaking platform. But there is an

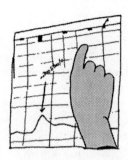

Figure 9. . Karen points to a second inscription layered onto her graphs. These inscriptions signify the amount of rainfall. As she begins her explanation, Walter interjects his own hypothesis as to an inference that can be drawn about the relation between the two graphs.

additional tension arising from the fact that the conversational topic can be shifted to be about something else, here the entire valley and its water resources. Karen began in display mode, and continued in her attempt to retain the knowledge display mode rather than engaging in an open interaction. This changes when the topic moves to consider the watershed itself rather than the sign that mediates the knowledge about it – at least in as far as Hagan Creek is concerned. A few minutes after the above exchange, Walter indicates that he also lives in the valley and that he has one of the water licenses. Subsequently, the interactions between the Karen and Walter change in kind. They begin to talk not only about the graph, but also about the issues for which the graph stands in a reflexive relation to the water, valley, history of settlement, and changes in farming. At this point, both own the issues, and thereby construct each other as equal contributors.

The following episode begins when Karen talks about irrigation and vertical jumps in the graph that stand in a reflexive relationship with irrigation practices.

62   K: These very, you know, ninety degree angles in the lines, that's definitely
63   straight, straight drops. That's definitely irrigation that decreases, peo-
64   ple are all stopping at the same time, starting at the same time. And the
65   conditions, it's dry for a while here. ((Gesture as in Fig. 9))
66   W: Yeah, a lot of hay, people are into the hay.
67   K: Yeah, a lot of people cut it at the same time.
68   W: Further, you go towards the Fellow's farm. Down Hagan Creek. Be-
69   cause once you get past Fellow's, it stops. There is corn. But of course,
70   nowadays, there is late corn, too.
71   K: Yeah, they grow different varieties.
72   W: I think they grow mostly early corn on the fields that are around Hagan
73   Creek.
74   K: Corn has a lot, requires lots of water, doesn't it? Compared to hay.

In this episode, Karen introduces the topic of irrigation, which goes with particular vertical discontinuities (jumps) in the graph. But it is not just that these jumps are signs that stand in a signifying relation to the water level changes caused by irrigation. Rather, irrigation also stands in relation to the second, layered graphical information on the top border of the graph (Figure 9). Presently, Karen and Walter stand in front of that part of the roll that was recorded during the summer. There are no rainfall events marked on the top part of the paper roll. Thus, the jumps attributed in this episode to irrigation exist in relation to the time of recording (summer), the number and size of the (here lacking) rainfall events. Most importantly, the topic in the episode is not some feature of the graph, but the farming practices and irrigation that obtain in the valley at the present time. Understanding now concerns the speakers' organic relationship in and with the valley (Figure 2), its people, their livelihoods, and the climate. That is, faced with the graph, their understanding has been reflected back onto itself: "consciousness pf am "other", of an object [here graph] in general, is itself necessarily *self-consciousness*, a reflectedness-into-self, consciousness of itself in its otherness" (Hegel, 1977, p. 102). Yet all this is part of the thick layer of knowledge and experience that brings forth the extraordinary competence in the first place. Here, and as a seventeen-year inhabitant of the valley, Walter is a knowledgeable conversation participant. He is as familiar as Karen with the hay farming that goes on in the summer, which requires the dry conditions of (late) summer in this part of the world. Karen then suggests that many farmers begin and stop irrigation at about the same time, a fact again related to the weather patterns in the valley and haying practices that require a dry period for each harvest.

Walter subsequently adds that not all of the farms grow hay, but that they also grow (different types of) corn. He even provides a description of the specific farm where the corn crops begin to dominate the fields (lines 68–70). Karen then makes a statement – which can be heard as a question to Walter who had previously already talked considerably about strawberry farming practices – that corn takes more water to grow than hay. This, in turn, would have significant impact on the irrigation practices (especially if there are different types of corn) with a resultant effect on the water levels and Karen's charts.

This episode shows that graphs are not just signs standing in a unique and unambiguous relationship to objects. In this situation, the graphs are both topic of and ground for their interaction, an important aspect in aligning the interaction participants and in achieving intersubjectivity. These graphs are not just objects of knowledge in the way that past developmental research in mathematics treated them. Rather, as the analyses show, they are the primary means of interaction between Walter and Karen is the creek and the surrounding valley in which it is located. The graph is but an object that anchors the social space in which the two collectively engage in the construction of the watershed for the purposes at hand.

TO KNOW GRAPHS

In the foregoing sections, I articulated different aspects of knowing graphs. These different episodes show that mathematics in everyday practice is constituted in a noisy field of practical action and discursive relations. In these practices, graphs do not exist as ideal Platonic objects with definite structure and elements. Rather, in the context of particular practices, graphs make available what is necessary in the situation at hand. Other structural aspects that a theorist may identify remain undisclosed. For example, Karen needs neither to read individual data values nor to identify the slopes of the graphs. What matters in the context of her work are those differences that make a difference; that is, differences that contribute to the relations that constitute the heuristic entities in the mediational triangle (e.g., subject, object, tools, and division of labor). Thus, it matters in the Karen-creek-graph relation that a particular graphical feature arises from a clogged pipe in the instrument or the lifting of a dam rather than some other event in the watershed.

The graphs do not just serve to express something about nature (in this instance the watershed). Rather there are very different, economic and personal matters in which these graphs are inscribed. Here, the proposal from which the three graphs in Figure 7 were culled was seemingly written to seek funding for monitoring the water budget in the watershed. But at another level, the technician to be employed with the funding received is Karen herself. The graph that Karen reads to different audiences is not just a representation: it is lived as a relation within a range of practices and her life of being a water technician; it is part of her everyday working life, just as the pen chart recorder, the tractors on the farm, the trout she can make jump, and the trees that shade the creek. This graph exists in relation to the ending contract that provides for her subsistence and a new contract with the prospects of continuing her work at a place that she has come to be very familiar with.

"Context" has been one of the focal points in the discussion of how to make mathematics more relevant. We may ask, "Where is the context in contextual word problems?" The present chapter contributes new answers. It is evident that situated cognition does not mean that people think differently in different contexts. Although signifiers (graphs) may be the same in different contexts, they in fact contribute to constituting the context in different ways. In Karen's everyday practice, the many different relations contribute to an over-determination of any individual relation and the objects and tools involved. At the same time, unlike former assumptions concerned only with the relation between sign and world (Figure 3a) or sign, world, and interpretant community (Figure 3b), the change in objects and tools also changes the way in which subjects are constituted. Thus, Karen's subjectivity changes over time (Figure 6a), through interactions related to division of labor (Figure 6b), and in individual interactions. Thus, Karen is constructed differently as a subject in her interaction with Nadely (expert) than with Walter who, along a number of dimensions, is more familiar with and knowledgeable about the valley, community, creek, farming practices, or watershed. Without considering the relations, we would draw inappropriate inferences about the nature and extend of someone's knowledge based on analyses of the data we have at hand.

From a phenomenological point of view, what imports is the lifeworld, the world perceived and acted in by the person-in-activity. This familiar world of practical understanding constitutes the very ground that allows a person to work with a graph, only to be reflected into itself but now, augmented by the explanatory effort, in a more articulated way. The chapter showed that the concrete embeddedness and meaning of activity could not be accounted for by analysis of the immediate situation because the concrete social institutions and relations were characterized by historically emerging contradictions. But they emphasize, at the same time, that objectively existing social structures do not have a determinate effect. Any meaning is socially constituted in relations between activity systems and persons acting in the world. Meaning always has this relational character.

It therefore does not bring us much further if we view context as a container that can be grafted intact onto cognition or cognitive development. The social is more than a container of the psychological, but each of the two arises from complex dynamics by means of which they are constituted in actual practice. Signs are produced and used within the dynamic intersection of actions, objects, and speech within a practice and therefore function as relations within the practice. Signification, therefore, cannot be reduced to representation. Participants themselves become in and through the relations in which they are embedded. Karen is who she is in relation to her employer, the water conservation and creek restoration efforts of her activist group, and the new teacher Nadely, who has sought her as a consultant for a school-related project. "Karen" also emerges from the relations with the First Nations people, the creek that she so intimately knows, and the Mayor, Walter, who participate in the reading of graphs in relation to the community.

In the episodes featured earlier, Karen navigates the ontological gap that exists between (features of) the graph and those features of the Hagan Creek watershed with which it stands in an indexical and reflexive relationship. When she talked with Walter about the irrigation, neither individual had a problem talking about the vertical jumps in the graph in terms of the irrigation. In fact, the conversation shifted and was concerned with the object, Hagan Creek (watershed), the knowledge about which is mediated by the graph. That is, the ontological gaps do not exist in praxis: they disappear in the movement consciousness to the object (graph) and back into itself, both constituting but contradictory moments in the movement of understanding (Hegel, 1977). In Karen's work and interactions with others, the graph seems to be transparent, providing her with a window on the world of the watershed. At this point, a troublesome question demands attention. How did Karen get there? This question has to be central to the activities of mathematics educators, for if, as pointed out earlier, there are ontological gaps between representations and the things they are said to stand for, then how do individuals ever come to the point of using graphs as if these gaps did not exist?

IMPLICATIONS FOR LEARNING AND DEVELOPMENT

Heeding the Ontological Gap

Past research on graphing made (sometimes implicitly, sometimes explicitly) use theoretical frames in which graphs (as sign, symbol) have an implicit relationship to the world or some other sign. Thus, in the research on graphing, investigators often ask students to interpret a graph or select among graphs the one that referred to some situation. These students were frequently untutored (not instructed) in graph use, and had few opportunities to engage in representation practices. A typical task asks students to walk across the room and return to their starting point upon which they are asked questions about graphs or asked to select that graph which best represented their trip across the room in terms of distance or position and velocity. Not surprisingly, large numbers of students answered inappropriately or selected graphs that were inconsistent with scientific practices. In other studies, a winch was used as a pedagogical device to allow students first-hand experience with a phenomenon that can be modeled mathematically by using linear functions – i.e., height $= f$(turns) (Greeno, 1988; Kaput, 1988). Many mathematics teachers and educators assume that exposure to such (hands-on) activities is sufficient for learning mathematics. This assumption is justified if we assume that there exists an isomorphism between the world (here the winch) and mathematics. Counting turns and measuring the length of string wound onto the winch share deep structure; measuring length can be reduced to counting equidistant intervals. However, turning and getting a bucket of water from a deep well are not inherently mathematical. If this assumption does not hold, we have little reason to expect that students infer mathematical knowledge from interacting with the device. What educators forget is that our network of (discursive, mathematical, and material) practices is so extended and so habitual that we no longer remark the ontological gaps that separate them.

A central assumption in cognitive research on mathematics is that structures are inherent across contexts. Thus, any linear function would be constant if it involved turning the crank of a stilling well to bring up the water bucket a certain way, increasing the velocity of a ball as it rolls down an incline, or increasing the height of a stack by adding books all. However, this chapter shows that we need to examine these relations as relations of signification. It then becomes evident that each practice is different though relations between them can be specified. In this case, situated cognition is not something people do when they think in different contexts; situated cognition means that subjects produce different outcomes in different settings. Certain transformations are therefore necessary to turn non-school practices into school mathematics practices.

When we take a traditional perspective and assume logical relations to exist between different sign systems, or even within sign systems, we might come to the conclusion that these students are not able to derive the relationship between walk and graph. That is, these students lack the skill or capacity for making logical inferences. They then are said to be stricken with cognitive deficiencies, mental deficits, misconceptions, and so on. It is easy to understand such conclusions, because they derive from sign-referent relationships that are taken to exist a priori. We come to entirely different conclusions, however, if we take a sociomaterial-practice perspective on ordering and representing activities. There are, therefore, no inherent logical grounds that link a sign (graph) and the world, but merely negotiated and shared ways of engaging in particular activities where the signs (graphs) are an integral part. From such a perspective, we do not expect individuals to derive the relation between two representations or between worldly events (walking across the room, turning a winch) and some mathematical representation. Rather, we might ask questions about the extent to which these individuals have participated in the practices. If there had been little prior participation, we might expect to see little resemblance between established practices and the activities that the individuals engaged in. It is not surprising, then, especially within the psychological frame applied, that this research focused on the deficiencies people bring to the task of relating signs and aspects of the world.

From Inside to Outside

Graphs are social objects in at least two senses. First, graphs only exist and have a sense in relation to the place they take in some sociomaterial practice. They are used in such places as poster displays, scientific articles, newspapers, or books. Here, readers who have previously participated in reading and graphing practices disclose through the process of their reading what the author intended the graphs to communicate: but in this reading, they really disclose their own practical understanding of the familiar world that they take as shared with the graph's author. As such, graphs only exist in and as of their relation to sign-related practices. Second, graphs can become the site of face-to-face interactions between people who negotiate, in real time, what graphs are meant to express, how they inscribe themselves in the issues at hand, and so forth. Thus, important understandings of graphing practices arose in the context of a micro-analytic study of mathematical representation practices in an eighth-grade classroom where students transformed nature into different sign forms, and interpreted the sign forms created by their peers (Roth, 1996). It turned out that these students developed considerable competence in transforming the material-form elements from Figure 3c in both directions: on tests, students easily moved from mathematical representations to their understanding of the natural world, whereas in their research, students easily moved from the natural world through cascades of representation to some final inscription. That is, on the one hand, they developed increasing competence in using graphs and statistics as a way to construct and express understandings about 35-m^2 plots of nature. On the other hand, they equally developed a tremendous competence in interpreting existing representations, that is, to create verbal descriptions of natural situations that could have been the origin of the graph.

In the context of this work, I conducted a quantitative study to compare their competencies to those of college science graduates enrolled in a fifth-year teacher education program. The task was based on pairs of numbers (light intensity, plant density) that were entered in each section of a subdivided plot of land; participants were asked whether there was a relationship between the two measures and how they could support their answers. There was a statistically higher use of graphs and statistics in the eighth graders' responses than in those college science graduates provided. I do not use mental deficiency to explain why college students do less well than eighth graders on data interpretation tasks. Rather, I suggest that the eighth-grade students were much more familiar and had more opportunities to enact the representation practices.

My research on graphing began in science classrooms assuming that scientists were experts that we could use to constitute a normative frame for expertise. The interviews with thirty-seven scientists (ecologists, physicists) taught me to rethink my assumptions, for there are many instances in my database where scientists do not provide expert interpretations. Rather, although the graphs have been culled from undergraduate textbooks in their own domain, scientists often read graphs in ways that mathematics research has come to denote with "iconic errors", "slope-height confusions", and more generally, with "misconceptions" (e.g., Roth & Bowen, 2003). Furthermore, rather than engaging in an inductive process where the referent of a graph is disclosed in an unfolding manner, we observed a dialectical process in which ecologists articulated knowledge as the outcome of a continuous movement between familiar ecological systems and tentative articulations of graphical signs: repeated return trips from perceived signs to memory traces of past experience and back to the perception of signs. At the same time, we found profound differences in the graph reading activities when scientists talked about graphs that arose from their own work. Here, they began by providing minute details of the local situations they had investigated, instruments they had used, and transformation that their data were subjected to. In these accounts, the graphs were transparent means, placeholders for an extended experience in the field and laboratory. That is, even scientists do not transfer skills from one domain of graphing to another; transfer of cognitive and linguistic operations across contexts is not as frequent as some educators and researchers would lead us to believe.

From my (sociomaterial) practice perspective, "individual" cognitive development is deeply bound up with changes of participation in sociomaterial practices of a culture: in their actions, individuals realize cultural possibilities in concrete ways, but, because an action "is indivisibly the action of one as well as of the other" (Hegel, 1977, p. 112), they do so because the cultural possibilities are available at a general, collective level. Schools are primary institutions for bringing about and fostering the enculturation into practices. Received conceptions of graphing competencies have led to educational misconceptions of what students should know and be able to do at particular points during their schooling. These misconceptions have led to ill-conceived pedagogical practices. If there is an ontological gap, relations between two domains cannot be derived on logical grounds. These relations are grounded in and given by the practices enacted by competent individuals; as shown, these relations are developed over time by participating in practice. We need to keep in mind here that out-of-school mathematical practices are inherently different from in-school practices because of the differences in the products of the practices, the relations of signification, the regulation of practices, the positioning of subjects, and the emotional investment. Calculations within everyday out-of-school practices exist in a different way than in school; but the calculations are often not the point of the activity. This leads to a new fusion of signifier and signified.

Everyday Mathematics, Inside

In relation to schooling, it is often assumed that students can learn practices independent of the settings in which they are used. The notion of "authentic mathematics" has been in circulation for some time. However, this notion makes little sense when we regard what Karen does as authentic mathematics (at least in relation to graphs). Let us assume that some teacher introduces the graphs Karen works with in order to make her classes more "authentic" or more "contextual". We can already say that she would not be able to bring children anywhere near to what Karen represents, for most of the relations present in Karen's activity will not be present in that of the children. What school children do seldom has a relation to other practices that we observe in Karen's case. One alternative to traditional teaching is to expand the range of activities and related practices that provide longer chains and denser networks of signifying practices. Graphing would then still be a school-related practice: it would no longer stand on its own but exist in relation to many other practices (material, signifying). The implication of my work is that out-of-school mathematics cannot become in-school mathematics, because the relations instantiated outside are so dissimilar from those instantiated inside schools. The best we can do is provide rich contexts in which activity structures are set into motion that allow new sets of (desirable) relations not-yet existing in the schools. The real trick is not one of finding everyday problems that bear some correspondence to school problems, but in finding problems that are truly problematic and therefore engaging to children. This involves considerable levels of control that children have to have over framing problems and solutions, even if this sometimes means that they abandon framing and solving altogether.

ACKNOWLEDGMENTS

The research and writing in the chapter were made possible in part by research grants 410-96-0681 and 410-99-0021 from the Social Science and Humanities Research Council of Canada. I thank Daniel Lawless for his careful reading and feedback on previous versions of this chapter and Sylvie R. Boutonn, G. Michael Bowen and Stuart H. Lee for their help during the data collection and transcription of the materials.

NOTES

[1] As is custom in the social studies of science, I choose to link the social and material rather than the social and historical, or the social and the cultural because I view all social practices as historically contingent and embedded in some culture. However, the material aspects of cognition are seldom enough emphasized or, as in traditional cognitive science completely left out of the modeling of knowing and learning.

[2] In dialectical logic, the activity system constitutes the middle term, the irreducible whole, which expresses itself one-sidedly in any element identified (Hegel, 1977). These elements therefore have metonymic relations to the whole (activity system).

[3] Traditional graphing research, which focuses on the relation between sign and some referent only therefore misses most aspects that constitute the competence in graphing among the scientists, technicians, and students in our studies.

[4] My former graduate students Michelle McGinn and Michael Bowen participated in this large-scale study of scientific representation practices.

[5] Two other relations are notable in the transcript. First, Karen's reading of the graph is mediated by another graph not present in the setting. As a form of division of labor, Environment Canada technicians have determined this function and also convert the water level chart into volume charts each year. Second, Karen's hand-finger movements across the paper stand in an iconic relation to the movement of the pen. That is, Karen's reading of the graph also exists in the context of her embodied understanding of the instrument that records the graphs. Both of these relations are discussed below.

[6] Such dependencies force us to reconsider the notion of context in school mathematics.

REFERENCES

Cole, M. & Engeström, Y. (1993). A cultural historical approach to distributed cognition. In G. Salomon (Ed.), *Distributed cognitions: Psychological and educational considerations* (pp. 1–46). Cambridge: Cambridge University Press.

Greeno, J.G. (1988). Situated activities of learning and knowing in mathematics. In M. Behr, C. Lacampagne & M.M. Wheeler (Eds.), *Proceedings of the 10th Annual Meeting of the PME-NA* (pp. 481–521). DeKalb, IL: International Group of Psychology of Mathematics Education.

Hegel, G.W.F. (1977). *Phenomenology of spirit* (A.V. Miller, Trans.). Oxford: Oxford University Press.

Heidegger, M. (1977). *Sein und Zeit [Being and time]*. Tübingen, Germany: Max Niemeyer.

Kaput, J.J. (1988). *Truth and meaning in representation situations: Comments on the Greeno contribution.* Paper presented at the annual meeting of the North American Chapter of the International Group for Psychology of Mathematics Education, DeKalb, IL.

Latour, B. (1993). *La clef de Berlin et autres leçons d'un amateur de sciences [The key to Berlin and other lessons of a science lover]*. Paris: Éditions la Découverte.

Lave, J. (1988). *Cognition in practice: Mind, mathematics and culture in everyday life.* Cambridge: Cambridge University Press.

Lemke, J.L. (2000). Opening up closure: Semiotics across scales. In J. Chandler & G. van de Vijver (Eds.), *Closure: Emergent organizations and their dynamics* (pp. 100–111) New York: New York Academy of Science Press.

Lemke, J. (2002). Mathematics in the middle: Measure, picture, gesture, sign, and word. In M. Anderson, A. Saenz-Ludlow, S. Zellweger & V. Cifarelli (Eds.), *Educational perspectives on mathematics as semiosis: From thinking to interpreting to knowing* (pp. 215–234). Ottawa: Legas Publishing.

Lynch, M. (1991). Method: Measurement – ordinary and scientific measurement as ethnomethodological phenomena. In G. Button (Ed.), *Ethnomethodology and the human sciences* (pp. 77–108). Cambridge: Cambridge University Press.

Marx, K. (1976). *Capital volume I.* London: Penguin Books.

Merleau-Ponty, M. (1945). *Phénoménologie de la perception [Phenomenology of perception]*. Paris: Gallimard.

Nöth, W. (1990). *Handbook of semiotics.* Bloomington: Indiana University Press.

Roth, W.-M. (1996). Where is the context in contextual word problems?: Mathematical practices and products in Grade 8 students? Answers to story problems. *Cognition and Instruction, 14*, 487–527.

Roth, W.-M. (2000). From gesture to scientific language. *Journal of Pragmatics, 32*(11), 1683–1714.

Roth, W.-M. (2003). *Toward an anthropology of graphing: Semiotic and activity-theoretic perspectives.* Dordrecht: Kluwer Academic Publishers.

Roth, W.-M. (2004). Emergence of graphing practices in scientific research. *Journal of Cognition and Culture, 4*, 595–627.

Roth, W.-M. & Bowen, G.M. (1999). Digitizing lizards or the topology of vision in ecological fieldwork. *Social Studies of Science, 29*, 719–764.

Roth, W.-M. & Bowen, G.M. (2001). Professionals read graphs: A semiotic analysis. *Journal for Research in Mathematics Education, 32*, 159–194.

Roth, W.-M. & Bowen, G.M. (2003). When are graphs ten thousand words worth? An expert/expert study. *Cognition and Instruction, 21*(4), 429–473.

Roth, W.-M. & Lee, Y.J. (2004). Interpreting unfamiliar graphs: A generative, activity-theoretic model. *Educational Studies in Mathematics, 57*, 265–290.

Roth, W.-M. & Middleton, D. (2006). The making of asymmetries of knowing, identity, and account-ability in the sequential organization of graph interpretation. *Cultural Studies of Science Education, 1*.

Vygotsky, L.S. (1986). *Thought and language.* Cambridge, MA: MIT Press. (Originally published in 1934.)

Walkerdine, V. (1988). *The mastery of reason.* London: Routledge.

Wolff-Michael Roth
Applied Cognitive Science
University of Victoria, Canada

GEORGENE L. TROSETH

LEARNING FROM VIDEO: EARLY UNDERSTANDING AND USE OF A SYMBOLIC MEDIUM

INTRODUCTION

The inclusion of a chapter on video in a book about notational knowledge may need some explanation. Preschool-aged children might learn letters and numbers from viewing television programs such as Sesame Street, but the focus of this chapter is not the learning of notation from video. I will argue that understanding and using video images is related to notational knowledge because both video and notations are kinds of symbolic artifacts. Video images are some of the first symbols that many young children encounter. The insights that children gain in learning to get information from video may help prepare them to master notational systems such as writing.

Historically, the term "symbol" has been used in a variety of different, often conflicting, ways (see DeLoache, 2002, for a comprehensive review). The meaning used here is the one suggested by DeLoache: A symbol is something that someone intends to stand for or represent something other than itself. This definition combines Goodman's (1976) assertion that virtually anything can serve a symbolic function with Werner and Kaplan's (1963) requirement that symbolization involve "an intentional act of denotative reference" (p. 21). It also emphasizes human intention: an object only becomes a symbol by virtue of a person employing it to record or communicate information. From this perspective, symbols include both spoken language and a wide variety of objects, markings, and images with a primary function of representation (e.g., models, diagrams, calendars, graphs, and pictures).

The subclass of symbols that should be considered notations has been defined in several ways. According to Lee and Karmiloff-Smith (1996), notations are visual symbols that leave a trace (thus excluding, for example, gestures and spoken words); notations continue to exist independent of the person who created them. Bialystock (1992) uses the term to mean the written form of external symbols. Iconic representations such as drawings and photographs (and by extension, video images) sometimes are included as kinds of notations that follow a different set of rules or constraints than those applying to writing and numbers (e.g., Lee & Karmiloff-Smith, 1996; Tolchinsky-Landsmann & Karmiloff-Smith, 1992). However, the philosopher Goodman (1976) excludes pictures from the class of notations because they do not meet his formal syntactic and semantic constraints on notationality: pictorial images are not easily decomposed into a set of discrete characters that can be correlated with individual elements of a field of

E. Teubal et al. (eds.), Notational Knowledge, 209–232.

reference (also see Gardner, Howard & Perkins, 1974; Karmiloff-Smith, 1996). Other common notational systems (even written inscriptions) fail to completely meet Goodman's ideal of notationality (Gardner et al., 1974).

Each symbol system, whether strictly notational or not, has a unique set of conventions that children must discover in order to correctly interpret the intended meaning. Under the surface differences between symbol types, however, there is deep similarity stemming from "the kind of mental representation needed for children to manipulate symbolic artifacts" (Bialystok, 1992, p. 270). Symbol use requires that children first perceive and interpret the symbolic object or marking itself, and then mentally represent whatever it is that the concrete artifact refers to. To achieve *dual representation* (DeLoache, 2002), children must recognize that an object stands for or directs attention to something else (usually, something that is not physically present). Because all symbol use involves this kind of mental representation, experience with depictions (video, photos, and drawings) may prepare children to understand and produce notations (DeLoache, 1995; Marzolf & DeLoache, 1994; Troseth, 2003b).

Early Exposure to Symbolic Artifacts

Years before children in Western societies begin to master the formal conventions of writing and number notation, they are surrounded by pictorial symbols, including video images on the family TV set, decals on their high chairs, appliquĆs on their clothing, and family photos on the walls. The average American toddler watches 2 to 3 hours of television and videos per day (Huston, Wright, Marquis, &Green, 1999; Jordan & Woodward, 2001), including programs that have been developed with infants and toddlers as the target audience such as *Baby Einstein*, *Tellytubbies*, and *Blues Clues*. Many middle-class infants and toddlers also spend time every day "reading" picture books with their parents (Gelman, Coley, Rosengren, Hartman & Pappas, 1998; Ninio & Bruner, 1978; Whitehurst, Arnold, Epstein, Angell, et al., 1994). Computers, digital cameras, and camcorders provide young children with other opportunities to be exposed to still and moving pictures.

Pictorial representations may seem extremely simple to understand. For instance, a video image of a real event may appear to be transparent, providing children with much of the same information they would obtain from directly experiencing the event (see Gibson, 1979). Recent research, however, has shown that substantial development is involved in very young children's understanding and use of video images, even highly realistic video of real events (e.g., Barr & Hayne, 1999; Deocampo, 2004; Deocampo & Hudson, 2005; Hayne, Herbert & Simcock, 2003; Schmitt & Anderson, 2002; Troseth, 2003a, 2003b; Troseth & DeLoache, 1998). The decrement in toddlers' learning from video, compared to their learning from direct experience, has been characterized as a video deficit (Anderson & Pempek, 2005).

Beyond learning from straightforward, realistic video, further challenges include the need to interpret what theorists dub the *grammar* and *syntax* of video

(Greenfield, 1984; Van Evra, 1990; c.f. Wolf & Gardner, 1981; Wright & Huston, 1981). Examples include conventional devices such as cuts, pans, montage, and camera angles that convey spatial and temporal relations as well as aspect or viewpoint. To fully understand the intended meaning of video images, children must discover and learn to interpret these conventional elements (see Bamberger, this volume). Experienced viewers use formal features such as these to differentiate realistic-looking fictional dramas from real news coverage and documentaries (Wright, Huston, Reitz & Piemyat, 1994; Wright, Kunkel, Pinon & Huston, 1989). A mature understanding of video thus requires mastery of a set of conventions, as does understanding other, more strictly notational symbol systems such as writing.

This chapter will focus on children's understanding and use of video images, although development is very similar for static pictures (see DeLoache, Pierroutsakos & Troseth, 1996; Troseth, Pierroutsakos & DeLoache, 2004, for reviews). Children must *comprehend* depictions before they can begin to produce even the simplest of notations described in this volume (e.g., Triona & Klahr, this volume). In the following section, I will outline the complexity inherent in the obvious-seeming relation between a video image and reality. Next I will review studies of children's early difficulties using realistic video as a source of information, and describe later developments involving children's learning of the formal features of video.

THE COMPLEXITY OF VIDEO IMAGES

During one of my studies, a 2-year-old participant was watching a home video of herself and her family building a tower of books and blocks. She retrieved a block and tried to hand it to the people on the set, saying, "Here". Jaglom and Gardner (1981) describe a 2-year-old going to fetch a paper towel after seeing an egg break on television. Somewhat older children continue to express some confusion about video images and picture, as when 3-year-olds told Flavell and his colleagues (Flavell, Flavell, Green & Korfmacher, 1990) that a bowl of popcorn in a video or picture would spill if the TV or photo were turned over. These examples point to one aspect of the complexity of video images – their dual nature. Images, whether kinetic or static, include both a surface (e.g., a flat, moving pattern of color behind a glass screen) and some content (what is depicted). Several theorists (e.g., Gregory, 1970; Potter, 1979; Sigel, 1979) have commented on the paradoxical dual nature of pictorial images. For instance, James Gibson (1979, p. 282) states:

> A picture is both a surface in its own right and a display of information about something else. [It] always requires two kinds of apprehension that go on at the same time ...

Ittelson (1996) elaborates: a picture simultaneously presents "information that would be provided by viewing the pictured real-world scene" and "information unrelated to the pictured scene, [coming] from the real-world surface on which the picture appears" (p. 175). Thus, to respond appropriately to a video image, children must hold in mind both the content of the image (e.g., tower-building by family members) and information indicating that this is merely a representation (flatness cues from the image itself, the glass surface of the screen, the surrounding plastic box, buttons, etc.). The young viewers in the examples above recognized the content of the image, but did not seem to clearly represent that what they saw was a depiction. As I will document in this chapter, the need to accurately represent both the image itself and its relation to something else – what DeLoache (2000) terms *dual representation* – provides a substantial challenge to young viewers.

Another level of complexity stems from the many symbolic relations possible between video and reality. First, video has the capacity to depict *ongoing, current reality*. Video monitors attached to security cameras in stores offer children brief, fascinating glimpses of themselves "on TV". Several years ago, during a visit to the Indianapolis Children's Museum, I observed a crowd of children (and adults) at a technology exhibit mesmerized by live video of themselves. The closed-circuit image of viewers was combined on the screen with a pre-taped background of an underwater scene, so that viewers appeared to be walking among the coral reefs – an unusual blending of current reality and fantasy.

Although video is capable of depicting entities and events that are immediately present, it more commonly relates to the real world "at a distance". For instance, video can present *real events that are spatially distant*, enabling viewers in their living rooms to watch a sporting event occurring in a stadium in another city. Video can depict *real events that are distant in time*, from the momentous (e.g., historical footage of the American Civil Rights Movement) to the mundane (e.g., other people's home videos). Video also has the capacity to depict *events that bear little or no relation to reality*, including dramas and cartoons. With the advent of computer animation, the ability to perceptually discriminate fantasy from reality has become more difficult: Viewers have watched apparently living, breathing dinosaurs interacting with humans as well as convincing film footage of Starfleet battles in deep space. The popular children's program *Blues Clues* presents a real actor in a cartoon environment interacting with cartoon objects and conversing with a cartoon dog. In developing a mature understanding of video, children must learn to identify these various relations between video and reality.

Another aspect of complexity in interpreting video images involves the *representational specificity* of a realistic image. For instance, in a video of zoo animals, the image of a mother panda and her baby can represent the kind "panda" *in general*, but in a newscast, the same image could depict a *specific* mother animal that has just given birth in captivity (see Rakoczy, Tomasello & Striano, in press, regarding "denoting" symbolic acts). Thus, the same image can serve as a specific or a generic representation, depending on the intention of the person who filmed the video and/or the person who displays it (DeLoache & Burns, 1994; Goodman, 1976; Troseth, 2003b). Using Werner and Kaplan's (1963) terminology, a single video image can express various intentional acts of denotative reference. A mature understanding of video involves detecting the intended meaning of an image used in a specific context (see Roth, this volume, on interpreting graphs in context).

Conceptual Knowledge about Video

DeLoache, Pierroutsakos and Troseth (DeLoache et al., 1996; Troseth, Pierroutsakos & Deloache, 2004) have used the expression the picture concept to refer to conceptual knowledge about pictures that is learned through experience. Children who are exposed to video, usually in the form of television, will develop similar conceptual knowledge about video. An initial development is the realization that video is an image – although real looking, it is two-dimensional, non-tangible, not real. To paraphrase the account we presented for pictures (Troseth et al., 2004), when viewing a video image, the child forms a two-part mental representation: "*x*" and "*on TV*". Seeing a video calls to mind information about what is depicted just as directly viewing the real thing would (it brings to mind a mental representation of "*x*"). Simultaneously, the mental representation "*on TV*" draws on conceptual knowledge arising from television-watching experience. It indicates that part of the viewer's mental representation of the concept "*x*" does not apply in this situation; for instance, one cannot really clean up the egg or give the block to the people on TV.

The act of forming that mental representation *on TV* is similar to what theorists (Harris & Kavanaugh, 1993; Leslie, 1987) propose children do to keep an object's pretend identity (e.g., "we pretend this is a telephone") separate from its real identity (e.g., "it is really a banana"). By representing a stimulus as "*x*" "*on T*", viewers note that only part of the normal mental representation of *x* applies. The combination of the two representations – *x* and *on TV* – tells a mature viewer how to respond to a video image: Get information from the image, but do not direct your actions toward it. Because of toddlers' immature concepts about video images, their mental representation of "*x*" (for instance, *people building with blocks*) sometimes may not clearly be designated as "*on TV*" and they may respond inappropriately.

Part of the conceptual knowledge of mature viewers involves a wide variety of potential functions of video images. Video serves as an important *source of information* to many with access to this technology. Much of what we know of distant places and current events in the world (e.g., wars and natural disasters, the stratagems of politicians and the escapades of celebrities) has not been the result of direct experience, but rather was obtained by viewing video. Adults routinely use information from video to make plans and decisions. Watching the weather channel, we know what preparations to make for the day – activities to anticipate or avoid, whether to take an umbrella or sunglasses. Seeing a live "eye-in-the-sky" traffic report may cause us to change travel plans. We can also learn new skills (e.g., how to improve our golf swing or cook a gourmet meal) by watching an instructional video or television program.

Another function of video is to *commemorate* meaningful events such as weddings and birthdays. Video has *evocative* power, stimulating emotions such as fear in the case of a horror film and laughter at the antics of the Three Stooges. Because video can *influence people*, advertisers spend enormous amounts of money producing and airing television commercials. In becoming mature viewers of video and deciphering its various functions, children must learn the intention behind commercials and how commercials differ from television programs (Butter, Popovich, Stackhouse & Garner, 1981; Donohue, Henke & Donohue, 1980; Huston & Wright, 1983).

Given the many functions of video images and their varied relations to reality, figuring out the appropriate response to a particular video image requires both a certain amount cognitive flexibility and conceptual knowledge gained through viewing experience (just as the use of writing or diagrams requires practice relating notation to referent – Eskritt & Lee, this volume). While children are learning about video, they sometimes respond to it in ways that reflect their incomplete understanding. In the next section, I will describe a combination of competence and lack of understanding that characterizes infants' response to video.

NOVICE VIEWERS: INFANTS AND VIDEO

The novice viewer is highly competent at one skill needed to understand video: *perceiving the similarity* between a two-dimensional image and what it depicts. Infants' competence has been documented with both still and moving pictures. In research with photographs, 5-month-old infants who habituate to a real doll later transfer their habitation to a photo of the doll (they evidently view it as "the same old doll"), looking longer at the photo of a novel doll (DeLoache, Strauss & Maynard, 1979; see Troseth et al., 2004, for a review of the picture research). Two- to five-month-old infants respond to the video image of another person with smiles and increased activity, much as they would to the actual person (Bigelow, 1996; Bigelow & Birch, 2000; Gusella, Muir & Tronick, 1988; Hayes & Watson, 1981; Muir, Hains, Cao & D'Entremont, 1996; Murray & Trevarthen, 1985). Also, 5-month-olds appear to recognize images of their own moving legs (Rochat & Morgan, 1995). Thus, infants are able to make sense of two-dimensional still and moving images.

Infants also *discriminate* video images of people and objects from the real things. Four- to six-month-old infants smile more at a real person than at a live, contingent video view of that person (Hains & Muir, 1996). Nine-month-olds differentiate video images of people, objects, and events from their real counterparts, looking longer at a live presentation of these entities than at a video of them (Pierroutsakos, Diener & Roberts, 2003). Similar results have been found with still pictures (DeLoache et al., 1979). Thus, perception of video images and pictures appears relatively automatic – young infants are able to both recognize similarities and discriminate differences between real objects and images of those objects.

However, there are suggestions from informal reports that infants do not understand the meaning of the differences they perceive. An acquaintance told us that when her son was around 14 months old, he tried to pluck a milk bottle shown on a commercial from the TV screen, screaming, "Ba-ba!" when he was unable to do so. Perner (1991) described his 16-month-old son intently trying to step into a picture of a shoe. In a study of mother-child picture book interactions, Murphy (1978) reported that the 9-month-old children "hit the pictures in the book and scratched at the pages as if trying to lift the picture from the page" (p. 379). One child observed over a 10-month period (8 to 18 months) initially scratched at and attempted to grasp the pictured objects on the page (Ninio & Bruner, 1978). During subsequent months, these behaviors decreased.

Were these the temporary lapses of a few young children, or did such reports reflect a general phenomenon – a pervasive lack of understanding of the nature of depictions during infancy? To explore this issue with pictures, DeLoache, Pierroutsakos, Uttal, Rosengren, and Gottlieb (1998) presented 9-month-old infants with highly realistic photos of single objects (e.g. a bottle, a rattle) and systematically examined the infants' responses. In a similar procedure with video, Pierroutsakos and Troseth (2003) sat 9-month-olds in front of a TV screen and showed them a video of a woman's hand placing the same objects (from the picture research) on a tabletop, one at a time, and then removing them. We also included two moving toys – a rocking Big Bird and a mechanical snail that lumbered across the screen.

It was not clear whether to expect exploratory behaviors to be directed toward the videos and photos in a brief experimental session, as these might be rare occurrences. However, every one of the ten 9-month-old infants in the original study, and most children in several replications, manually investigated the pictured objects, rubbing and sometimes hitting at the surface of the pictures. They even grasped at the pictures as if trying to pick up the depicted objects. The children in the video study behaved similarly toward the objects on the TV screen. In Figure 1, a 9-month-old boy attempts to pick up a depicted toy, his pincer grasp clearly visible in the small inset picture. The children were particularly persistent with the moving objects, often following the snail off the screen, repeatedly grasping at it.

Why do 9-month-old infants manually investigate objects depicted on video? Given the well-established ability of even younger infants to discriminate between pictures and objects, it seems unlikely that 9-month-olds cannot perceive the difference between depiction and reality and fully expect to be able to pick up the object on a TV screen. To confirm that 9-month-old infants could differentiate two-dimensional video images from three-dimensional real entities, Pierroutsakos, Diener and Roberts (2003) presented 9-month-olds with real objects and events – people's faces, masks, toys that lit up – alongside a video image of the same people and events. In this direct comparison, the babies looked reliably longer at the live than at the video view of these entities. Children of this age also reached for an object in preference to a picture of the same object, showing that they perceived the difference (DeLoache et al., 1998). Thus, when 9-month-olds rub, hit, and grab at the objects on a video screen, this behavior does not simply reflect an inability to discriminate between images and objects.

A second possibility is that the manual behavior exhibited by 9-month-olds stems from the dual nature of images. The babies perceive a depicted object that in many ways looks like a real object. In other ways, of course, it does not. A

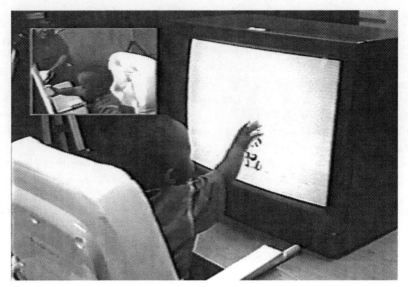

Figure 1. A 9-month-old infant tries to grasp a depicted object. In the inset (side view) picture, the infant's pincer grasp is visible.

two-dimensional image lacks motion parallax (moving the head does not change what is visible) and binocular disparity is missing – there is virtually no difference in the images detected by the two eyes. Nine-month-old infants evidently do not understand the significance of these perceptual differences for their behavior; they do not know what the functional limitations of images are. As a result, they respond to a depicted object as if it were a real object, attempting to manually explore it, although more tentatively than they would the object itself.

When the depicted object turns out not to be manipulable, the infants' lack of affective reaction (none appeared upset or even surprised) indicates that they are not committed to the belief that pictured objects are just like real ones. Infants' manual exploration of pictorial representations thus appears to be the same kind of exploratory behavior that they direct toward other aspects of the environment.

Infants' Emotional Response to Video

Pierroutsakos, Diener and Roberts (2003) subsequently compared 9-month-old infants' emotional reactions to a series of live events with their reactions to video images of those events, including presentation of a series of masks and toys and of a person speaking to them. Infants were very interested in the video presentation: they looked at it, reached for the depicted entities, and vocalized in response to it. Infants also reacted affectively to the video, showing fear in response to scary masks and interest and positive affect toward an electronic game that produced a series of lights and musical tones, and to a person playing peek-a-boo. Video clearly has an emotional impact even in infancy. Infants' reactions to the live presentation were somewhat stronger, however, suggesting that the infants discriminated the videotaped events from the real ones.

A recent study (Mumme & Fernald, 2003) indicates that infants also can interpret the emotional responses of people on video. One-year-olds were shown a videotape of an adult reacting either positively or negatively to a toy. When later given the opportunity to play with the same toy, infants who saw the adult's negative reaction via video were less likely to play with the toy and showed more negative affect. They used the video as a source of specific social and emotional information.

In summary, it is clear that infants find video presentations meaningful. They extract information from video and learn from these presentations. Furthermore, they respond to video with the same kinds of emotions and manual behavior that they produce in response to actual objects and events.

Developmental Course

Infants presumably learn the significance of two-dimensionality through experience with depictions. Thus, one would expect that older infants would manually investigate less, since they have had more opportunities to interact with and learn about pictures and video. We examined the developmental course of children's investigation of video images (Pierroutsakos & Troseth, 2003) and pictures (DeLoache et al., 1998) comparing the behavior of 9-, 15-, and 19-month-old infants.

Figure 2 shows the mean number of actions the children directed at the video images in this study. Exactly the same pattern of results was found with pictures, except that 9-month-olds directed somewhat more manual behavior toward video images than pictures. With age, the level of manual investigation decreased. The 9-month-olds frequently rubbed and grasped at the video images, just as children of this age did in the initial study. Older children were more likely to point at the objects in video images and pictures instead of manually exploring them. In fact, 19-month-olds almost never grasped at the pictured objects, but pointed and vocalized instead. The results for 15-month-olds were intermediate. Thus, the tendency to physically explore the surface of the image is gradually replaced by communication about its referent, in much the same way that children direct others' attention to real objects starting at around 10 months (Carpenter, Nagell & Tomasello, 1998). Through experience, infants learn that what is depicted is not a real object – it is not manipulable or eatable. They learn to point to and label objects in video and pictures as their parents do. Only in rare instances do older children lose sight of the fact they are viewing a depiction, as did the 2-year-old who tried to hand a block to the people in a home video.

USING VIDEO AS A SOURCE OF INFORMATION

Along with figuring out the basic nature of depictions, children learn how video images and pictures are commonly used. One important function of pictorial rep-

Manual Investigation

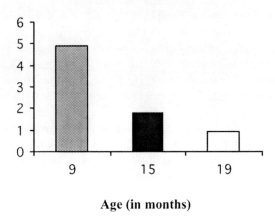

Age (in months)

Pointing

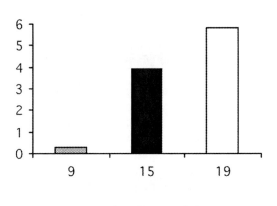

Age (in months)

Figure 2. Mean number of manual behaviors and points (per child) directed at objects on video by 9-, 15-, and 19-month-old infants.

resentations, and of symbols in general, is to serve as a source of information about the real world. Mature viewers know that video can provide useful information. I have been especially interested in whether young children can use video as a source of information when appropriate.

To examine this issue, my colleagues and I have employed a general procedure used previously with other representations – pictures, scale models, and maps (DeLoache, 1987, 1991; DeLoache & Burns, 1994; Marzolf & DeLoache, 1994). We give 2- and 2-1/2-year-old children a problem to solve that requires the use of information from video. Specifically, children watch a "live" video presentation of a toy being hidden in the room next door and then try to retrieve the toy. To find it, children must use what they have learned from a representation (the video image) to form an inference about a real situation (the location of the toy in the next room). Searching for hidden objects is a task that engages the interest of 2-year-olds. This task is also age-appropriate because understanding the instructions and solving the problem do not rely heavily on verbal information.

In our initial experiments (Troseth & DeLoache, 1998), we tried to demonstrate to children how live video relates to ongoing reality. During an extensive orientation, the children saw themselves, their parents, the experimenter, the furniture in the room (hiding places), and the toy on the video screen. Most children loved seeing themselves "on TV", and many became very engaged in interacting with their own video image. They often said "mommy" or "daddy" on seeing their parents on the screen, said their own name, and sometimes labeled depicted objects. We pointed out the correspondence between the images on the screen and the real people and objects in the room.

Next, the children participated in four retrieval trials. As they watched, the assistant walked out the door into the next room (closing it) and appeared on the video screen, hid the toy, and returned. The experimenter directed children's attention to the events appearing on the monitor, narrating the assistant's behavior without labeling the hiding place. Finally, the children were asked to go find the toy in the room.

After watching the live video presentation, the 2-1/2-year-old children usually knew where to search for the toy, retrieving it on 79% of trials (we counted as correct only errorless retrievals, that is, searching first in the right location). In contrast, the 2-year-olds frequently did not use what they saw on the video screen to guide their search, finding the toy only 44% of the time (Figure 3, *Standard Video*). Only two of the twelve 2-year-olds in the initial study were highly successful. The younger children's poor performance on the video search task has been replicated by us (Troseth, 2003b; Troseth & DeLoache, 1998, experiment 3) and independently by other researchers using very similar procedures (Deocampo & Hudson, 2005; Schmitt & Anderson, 2002).

The same age difference was found when children were asked to use pictures (photographs and line drawings) as a source of information (DeLoache, 1987, 1991; DeLoache & Burns, 1994). In a series of experiments, after an adult pointed to a picture to show children where a toy was hidden, 2-1/2-year-olds easily found the toy (about 80% correct) but 2-year-olds had great difficulty (only 6% to 27% correct). Thus, 2-year-old children do not easily get information from a depiction and apply it to a real situation.

A Novel Use of Video

By the time children participate in our search tasks, they easily recognize depicted objects. They no longer attempt to grasp at video images and pictures of objects but point at them and attempt to talk about them. Toddlers also realize that when adults point at and label pictures, they are talking about the depicted objects and not just the images themselves (Ganea & DeLoache, 2005; Preissler & Carey,

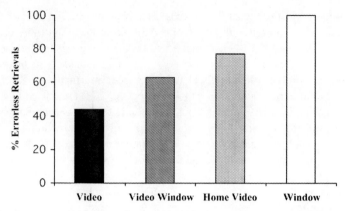

Figure 3. Percentage of errorless retrievals achieved by 2-year-olds who searched for a toy in four information conditions: live video of hiding events (Standard Video); monitor hidden, live video visible through window (Video Window); live video experience at home before search task (Home Video); direct view through a window (Real Window).

2004). They therefore seem to be figuring out (at least, in the familiar contexts of picture book reading and sharing pictures) that two-dimensional images are representations that direct attention to something else. Why, then, did 2-year-olds not realize that the live video presentation pointed to events happening in the adjoining room, get information from the video, and succeed at the search task?

While apparently simple, this task actually requires children to use video in a way they probably have never done before. To find the toy, children must take what they see on a television screen as a source of information *about present reality*. They need to form a mental image of a real, current situation (the location of the toy in the room) based on what they see on the video monitor. This novel use of video requires children to respond flexibly to a familiar medium. Because this is a situation outside their previous experience, 2-year-old children might need some additional training to figure out how live video relates to the current situation, similar to the way that older children need explicit teaching to make the leap between notation and referent (see Eskritt & Lee, this volume; Roth, this volume). We therefore carried out studies to examine what kind of experience (if any) would help children of this age to use video-presented information.

One study was designed to emphasize the correspondence between video and reality. During four training trials, a door between the hiding room and the adjoining viewing area was left open so that children (in the viewing area) could watch the assistant hide the toy in the room directly through the doorway and on the video monitor at the same time. The experimenter directed the children's attention to the two views of the hiding event. After a brief delay (during which the experimenter stood in the doorway to block children's view of the room), children were sent in to find the toy. On the four training trials, when they could directly watch the hiding of the toy, the children almost always found it (91% correct). Immediately after this training, the children participated in four standard video trials with the door closed so that the only source of information was video.

On the video trials, their mean level of retrievals was as low (41%) as that of 2-year-olds who did not receive training (Troseth, 2003a, experiment 1).

Potential Sources of Difficulty

The results of the training study suggest that children's failure to use information from video cannot be attributed to poor memories or to an inability to inhibit returning to the previous location: the same children had no difficulty finding the toy when the door was open and they could watch directly as it was hidden. In another study, 2-year-olds watched the hiding of the toy through a window that was the same size and location as the video screen had been (Troseth & DeLoache, 1998, experiment 2). Everything else about the procedure was the same as in the original experiment, except that the children observed the hiding event directly through the window rather than via the video monitor. The children who watched through the window always retrieved the toy – 100% correct performance (Figure 3 – *Real Window*). Thus, minus the need to use video, they had excellent memories for the location of a toy hidden in the adjoining room and exhibited no tendency to perseverate.

Similar results were reported by Deocampo (2004) in research exploring 2- and 2-1/2-year-old children's solutions to means-end problems presented on video. Children were trained to criterion to use three different tools to remove prizes from specific containers (e.g., using a key to unlock a transparent box). Then, with the tools in front of them, the children watched either on a video monitor or directly through a window as an adult in the next room baited one of the three containers. While watching, they were encouraged to pick the tool they needed to get the treat. Children picked the correct tool more frequently after watching through a window (younger, 78%; older, 96%) than after watching on a video screen (younger, 52%; older, 64%; chance = 33%). In the video condition, only 3 younger and 5 older children (out of groups of 11) picked the correct tool at a rate significantly above chance. More than twice as many children of each age were above chance in the window condition. Again, children did not treat information from video and from direct experience as equivalent. A similar video deficit (Anderson & Pempek, 2005) was recently found in children's learning of words from a person who addressed them "face to face" or from a video screen (Krcmar, Grela & Lin, 2004; see also Kuhl, Tsao & Liu, 2003, regarding a video deficit in maintaining non-native speech sound contrasts from video versus live exposure).

The success of the 2-year-olds in the problem-solving tasks when they watched through a window also indicated that they wanted to find the toy (or to open the container and retrieve the prize). We produced further evidence that motivation was not a problem by ensuring that children were highly motivated to search successfully. After adding some larger hiding places to the room, we asked *parents* to serve as the "hidden object". Two-year-old children intently watched on the video monitor as their parents hid in the next room (e.g., crawled under a card table covered by a tablecloth, crouched behind a screen, etc.). All of the children were *extremely* eager to find their parents and rejoiced when they finally (with assistance) found them. Nevertheless, the children looked first in the right place on only 31% of trials (Troseth & DeLoache, 2003). Thus, lack of motivation does not seem to be causing 2-year-olds' difficulties with video.

A third possibility is that young children's problems result from difficulty assigning meaning to a two-dimensional image. There are several indications that this is not the case. As described earlier, young infants behave toward a video image much as they would toward the depicted entities and events, smiling at video images of people, attempting to grasp interesting toys, and displaying fear toward scary masks. Twelve-month-old children recognize the emotional expression a person on video directs toward a novel toy, and this information affects their response to the real toy (Mumme & Fernald, 2003). In addition, children as young as 14 months of age imitate novel actions they see on video, although they imitate more frequently after a person directly models the actions (Barr & Hayne, 1999; Hayne et al., 2003; McCall, Parke & Kavanaugh, 1977; Meltzoff, 1988). Children who participate in our video experiments frequently label the people and items they see on the monitor screen, indicating that they make sense of the video image. A video presentation also helps young children remember behaviors they learned earlier. Hudson and Sheffield (1999) taught 18- and 24-month-old children eight novel actions (e.g., pressing a toy bear's paw to make it talk), and then brought them back to the lab after a 10- to 16-week delay. The children were shown a video of a preschool child carrying out the actions they had learned previously. When they were tested the next day, the children re-enacted the behaviors at a significantly higher rate than did children who had not received the video reminder. For all of these reasons, it appears likely that our video presentation is meaningful to our 2-year-old research participants.

However, Evans, Crawley and Anderson (2004) voiced a specific concern about the meaningfulness of a video image for object retrieval. Their question was whether very young children had trouble assigning meaning to a two-dimensional representation of a complex, three-dimensional space. Perhaps children's problem with video (and pictures) in the search task is that a depiction of spatial relations on a flat surface does not allow them to reconstruct the relations between the locations in the room. Hypothetically, this could hinder children's ability to use information from video to find a toy hidden in the room. To test this account, Evans and her colleagues presented 2-year-old children with a verbal cue rather than a complex pictorial one. Children did not see the experimenter on video hide a toy in the room; instead, she appeared on camera against a neutral background and simply told children where the toy was hidden. In another condition, the experimenter stood right in front of children while giving the verbal information. Although this task did not require 2-year-olds to make sense of a complex array of spatial relations from video, they still did not use information from video to find the toy (only 20% correct). Children who directly saw and heard the experimenter give the verbal prompt were much more successful (64%). Using Evans et al.'s procedure, we recently replicated this difference between direct and video-presented verbal information as part of a larger study (Troseth, Saylor & Archer,

2006). Two-year-old children apparently do not evaluate verbal cues occurring on video as equivalent to cues they hear directly.

Representing Symbolic Relations

Given that 2-year-old children's difficulties in the video tasks do not stem from problems of memory, motivation, or understanding the meaning of something seen on video, what does make these problem-solving tasks so difficult for them? We think the problem arises from the need for dual representation (DeLoache, 1987, 1991, 2000; DeLoache, Miller & Rosengren, 1997). To solve a problem using information from video, children must mentally represent both the video event actually seen (an event "on TV") and the real event it stands for. In other words, they must recognize the symbolic relation between an image on a television screen and reality. Based on what they see on the video screen, they must construct a mental model of the real event happening in the next room and use this representation to guide their search. On subsequent trials, they must update their mental representation of current events in the room using information from video, rather than relying on an outdated memory (the location of the toy on the previous trial). We think the 2-year-olds' problems in the object-retrieval task are attributable in large part to difficulty in achieving dual representation. Children watch and interpret the video event, but fail to relate it to the real event.

To test this claim, we attempted to remove the need for dual representation from the video task. To do this, we tried to convince children that they were watching hiding events directly through a window, when they were actually watching a video screen (Troseth & DeLoache, 1998, experiment 3). If children did not realize they were watching video, they would not need to represent the "stands for" relation between the video image and the actual event, and the task should therefore be easier. They would need to represent only what they saw – an event visible through a window. The logic is similar to that in a study of older children's understanding of a scale model in which a "shrinking machine" eliminated the need for children to represent a symbolic relation (DeLoache et al., 1997).

The key to the video window study was that the child never saw the video camera or monitor. The experimenter took the child to the adjoining area to "watch through the window" as the assistant hid the toy. She opened the curtain covering the window and directed the child's attention to the hiding event seen through the window. Then she closed the curtain. After a 10-second delay, the child was asked to retrieve the toy. Everything was as similar as possible to the procedure of the study in which children watched the hiding events directly through a window (except that the hiding event visible in the window was actually a video image).

Behind the scenes, feverish activity produced this apparently seamless display. As soon as the experimenter and child entered the adjoining area and closed the door, the assistant rolled a cart containing the monitor and video camera out of a hiding place and positioned the monitor directly in front of the window. The video screen, but not the rest of the monitor, was visible through the window. When the monitor was in place (10 seconds later) the experimenter opened the curtain. After

223

the child watched the hiding event, the experimenter closed the curtain, and the assistant removed the cart before opening the door and inviting the child to search for the toy. This sequence was repeated for each trial, so the child never saw the monitor or video camera.

The children were watching a two-dimensional video image, just like in the other studies, but this time they were told they were watching through a window. Perceptually, the image was the same in both cases, but all of the typical contextual cues indicating that the image was "*on TV*" (e.g., surrounding plastic case, buttons and display lights) were missing, obscured by the curtain and window frame as well as by the verbal suggestions. Nevertheless, if the children noticed the flatness cues, they still might mark the event as "on TV" despite our statement that this was a window.

We compared the children's performance to that of a new group of 2-year-olds in the standard video situation who saw the video on a TV set. The performance of the children who knew they were watching video (41%) was as inaccurate as in the original study (only 3 of 16 children were correct on every trial). When the source of the information was obscured, however, performance was more accurate (63%; Figure 3, *Video Window*), and significantly more children succeeded (9 of 16 children were always correct). The results of this study thus support the dual representation hypothesis: More children made use of the information from video when they did not need to mentally represent the symbolic relation between the video image and the actual event.

Symbolic Experience

Why do children fail to use relevant information if they know it comes from video? Children's prior experience with television may be involved. Children's experience with video (and pictures) is largely, if not entirely, with images that are not immediately relevant to the world outside the edge of the screen or the frame of the picture – the images are "decontextualized" (Ittelson, 1996, p. 173). Most programs on television depict people and events the child has never encountered. For instance, Mr. Rogers talked directly to the boys and girls watching, but he was never in the same room with them and did not answer if they responded to his statements; there was no relation between their behavior and his. Even home videos and family photos, which depict familiar people and entities, typically are not related to the present, but to past birthday parties, grandparent visits, and holiday trips. Furthermore, children's TV shows and books are often pure fantasy – cartoons showing violations of physical and biological principles, with people flying through the air and dogs driving cars.

I think young viewers decide that events occurring on TV are not relevant to the current context: They have learned that they cannot really grab the toy from the commercial, pat the kitty in the video, or taste the food on TV, and that a speeding car appearing on the screen is not going to come through their living room. As they try to figure out the appropriate response to this strange kind of object that depicts something that is not really there, children form a concept that sums up their many individual experiences with video. The conceptual tag *"on TV"* leads them to treat video images as irrelevant to current reality. Reporting an instance of this segregation of video from reality, the mother of a 2-year-old related that her daughter acted confused while watching mommy working out along with an exercise video. The child repeatedly looked back and forth between her mother and the screen, as if surprised to see a relation between the two. For most 2-year-olds, their (incomplete) concept *on TV* may lead them to discount the relevance of the video presentation in the lab to the real, immediate problem they are trying to solve (finding the hidden toy).

One kind of experience that might be expected to make the connection more apparent to children is *live video of themselves*. Previous research suggests that the relation between a live video image and children's own motions may be central to self-recognition (e.g., Bahrick & Watson, 1985; Lewis & Brooks-Gunn, 1979; Povinelli, Landau & Perilloux, 1996). Contingency between children's own movement and what they see on the monitor also may convince them that events on a TV screen can be related to the real world around them and hence can be informative about it.

To determine the impact of this kind of experience with live video, I had parents connect their camcorder to their family television set, and children saw themselves and their families (their parents, siblings, and pets) "live" on TV for two weeks (Troseth, 2003b). During five 10-minute sessions, as children played with toys (e.g., built and knocked over a tower of blocks), their every movement and the consequences of their actions were pictured on the screen. When they came to the lab, 2-year-old children with this prior experience used information from live video to find the hidden toy; in fact, their performance (77% correct – Figure 3, *Home Video*) matched that of children six months older (2-1/2-year-olds) in the original studies.

The experienced children also performed impressively on a subsequent transfer task with still pictures. After the experimenter pointed to a photograph of the hiding place, the children found the toy 60% of the time – much more often than 2-year-olds did in the earlier picture research (DeLoache & Burns, 1994). A control group of children who did not get the live video experience performed inaccurately on both tasks (video: 23% correct; pictures: 15%).

Experiencing repeated opportunities to see their own contingent actions depicted on the video screen, children apparently came to realize that video images could represent real events. Children then used a video image for information even when they themselves were not on the screen (i.e., during the hiding events at the lab) and many went on to detect the relation between a static picture and a real situation. These results demonstrate that, through experience, very young children learn and can generalize important symbolic functions, such as using depictions as sources of information.

Recently we examined the relation between 2-year-old children's naturalistic, everyday symbolic experiences and their success on our object retrieval tasks (Troseth et al., 2005). Parents of 120 participating children filled out an extensive questionnaire regarding their children's exposure to a variety of symbolic entities – television, home video, pictures, the alphabet, drawing, pretending, etc. – and their children participated in the video and picture tasks. In our sample, the average primary caregiver education was a bachelor's degree (the range was "some high school" to "graduate/professional degree") and average family income (based on census tract data) was between $50,000–$75,000 USD (spanning a range of $30,000 to over $100,000). In regression analyses, task success (on both video and picture tasks) was predicted by children's exposure to live video on the LCD display screens of their parents' video cameras and on store security monitors, after controlling for variables such as child vocabulary, parent education, and family income. The children's use of video for information was also predicted by their early understanding of writing and drawing (specifically, by their pretending to draw pictures and write their name or the ABCs, or by actually producing these symbols) – evidence that they may have begun to understand the notion of graphic representation (Kellogg, 1969). Thus, we found patterns of relation between the children's task success and prior exposure to specific symbolic experiences. Both experimental and correlational studies therefore suggest that symbolic experience is one factor promoting children's symbolic development.

With age, children need less experience with live video to figure out the novel symbol-referent relation inherent in our task. After only a 5-minute orientation to live video, older participants (2-1/2-year-olds) readily recognized that a video image could inform them about the real events in the room next door (Troseth & DeLoache, 1998). Several factors may be involved in this age-related advance in symbol use, including greater experience with a wide variety of symbolic artifacts, advancing language ability that allows children to grasp other people's symbolic intentions (see Tomasello, 1999), and increased working memory and representational capacity facilitating the achievement of dual representation (DeLoache, 2002; DeLoache, Simcock & Marzolf, 2004). As children continue to watch video with these increased capacities, their concept of the medium may broaden to include the various ways that video can relate to reality.

MASTERING THE CONVENTIONS OF VIDEO

After children begin to understand the relation between a live video image and a real event, there is still much to learn about this representational medium. To understand the variety of video images they will encounter, children need to master a set of conventions comprising the "grammar" of video (Van Evra, 1990). As word order and morphology convey meaning in written language, a set of formal features conveys relational information and point-of-view in video, directing focus to particular aspects of a referent situation (Greenfield, 1984; see also Wright & Huston, 1981; Wright & Huston, 1983; see also Bamberger, this volume). For instance, cuts convey a change of perspective on a scene; zooms show how a detail fits into its surrounding context; a dissolve signifies a change of scene or time. Montage (cutting back and forth between two shots) signifies comparison, approach, or convergence. Camera position conveys point of view.

"Symbolic conventions like these, taken together, form a code the viewer must know in order to comprehend what happens on the screen" (Greenfield, 1984, p. 10).

When children first encounter video that includes formal features, there are many opportunities for misunderstanding. Children must learn that a close-up does not indicate that a depicted object (e.g., an insect) is huge. They need to learn that instant replay does not indicate the repetition of an action – something quite difficult for preschool-aged children to understand (Rice, Huston &Wright, 1986). Processing the code of formal features takes cognitive resources, leaving the novice viewer few resources to direct toward understanding the contents of programs. As in learning from conventional notation systems such as writing, mastery of a formal code is necessary for children to comprehend educational content from many television programs (Fisch, 2000).

Once children have achieved a degree of television literacy (Greenfield, 1984), they can use the presence or absence of formal features to interpret the contents of a video: Is this documentary or fantasy? It is a dramatization or live coverage of a real event? In a study by Wright, Huston, and their colleagues (1994), 5- and 7-year-old children showed that they had begun to master this *genre factor*; for instance, they distinguished dramas from documentaries on the basis of formal features such as dramatic music and close-ups. Children who were interviewed shortly after the space shuttle Challenger disaster used the absence of formal features ("No music, no close-ups") to interpret the video they saw as being real rather than fiction (Wright et al., 1989, p. 33). Substantial evidence indicates that preschool-aged children have begun to figure out the code and benefit from information presented in educational programs (e.g. Anderson et al., 2000; Anderson, Huston, Schmitt, Linebarger & Wright, 2001; Crawley, Anderson, Wilder, Williams & Santomero, 1999; Mielke, 2001; Rice, Huston, Truglio & Wright, 1990; Rice & Woodsmall, 1988; Wright et al., 2001; Zill, 2001).

CONCLUSION

This discussion has pointed out areas of similarity between video and notational systems such as writing and numbers. First, understanding and using a pictorial symbol like a video image may require the same kind of underlying mental representation as that which is needed for abstract notation: One must perceive and interpret the concrete entity (object, marking, image) itself and represent the "stands for" relation between that object and what it represents. In addition, substantial mapping and decoding are required to interpret both the formal features of video and the conventions of notation.

The many functions of video images illustrate the fact that any representation is "a construal of an object" and that making and displaying a depiction "is not a matter of copying [reality] but conveying" (Goodman, 1976, p. 9; see also Bamberger, this volume; Roth, this volume). A single video image can convey different meanings in different contexts. It can provide information about the past or the present, about specific entities or a general class of objects, about real events or total fabrications. One of the main challenges for young children is figuring out the particular interpretation to put to a video image in order to get the information intended by its creator.

Because it appears likely that video and other symbol systems rest on the same kind of mental representation, experience with one kind of symbol may help the novice figure out how to use another. My research shows that very young children learn from their experience with video and transfer what they learn to still pictures (Troseth et al., 2005; Troseth, 2003b). Planned longitudinal studies will establish whether children's early understanding and use of simple symbols such as video images and pictures relates to their learning about notations as they approach and enter the school years. Also, training studies may establish the kind of early symbolic experience that best facilitates the acquisition of notational knowledge. Liben (1999) suggests that as children gain experience with multiple depictions of the same thing (e.g., a home video of a dog, a photo of a dog in an advertisement, a drawing of a dog in story book, a toy replica of dog – all labeled with the word that is used for the real referent), they may develop an abstract notion of symbolization. When they encounter the written inscription "d-o-g", their concept of how symbols work may help them to master the formal notation.

REFERENCES

Anderson, D.R. & Pempek, T.A. (2005). Television and very young children. *American Behavioral Scientist, 48*(5), 505–522.

Anderson, D.R., Bryant, J., Wilder, A., Santomero, A., Williams, M. & Crawley, A.M. (2000). Researching Blue's Clues: Viewing behavior and impact. *Media Psychology, 2*(2), 179–194.

Anderson, D.R., Huston, A.C., Schmitt, K.L., Linebarger, D.L. & Wright, J.C. (2001). *Early childhood television viewing and adolescent behavior: The recontact study.* Monographs of the Society for Research in Child Development, Vol. 66, No. 1, Serial No. 264, pp. vii–147.

Bahrick, L.E. & Watson, J.S. (1985). Detection of intermodal proprioceptive-visual contingency as a potential basis of self-perception in infancy. *Developmental Psychology, 21*(6), 963–973.

Barr, R. & Hayne, H. (1999). Developmental changes in imitation from television during infancy. *Child Development, 70*(5), 1067–1081.

Bialystok, E. (1992). Symbolic representation of letters and numbers. *Cognitive Development, 7*(3), 301–316.

Bigelow, A.E. (1996). Infants' memory for contingently responding persons. *Infant Behavior and Development, 19* (Special ICIS Issue), 334 pp.

Bigelow, A.E. & Birch, S.A.J. (2000). The effects of contingency in previous interactions on infants' preference for social partners. *Infant Behavior and Development, 22*(3), 367–382.

Butter, E.J., Popovich, P.M., Stackhouse, R.H. & Garner, R.K. (1981). Discrimination of television programs and commercials by preschool children. *Journal of Advertising Research, 21*(2), 53–56.

Carpenter, M., Nagell, K. & Tomasello, M. (1998). *Social cognition, joint attention, and communicative competence from 9 to 15 months of age.* Monographs of the Society for Research in Child Development, 63(4, Serial No. 255).

Crawley, A.M., Anderson, D.R., Wilder, A., Williams, M. & Santomero, A. (1999). Effects of repeated exposures to a single episode of the television program Blue's Clues on the viewing behaviors and comprehension of preschool children. *Journal of Educational Psychology, 91*(4), 630–637.

DeLoache, J.S. (1987). Rapid change in the symbolic functioning of very young children. *Science, 238*(4833), 1556–1557.

DeLoache, J.S. (1991). Symbolic functioning in very young children: Understanding of pictures and models. *Child Development, 62*(4), 736–752.

DeLoache, J.S. (1995). Early understanding and use of symbols: The model model. *Current Directions in Psychological Science*, *4*(4), 109–113.

DeLoache, J.S. (2000). Dual representation and young children's use of scale models. *Child Development*, *71*(2), 329–338.

DeLoache, J.S. (2002). The symbol-mindedness of young children. In W. Hartup & R.A. Weinberg (Eds.), *Child psychology in retrospect and prospect: In celebration of the 75th anniversary of the Institute of Child Development* (Vol. 32, pp. 73–101). Mahwah, NJ: Lawrence Erlbaum Associates.

DeLoache, J.S. & Burns, N.M. (1994). Early understanding of the representational function of pictures. *Cognition*, *52*(2), 83–110.

DeLoache, J.S., Miller, K.F. & Rosengren, K.S. (1997). The credible shrinking room: Very young children's performance with symbolic and nonsymbolic relations. *Psychological Science*, *8*(4), 308–313.

DeLoache, J.S., Pierroutsakos, S.L. & Troseth, G.L. (1996). The three 'R's' of pictorial competence. In R. Vasta (Ed.), *Annals of child development* (Vol. 12, pp. 1–48). London: Jessica Kingsley Publishers.

DeLoache, J.S., Pierroutsakos, S.L., Uttal, D.H., Rosengren, K.S. & Gottlieb, A. (1998). Grasping the nature of pictures. *Psychological Science*, *9*(3), 205–210.

DeLoache, J.S., Simcock, G. & Marzolf, D.P. (2004). Transfer by very young children in the symbolic retrieval task. *Child Development*, *75*(6), 1708–1718.

DeLoache, J.S., Strauss, M.S. & Maynard, J. (1979). Picture perception in infancy. *Infant Behavior and Development*, *2*(1), 77–89.

Deocampo, J.A. (2004). A new paradigm for testing dual representational understanding with different representational demands. *Dissertation Abstracts International: Section B: The Sciences and Engineering*, *64* (9B), 4652 (UMI No. AAI3105440).

Deocampo, J.A. & Hudson, J.A. (2005). When seeing is not believing: Two-year-olds' use of video representations to find a hidden toy. *Journal of Cognition and Development*, *6*(2), 229–260.

Donohue, T.R., Henke, L.L. & Donohue, W.A. (1980). Do kids know what TV commercials intend? *Journal of Advertising Research*, *20*(5), 51–57.

Evans Schmidt, M., Crawley, A.M. & Anderson, D.R. (in press). Two-year-olds' object retrieval based on television: Testing a perceptual account. *Media Psychology*.

Fisch, S.M. (2000). A capacity model of children's comprehension of educational content on television. *Media Psychology*, *2*(1), 63–91.

Flavell, J.H., Flavell, E.R., Green, F.L. & Korfmacher, J.E. (1990). Do young children think of television images as pictures or real objects? *Journal of Broadcasting and Electronic Media*, *34*(4), 399–419.

Ganea, P.A. & DeLoache, J.S. (2005). *From picture books to the real world: Pictorial realism affects young children's generalization from depicted to real objects.* Manuscript submitted for publication.

Gardner, H., Howard, V. & Perkins, D. (1974). Symbol systems: A philosophical, psychological, and educational investigation. In D.R. Olson (Ed.), *Media and symbols: The forms of expression, communication, and education. The 73rd yearbook of the National Society for the Study of Education* (pp. 27–55). Chicago: University of Chicago Press.

Gelman, S.A., Coley, J.D., Rosengren, K.S., Hartman, E. & Pappas, A. (1998). *Beyond labeling: The role of maternal input in the acquisition of richly structured categories.* Monographs of the Society for Research in Child Development, 63(1, Serial No. 253).

Gibson, J.J. (1979). *The ecological approach to visual perception.* Boston: Houghton Mifflin.

Goodman, N. (1976). *Languages of art: An approach to a theory of symbols* (2nd edn.). Indianapolis, IN: Hackett Publishing.

Greenfield, P. (1984). *Mind and media: The effects of television, video games, and computers.* Cambridge, MA: Harvard University Press.

Gregory, R.L. (1970). *The intelligent eye.* New York: McGraw-Hill.

Gusella, J.L., Muir, D. & Tronick, E.A. (1988). The effect of manipulating maternal behavior during an interaction on three- and six-month-olds' affect and attention. *Child Development*, *59*(4), 1111–1124.

Hains, S.M.J. & Muir, D.W. (1996). Effects of stimulus contingency in infant-adult interactions. *Infant Behavior and Development*, *19*(1), 49–61.

Harris, P.L. & Kavanaugh, R.D. (1993). *Young children's understanding of pretense*. Monographs of the Society for Research in Child Development, 58(1, Serial No. 231).

Hayes, L.A. & Watson, J.S. (1981). Facial orientation of parents and elicited smiling by infants. *Infant Behavior and Development, 4*(4), 333–340.

Hayne, H., Herbert, J. & Simcock, G. (2003). Imitation from television by 24- and 30-month-olds. *Developmental Science, 6*(3), 254–261.

Hudson, J.A. & Sheffield, E.G. (1999). The role of reminders in young children's memory development. In C. Tamis-Lemoude & L. Balter (Eds.), *Child psychology: A handbook of contemporary issues* (pp. 193–221). Philadelphia: Psychology Press/Taylor & Francis.

Huston, A.C. & Wright, J.C. (1983). Children's processing of television: The informative function of formal features. In J. Bryant & D.R. Anderson (Eds.), *Children's understanding of television: Research on attention and comprehension* (pp. 35–68). New York: Academic Press.

Huston, A.C., Wright, J.C., Marquis, J. & Green, S.B. (1999). How young children spend their time: Television and other activities. *Developmental Psychology, 35*(4), 912–925.

Ittelson, W.H. (1996). Visual perception of markings. *Psychonomic Bulletin and Review, 3*(2), 171–187.

Jaglom, L.M. & Gardner, H. (1981). The preschool television viewer as anthropologist. In H.H. Kelly & H. Gardner (Eds.), *New directions in child development: No. 13. Viewing children through television* (pp. 9–30). San Francisco: Jossy-Bass.

Jordan, A.B. & Woodward, E.H., IV. (2001). Electronic childhood: The availability and use of household media by 2- to 3-year-olds. *Zero to Three, 22*, 4–9.

Karmiloff-Smith, A. (1996). Internal representations and external notations: A developmental perspective. In D. Peterson (Ed.), *Forms of representation: An interdisciplinary theme for cognitive science* (pp. 141–151). Exeter: Intellect Books.

Kellogg, R. (1969). *Analyzing children's art*. Palo Alto, CA: National Press.

Krcmar, M., Grela, B.G. & Lin, Y. (2004). *Learning vocabulary from television: Toddlers, teletubbies, and attention*. Manuscript submitted for publication.

Kuhl, P.K., Tsao, F.-M. & Liu, H.-M. (2003). Foreign-language experience in infancy: Effects of short-term exposure and social interaction on phonetic learning. *Proceedings of the National Academy of Sciences of the United States of America (PNAS), 100*(15), 9096–9101.

Lee, K. & Karmiloff-Smith, A. (1996). The development of external symbol systems: The child as a notator. In R. Gelman & T.K. Au (Eds.), *Perceptual and cognitive development. Handbook of perception and cognition* (2nd edn.) (pp. 185–211). San Diego, CA: Academic Press.

Leslie, A.M. (1987). Pretense and representations: The origins of "theory of mind". *Psychological Review, 94*, 412–426.

Lewis, M. & Brooks-Gunn, J. (1979). *Social congnition abnd the acquisition of self*. New York: Plenum Press.

Liben, L.S. (1999). Developing an understanding of external spatial representations. In I.E. Sigel (Ed.), *The development of representational thought: Theoretical perspectives* (pp. 297–321). Hillsdale, NJ: Erlbaum.

Marzolf, D.P. & DeLoache, J.S. (1994). Transfer in young children's understanding of spatial relations. *Child Development, 64*, 1–15.

McCall, R.B., Parke, R.D. & Kavanaugh, R.D. (1977). *Imitation of live and televised models by children on to three years of age*. Monographs of the Society for Research in Child Development, 42(5, Serial No. 173).

Meltzoff, A.N. (1988). Imitation of televised models by infants. *Child Development, 59*, 1221–1229.

Mielke, K.W. (2001). A review of research on the educational and social impact of Sesame Street. In S.M. Fisch & R.T. Truglio (Eds.), *"G" is for growing: Thirty years of research on children and Sesame Street* (pp. 83–95). Mahwah, NJ: Lawrence Erlbaum Associates.

Muir, D., Hains, S.M.J., Cao, Y. & D'Entremont, B. (1996). Three-to six-month olds' sensitivity to adult intentionality: The role of adult contingency and eye direction in dyadic interactions. *Infant Behavior and Development, 19*, 200.

Mumme, D.L. & Fernald, A. (2003). The infant as onlooker: Learning from emotional reactions observed in a television scenario. *Child Development, 74*(1), 221–237.

Murphy, K.C. (1978). Painting in the context of shared activity. *Child Development, 49*, 371–380.

Murray, L. & Trevarthen, C. (1985). Emotional regulation of interactions between two-month-olds and their mothers. In T. Fields & N. Fox (Eds.), *Social perception in infants* (pp. 177–197). Norwood, NJ: Ablex.

Ninio, A. & Bruner, J. (1978). The achievement and antecedents of labelling. *Journal of Child Language*, 5(1), 1–15.

Perner, J. (1991). *Understanding the representational mind*. Cambridge, MA: The MIT Press.

Pierroutsakos, S.L., Diener, M. & Roberts, A. (2003). *Infants' manual and affective responses to live and video presentations*. Unpublished manuscript.

Pierroutsakos, S.L. & Troseth, G.L. (2003). Video verite: Infants' manual investigation of objects on video. *Infant Behavior and Development*, 26(2), 183–199.

Potter, M.C. (1979). Mundane symbolism: The relations among objects, names, and ideas. In N.R. Smith & M.B. Franklin (Eds.), *Symbolic functioning in childhood* (pp. 41–65). Hillsdale, NJ: Erlbaum.

Povinelli, D.J., Landau, K.R. & Perilloux, H.K. (1996). Self-recognition in young children using delayed versus live feedback: Evidence of a developmental asynchrony. *Child Development*, 67(4), 1540–1554.

Preissler, M.A. & Carey, S. (2004). Do both pictures and words function as symbols for 18- and 24-month-old children? *Journal of Cognition and Development*, 5(2), 185–212.

Rakoczy, H., Tomasello, M. & Striano, T. (in press). How children turn objects into symbols: A cultural learning account. In L. Namy (Ed.), *Symbol use and symbol representation*. New York: Erlbaum.

Rice, M.L., Huston, A.C., Truglio, R. & Wright, J.C. (1990). Words from "Sesame Street": Learning vocabulary while viewing. *Developmental Psychology*, 26(3), 421–428.

Rice, M.L., Huston, A.C. & Wright, J.C. (1986). Replays as repetitions: Young children's interpretation of television forms. *Journal of Applied Developmental Psychology*, 7(1), 61–76.

Rice, M.L. & Woodsmall, L. (1988). Lessons from television: Children's word learning when viewing. *Child Development*, 59(2), 420–429.

Rochat, P. & Morgan, R. (1995). Spatial determinants in the perception of self-produced leg movements in 3- to 5-month-old infants. *Developmental Psychology*, 31(4), 626–636.

Schmitt, K.L. & Anderson, D.R. (2002). Television and reality: Toddlers' use of visual information from video to guide behavior. *Media Psychology*, 4(1), 51–76.

Sigel, I.E. (1979). On becoming a thinker: A psychoeducational model. *Educational Psychologist*, 14, 70–78.

Tolchinsky-Landsmann, L.T. & Karmiloff-Smith, A. (1992). Children's understanding of notations as domains of knowledge versus referential-communicative tools. *Cognitive Development*, 7(3), 287–300.

Tomasello, M. (1999). The cultural ecology of young children's interactions with objects and artifacts. In E. Winograd & R. Fivush (Eds.), *Ecological approaches to cognition: Essays in honor of Ulric Neisser. Emory symposia in cognition* (pp. 153–170). Mahwah, NJ: Lawrence Erlbaum Associates.

Troseth, G.L. (2003a). Getting a clear picture: Young children's understanding of a televised image. *Developmental Science*, 6(3), 247–253.

Troseth, G.L. (2003b). TV guide: Two-year-old children learn to use video as a source of information. *Developmental Psychology*, 39(1), 140–150.

Troseth, G., Casey, A., Lawver, K., Walker, J. & Cole, D. (2005). *Naturalistic experience and the early use of symbolic artifacts*. Manuscript submitted for publication.

Troseth, G.L. & DeLoache, J.S. (1998). The medium can obscure the message: Young children's understanding of video. *Child Development*, 69(4), 950–965.

Troseth, G.L. & DeLoache, J.S. (2003). *Very young children's use of video to find a hidden parent*. Unpublished manuscript.

Troseth, G.L., Pierroutsakos, S.L. & Deloache, J.S. (2004). From the innocent to the intelligent eye: The early development of pictorial competence. In R.V. Kail (Ed.), *Advances in child development and behavior* (Vol. 32, pp. 1–35). San Diego, CA: Elsevier Academic Press.

Troseth, G., Saylor, M. & Archer, A. (2006). Young children's use of video as a source of socially relevant information. *Child Development*, 77(3), 786–799.

Van Evra, J. (1990). *Television and child development*. Hillsdale, NJ: Lawrence Erlbaum Associates.

Werner, H. & Kaplan, B. (1963). *Symbol formation: An organismic-developmental approach to language and the expression of thought*. Oxford, New York: Wiley.

Whitehurst, G.J., Arnold, D.S., Epstein, J.N., Angell, A.L., et al. (1994). A picture book reading intervention in day care and home for children from low-income families. *Developmental Psychology*, *30*(5), 679–689.

Wolf, D. & Gardner, H. (1981). On the structure of early symbolization. In R.L. Schiefelbusch & D.L. Bricken (Eds.), *Early language: Acquisition and intervention* (pp. 289–327). Baltimore, MD: University Park Press.

Wright, J.C. & Huston, A. (1981). Children's understanding of the forms of television. In H.H. Kelly & H. Gardner (Eds.), *Viewing children through television* (pp. 73–87). San Fransisco: Jossey-Bass.

Wright, J.C. & Huston, A.C. (1983). A matter of form: Potentials of television for young viewers. *American Psychologist*, *38*(7), 835–843.

Wright, J.C., Huston, A.C., Murphy, K.C., St Peters, M., Pinon, M., Scantlin, R. & Kotler, J. (2001). The relations of early television viewing to school readiness and vocabulary of children from low-income families: The early window project. *Child Development*, *72*(5), 1347–1366.

Wright, J.C., Huston, A.C., Reitz, A.L. & Piemyat, S. (1994). Young children's perceptions of television reality: Determinants and developmental differences. *Developmental Psychology*, *30*(2), 229–239.

Wright, J.C., Kunkel, D., Pinon, M.F. & Huston, A.C. (1989). How children reacted to televised coverage of the space shuttle disaster. *Journal of Communication*, *39*(2), 27–45.

Zill, N. (2001). Does Sesame Street enhance school readiness?: Evidence from a national survey of children. In S.M. Fisch & R.T. Truglio (Eds.), *"G" is for Growing: Thirty years of research on children and Sesame Street* (pp. 115–130). Mahwah, NJ: Lawrence Erlbaum Associates.

Georgene L. Troseth
Department of Psychology and Human Development
Vanderbilt University, USA

MICHELLE ESKRITT AND KANG LEE

THE IMPACT OF NOTATION ON COGNITION & ITS DEVELOPMENT: THEORETICAL PERSPECTIVES & EMPIRICAL EVIDENCE[1]

Theorizing about the influence of notational use on cognition has a long tradition. Interestingly, unlike modern views, notational use has not always been viewed positively. For example, Plato believed that external symbols would be detrimental to thought in the sense that literate people would merely be regurgitating information found in books rather than thinking about the information for themselves. Furthermore, literate individuals would come to rely on notations to act as their external memory store leading to the deterioration of internal memory. A more positive view of external symbols started to evolve during the Enlightenment. Philosophers at that time, such as John Stuart Mill, believed that external symbols were necessary for systematic thought (Mill, 1969). This position led to the rise of universal education as learning how to decode and produce alphanumeric symbols was believed to be of critical importance to an individual's intellectual and personal growth. At present, this positive view of the relationship between notation and cognition is widely held by individuals from all walks of life. For example, the public often regards illiteracy as being a problem similar to poverty or malnutrition. Policy makers and politicians see the increase of literacy levels as one of the main impetus to national and individual development.

Despite the prevalence of this commonsense view, there has been limited systematic theoretical analysis of the relationship between notation and cognition. Furthermore, the effect of notation on cognition has rarely been directly examined empirically. Theories and research on how notations may influence cognitive processing are scattered throughout a variety of fields of enquiry that often do not even reference one other. We would like to make the argument that literacy can have important implications for cognition and its development, and specifically, that adults' and children's use of notations will impact on their cognitive experiences. Before embarking on this argument, however, we would like to elaborate on our choice of terminology. A number of different terms have been used to describe this area such as "literacy", "symbolic literacy", "notation", "external symbols", "numeracy", and "writing". The most commonly used are "literacy" and "writing", which we would like to avoid. Literacy is usually thought of as the ability to read and write. While a number of theorists (Illich, 1991; McLane & McNamee, 1990; Olson, 1994) have argued that literacy involves more than just the ability to decode and produce words, this is still a common misconception.

Likewise, "writing" is again thought to be restricted to written words even though in modern societies many different types of written symbols can be found from charts and figures, to musical notation, to ideograms and icons. Therefore, to avoid confusion and to capture the issue to be discussed here in a broader sense, we choose to use the terms "notations" or "permanent external symbols".

The present chapter attempts to review what theoretical and empirical work has been done, and to piece together a picture of the relationship between notation and cognition. We will first examine the existing theoretical discussions on the relationship between notation and cognition from a historical perspective. Second, we will discuss the issue from the cross-cultural perspective, which will be followed by reviewing the existing empirical research on adults' production and use of notations and its impact on their cognitive processes. Then, the developmental evidence regarding the issue will be examined. Finally, we will discuss some key theoretical and methodological issues involved in this area of research and speculate on future research directions.

HISTORICAL PERSPECTIVE

During the 1960s, some theorists (Goody & Watt, 1963/1968; Havelock, 1963; McLuhan, 1962) suggested that writing actually alters the way individuals think. Their aim was to understand how the invention and use of permanent external symbols influenced different societies at different historic times. According to this view, individuals in a literate culture think in a qualitatively different manner from those in an oral, nonliterate culture.

> Without writing, the literate mind would not and could not think as it does, not only when engaged in writing but normally even when it is composing its thoughts in oral form. More than any other single invention, writing has transformed human consciousness. (Ong, 1982, p. 78)

These theorists revolutionized ideas about the influence of notation on thought. For example, McLuhan (1962) explored how thought is influenced by different media. He argued that the alphabet "changed the ratio of the senses" and altered the way that literate societies perceived the world, which was exacerbated by the invention of the printing press and other forms of mass media. Havelock (1963) examined Plato's *Republic* and put forth the argument that, while Plato thought negatively about the influence of writing, the invention of the alphabet radically changed the way the Ancient Greeks thought as compared to the earlier, oral society of Homer. Havelock suggested that in the *Republic*, Plato argued for a change in the educational system from the memorization and internalization of poems and epics to an emphasis on the separation of the "knower from known". That is, an individual must think of objects and concepts separate from their context; for example, to think about the concept of "justice" divorced from a particular situation.

Both Goody and Watt (1963/1968) and Ong (1982) argued that the invention of the alphabet influenced reasoning and logic. Goody and Watt (1963/1968) noted that the rise of literacy in Ancient Greece coincided with the development of two new disciplines: history and logic. They argued that writing allowed permanent records to be created so that the present could be compared to the past, which allowed for the development of the study of history. With the use of a writing system, inconsistencies that were not noticed in oral cultures become apparent in literate cultures, which led to scepticism. Scepticism in turn resulted in a search for alternatives that gave rise to logic and the syllogism. Ong (1982) suggested that in an oral culture, sustained thought could only be achieved through communication and that this thought was aggregative, participatory, and traditional. Literate thought, on the other hand, is analytic, objective and logical. While Ong did not dispute that all thought is to some degree analytical, he suggested that only with literacy comes the ability for "abstracting, sequential, classificatory, explanatory examination of phenomena or of stated truths" (p. 8).

These authors argued that literacy was the cause of the abstract, logical, scientific mind of Western society. However, Harris (1986) and Olson (1994) pointed out that many of these earlier theories tended to limit themselves to the influence of the alphabet and were vague about the specific mechanisms that led to this qualitative change. As a result, they have left themselves open to criticism from those taking a cross-cultural perspective who pointed to cultures that developed writing systems but did not develop in a manner similar to Western culture (e.g., Scribner & Cole, 1982) and to oral cultures that developed forms of abstract reasoning (e.g., Hutchins, 1983; Neisser, 1976) that are supposedly not available to those without a writing system.

More recent theories have rectified these problems and thus leave open the intriguing possibility that external symbol use may alter certain aspects of individuals' cognition in a specific manner. One of the contemporary theorists is Olson (1994), who provided a specific account of how notation influences cognition. He suggested that learning the alphabet affects metalinguistic knowledge by altering our perception of language and creating a new awareness of interpretation. Olson argued that writing allows language to become an object that can be studied; it provides a conceptual model for language. He argued that, unlike many of the earlier theories that focussed on the influence of the type of writing system used, it was the way that a text was read that influences thought. Notation can call attention to the distinction between what is said and what is meant. It is the awareness of the difference between the intention of the author and the external representation that leads to "the shift from thinking about things to thinking about representations of those things, that is, thinking about thought" (p. 282).

Unfortunately, the vast majority of evidence for the historical perspective comes from historical analysis rather than empirical research. While historical research can provide intriguing hypotheses, empirical research, when possible, is necessary to test these ideas. As Olson and Astington (1990) pointed out, when historians discuss the influence of literacy on cognition, they are referring to the "evolution of a literate mode of discourse that took perhaps a millennium to develop" (p. 708). Psychologists, on the other hand, are trying to determine the influence of learning this literate mode of discourse on the individual within a lifetime at most.

EVOLUTIONARY PERSPECTIVE

Donald (1991) has taken a much longer historical perspective by examining the evolution of cognition, including the development of permanent external symbols as a form of an external working memory. While some theorists mention that permanent external symbols enhance memory, they have argued that literacy is more than a memory aid. However, Donald argued that the ability to use permanent external symbols as working memory and storage is the key to understanding how permanent external symbols could alter thought. Memory is more than just passive storage; it is an integral part of all cognitive processes. The ability to use permanent external symbols to store information allows for the development of new memory strategies. Furthermore, permanent external symbols allow information to be transformed and organized in new ways. As an example Donald offered the "list":

> Oral listing is limited, owing to memory limitations; orally memorized lists tend to tie up working memory preventing further processing of the list. In contrast, visual lists can be arranged in various ways, and juxtaposed to simplify the later treatment of the information they contain. List arrangements can facilitate the sorting, summarizing, and classifying of items and can reveal patterns otherwise not discernable. (Donald, 1991, p. 288)

The invention of visuographic symbols led to the development of a number of different graphic conventions and notational systems. These in turn allowed for the development of an external symbolic storage system. Previously, humans relied on cultural information being stored in individual physical memory. Nonliterate cultures tend to rely on formulaic recital and group rituals, or visual imagination to store collective memories (Donald, 1993). While this can store impressive amounts of information, it has its limits. With the external symbolic storage system, collective memory can be stored in an external form. This "external memory" creates the possibility of a change in the role of memory and allows for new storage, retrieval, and processing strategies. Permanent external symbols can function both as a long-term and short-term memory. New ways of thinking have developed with external symbols such as formal arguments, systematic taxonomies, logic, and formal measurement. Donald (1991) argued that the ability to use the external symbolic storage system requires the development of a cluster of cognitive skills that are generally thought of as "literacy" skills. Evidence for these skills come from studies of neurophysiological damage such as acquired dyslexia, dysgraphias and acalculias.

By framing the invention and development of permanent external symbols in terms of cultural evolution can lead to the inappropriate conclusion that oral cultures are less "evolved" than literate cultures. To be fair, we do not believe this to be Donald's intent. He did postulate that the development of different notational systems was probably the result of a conceptual need. Some level of understanding was already present and the development of permanent external symbols provided a powerful tool for exploiting and developing further that understanding (see also Vasco, this volume). Donald's discussion of external symbol use can also suggest that the effects of notation on cognition are necessarily positive. But as Zhang (1993) argued, permanent external symbols "not only represent information; they also constrain, anchor, structure, and change people's cognitive behavior" (p. 775). As will be discussed later, the effects of permanent external symbols are too complex to be so simply pegged as always having positive effects.

THE CROSS-CULTURAL PERSPECTIVE

Early Western explorers, such as Livingston (1865), noted how differently oral cultures reacted to permanent external symbols.

> To all who have not acquired it, a knowledge of letters is quite unfathomable; there is nought like it within the compass of their observations; and we have no comparison with anything except pictures to aid them in comprehending the idea of signs of words. It seems to them supernatural that we see in a book things taking place, or having occurred at a distance. No amount of explanation conveys the idea unless they learn to read. (Livingston, 1865, p. 189)

Levy-Bruhl (1923) was one of the first to qualitatively describe the thought processes of "primitive" (i.e., oral) cultures. He argued from evidence of writings from early missionaries and anthropologists about encounters with different oral societies, that nonliterate cognition is mystical, primitive and concrete. According to Levy-Bruhl, most nonliterates believe that writing "speaks" to the literate individual and the literate individual must have some charm or magic to make the writing speak which accounts for the nonliterates' inability to "hear" what the writing has to say. Writing is also viewed as a mystical part of the literate cultures' religions. It has been thought to be able to tell the future or answer any question. Some peoples even believed that writing can "see" or is sentient in some way. For example, Levy-Bruhl related how one nonliterate was carrying a package containing a message and tobacco. On his way to deliver the package he removed the tobacco. When the person receiving the message asked about the tobacco, the messenger became quite indignant because he had hid the message in a tree trunk before taking the tobacco so that the message could not see the theft.

More recent work examining oral cultures has focussed on finding evidence against this ethnocentric view that oral thought is illogical, concrete, and primitive. Feldman (1991), for example, has examined different types of discourse from a number of oral cultures. She argued that a common assumption is that oral production in oral cultures is similar to that of Western society and that these productions are in the form of everyday conversation. In fact, oral discourse in oral cultures can have very distinctive forms because they do not have competition from written forms and these oral forms show evidence of quite sophisticated thought. As an example, Feldman (1991) discussed the Ilongot of the Philippines who developed a number of different types of oral genres, one of which is the *purang*. *Purang*, a type of formal oratory used to resolve disputes, has a distinctive sound and form. An important part of *purang* is to understand the underlying assumptions and mental states of others. Interpretation plays an important role as replies have to include the interpretation of the previous speakers' discourse. Feldman argued that *purang* demonstrates evidence of metalinguistic awareness because of the degree of interpretation involved. Furthermore, *purang* often includes discussion about words and discourse itself. Thus, not only literate cultures have an interest in interpretation and metalinguistics.

Two of the most well-known empirical studies that have examined the influence of permanent external symbols across cultures are by Luria (1976) and Scribner and Cole (1982). Luria (1976) examined the effects of the introduction of literacy to an isolated area of Russia, Uzbekistan. An experimenter sat in a teahouse or at a campfire with groups of individuals with differing amounts of exposure to schooling and literacy and had long conversations with them. Embedded in the conversations were questions pertaining to perception, logic, abstraction, and self-consciousness in the form of riddles, a familiar and natural part of these types of conversations. Luria found that even small amounts of schooling could have dramatic influence on the types of responses given. Those with even minimal amounts of education showed signs of abstract, theoretical, logical thinking compared to the nonliterates who were more practically, situationally orientated. The most common example given of Luria's work is the nonliterates' answers when asked to respond to syllogisms:

> The following syllogism is presented: **In the Far North, where there is snow, all bears are white. Novaya Zemlya is in the Far North and there is always snow there. What color are the bears there?**
>
> > "There are different sorts of bears".
> > *Failure to infer from syllogism.*
> > The syllogism is repeated.
> > "I don't know; I've seen a black bear, I've never seen any other colors ... Each locality has its own animals: if it's white, they will be white; if it's yellow, they will be yellow".
> > *Appeals only to personal graphic experience.*
> > **But what kinds of bears are there in Novaya Zemblya?**
> > "We always speak only of what we see; we don't talk about what we haven't seen".
> > ... (Luria, 1976, pp. 108–109).

As nonliterates' answers were qualitatively different not only for questions about reasoning, logic, and abstraction but also for perception, self-consciousness, and imagination, Luria argued that notation influences both our external reality and our "own inner world as shaped in relation to other people" (p. 159). It is important to note that Luria was not arguing that the thinking patterns of the nonliterate were lesser in any way to those who had received schooling, just that their way of thinking was qualitatively different.

The Vai, a small group of people living in rural Liberia, have developed their own syllabary writing system and learn their own script on an individual basis (i.e., one on one instruction) rather than in schools. Their writing system is used primarily to write letters for both personal and commercial use. Scribner and Cole (1982) hoped to use this opportunity to determine if the differences in thought processes suggested by such authors as Luria, Goody and Watt, and Havelock, would be found between those literate and illiterate of the Vai script. Scribner and Cole tested abstraction, classification, memory, logic, and communication with literate and illiterate individuals with the Vai writing system, those literate with the Qur'an, and those who had received schooling in English. For the most part, the only group that showed superior performance on the tests were those who had received schooling. This superior performance was for the most part limited to tasks related to verbal exposition.

From these results, Scribner and Cole argued that it was not permanent external symbols per se that changes thought, but schooling. Support for this view also comes from research by Greenfield and associates who found that different aspects of cognitive development are influenced by schooling (for review see Greenfield & Bruner, 1969). Luria's study was confounded with influence of schooling and permanent external symbols. Scribner and Cole argued that while literacy in a particular writing system may enhance cognitive abilities related to the particular way that writing system is used, permanent external symbols in no way alter thought processes.

However, a flaw with their argument is that schooling is a product of a literate culture (Donald, 1991). Literacy and schooling are not independent from one another. Unlike some cognitive abilities such as language that often comes naturally and easily, learning to comprehend and produce an external symbol system is a painstaking task. The school system was created to teach individuals the skills necessary for a literate culture, of which reading and writing are only a part. As Olson and Astington (1990) wrote, "the cognitive consequences of literacy are tied to the involvement in a literate culture and not directly to the skills of reading and writing" (p. 711).

Educational Psychology

One area in educational psychology has taken a practical approach to examining the influence of permanent external symbols on cognition. Researchers within this field have studied the ability of undergraduates to use note-taking to learn the contents of a lecture. Over 99% of students, when questioned, said that they take notes during lectures (Palmatier & Bennet, 1974), and Meter, Yokoi, and Pressley (1994) found that students reported taking notes to help themselves pay attention in class, to organize the lecture material, and to use them later as a study aid. These different goals of note-taking illustrate a distinction made by Di Vesta and Gray (1972) about the possible functions of note-taking. According to the *encoding hypothesis*, note-taking is used to aid in the encoding of the lecture material. That is, the process of note-taking itself is important for learning new information. Kiewra (1985, 1989), in reviewing the existing literature, found that in 35 studies, note-takers performed significantly better on a subsequent test compared to those that did not take notes. Another 23 studies found no difference between these two groups, and 3 found note-taking to be detrimental to performance. A number of different variables can influence the effect of note-taking on performance such as density of information presented (e.g., Aiken, Thomas & Schennum, 1975; Peters, 1972), rate of presentation of materials (e.g., Aiken et al., 1975; Peters, 1972), format of the lecture (e.g., Aiken et al., 1975), and type of test given to evaluate learning (e.g., Barnett, Di Vesta & Rogozinski, 1981; Peper & Mayer, 1978).

The other possible function of note-taking is as a form of external storage. According to the *external storage hypothesis*, students take notes to have a permanent record of the lecture material to study at a later date. Kiewra (1985, 1989) reported that in 24 studies, students allowed to review their notes did better than those who did not review. While no study found review to be detrimental, another eight studies found no difference between those that reviewed and those that did not review. In this type of study, there are usually two groups; both groups take notes during the lecture but one group is given the opportunity to review their notes before a later test while the second group is not. There are at least two major confounds with these studies. Students who reviewed their notes: (1) had two exposures to the lecture material (i.e., once hearing the lecture and once while studying their notes) as opposed to those in the no review condition who only had one exposure, and (2) had the opportunity to use note-taking to both encode the information (i.e., taking notes during the lecture) and as external storage (i.e., studying their notes).

The solution to these confounds that later research has often taken is to provide ready-made notes for those reviewing. For example, Benton, Kiewra, Whitfall, and Dennison (1993) included in their study a group of participants that attended the lecture but review provided notes. Unfortunately, a problem arises as to what type of notes to provide the students to study. For example, studies have found that students record less than 40% of the information provided in lecture material (e.g., Hartley & Cameron, 1967; Howe, 1970) and students did better on a later test if they reviewed the instructors' notes rather than their own (e.g., Kiewra, 1983; Maqsud, 1980). Not surprisingly, different studies have found different effects of note-taking depending on the type of notes provided and the length of delay between the review and test (Benton et al., 1993; Kiewra et al., 1989; Morrison, McLaughlin & Rucker, 2002).

None of the above studies examined how undergraduates would spontaneously produce and use notations. To address this neglected issue, Eskritt, Lee, and Donald (2001) had undergraduates play a memory card game, Concentration. In Concentration, players must remember the identity and location of pairs of cards placed face down in an array. For one game the students were given the opportunity to produce notations (Notation condition), and in the other they were not (No Notation condition). The majority of participants (83%) made notations when given the opportunity. All of the students who made notations did significantly better in the Notation versus the No Notation condition. Next, Eskritt et al. wanted to determine why the use of notations was beneficial by asking whether the undergraduates spontaneously used their notations for encoding information or external storage. Before having the students play Concentration, they were shown the identity and location of cards ahead of time. Half of the students were told they could make notations (i.e., the Notation group) while the other half of the students studied the cards (i.e., the Study group). Then the cards were turned over in the exact same position and the notes were unexpectedly taken away from the Notation group. If the encoding hypothesis is correct then the removal of the notations should have no impact on performance. In contrast, if the students were using their notations as an external store, as suggested by the external storage hypothesis, the performance of undergraduates in the Notation group should be poorer than undergraduates in the Study group. The results supported the external storage hypothesis; students in the Notation group took significantly longer to win the game than students in the Study group.

However, this answer turned out to be too simplistic. In another experiment, Eskritt et al. (2001) discovered that both hypotheses might be correct to a certain degree. Undergraduates were again shown the cards face up in the array and divided into two groups. The Notation group was allowed to take notes, while the Study group was given an equal amount of time to memorize the same information. After the cards were turned over, the notations were unexpectedly taken away and students were shown flashcards of the deck of cards they had seen as well as a new deck and asked whether they recognized the card. If they did, they were asked to locate the pair within the array in front of them. Thus, Eskritt et al. were able to differentiate undergraduates' memory for the identity of the cards from that for their location. They found that the students were not placing all information in their notations. As in the previous experiment, undergraduates in the Study group performed significantly better than students in the Notation group but only for the location information. Students in both groups reached ceiling on their ability to recognize the identity of the cards they had seen. This finding demonstrates that the students in the Notation group were storing identity information in memory while relying on their notations for the location information. Thus, these students used a split-storage strategy for remembering different types of information.

The results of this study help illuminate one of the problems the note-taking literature has had in distinguishing whether students should use their notations for external storage or encoding. It is clearly not an either-or sort of issue. Donald (1991) suggested that to use notations effectively, an individual must maintain in memory the information necessary to use the notations. This idea fits nicely with the findings of Eskritt et al. (2001) that undergraduates used a split-storage strategy. Consistent with some suggestions in the note-taking literature, the optimal way of using permanent external symbols as a memory aid is perhaps to employ notations for both encoding and external storage. However, Eskritt et al.'s study was a memory task as opposed to testing students' understanding of lecture material. Further research is necessary to explore this issue.

Cognitive Psychology

An area within the field of cognitive psychology is concerned with how internal and external representations interact. The term "external representation" is usually used to describe permanent external symbols but also any cognitive artifact that can be used to aid cognitive processes (e.g., an abacus). Research in this field has focussed on how different types of external representations can influence performance. As Norman (1991) pointed out, different types of representations represent different aspects of information at the expense of other information. Furthermore, information can be represented to suggest to an individual a possible set of interpretations that are not as obvious with another type of representation. The distinction that is frequently made by researchers is between linguistic representations and graphical representations (e.g., Cox, 1999; Larkin & Simon, 1987; Lemke, 1998; Stenning & Oberlander, 1994). It is important to note, however, that one class of representations is not necessarily superior to another, but that in a particular situation some representations may be more appropriate than others.

The majority of participants will make notations if given the opportunity during problem-solving or reasoning tasks (Cox & Brna, 1995; Schwartz, 1971). The production of notations is related to a cost-benefit analysis (Cary & Carlson, 1999). Participants need to feel that the benefit of producing notations outweighs the cost or effort of their production. A number of studies have found that performance in a problem-solving task can be affected by the type of external representation used in the task (Eskritt & Arthurs, in press; Zhang, 1997; Zhang & Norman, 1994). For example, Zhang (1997) used different isomorphs of the game Tic-Tac-Toe to discover if the different external representations of the game would influence adults' performance. For example, one isomorph was the Number variation. In this version, players pick numbers from 1 to 9 and the first who gets three numbers that adds up to 15 wins. A number can only be picked once by the players. Zhang found that, despite the fact that the underlying structure of the games was identical, some isomorphs of Tic-Tac-Toe were more difficult than others. Participants took significantly longer to discover winning strategies with some external representations of the games than others.

RESEARCH WITH CHILDREN

A great deal of research has been done on children's comprehension of different types of notational systems and some research has been conducted on children's production of different types of notational systems (for review see Lee & Karmiloff-Smith, 1996a; Tolchinksy, 2003). However, when the interaction between cognitive and notational development are examined, it is usually to explore how children's notations reflect their cognitive development (e.g., Piaget & Inhelder, 1948/1956) or how cognitive development influences children's comprehension and use of permanent external symbols (e.g., Bamberger, 1982; DeLoache, 1989; Karmiloff-Smith, 1992). Very little research has examined how the developing ability to use permanent external symbols may influence cognition (see Tolchinsky, 2003).

Metalinguistic Knowledge

Different types of orthographies have been found to influence lower level visual information processing (Hung & Tzeng, 1981). For example, visual scanning patterns can be influenced by the type of script an individual learns to read. Thus, the direction that an individual is taught to read can carry over into other tasks such as the exploration of patterns (Elkind & Weiss, 1967; Kugelmass & Lieblich, 1979). However, some research has gone further to suggest that children's perceptions of language change as they learn to read. These studies appear to indicate that children's developing ability to read influences their metalinguistic knowledge (Olson, 1994, 1996). For example, Magnusson and Naucler (1993) found that with learning to read comes a growing phonemic awareness. In a task where "sounds" are to be deleted from words, such as the /f/ from "fish" to make "ish", pre-readers find these tasks almost impossible while readers find it rather simple. This effect has not only been found with children, but also when comparing literate and nonliterate adults (Bertelson, de Gelder, Toufouni & Morais, 1989; Morais, Cary, Alegria & Bertelson, 1979; Prakash, Rekha, Nigam & Karanth, 1993)

Children's conception of a word or sentence is also influenced by learning to read (Francis, 1975). For example, Homer and Olson (1999) read a story to children between the ages of 4 to 6 years of age. Occasionally the narrator would pause and ask the child what was the last word that had been said. They found 6-year-olds performed significantly better on the task than the younger children and were more likely to identify words such as "of" or "the" as words. Performance on this task was significantly related to a similar text-based task. In that task, children were shown a picture with a phrase underneath. The experimenter would read the phrase and then cover up one word and ask what the phrase now said. Again older children were significantly better at this task. This research complements the cross-cultural research with scripts that do not use conventional markings for word boundaries such as used by the Vai (Scribner & Cole, 1983) and the Chinese (Miller, 2002). Homer and Olson argued that it is learning to read a writing system that differentiates words in notation that such a concept arises.

Memory

One obvious area that permanent external symbols are assumed to influence cognition is the area of memory. Plato thought that permanent external symbols would have a negative impact on memory while others such as Donald (1991) and Vygotsky and Luria (1994) have suggested that permanent external symbols could change the memory strategies used for a task and therefore enhance memory performance. With adults, a few studies have collected questionnaire data on the frequency in which people use different types of memory strategies. A couple of studies (Harris, 1982; Intons-Peterson & Fournier, 1986) have found that adults reported using more external memory strategies (e.g., writing a note, asking someone to remind you) than internal memory strategies (e.g., rehearsal, mental retracing) and thought they were more reliable. Similarly, research with children found that they were more likely to offer suggestions of external memory strategies than internal memory strategies to help remember to perform a certain act (Kreutzer, Leonard & Flavell, 1975). These findings suggest that both adults and children are at least aware of the usefulness of such external memory strategies as note-taking.

Nevertheless, little research has been done on children's production of permanent external symbols to aid their own memory. Although several studies have examined children's notation production in a memory task (Cohen, 1985; Karmiloff-Smith, 1979), they only focused on the types of notations produced by the children rather than how the notations affected their memory performance. One exception was a research project by Brown and Smiley (1978) who examined how well children at different ages could use permanent external symbols and other external aids (e.g., highlighting) to summarize text. In one experiment, Brown and Smiley (1978) read a passage to children from grades 5 to 12. Afterwards, children were asked to recall the gist of the passage. Then the students were given pens and a copy of the passage to study and were told they would be asked to recall the passage again. They found that very few grade 5 and 7 students made notes or underlined the text, while 50% of senior high school students did. Recall of the passage improved for the grade 7 and 12 students but not for grade 5 students. Unfortunately, this study is confounded by the possibility of a practice effect or other memory strategies. This explanation is especially likely considering that only 12% of grade 7 students made notes and yet grade 7 students as a whole were much better at recall than grade 5 students.

With regard to the emergence of notational production, Luria (1978) asked preschool children, starting at 3 to 4 years of age, to remember a list of words and sentences and to write down the words and sentences to help recall. He found that at first, children's 'writing' looked superficially like adults' but the different sentences the children wrote could not be differentiated. Children also did not attempt to 'read' what they had written when asked to recall the sentences. After a couple of sessions, 4- and 5-year-olds began to relate their 'writing' to what they heard. Long sentences resulted in longer lines of scribbles, and for words, shorter lines. During recall, children now started to refer to their notations as a memory aid and the recall of sentences did improve somewhat.

It was the presence of quantity or concrete shapes or size in the sentences that eventually led children to develop more usable notations. Picture-writing became fully developed by the time children reached 5 or 6 years of age. However, once children started to learn formally how to write they would rely totally on writing and drop picture-writing altogether. They did this regardless of how well they knew the alphabet or how to spell. For example, one child knew only the letters "A" and "I" and so for each sentence he was given to remember he would write down one of these letters even though they could not help him recall the sentences.

Luria's (1978) study, though very informative, was reported only with examples and description. No details were provided about the number of subjects tested, how many sessions they were tested for, and whether the same children were studied from 3 years of age until they were 6 years old. Thus, it is unclear how many children went through each of the transitions and whether children's productions actually affected their recall. Though Luria implied that as children's notations improved, their ability to recall improved, this might be due to a practice effect. Children might have learned to recall sentences better over time and the improvement was unrelated to children's ability to notate. It should be noted that this lack of information was not due to Luria's report style. Rather, the reason for the vagueness in Luria's report was because at the time of his report, the Soviet Union had a strict policy of prohibiting the dissemination of numeric data about Soviet people to the West because they were considered a state secret.

A couple of studies have also been conducted to examine numeracy in preschool children. Hughes (1986), and Bialystok and Codd (1996) examined 3- to 5-year-olds' ability to produce notations to remember the number of objects within several containers. Children produced three different types of notations. Some of the children produced nonmnemonic notations that did not serve any obvious memory value, such as drawing a picture. Other children drew a token for each item within the container, such as three lines, one for each of the hidden objects. And the third type of notation was to write the numerical symbol for the amount of objects. Hughes (1986), and Bialystock and Codd (1996) found that the type of notations produced influenced their impact on memory performance. For example, the children who drew pictures did not improve their memory, while the children who wrote the number of objects inside the container benefited.

Eskritt and Lee (2002) had older children between the ages of 6 to 12 years of age make notations to aid them in playing the memory card game, Concentration. Eskritt and Lee also found that children produced different types of notations and the beneficial effects of the notations were dependent on the types of notations produced. The younger children were more likely to produce nonmnemonic notations that tended to be *detrimental* to memory performance. These children did better when they did not have the opportunity to make notations compared to when they did. Older children produced notations similar to adults and these notations improved their memory performance.

Eskritt and Lee (2002) further investigated whether older children would also use a split-storage strategy for remembering the cards and their location like the undergraduates in Eskritt et al. (2001). They showed 11- and 12-year-olds the cards face up in the array and divided into a Notation and Study group. They were shown flashcards of the cards they had seen as well as from a new deck and asked children whether they recognized the card and where the pair was located. As with undergraduates, Eskritt and Lee determined that children were not placing all the information in their notations. Children in both groups reached ceiling on their ability to recognize the identity of the cards they had seen, while the Study group did significantly better at locating the cards within the array. It seems that children at least as young as 11 to 12 years of age use their notations adaptively.

For the Concentration task, they use their memory to store identity information and their notations to store location information.

These studies can provide some insight into the conflicting results found in note-taking literature in the area of educational psychology. They show that it is the quality of the notations, not simply note-taking itself that needs to be examined. The results of Luria (1978), Hughes (1986), Bialystok and Codd (1996), and Eskritt and Lee (2002) suggest that if undergraduates are not making adequate notations, then the notations they produce will not aid performance. Furthermore, Eskritt and Lee's study suggests that students' poor notations may even harm performance, which is consistent with the findings of several studies in the adult note-taking literature (Kiewra, 1985, 1989).

Problem-Solving and Reasoning

With a few exceptions (e.g., Gauvain, de la Ossa & Hurtado-Ortiz, 2001; Kelly, Miller, Fang & Feng, 1999), the majority of research on children's understanding of permanent external symbols and problem-solving has focused on mathematics and scientific reasoning (e.g., Cobb, Yackel & McClain, 2000). Theorists within this perspective have questioned the strict division between external and internal representations (Cobb, 2000; Johnson & Lesh, 2003; Yachel, 2000; see also Roth, this volume). They have argued that permanent external symbols are an integral part of thinking about mathematics, and mathematical reasoning does not necessarily take place entirely internally, an idea that has also been expressed by some cognitive scientists (Clark, 1997; Hutchins, 1995). Furthermore, there is a reiterative relationship between external symbol use and understanding of concepts. Sfard (2000) argues there is interplay between understanding mathematical symbols and mathematical concepts so that it is uncertain which comes first.

To illustrate, Lehrer et al. (2000) examined children's use of graphs to illustrate plant growth. They found that children's notations were influenced by the questions they asked about plant growth but also, the questions they asked were influenced by the notations they produced. At first children were mostly concerned with measuring height, but gradually came to realize that different types of notations included other types of information (e.g., width, volume) and they discovered patterns in the data they would not have noticed otherwise (e.g., growth was variable over time). Children's ideas about plant growth were closely linked to the gradual sophistication of the notations they used to illustrate growth. Therefore, Lehrer et al. found that changes in notations were related to changes in conceptual understanding.

Research done in this field of inquiry tends to look at collaborative learning and how children's interactions with a teacher or other students and permanent external symbols will influence their understanding of different mathematical or scientific concepts (Lehrer et al., 2000; Zawojewski, Lesh & English, 2003). Furthermore, researchers tend to examine children's modification and adaptation of their external representations over time and how the interaction between external representation development and conceptual understanding occur together. This

246

research has demonstrated that children can learn concepts thought beyond their grasp at an early age (Lehrer & Schauble, 2003; Petrosino, Lehrer & Schauble, 2003) and that the understanding of external representations can be an integral part of mathematical and scientific thinking (Cobb & McClain, 2001).

Attention and Behaviour Regulation

To the best of our knowledge, only one study has examined the use of permanent external symbols to aid attention and behavioural regulation. Leont'ev (1994), a contemporary of Luria, had children and adults play a question game where the experimenter asked the participants eighteen questions they had to answer the questions as quickly as possible. For half of the questions, the correct answer was a color name, and for the other half, the answer was a "yes" or "no" response. To win the game participants had to follow two rules. Participants could not use the same color name more than once, nor could they use two "forbidden" color names. Participants were given cards, each with a different color on it, to aid them in the task.

As with the study conducted by Luria on preschooler's use of writing to re-member phrases, Leont'ev also reported his study with mostly descriptions and anecdotes. Leont'ev found that preschoolers (i.e., 5-year-olds) did not use the cards to help them play the game, or if they did, the cards distracted the child and hindered performance. The preschoolers frequently answered with the same color name or used the forbidden colors. The problem was not in the younger children's ability to remember the rules, as they were able to recall them when asked at the end of the game.

For the older, school-aged children, a number of different strategies were used. Some of the children still failed to use the cards just like the preschoolers. The rest of the children put aside or turned over cards containing the colors they could no longer use as an answer. These children could be further divided into two groups. One group of children only referred to the cards *after* they had given an answer. The other group of children used the cards to help provide an answer to the question. For these children, the use of the cards aided performance.

Some of the adults also turned over cards of the colors that they had already used. However, some adults kept all of the cards face up in front of themselves and just looked at them when giving an answer. Leont'ev asked these adults if the cards had helped performance and the adults replied that, despite not physically manipulating the cards, they still used them to keep track of which color names they were not permitted to use. Leont'ev argued that adults had internalized the external signs so that they could use them mentally without having to manip-ulate them externally. Children, in contrast, may yet develop the ability to use permanent external symbols to regulate their attention and behaviour.

247

SUMMARY

In this chapter we have reviewed the influence that notation may have on cognition and its development. We pointed out that ideas concerning how permanent external symbols might influence cognition have a long history and yet only recently have theorists and researchers begun to examine the issue closely. During the 1960s, a number of theorists discussed, from a historical point of view, how the use of notations has altered the "consciousness" of Western society (Goody & Watt, 1963/1968; Havelock, 1963; McLuhan, 1962). The cross-cultural perspective has examined the differences between oral and literate peoples with the assumption that different types of responses are evidence of different thought processes as a result of experience with permanent external symbols. Typically the theories espousing the view that permanent external symbols have an effect on cognition view this effect as beneficial. However, empirical research concerning how permanent external symbols may affect cognition is scarce. Many of the studies that might be used to address this issue were not conducted with this question in mind and come from a variety of different fields that often do not reference one another. Nevertheless, this limited body of research has revealed that permanent external symbols can benefit task performance on various tasks such as attention (Leont'ev, 1994), memory (e.g., Bialystok & Codd, 1996; Eskritt & Lee, 2002; Eskritt et al., 2001; Hughes, 1986; Luria, 1978), and problem-solving and scientific reasoning (e.g., Cobb et al., 2000; Zhang, 1997; Zhang & Norman, 1994). However, some of the research has indicated that the effects of permanent external symbols are not so clear-cut. A few studies have demonstrated that permanent external symbols are not necessarily beneficial for either children or adults (Eskritt & Lee, 2002; Kiwera, 1989; Lehrer et al., 2000; Leont'ev, 1994; Zhang, 1997).

While research has demonstrated that permanent external symbols can influence task performance, is this evidence that they can enhance cognition? Norman (1991) argued that permanent external symbols do not enhance cognition; that is, they do not increase a person's cognitive capacities. A microphone enhances the volume of one's speech by making it louder. However, a pulley does not increase an individual's strength. Rather, it alters the task so that individuals will find it easier to lift an object with their own strength. Permanent external symbols could be like the pulley; they can change the nature of the task so that it is easier for an individual to perform (though see Bamberger, this volume). However, while permanent external symbols may act as a powerful tool, if an individual does not know how to use them effectively or if they are not applicable to the task, they will not help performance. They are only as effective as the person knows how to use them. As some research has suggested, they can even hinder performance (Eskritt & Lee, 2002; Lehrer et al., 2000; Leont'ev, 1994; Zhang, 1997). The research by Scribner and Cole (1983) demonstrated that the way permanent external symbols can affect performance is dependent on the way they are viewed and used by the culture, and practices that surround them. Permanent external symbols obtain their significance from the culture they are in (Mead, 1934). The cognitive consequences of permanent external symbols therefore depend on the purpose and context within which they are used.

There are many possible reasons and ways that permanent external symbols may influence cognition and its development. For example, permanent external symbols can aid in organizing the display of otherwise disorganized information, such as the list (Donald, 1991). Permanent external symbols can also reveal relationships and structures about the information they encode and hence make explicit knowledge that may have been implicit (Karmiloff-Smith, 1992). Novel information can be "discovered" in the development of the permanent external symbols themselves, such as metalinguistic awareness (Olson, 1994), mathematics (Lehrer et al., 2000), or musical knowledge (Bamberger, 1982).

FUTURE DIRECTIONS

Given the prevalence of permanent external symbols in modern society and theorists' emphasis of their critical role in cognitive development at both societal and individual levels, one would anticipate a large body of empirical research on the influence of permanent external symbols on cognition and its development. Surprisingly, this is not the case. Limited empirical research notwithstanding, existing evidence to date has revealed some interesting findings (e.g., the possibility that under some circumstances permanent external symbols can be detrimental to performance). Such findings illustrate the necessity for more research to obtain a better understanding of the effects of permanent external symbols on cognition and its development.

Specifically, further research is needed to examine how permanent external symbols impact memory, problem-solving, and attention and behavioral regulation. Regarding the issue of the relation between notation and problem-solving and that between notation and attention/behavioral regulation, empirical research has been almost nonexistent except for the instruction of children in mathematical and scientific notation. Existing studies have their adult and child participants use external representations provided by the experimenter (Leont'ev, 1994; Zhang, 1997; Zhang & Norman, 1994) or did not examine how participants' self-produced notations may affect their performance (e.g., Cox, 1999; Schwartz, 1971). Further study is needed to determine what types of notations adults and children will produce themselves to aid their problem-solving and attention, and what influence these notations have on performance and understanding of tasks in hand. Research on how permanent external representations can influence mathematical and scientific reasoning illustrates the potential reiterative relationship that can exist (Sfard, 2000). How children might produce and use permanent external symbols to regulate behavior also needs to be examined. For example, whether children can use the production of notations to inhibit behavior or resist temptation.

In the area of memory, researchers have started to examine the types of permanent external symbols produced by adults and children and how these notations influence memory performance (Bialystok & Codd, 1996; Eskritt & Lee, 2002; Eskritt et al., 2001; Hughes, 1986; Kiewra, 1985; Luria, 1978). However, more research is necessary to determine how these notations impact adults' and children's choice of memory strategies. The study by Eskritt et al. (2001) and Eskritt and Lee (2002) revealed that notational production led adults and older children to store identity information in memory and location information in their notations for a Concentration game. Future research could investigate how generalizable these findings are to other tasks. Studies need to be developed that examine whether the type of information stored in memory varies depending on the type of memory task, or even whether some types of information may be better stored in memory when producing notations compared with other types of mnemonic strategies, such as rehearsal. Also, one could investigate at which age such information division strategy emerges and how it develops.

Another issue that deserves more attention is adults' and children's adaptability in using and producing notations for different tasks (Kress, 1997; see also Triona & Klahr, this volume). The skills to use some types of permanent external symbols in Western culture has been developing for many centuries (Olson & Astington, 1990), and several different types of notational systems have evolved and been adaptively applied to various situations. The way that the adults and children in many of the previously mentioned studies were so quick to develop notations to the novel tasks presented by experimenters attests to the adaptability, especially considering that some participants were rather novice users. Furthermore, the experiments by Luria (1978) and Eskritt and Lee (2002) suggest that children are also quite capable of adapting their own cognitive processes (i.e., memory strategies) to fit with the purpose of their notational productions. Research on adults' and children's adaptability in using and producing notations should elucidate the two-way interaction between cognition and notation.

The research presented in the present chapter has focused on how notations may interact and change an individual's cognitive processes. Another, equally important consequence of notations is the distribution of cognitive resources among individuals. Notation does not only impact cognition at the individual level. The function that is most commonly thought of for producing and using notations is that of communication (e.g., Callaghan, 1999; Lee & Karmiloff-Smith, 1996b; Lee, Karmiloff-Smith, Cameron & Dodsworth, 1998). Permanent external symbols can be involved in more than just a dyadic interaction. In a problem-solving task involving more than one individual and permanent external symbols, permanent external symbols can be used in a triadic or multiriadic interaction (Lehrer et al., 2000; Zawojewski et al., 2003; see also Roth, this volume). More research is necessary to determine how individuals distribute their cognition among not only permanent external symbols but also other people in the environment. Such an approach would examine how permanent external symbols affect both the social processes as well as the cognitive processes of the individuals involved. Hutchins (1996) argued that distributed cognition has properties different from those of any one individual within the distribution. By distributing cognition, the computational load is shared, reducing the difficulty of the task. Hutchins (1995) illustrated how such a system may work by examining the behavior of pilots in landing a plane. He described the interaction between individual pilots with one another and the external representations in the cockpit. Donald (1991) suggested that this ability to link with permanent external symbols to form a network of resources allows for cognitive operations that would not be possible for an individual in isolation (see also Clark, 1997). Furthermore, the accumulation of notations creates a culturally shared pool of information and knowledge. As Bruner (1990) wrote,

> A 'person's' knowledge is not *just* in one's own head, in 'person solo', but in the notes that one has put into accessible notebooks, in the books with underlined passages on one's selves, in the handbooks one has learned how to consult, in the information sources one has hitched up to the computer, in the friends one can call up to get a reference or a 'steer', and so on almost endlessly. (p. 106)

In essence, notation enables cognition to evolve from a personal affair to become a collective enterprise that allows for a culture to accelerate the expansion of its reservoir of knowledge, and for individuals in the culture to gain cognitive experiences with the refinement of time and space.

NOTE

[1] This chapter was supported in part by two separate grants from Social Sciences and Humanities Research Council of Canada to the two authors and a NICHD grant (1 RO1 HD46526-01) to the second author. Correspondence should be addressed to Dr. M. Eskritt, Department of Psychology, Mount Saint Vincent University, Halifax, NS, B3M 2J6, Canada. E-mail: michelle.eskritt@msvu.ca.

REFERENCES

Aiken, E.G., Thomas, G.S. & Shennum, W.A. (1975). Memory for a lecture: Effects of notes, lecture rate, and informational density. *Journal of Educational Psychology, 67*, 439–444.

Appel, L.F., Cooper, R.G., McCarrell, N., Sims-Knight, J., Yussen, S.R. & Flavell, J.H. (1972). The development of the distinction between perceiving and memorizing. *Child Development, 43*, 1365–1381.

Bamberger, J. (1982). Revisiting children's drawings of simple rhythms: A function for reflection-in-action. In S. Strauss (Ed.), *U-shaped behavioral growth*. Academic Press.

Barnett, J.E., Di Vesta, F.J. & Rogozinski, J.T. (1981). What is learned in note taking? *Journal of Educational Psychology, 73*, 181–192.

Benton, S.L., Kiewra, K.A., Whitfall, J.M. & Dennison, R. (1993). Encoding and external-storage effects on writing processes. *Journal of Educational Psychology, 85*, 267–280.

Bertelson, O, de Gelder, B., Toufouni, L.V. & Morias, J. (1989). The metaphonological abilities of adults illiterates: New evidence of heterogeneity. *European Journal of Cognitive Psychology, 1*, 239–250.

Bialystok, E. & Codd, J. (1996). Developing representations of quantity. *Canadian Journal of Behavioural Science, 28*(4), 281–291.

Brown, A.L. & Smiley, S.S. (1978). The development of strategies for summarizing texts. *Child Development, 49*, 1076–1088.

Bruner, J. (1990). *Acts of meaning*. Harvard University Press.

Callaghan, T. (1999). Early understanding and production of graphic symbols. *Child Development, 70*, 1314–1324.

Cary, M. & Carlson, R. (1999). External support and the development of problem-solving routines. *Journal of Experimental Psychology: Learning, Memory, and Cognition, 25,* 1053–1070.

Clark, A. (1997). *Being there: Putting brain, body, and world together again.* Cambridge, MA: MIT Press.

Cobb, P. (2000). From representations to symbolizing: Introductory comments on semiotics and mathematical learning. In P. Cobb, E. Yackel & K. McClain (Eds.), *Symbolizing and communicating in mathematics classrooms: Perspectives on discourse, tools, and instructional design.* Mahweh, NJ: Erlbaum.

Cobb, P., Yackel, E. & McClain, K. (Eds.) (2000). *Symbolizing and communicating in mathematics classrooms: Perspectives on discourse, tools, and instructional design.* Mahweh, NJ: Erlbaum.

Cobb, P. & McClain, K. (2001). An approach for supporting teachers' learning in social context. In F.L. Lin & T. Cooney (Eds.), *Making sense if mathematics teacher education.* Dordrecht: Kluwer.

Cohen, S.R. (1985). The development of constraints on symbol-meaning structure in notation; Evidence from production, interpretation, and forced-choice judgements. *Child Development, 56,* 177–195.

Cox, R. (1999). Representation construction, externalised cognition and individual differences. *Learning and Instruction, 9,* 343–363.

Cox, R. & Brna, P. (1995). Supporting the use of external representations in problem solving: The need for flexible learning environments. *Journal of Artificial Intelligence in Education, 6,* 239–302.

DeLoache, J.S. (1989). The development of representation in young children. *Advances in Child Development and Behavior, 22,* 1–39.

Di Vesta, F.J. & Gray, G.S. (1972). Listening and note taking. *Journal of Educational Psychology, 63,* 8–14.

Donald, M. (1993). Human cognitive evolution: What we were, what we are becoming. *Social Research, 60,* 143–170.

Donald, M. (1991). *Origins of the modern mind: Three stages in the evolution of culture and cognition.* Harvard University Press.

Elkind, D. & Weiss, J. (1967). Studies in perceptual development: III. Perceptual exploration. *Child Development, 38,* 1153–1161.

Eskritt, M. & Arthurs, C. (in press). Analytical reasoning skills: Does the use of notations improve performance? *Canadian Journal of Education.*

Eskritt, M. & Lee, K. (2002). 'Remember where you last saw that card': Children's production of external symbols as a memory aid. *Developmental Psychology, 38,* 254–266.

Eskritt, M., Lee, K. & Donald, M. (2001). The influence of symbolic literacy on memory: Testing Plato's hypothesis. *Canadian Journal of Experimental Psychology, 55,* 39–50.

Feldman, C.F. (1991). Oral metalanguage. In D.R. Olson & N. Torrance (Eds.), *Literacy and orality.* Cambridge University Press.

Flavell, J.H. (1971). First discussant's comments: What is memory development the development of? *Human Development, 14,* 272–278.

Francis, H. (1975). *Language in childhood: Form and function in language learning.* Paul Elek.

Gauvain, M., de la Ossa, J.L. & Hurtado-Ortiz, M.T. (2001). Parental guidance as children learn to use cultural tools: The case of pictorial plans. *Cognitive Development, 16,* 551–575.

Goody, J. & Watt, I. (1968). The consequences of literacy. In J. Goody (Ed.), *Literacy in traditional societies.* Cambridge University Press. (original published in 1963)

Greenfield, P.M. & Bruner, J.S. (1966). Culture and cognitive growth. *International Journal of Psychology, 1,* 89–107.

Harris, J.E. (1982). External memory aids. In U. Neisser (Ed.), *Memory observed: Remembering in natural contexts.* Freeman & Co.

Harris, R. (1986). *The origin of writing.* Duckworth.

Hartley, J. (1983). Note-taking research: Resetting the scoreboard. *Bulletin of British Psychology, 36,* 13–14.

Hartley, J. & Cameron, A. (1967). Some observations on the efficiency of lecturing. *Educational Review, 20,* 3–7.

Havelock, E.A. (1963). *Preface to Plato.* Cambridge, MA: Harvard University Press.

Homer, B. & Olson, D.R. (1999). Literacy and children's conception of words. *Written Language and Literacy, 2,* 113–140.

Howe, M.J. (1970). Using student notes to examine the role of the individual learner in acquiring meaningful subject matter. *Journal of Educational Research, 64,* 61–63.

Hughes, M. (1986). *Children and number: Difficulties in learning mathematics.* Blackwell Publishers.

Hung, D.L. & Tzeng, O.J.L. (1981). Orthographic variations and visual information. *Psychological Bulletin, 90,* 377–414.

Hutchins, E. (1995). *Cognition in the wild.* MIT Press.

Hutchins, E. (1983). Understanding Micronesian navigation. In D. Gentner & A.L. Stevens (Eds.), *Mental models.* Erlbaum.

Hutchins, E. (1995). How a cockpit remembers its speed. *Cognitive Science, 19,* 265–288.

Illich, I. (1991). A plea for research on lay literacy. In D.R. Olson & N. Torrance (Eds.), *Literacy and orality.* Cambridge University Press.

Intons-Peterson, M.J. & Fournier, J. (1986). External and internal memory aids: When and how often do we use them? *Journal of Experimental Psychology: General, 115,* 267–280.

Johnson, T. & Lesh, R. (2003). A models and modeling perspective on technology-based representational media. In R. Lesh & H.M. Doerr (Eds.), *Beyond constructivism: Models and modeling perspectives on mathematics teaching, learning, and problem solving.* Mahweh, NJ: Erlbaum.

Karmiloff-Smith, A. (1979). Micro- and macrodevelopmental changes in language acquisition and other representational systems. *Cognitive Science, 3,* 91–118.

Karmiloff-Smith, A. (1992). *Beyond modularity: A developmental perspective on cognitive science.* MIT Press.

Kelly, M.K., Miller, K.F., Fang, G. & Feng, G. (1999). When days are numbered: Calendar structure and the development of calendar processing in English and Chinese. *Journal of Experimental Child Psychology, 73,* 289–314.

Kiewra, K.A. (1983). The process of review: A levels of processing approach. *Contemporary Educational Psychology, 8,* 366–374.

Kiewra, K.A. (1985). Investigating notetaking and review: A depth of processing alternative. *Educational Psychology, 20,* 23–32.

Kiewra, K.A. (1989). A review of note-taking: The encoding-storage paradigm and beyond. *Educational Psychology Review, 1,* 147–172.

Kiewra, K.A., Dubois, N.F., Christensen, M., Kim, S. & Lindberg, N. (1989). A more equitable account of the note-taking functions in learning from lecture and from text. *Instructional Science, 18,* 217–232.

Kress, G. (1997). *Before writing: Rethinking the paths to literacy.* Routledge.

Kreutzer, M.A., Leonard, C. & Flavell, J.H. (1975). *An interview study of children's knowledge about memory.* Monographs for the Society for Research in Child Development, Vol. 40 (Serial no. 159).

Kugalmass, S. & Lieblich, A. (1979). Impact of learning to read on directionality in perception: A further cross-cultural analysis. *Human Development, 22,* 406–415.

Larkin, J.H. & Simon, H.A. (1987). Why a diagram is (sometimes) worth ten thousand words. *Cognitive Science, 11,* 65–99.

Lee, K. & Karmiloff-Smith, A. (1996a). The development of external symbols systems: The child as the notator. In E.C. Carterette & M.P. Friedman (Eds.), *Handbook of perception, Vol. 13, Perceptual and cognitive development* (R. Gelman & T. Au, volume eds.). Academic Press.

Lee, K. & Karmiloff-Smith, A. (1996b). The development of cognitive constraints on notations. *Archives of Psychologie, 64,* 3–26.

Lehrer, R. & Schauble, L. (2003). Origins and evolutions of model-based reasoning in mathematics and science. In R. Lesh & H.M. Doerr (Eds.), *Beyond constructivism: Models and modeling perspectives on mathematical teaching, learning, and problem solving.* Mahweh, NJ: Erlbaum.

Lehrer, R., Schauble, L., Carpenter, S. & Penner, D. (2000). The innerrelated development of inscriptions and conceptual understanding. In P. Cobb, E. Yackel & K. McClain (Eds.), *Symbolizing and communicating in mathematics classrooms: Perspectives on discourse, tools, and instructional design.* Mahweh, NJ: Erlbaum.

Leont'ev, A. (1994). The development of voluntary attention in the child. In R. van der Veer & J. Valsiner (Eds.), *The Vygotsky reader.* Blackwell.

Levy-Bruhl, L. (1923). *Primitive mentality* (L.A. Clare, Trans.). Macmillian.

Livingston, D. (1865). *Missionary travels and researches in South Africa: Including a sketch of sixteen years' residence in the interior of Africa.* Harper Brothers.

Luria, A.R. (1976). *Cognitive development: Its cultural and social foundations* (M. Lopez-Moriallas & L. Solotaroff, Trans.). Harvard University Press.

Luria, A.R. (1978). The development of writing in the child. In M. Cole (Ed.), *The selected writings of A.R. Luria*. M.E. Sharpe.

Magnusson, E. & Naucler, K. (1993). The development of linguistic awareness. *First Language, 37,* 93–112.

Maqsud, M. (1980). Effects of personal lecture notes and teacher notes on recall of university students. *British Journal of Educational Psychology, 50,* 289–294.

McLane, J.B. & McNamee (1990). *Early literacy*. Harvard University Press.

McLuhan, M. (1962). *The Gutenberg galaxy*. Toronto University Press.

Meacham, J.A. & Leiman, B. (1982). Remembering to perform future actions. In U. Neisser (Ed.), *Memory observed: Remembering in natural contexts*. Freeman and Co.

Mead, G.H. (1934). *Mind, self and society*. University of Chicago Press.

van Meter, P., Yokoi, L. & Pressley, M. (1994). College students' theory of note-taking derived from their perceptions of note-taking. *Journal of Educational Psychology, 86,* 323–338.

Mill, J.S. (1969). *Autobiography*. Oxford University Press.

Miller, K.F. (2002). Children's early understanding of writing and language: The impact of characters and alphabetic orthographies. In W. Li, J.S. Gaffney & J.L. Packard (Eds.), *Chinese children's reading acquisition: Theoretical and pedagogical issues*. Boston: Kluwer.

Morais, J., Cary, L., Alegria, J. & Bertelson, P. (1979). Does awareness of speech as a sequence of phonemes arise spontaneously? *Cognition, 7,* 323–331.

Morrison, E. H., McLaughlin, C. & Rucker, L. (2002). Medical students' note-taking in a medical biochemistry course: An initial exploration. *Medical Education, 36,* 384–386.

Nelson, K. (1996). *Language in cognitive development: The emergence of the mediated mind*. Cambridge University Press.

Neisser, U. (1976). *Cognition and reality: Principles and implications of cognitive psychology*. Freeman.

Norman, D.A. (1991). Cognitive artifacts. In J.M. Carroll (Ed.), *Designing interaction: Psychology at the human-computer interface*. Cambridge University Press.

Olson, D.R. (1996). Towards a psychology of literacy: On the relations between speech and writing. *Cognition, 60,* 83–104.

Olson, D.R. (1994). *The world on paper*. Cambridge University Press.

Olson, D.R. & Astington, J.W. (1990). Talking about text: How literacy contributes to thought. *Journal of Pragmatics, 14,* 705–721.

Olson, D.R. & Torrance, N. (1991). *Literacy and orality*. Cambridge University Press.

Ong, W.J. (1982). *Orality and literacy: The technologizing of the word*. Methuen.

Palmatier, R.A. & Bennett, J.M. (1974). Note taking habits of college students. *Journal of Reading, 18,* 215–218.

Peper, R.J. & Mayer, R.E. (1978). Note-taking as a generative activity. *Journal of Educational Psychology, 70,* 34–38.

Peters, D.L. (1972). Effects of note-taking and rate of presentation on short-term objective test performance. *Journal of Educational Psychology, 63,* 276–280.

Petrosino, A.J., Lehrer, R. & Schauble, L. (2003). Structuring error and experimental variation as distribution in the fourth grade. *Mathematical Thinking and Learning, 5,* 131–156.

Piaget, J. & Inhelder, B. (1956). *The child's conception of space*. Routledge & Kegan Paul. (Original work published in 1948.)

Plato (1985). *Dialogues*. (Translated by B. Jowett). New York: MacMillian & Co.

Prakash, P., Rekha, D., Nigam, R. & Karanth, P. (1993). Phonological awareness, orthography, and literacy. In R. Scholes (Ed.), *Literacy and language analysis*. Erlbaum.

Scribner, S. & Cole, M. (1981). *The psychology of literacy*. Harvard University press.

Sfard, A. (2000). Symbolizing mathematical reality into being – or how mathematical discourse and mathematical objects create each other. In P. Cobb, E. Yackel & K. McClain (Eds.), *Symbolizing and communicating in mathematics classrooms: Perspectives on discourse, tools, and instructional design*. Mahweh, NJ: Erlbaum.

Stenning, K. & Oberlander, J. (1994). A cognitive theory of graphical and linguistic reasoning: Logic and implementation. *Cognitive Science, 19,* 97–140.

Schwartz, S.H. (1971). Modes of representation and problem solving: Well evolved is half solved. *Journal of Experimental Psychology, 91*, 347–350.

Tolchinksy, L. (2003). *The cradle of culture and what children know about writing and numbers before being taught.* Mahwah, NJ: Erlbaum.

Vygotsky, L. & Luria, A. (1994). Tool and symbol in child development. In R. van der Veer & J. Valsiner (Eds.), *The Vygotsky reader.* Blackwell.

Yackel, E. (2000). Introduction: Perspectives on semiotics and instructional design. In P. Cobb, E. Yackel & K. McClain (Eds.), *Symbolizing and communicating in mathematics classrooms: Perspectives on discourse, tools, and instructional design.* Mahweh, NJ: Erlbaum.

Zawojewski, J.S., Lesh, R. & English, L. (2003). A models and modeling perspective on the role of small group learning activities. In R. Lesh & H.M. Doerr (Eds.), *Beyond constructivism: Models and modeling perspectives on mathematical teaching, learning, and problem solving.* Mahweh, NJ: Erlbaum.

Zhang, J. (1997). The nature of external representations in problem solving. *Cognitive Science, 21*, 179–217.

Zhang, J. (1993). External representation: An issue for cognition. *Behavioral and Brain Sciences, 16*, 774–775.

Zhang, J. & Norman, D.A. (1994). Representations in distributed cognitive tasks. *Cognitive Science, 18*, 87–122.

Michelle Eskritt
Mount St. Vincent University
Halifax, Canada

Kang Lee
Department of Psychology
University of California, San Diego, USA

NAME INDEX

Acredolo, L., 169
Aiken, E., 240
Alegria, J., 144, 243
Anderson, D., 210, 219, 221-222, 227
Angell, A., 210
Antel, A., 146
Apel, W., 57-58
Arbib, M., 41n
Archer, A., 222
Archimedes, 33, 41n
Aristotle, 18, 51-53, 56
Arnheim, R., 113
Arnold, D., 210
Aronoff, M., 136
Arthurs, C., 242
Astington, J., 235, 239, 250
Atwood, M., 165
Aubrey, C., 125
Aurillac, G. de (Sylvester II), 23

Bahrick, L., 225
Bamberger, J., 6-7, 9, 30, 49, 63, 81-112, 164, 172, 177, 211, 226-227, 243, 248-249
Barbosa, M., 41n
Barnett, J., 240
Barr, R., 210, 222
Bartlett, F., 82, 98, 100, 103, 107
Bateson, M., 111
Bednarz, N., 150
Benenson, J., 146
Bennett, J., 239
Benton, S., 240
Bergamini, D., 28, 41n
Berger, 49
Bertelson, O., 243
Bertelson, P., 144
Berthoud-Papandropoulou, I., 140
Bialystock, E., 30, 209, 245
Biber, D., 15
Bigelow, A., 214
Birch, S., 214
Black, J., 173

Blanche-Benveniste, C., 137, 140
Bluestein, N., 169
Boethius, 18, 33
Boutonn_, S., 205
Bolger, F., 130, 159, 165-166, 170-173
Bowen, G., 183, 187, 194, 204
Bowen, M., 206
Boyer, C., 39n
Boysen, S., 3, 20, 40n
Braisby, N., 124
Braswell, G., 168
Brenneman, K., 117-118, 124
Brna, P., 242
Brook-Gunns, J., 225
Brown, L., 3
Bruce, B., 22, 26
Brun, J., 148
Bruner, J., 135, 210, 215, 251
Bryant, P., 149
Burns, N., 212, 218-219, 225
Butter, E., 214

Cajori, F., 31-33, 39n
Callaghan, T., 159, 162, 164-165, 167-168, 172, 250
Callanan, M., 168-169
Cameron, A., 240
Cameron, C., 116
Campbell, R., 124
Cantor, G., 21, 40n
Cantor, M., 39n
Cao, Y., 214
Caplin, W., 50
Cardano, G., 40n
Carlson, R., 242
Carpenter, M., 217
Carter, R., 148
Cary, L., 144, 243
Cary, M., 242
Carey, S., 219
Capaldi, E., 3, 20, 40n
Casey, A., 231
Catach, N., 137

Champollion, J., 70
Chemla, K., 22
Chervel, A., 137
Clark, A., 246, 251
Clark, E., 118, 124
Clark, G. de, 149
Clemente, A., 139
Cobb, P., 246-248
Codd, J., 30, 126, 128, 172, 245-246, 248, 250
Cohen, S., 159, 163-164, 166, 171-172, 244
Cole, M., 185, 235, 238-239, 243, 248
Coley, J., 210
Collins, A., 16
Colston, H., 153
Cooper, R. Jr., 146
Cowan, R., 125, 131n
Cox, M., 162, 168
Cox, R., 242, 249
Crawley, A., 222, 227
Curtiss, L., 146

Davis, A., 118
Davis, H., 20
Dehaene, S., 3, 19-20, 40n, 135
Deloache, J., 128, 209-226, 243
Dennison, R., 240
Deocampo, J., 210, 219, 221
Desborde, F., 137
Diener, M., 214-216
Dockrell, J., 6, 113-134, 148
Dodsworth, P., 116, 250
Doman, G., 20, 40n
Doman, J., 40n
Dominin, D., 168
Donald, M., 3, 9, 135, 163, 236-237, 239-241, 243, 249, 251
Donaldson, M., 117-119
Donohue, T., 214
Donohue, W., 214
Downs, R., 169
Duval, R., 14-16, 20

Elkind, D., 243
Engeström, Y., 185
English, L., 246
Entremont, B. de, 214
Epstein, J., 210
Eskritt, M., 9, 159, 163, 168-170, 172, 214, 220, 233-255
Euclid, 18
Evans, M. Schmidt, 222
Evra, J. van, 211, 226
Ewers-Rogers, J., 125

Fang, G., 246
Fauvel, J., 39
Fayol, M., 117, 124
Feldman, C., 237-238
Feng, G., 246
Fernald, A., 217, 222
Ferreiro, E., 113, 115, 119, 126, 139-140
Fisch, S., 227
Flavell, E., 211
Flavell, J., 211, 244
Fournier, J., 244
Francis, H., 243
Franco of Cologne, 50-60, 62
Frege, G., 46
Freudenthal, H., 21-22
Funkenstein, A., 58
Fuson, K., 41n

Gallistel, C., 41n
Ganea, P., 219
García, R., 13, 39
García Hidalgo, I., 140
García-Milá, M., 30, 116, 118
Gardner, H., 210-211
Garner, R., 214
Gauvain, M., 246
Gelder, B. de, 243
Gelman, R., 41n, 117
Gelman, S., 210
Gibson, J., 210-211
Giossi, J., 148
Goerzel, B., 16

Goes, C. de, 117
Goldin-Meadow, S., 123
Golomb, C., 162, 168
Gombert, J., 117, 124
Goodman, N., 1, 115, 209-210, 212, 227
Goody, J., 234-235, 239, 248
Gottlieb, A., 215
Grattan-Guinness, I., 22-24, 39n
Gray, G., 239
Green, F., 211
Green, S., 210
Greenfield, P., 211, 226-227, 239
Greeno, J., 183, 202
Gregory, R., 211
Grela, B., 221
Guedj, D., 23, 39n
Gullberg, J., 19, 36, 39n
Günther, 61
Gusella, J., 214

Hains, S., 214
Harley, B., 3
Harris, J., 244
Harris, P., 213
Harris, R., 235
Hartley, J., 240
Hasty, C., 87, 111
Hartman, E., 210
Hatano, G., 132n
Havelock, E., 234, 239, 248
Hayes, L., 214
Hayne, H., 210, 222
Hegel, G., 186, 199, 201, 204, 205n
Heidegger, M., 186
Henke, L., 214
Henriques, A., 148
Herbert, J., 210
Hirst, K., 3
Hofstadter, D., 40n
Homer, B., 243
Howard, V., 210
Howe, M., 240
Hudson, J., 210, 219, 222

Hughes, M., 30, 114, 125, 148, 172, 245-246, 248, 250
Hung, D., 243
Hurtado-Ortiz, M., 246
Huston, A., 210-211, 214, 226-227
Hutchins, E., 235, 246, 250

Ifrah, G., 39n
Illich, I., 233
Inagaki, K., 132n
Inhelder, B., 242
Intons-Peterson, M., 244
Ittelson, W., 211, 224

Jacobson, C., 169
Jaglom, L., 211
Janvier, B., 150
Jeffries, R., 165
Jipson, J., 169
Johannes de Muris, 58-63
Johnson, T., 246
Jolley, R., 118
Jordan, A., 210
Joseph, G., 22, 39

Kagan, J., 146
Kamii, C., 148-149
Kaplan, B., 209, 212
Kaplan, D., 173
Kaput, J., 1, 202
Karanth, P., 243
Karmiloff-Smith, A., 2, 9, 113, 115-118, 124, 128, 130-131, 146-147, 159, 164-174, 209-210, 242-244, 249-250
Kavanaugh, R., 213, 222
Keating, D., 146
Kellogg, R., 226
Kelly, M., 246
Kemeny, V., 169
Keselman, A., 173
Kiewra, K., 240, 246, 250
Klahr, D., 7, 159-178, 211, 250
Klein, E., 131
Klein, J., 55

Scheuer, N., 148, 150
Schmandt-Besserat, D., 41n
Schmitt, K., 210, 219, 227
Schwartz, S., 242, 249
Scribner, S., 235, 238-239, 243, 248
Schön, D., 90
Sebeok, T., 1
Sebokht, S., 23
Selin, H., 16, 35, 39n
Sfard, A., 246, 249
Sheffield, E., 222
Shrager, J., 173
Siegler, R., 173
Siegrist, F., 114, 125, 148
Sigel, I., 211
Silk, A., 113, 118
Simcock, G., 210, 226
Simon, H., 242
Sinclair, A., 114, 125, 148
Sinclair, H., 114
Sirat, C., 137
Slobin, D., 139
Smiley, S., 244
Soennichsen, M., 169
Sophian, C., 125
Sorsby, A., 123
Spade, P., 56
Stackhouse, R., 214
Starkey, P., 146
Stenning, K., 242
Stone, A., 61-62
Strauss, M., 146, 214
Striano, T., 212
Strom, D., 169
Sulzby, E., 117
Svetina, M., 173

Taboada y Ulloa, J., 19
Tanay, D., 5, 45-64, 112n
Teale, W., 117
Teberosky, A., 30, 113, 116, 118, 139
Teubal, E., 6, 113-134, 147-148
Thomas, G.S., 240
Thomas, G.V., 113, 118

Threlfall, J., 22, 26
Tolchinsky, L., 1-10, 14, 19, 22, 113-117, 124, 135-159, 209, 243
Tomasello, M., 212, 217, 226
Toufouni, L., 243
Treitler, L., 48, 54
Trevarthen, C., 214
Triona, L., 7, 159-178, 211, 250
Tronick, E., 214
Troseth, G., 8, 9, 209-232
Truglio, R., 227
Tsao, F-M., 221
Tuson, J., 4-5, 65-78
Tzeng, O., 243

Uttal, D., 128, 169, 215

Vasco, C., 4-5, 9, 13-43, 237
Vesta, F. di, 239-240
Villani, V., 114
Vogel, I., 135
Vong, K., 125
Vygotsky, 14, 38, 115, 117, 123, 185, 243

Wagner, S., 123
Walkerdine, V., 182, 186
Watson, J., 214, 225
Watt, I., 234-235, 239, 248
Weiss, J., 243
Werner, H., 82, 209, 212
Whitehurst, G., 210
Whitfall, J., 240
Wiese, H., 135, 145-146
Wilder, A., 227
Willats, 2
Williams, M., 227
Witmer, T., 40n
Wittgenstein, L., 46, 112n
Wright, J., 210-211, 214, 226-227
Wolf, D., 211
Wood, A., 125
Woodsmall, L., 227
Woodward, D., 3
Woodward, E. IV, 210

Yackel, E., 246
Yokoi, L., 239

Zawojewski, J., 246, 250
Zhang, J., 237, 242, 248-249
Zill, N., 227
Zwicky, A., 138, 156n

SUBJECT INDEX

A

abacus, 16, 17, 31, 242,
abbreviating numerals, 27
ambiguity of natural language, 46
absolute value, 151, 152
abstract numbers, 25, 40
    number concept, 25
    notation, 227
    notion of symbolization, 228
acalculias, 236
accounting systems, 4, 65
accumulation of notations, 251
acrophonic, 31
acrophony principle, 68, 77
action path, 87, 88, 93, 95, 96, 97, 98, 100, 107
    temporal, 97
activity-theoretic terms, 185
action notation, 104
acquiring conventional systems, 7
    Conventions of Writing, 138, 142, 210
    Conventions of the Written System of Numbers, 146
acquisition of notational knowledge, 228
additive bases, 35
    composition of the system, 149, 152
    convention, 34
    multiplicative bases, 35
    ordering, 20
adult interventions, 81
Adults' Use of Notations to Influence Cognition, 239
alephat, 31
algebra, 17, 40, 47, 64
algebraic integers, 20
alphabet, 4, 31, 32, 33, 36, 37, 55, 65, 68, 70, 71, 72, 77, 136, 226, 234, 235, 244

alphabet adaptations, 71
alphabetic systems, 71, 72, 144
alphabetic orthographies, 136
    principle, 68
    rather, 70
    writing, 67, 68, 71, 135
alphanumeric registers, 35
    symbols, 37, 233
amphibious artifacts, 14
analogical graphic representation, 147
appliques, 210
apprehended movement, 106
appropriation of the notational systems, 7, 131
aquifer, 189,192
Arabic alphabets, 71
    language, 19, 28
    manuscripts, 23
    numeration system, 23
    numeral, 17, 18, 27, 33, 36
Arabs, 23
Aramaic, 31
arbitrary chains of, 54 (also ligatures, 54)
    referent system, 75
    symbols, 3, 168
Aristotelian qualitative discourse, 53
    qualitative rather than quantitative physics, 51
    system, 51
ars cantus mensurabilis, 50, 63
ars nova, 58
artificial language, 5, 45, 46
    distinction between natural language, 46
art of notation, 59
ASCII code, 35, 37
Attention and Behaviour Regulation, 247
Attic, 32
auditory and visual discrimination, 136
    domain, 74, 76, 77

perspective, 3
performance, 118
processes, 113
progression in notations, 127
progression, 167
psychology, 8
trajectories, 113
development of alphabet, 73
events, 66
early notations, 115
notational systems, 114
number systems and numerical notations, 13
numerical notations, 124
permanent external symbols, 236
representational capacities, 113
writing, 5, 69
writing systems, 137
diachronic perspective, 3
reading, 14
reading of history, 28
Didactical Research Implications, 13, 19
didactics of mathematics, 13, 15
Discovering the Rules through Interaction with the Written System, 150
Distinguishing Numeracy from Literacy: Evidence from Children's Early Notations, 6, 113
directionality, 104, 136, 145
discharge measurements, 192
discreteness, 136
discrete rhythmical duration, 5, 46
discursive, mathematical, and material) practices, 202
discursive relations, 199
display mode, 198
dissolved-oxygen (DO) content, 181
distinction between actual realizations and conceptual categories, 1
distinction between natural and artificial language, 46
distributive numbers, 26
diversified rhythmic texture, 54
division strategy, 250
domain auditory, 74

of knowledge of external representation, 8
oral, 116
notational, 5, 6, 116, 123, 124, 130
numerosity, 129
sensory, 5, 73
domain-specific constraints, 130
double face, 1-3, 8
drawing symbols, 113
driving forces behind quantification, regulation , standardization of the different duration of musical sounds time for musical, 47
dual representation, 210, 212, 223, 226
hypothesis, 224
dual value, 67
dyadic interaction, 250
dyslexia, 236
dysgraphias, 236

E
early notational productions, 113
eccentric rhythmic style, 61
ecological system, 190, 204
economic histories, 188
educational psychology, 9, 239, 246
implications, 110, 111
research, 39
research implications, 13, 19
research on numbers, numeration and numeracy, 14
efficacy and semiotic behaviour of the modal notation, 49
effect of notation on cognition, 233
Egypt, 68- 70
Egyptian writing, 70, 77
encoding hypothesis, 239, 241
endurance, 2, 8
emergence and subsequent evolution of certain systems, 4
emergency and development of different systems, 3
embodied notation, 104, 110
embodiment, 98, 100, 104, 194
physical, 85
embryology and phylogeny, 39
empiricist attitude, 63

empirical research, 234, 235, 248, 249
epistemic tools, 2, 3, 135
epistemology, 58
events (landmarks), 89
evolving conceptions, 98
evolutionary perspective, 3, 9, 236
evolution of cognition, 236
ethnographic study, 184
ethnographies, 187
Etruscan, 71
expansion of the alphabet, 71, 77
experiences and interpretations of the notations, 114
extending registers, 29
extensive orientation, 219
external manual operations, 116
external memory, 233, 236, 244
external notational stimuli, 114
external representations, 1-3, 7-9, 15, 38, 114, 129, 159, 242, 246, 247, 249, 251
    creation and interpretation of, 2
external storage hypothesis, 240, 241
external symbolic storage system, 236
external symbols, 9, 20, 209, 231, 234, 236-239, 241-244, 246-251
external working memory, 236
extracortical, 3
extra-linguistic context, 5
external representations on human development (analysing the effect of), 3
external representations, appropriation of, 1
    humans' creation of, 1
    appropriation, 1
    understanding, 1
    use of, 1

F
face-to-face interactions, 197, 203
face value, 145, 148, 151, 152
features of writing systems and written number systems, 135
figural boundary, 85
figural group, 99
    grouping structure, 104

motivic grouping boundaries, 95
motivic structure, 102
    representations, 173, 174
    structure of the tune, 85
fin de siècle, 61
finger-and-toe registers, 28
finger figures, 29
    numerals, 27, 29
    numeral registers, 28, 29
    registers, 28
first stages of acquisition of conventional writing, 140
fixed reference, 6, 88, 102, 111
    reference structure, 87, 88, 94, 106
flatness cues, 212, 224
focus of attention, 107, 108
formal arguments, 236
    constraints, 116, 147
    features of video, 211, 227
    measurement, 236
    notational knowledge, 123
fractions, 22, 40, 61
Franconian notation, 50-52, 54, 55, 57, 59
Franconian symbols, 52
    semiotic behaviour of, 55
framework, 7, 8, 14, 17, 46, 103, 119, 159, 160, 161, 164, 167, 172, 175-177, 182
function of the numeral system, 124
    word, 140, 141, 143, 139
functional registers, 15
    writing, 71
    words, 141, 143
functional-communicative tools, 3
functionally equivalent pairs, 99, 100
functioning fixed reference grid, 110
functioning of written numbers, 152
functions of video images, 8, 213, 214, 227
Fundamental Structure, 182

G
general notational domain, 123
genre factor, 227
gestural registers, 4, 28

map-maker, 6, 7, 81, 83, 87-90, 92, 94, 95, 102, 106, 110, 111
map-makers' notation, 94, 95, 102
map-making, 6, 81, 88, 108, 110, 111
mastery of a formal code, 227
material and social dimensions, 186
materialized numerals, 17
mathematical cognition, 184, 197
    development, 197
    education, 4, 13, 20, 25, 26, 28, 36, 37, 39, 182, 183
    notation, 5, 39, 55
    reasoning, 246
    structure, 182
maxima, 59, 63, 142, 193
Maya, 13, 23, 34, 35
mediated relations, 180, 186, 194
mediating artifact, 185, 186, 191, 194
Mediating Artifacts, Tools, and Division of Labor, 191
medieval linguistic theories, 54
Memory, 34, 35, 48, 68, 72, 74, 114, 160, 162, 163, 168, 169, 204, 236, 239, 241-243, 245, 246, 248-250
    collective, 65, 236
    external, 233, 236, 244
    game, 163, 168, 169, 226, 240
    internal, 233, 244
    load, 26, 28, 29
    model of, 16
    personal, 65,
    strategies, 236, 243, 244, 250
    working, 168, 226, 236
mental artifacts, 14
mental construction, 38, 90, 106
mental numerals, 17
mental processes, 4, 65,
mental representation, 210, 131, 213, 227, 228
mental strategies, 65
Mesopotamia, 23, 65, 68, 69
Mesopotamian numeration, 66
Mesopotamian writing, 69, 77
meta-category of rhythmic perfection, 59
metalinguistic awareness, 9, 238, 249
metalinguistic knowledge, 235
metalinguistic knowledge, 235, 243

metalinguistic tasks, 144
metaphoric spatial/temporal language, 106
meters (time; see also time signatures), 45
meter, 45, 54, 60, 62, 181, 190, 239
methodological artefact, 117
methodological confounds, 118
methodological consideration, 117, 118
methodological perspectives, 118
methodology, 117, 118
metric cycles, 45
metric structure, 45, 47
metrical accentuation, 45, 46
    binary, 54
    ternary, 54
micro-analytic study of mathematical representation practices, 203
minima, 58, 59, 61, 63,
minimalist systems, 68
minimal basic-word or gesture lists, 28
    sound units (alphabets), 77
mixed systems, 72
models: hieroglyphic, 70
    hieratic, 70
    demotic, 70

monastic scriptorium, 137
monoconsonantal signs, 71
monophony, 47
morpheme, 67, 136, 139
morphological levels, 67
    units, 66
Morse, 31
motion parallax, 216
motivic grouping, 85
motor competence, 129
    skill, 129, 168
movable-counter registers, 31
multi-digit numeral, 149
multiple functions of external representations, 1
multisensory domain, 76
multi-unit structure, 149
musical compositions, 45, 47, 48, 60
    perception and cognition, 49
    time, 45, 47, 50, 51, 61
    map-makers, 6, 87, 89

and Spatial Path-Makers, 87
music notation conventions, 107

N
national development, 233
natural foundation of medieval notation, 55
natural language, 5, 45- 47
natural numbers, 19, 21, 35, 38, 40
nature of the stimulus, 129
new framework for understanding how young children create external representations for puzzles and problems, 7, 159
neural basis of cognitive functioning, 20
neurological basis of notational knowledge, 3
neurophysiological damage, 236
Noesis, 14, 15, 21
noetic constructions, 4, 16, 18, 38
noetic activity, 21
non-canonical partitions, 150
non-conventional notations, 150
nonliterate cognition, 237
nominalism, 57, 58
nominalist rejection of mental constructs, 63, 131
non-iconic representation, 75, 131
nonmnemonic notations, 245
non-mnemonic representations, 163, 245
No Notation condition, 241
notations, 1, 3, 5-7, 18, 39, 55, 81, 86, 95, 103, 107, 111, 113-131, 148, 159, 162-166, 172 176, 209, 228, 233, 234, 240-242, 244-248, 250, 251
    and cognition, 9, 233, 234
    condition, 240
    creation, 163
notational abilities, 7, 113, 159, 160, 161, 175
    challenge, 57
    competence, 113, 117, 118, 119
    competency, 166
    complexities, 62
    constraints, 127
    conventions, 106, 111

conventions and inventions, 111
development, 4, 7, 8, 114, 123, 131, 242
elements, 7, 155
forms, 117, 119, 123,124, 128,
functions, 5, 115
forms, 115
innovations, 61
inventions, 90, 111
level, 128, 130
opportunities, 129
output, 127
notations may influence cognitive processing, 233
notational proposals, 5
notational problems, 126
notation-path, 104, 107
notation path is no longer iconic but rather symbolic, 88
notational responses, 124, 128
notational strategy, 7, 160, 175, 176
    figural, 7
    linguistic, 7
Notations systems, 114, 236
notational symbol systems, 211
notational tasks, 117, 118, 159, 160-162, 167-169, 172, 175, 176
notational task performance, 160
notational types, 114
notational use, 233
notations for numerosities, 129
Notch registers, 25, 31
note-shape, 5, 47, 51, 52, 54, 57, 58, 60-62
notion of graphic representation, 226
null quantity display, 128
number assignments, 154
number-like representations, 121, 126, 127
number scheme, 106
number systems as conceptual constructions and numeration systems as semiotic registers, 4
number systems, 4, 6, 16 , 18, 20, 21, 40, 135
numeracy, 13, 233, 245
numeracy from literacy, 6, 113

numeric notations, 118, 120, 122, 125
numerical operations afford, 129
numerical magnitude, 154
numerical sequence, 153
numerical values, 180
numerical writing, 155
numerosity, 21, 126, 127, 131, 148
numerosities, 127, 129, 146
numeral type, 15-18, 36,
numerals, 1, 3-6, 9, 14, 15, 17, 18, 20, 33

O

object and location representations, 162, 163, 165, 167, 170-172
object information, 167-169, 171, 172,
object representations, 162, 165, 167, 168
object-retrieval task, 223
object symbolization tasks, 7
OCR-software failed, 33
one-to-one dot register, 25
one-to-one vertical-stroke numerals, 27
Old Hebrew, 32
ontogeny, 13, 39
ontological commitment, 55
Ontological Gap, 183, 184, 201, 202, 204
operational cognitive-motor
components of semiotic registers, 18
oral and auditory domain of speech, 65
"oral based notations", 153
oral numerals, 23
oral word numeral, 15, 24, 28
oral word register, 16, 30
Oral-Word Semiotic Registers, 27, 28
order of occurrence, 6, 84, 85, 88, 92, 107,
ordinal numbers, 25, 26, 104, 112
ordinality, 22
ordinality genus, 22
ordinal placement numbers, 26
organic development, 98, 100, 103
orthographic systems, 116
orthographic traditions, 71
orthography, 137

P

Palmyran, 31
parallelism, 13, 38, 39
        between ontogeny and
phylogeny, 39
        between sociogenesis and
psychogenesis, 39
        of ontogenesis and
phylogenesis, 38
particulars, 57, 58, 63
path-maker, 6, 7, 81, 83-89, 91 – 93, 111
path-making, 6, 7, 81, 83, 110, 111
pedagogical device, 202
perceived pitch, 92
perfect triple note values, 62
permanent external symbols, 234, 236-239, 241-244, 246-251
phases, 24, 61, 81, 91, 114, 116, 130
phases as the conceptual, the formal and the symbolic, 116
phenomena examination, 235
        abstracting, 235
        explanatory, 235
        classificatory, 235
        sequential, 235
phenomenological point of view, 200
Phoenician, 31, 68, 70, 71
phonemes, 136
phonetic coding, 32
        value, 70
        variant, 26, 28
Phonic Registers, 30
        value, 138
phonographic conventions of the
written system, 138
phonological awareness, 144
        or alphabetic writings, 68
        segments, 136
        systems, 71
        units, 71
        writing, 67
phylogeny, 13, 39
physical characteristics of heat capacity,
and ecological relationships, 190
        embodiment, 85, 104
        system, 190
Piagetian, 13, 149

pictograms, 67, 77
pictographic (or iconic), 69
pictographic and syllabic writing, 69
pictorial images, 209, 211
    representations, 131, 210, 216,
pitch direction, 107
    functions, 85, 111
    properties, 7, 84, 88, 92, 94,
    100, 108, 110
    relations, 106, 107
place value, 6, 29, 33, 34, 36, 37, 133,
145, 148
Planned longitudinal studies, 228
political histories, 188
polynomial base, 35-37
    semiotic register, 35
polyphonic compositions, 50
    music, 48, 57
polyphony, 47
positional principle, 136, 145, 155
    value, 23, 145, 149, 152, 155
practical action, 199
precursors of writing, 4
prepositions, 137-139
presentations, 113
presentation strategies, 236
present-day oral and gestural
numeration systems, 28
    archeology of, 28
    ethnology of , 28
preservation of logographic and syllabic
systems, 77
primus gradus, 59
principle of place value in written
numeration, 6, 135
Principle of Place Value in the Written
Number System, 145
principles underlying the different
systems evolve, 4
printing, 73, 137, 234
problem solution sequences, 7
problem solving level, 128, 130
Problem-Solving and Reasoning, 246
problem-solving or reasoning tasks, 242
problem-solving tasks, 165, 170, 221,
223
problem space, 2, 113, 116, 118

production of notations, 6, 114, 119,
242, 249
production and use of notational
systems, 115
projective semiosis, 14, 15, 33
pronominal clitics, 140, 141, 156
pronouns, 139, 141, 143, 144, 156
property invariance structures, 111
property-ordered structure, 88
psychogenesis, 13, 25, 39
Psychogenetic Research Implications,
13, 19
psycholinguistic studies, 139
psychological research, 39
psychology of mathematics education,
182
pulse biological, 48
    physiological, 48
punctuation marks, 137
Purang, 238
Pythagorean figural numbers, 25, 30

Q
quality of suppositio, 56
quantifying musical time, 47
quartus gradus, 59

R
rational amplifier, 20
rational numbers, 20, 38, 40
rational number systems, 21
real numbers, 19, 21, 38
realm of abstract universals, 63
reference structure, 88, 94, 106
referent, 6, 8, 56, 74-76, 83, 118, 120,
123, 130, 131, 149, 181, 183, 185, 204,
214, 217, 220, 226, 228
referential-communicative situations,
148
    use of notations, 117
    function, 119
    tool, 6, 117, 130, 135
referential content, 140
    mapping component, 130
reflexive relationship, 198, 201
regression analyses, 226
regulative function of the perfect long,
54

relational character, 201
relationship between notation and cognition, 9, 233, 234
    between notation and cognition from a historical and evolutionary perspective, 9
relations between numerals, 151, 152
relations in praxis, 187
    of signification, the regulation of practices, the positioning of subjects, and the emotional investment, 204
    material, 185
    linguistic, 185
    practical, 185
relative durational value, 48, 51
    integers, 40
    size, 136
representational capacity, 132, 226
    drawing, 168
    medium, 226
    specificity, 212
representations of numerals, 130
representation practices, 186, 187, 202, 203, 206
representation of time in medieval music, 5, 45
    of the logical structure of the world, 46
    of written language, 130
representations, 113
representational systems, 115, 118
Representing Symbolic Relations, 223
Restructuring conceptual intuitions through invented notations, 6, 81
Restructuring conceptual intuitions through invented notations, from path-making to map-making, 81
retrieval strategies, 236
revisited conceptualization, 8
riffles, 181, 186, 190, 191, 196
riparian zones, 179, 186, 191
rhetorical figure, 73
    combinations, 54, 59
    concepts, 57
    division, 60
    ideas, 47
    inventions, 47

level, 59
meaning, 5, 45, 112
modes, 48, 49, 54, 55
motion, 54
motions or divisions, 61
notation, 5, 45, 47, 48, 50-55, 58, 60, 62, 63
options, 54
pattern, 47, 48, 50, 55
phrase, 5, 54
sign or note-shape, 46
terminology, 59
theory, 47
units, 45, 59
value, 5, 45, 58, 61, 62
vocabulary, 54
variants, 63
role of writing and written numbers, 155
Romans, 13, 34, 72
rotary press, 73
runes, 72

S
sacral resonance of music, 60
Sanskrit, 19, 23
schemata, 82, 103
schematic realism, 69
scholastic, 58
scientific reasoning, 246, 248, 249
scriptio continua, 137
secundus gradus, 59
segregation of video from reality, 225
selective attention, 83
semantic interpretation, 154
semibrevis, 51, 53, 58
Semiosis, 14, 15
semiotic abstraction and separation of physical references, 5
    activity, 14, 15
    approach, 8, 182
    approach to graphing, 182
    code, 45
    connection, 189
    field, 47, 52
    framework, 14, 17
    powers, 4, 38
    processes, 184

Registers, 4, 5, 15, 16, 18, 20, 21, 30, 34, 37, 38
    revolution, 4, 66, 72
    transfer, 5, 73, 74
sensorial aspects, 75
sensory domain, 5, 73, 76, 77
sensual representation of symbols, 46
sensori-motor actions, 196
    experience, 195
    processes, 196
    representations, 196
sensory domains, 5, 77
    independence of language, 76
    inputs, 73
    response, 82
    stimulation, 82
    stimuli, 82
sequence and object or location representations, 162
sequence, object, and location representations, 162
sequential building procedure, 85
    information, 164, 166, 167, 170-175
    order, 82, 145
    order of primitives, 145
    series of landmarks, 86, 87
sign functions, 8, 182
sign-reference relationship, 184
sign-referent relationships, 202
sign tokens, 15, 17, 18
    types, 17, 18
signed integers, 20, 21, 38, 40
signs and signing processes, 182
silent reading, 137
Sinaitic adaptation, 71
single musical note-shape, 51
situated cognition, 200, 202
situation-dependent, functional meanings, 110
situation-independent reference structures, 90
sliding-bead registers, 31
societal activity, 182
socio-cultural contexts, 114
    environment, 5, 115
    support, 120
sociogenesis, 13, 25, 39

social nexus, 181
sociomaterial situations, 182
sociomaterial world, 182, 186
sound symbols, 75, 76
spatial and temporal relations, 8, 211
    boundaries, 95
    grouping, 94, 102
    or temporal markers, 165
    structure, 85
spoken modality, 135
    numerals, 128
    and written numbers, 153
split-storage strategy, 241, 245
stage, 132
stated truths examination, 235
    abstracting, 235
    explanatory, 235
    classificatory, 235
    sequential, 235
stimulus, 128, 129, 213
stimulus presentation, 128, 129
storage strategies, 236
social histories, 188
strategy in notational research, 173
structural analysis, 95
    element, 85
    entities, 103
    equivalency, 183
    isomorphism, 182
structure of the numeral system, 124
study of representational objects, 3
subitized or counted integers, 20
superordinate and ordinate features of writing, 136
syllabaries and alphabets, 4, 65
syllabic writings, 67
syllables (syllabograms), 77
syllogism, 235, 238
symbolic and the referential-communicative tool, 117
    artifacts, 209, 226
    conventions, 111, 227
    development, 226
    domain, 75
    experiences, 224, 225
    functioning, 119
    functions, 225
    intentions, 226

literacy, 231, 233
medium, 8
numerals, 17, 18
representation, 51, 116
sequences, 33
systems, 113, 115, 116
symbol-referent relation, 226
symbols, 113
symbol system, 111, 210, 228, 239
symbol types, 210
syllabic writing, 67
syllabic systems, 68, 72, 77
synaesthetic game, 65
synaesthesia, 73
synchronic-descriptive perspective on external representations, 3
synchronic reading of history, 14
syntactic category of words, 139, 140
category of words, 140
Context, 141, 143, 144
environment, 143
levels, 67
rule, 34, 119
structure, 66
syntax, 112, 210
Syriach, 31
systemic network, 20
systematic and generalised concept of number, 135
taxonomies, 236

T
Task constraints: children's notational strategies, 172
technological and semiotic revolution, 72
temporal action paths, 82, 97
articulations, 47
experience, 45
events, 45
information, 172
meaning, 46
rhythmical meaning, 5, 46
structure, 45
[Ten]10-Trap, 36
tertius gradus, 59
ternary values, 60
textual environment, 141-143

theory building, 135
theoretical analysis of the relationship between notation and cognition, 233
and methodological considerations, 118
background, 81, 82
frame, 52, 201
perspectives and empirical evidence, 9
"the rhythmic modes", or "modal notation", 48
thumb-anchored register, 29
time interval, 4, 38, 45
signatures, 45 (meters)
topological semiotics, 184
touching registers, 29
transfinite cardinal numbers, 21
transformations, 81
treatment, 5, 16, 17, 20, 236
triadic or multriadic interaction, 250
trinitarian unit, 47
tributaries, 192
triple meters, 47
trochaic pattern of a long, 49, 54
tune-building strategies, 91
tune reflecting aspects, 95
tune structure, 107
typewriter, 73
typical contextual cues, 224

U
ultimate principle of rhythmic order, 54
unconventional separation, 141, 143
unitary conceptual structures, 149
units of segmentation, 135
universal perceptual principle, 49
universals, 57, 58, 63
unlimited semiosis, 184
use of numeric and writing systems, 115

V
verbal cue rather than a complex pictorial one, 222
verbally formulated negatives, 126
verbal instructions, 104
verbal/written notations, 120
verb particles, 139

vertical discontinuities, 198
video deficit, 210, 221
video presentation, 216-220, 222, 225
visual and auditory discrimination, 136
visual domain, 74-77
visual information processing, 243
visual sense, 5, 73
Visual-Tactile Registers, 31
vocal system, 76

W
whole rhythmic phrase, 5, 45, 112
Word-Category Counts, 139
word numerals, 17, 23-25, 28, 33, 34
world and mathematical structure, 182
writing and written numbers as source
of knowledge, 6, 135
writings: hieroglyphs, demotic and
Greek, 70
writing, number and music notation
from an historical perspective, 4
writing: the story of a cognitive
revolution, 4, 65
writing system, 6
written language notations, 115
written language and numbers, 135
written modality, 135
written number system, 6
written numerals, 4, 25, 27, 145, 146,
153, 154
written numeration as a source of
knowledge, 150
written outputs, 138

Z
zero stimuli, 128

Printed in the United Kingdom by
Lightning Source UK Ltd., Milton Keynes
137405UK00001B/34/A